The Heart of the Matter

Historical Materialism Book Series

The Historical Materialism Book Series is a major publishing initiative of the radical left. The capitalist crisis of the twenty-first century has been met by a resurgence of interest in critical Marxist theory. At the same time, the publishing institutions committed to Marxism have contracted markedly since the high point of the 1970s. The Historical Materialism Book Series is dedicated to addressing this situation by making available important works of Marxist theory. The aim of the series is to publish important theoretical contributions as the basis for vigorous intellectual debate and exchange on the left.

The peer-reviewed series publishes original monographs, translated texts, and reprints of classics across the bounds of academic disciplinary agendas and across the divisions of the left. The series is particularly concerned to encourage the internationalization of Marxist debate and aims to translate significant studies from beyond the English-speaking world.

For a full list of titles in the Historical Materialism Book Series available in paperback from Haymarket Books, visit: www.haymarketbooks.org/ series_collections/1-historical-materialism.

The Heart of the Matter

Ilyenkov, Vygotsky and the Courage of Thought

David Bakhurst

Haymarket Books
Chicago, IL

First published in 2023 by Brill Academic Publishers, The Netherlands
© 2023 Koninklijke Brill NV, Leiden, The Netherlands

Published in paperback in 2024 by
Haymarket Books
P.O. Box 180165
Chicago, IL 60618
773-583-7884
www.haymarketbooks.org

ISBN: 979-8-88890-216-5

Distributed to the trade in the US through Consortium Book Sales and
Distribution (www.cbsd.com) and internationally through Ingram
Publisher Services International (www.ingramcontent.com).

This book was published with the generous support of Lannan
Foundation, Wallace Action Fund, and the Marguerite Casey Foundation.

Special discounts are available for bulk purchases by organizations and
institutions. Please call 773-583-7884 or email info@haymarketbooks.org
for more information.

Cover art and design by David Mabb. Cover art is a detail from *Luibov
Popova Untitled Textile Design on William Morris Wallpaper for Historical
Materialism*, edition of 100, screen print on wallpaper (2010).

Printed in the United States.

Library of Congress Cataloging-in-Publication data is available.

Феликсу

‥

Contents

PART 3
Vygotsky

PART 4
Contemporary Applications

Preface

This book brings together the best of my essays on Russian philosophy and psychology. The focus is on the legacies of Evald Ilyenkov and Lev Vygotsky, though many other figures play significant roles in the story. I hope the book conveys the dramatic social and historical context in which these Russian thinkers lived and worked, making their ideas intelligible in their own terms, while bringing them into dialogue with themes and thinkers in Western philosophy to show how they illuminate philosophical issues of enduring significance.

The earliest essay, 'Social Memory in Soviet Thought', was written in 1989 and the most recent, 'Vygotsky's Concept of *Perezhivanie*', in 2018, so the volume represents the work of nearly 30 years. The essays appear more or less in their original form, though I have made minor modifications to avoid repetition, correct errors and bring the discussion up to date. I have also revised the references to reflect the many recent publications of writings by or about Ilyenkov and Vygotsky. At the end of each chapter, I have added a short bridge passage to segue into the next. If I have been successful, the collection should hang together as a coherent whole, though each of the essays can be read independently.

Ilyenkov was fond of the expression, '*sut' dela*', which has been variously rendered by his translators as the 'essence', 'crux' or 'gist' 'of the matter', though, in my view, the most attractive translation is often 'the heart of the matter'. Ilyenkov uses the expression to characterise the ends of thought. On his view, thinking should not rest content with a superficial characterisation of surface phenomena but aspire to transcend appearances and disclose the nature of things, thereby explaining both why things are as they are and why we tend to see them as we do. Thought, in other words, gets to the heart of the matter, and thus the phrase is a fitting title for this collection.

The idea of philosophy getting to the heart of the matter is central to Ilyenkov's understanding of dialectical thought and the unity of logic, dialectics and epistemology. For him, logic describes the 'laws of thought', but this is more than the articulation of argument forms and principles of inference. It requires us to bring to self-consciousness the fundamental categories, concepts and modes of inquiry by which thought discloses reality and arrives at knowledge. Logic, thus understood, is the science of thinking, which is, Ilyenkov tells us, the true subject matter of philosophy.

The passion to get to the heart of the matter is also central to Ilyenkov's educational philosophy, which focuses on the educators' responsibility to enable learners to acquire the power to think for themselves and to develop the courage to use it. In the Soviet Union, of course, such an affirmation of independence of mind was not always viewed positively, and Ilyenkov's career was scarred by many distressing brushes with authority. One of these followed the publication, in *Komsomol'skaya Pravda*, of a report on a roundtable on philosophy and education, in which Ilyenkov participated, along with a number of friends and colleagues. The article was called *'Muzhestvo mysli'* or 'The Courage of Thought' – hence my subtitle. To cultivate authentic thinking was, for Ilyenkov, the mission of philosophy, and he showed considerable fortitude in remaining true to his views despite what he had to endure.

Vygotsky was another thinker who had a tremendous passion for truth, enlightenment and independent thought. Like Ilyenkov, Vygotsky did not seek to understand the human mind for its own sake, but as part of the project of creating the conditions in which human flourishing can become a reality for all. For me this unity of theory and practice, unbridled intellectual inquiry and passionate moral conviction, makes their work so inspiring and their respective stories so moving.

This book is dedicated to my friend and mentor, Felix Mikhailov, another courageous thinker (and participant in the ill-fated Courage of Thought roundtable), without whom I would never have found my way in the curious world of Soviet philosophy. Felix was a wonderful person and a brilliant philosopher. We shared many great times and my debt to him is incalculable. Felix knew Vygotsky's psychology well and he was a close friend of Ilyenkov, who had died only a year before my first visit to Moscow, so much of what I know about Vygotsky and Ilyenkov I learnt from Felix. I relate the story of our friendship in Chapter 1.

I am lucky to have many other friends who have influenced and inspired me on this journey. I must mention Vladislav Lektorsky, Jonathan Dancy, David Wiggins, Jan Derry, Paul Standish, Andrew Davis, Mike Cole, Carol Padden (who co-authored with me 'The Meshcheryakov Experiment'), Cheryl Misak, Sebastian Rödl and Christine Sypnowich. Christine, my wife and colleague at Queen's, has been with me since the early days of my studies of Soviet philosophy – I remember finishing up 'Social Memory in Soviet Thought' at my parents' house in London a few days before we were married in 1989. Over the years, Christine has been a constant source of support, constructive criticism and wise counsel, and we've had a great deal of fun along the way. Our children Rosemary and Hugh also deserve my thanks; it is not always easy having philosophers for parents.

My career as an academic has afforded many opportunities to travel and discuss my work with friends and colleagues at symposia and conferences around the world. I am grateful for that, and for the many helpful comments and criticisms my work has received on such occasions. I am also indebted to my students at Queen's, who have been a pleasure to teach and supervise over the years. I must thank one in particular, Rogney Piedra Arencibia, who devoted a great deal of his time to helping me bring this book to completion. I benefitted enormously from his hard work, good humour and technical know-how, not to mention his considerable expertise on Ilyenkov. I am also very grateful Elena Illesh, Ilyenkov's daughter, for inviting me to visit her home where the Ilyenkov Archive resides, and to Andrey Maidansky, who accompanied me on that visit, and who later very kindly – and almost instantly – answered my numerous e-mail requests for materials, information and advice on translation. With Elena and Andrey at the helm, Ilyenkov's legacy is in good hands.

When I began working on Soviet philosophy, I was often advised to give it up in favour of a more mainstream area of specialisation. 'You'll never get a job', I heard more than once. The advice was no doubt well intentioned, but I am glad I was sufficiently reckless to ignore it. Philosophers are often suspicious of, and threatened by, unfamiliar traditions and quick to find reasons to disparage and ignore them. So it is very good for philosophers to be forced to immerse themselves in alien styles of thought and forge a meeting of minds. I am fortunate to have had this opportunity, and to have encountered so many fascinating interlocutors who made my study of Soviet thought, not just intellectually rewarding, but a thrilling adventure.

PART 1

Beginnings

∵

CHAPTER 1

The Riddle of the Self Revisited

This opening chapter pays tribute to my friend and mentor, Felix Trofimovich Mikhailov (1930–2006), without whom my studies of Russian philosophy would never have got off the ground let alone resulted in the writing of *Consciousness and Revolution in Soviet Philosophy*[1] and the various essays collected in this volume.

Mikhailov is best known for his book *Zagadka chelovecheskogo ya*. *Zagadka* is a remarkable book, written by a remarkable man. The book has its origins in the fertile years of the Khrushchev 'thaw' – it was first published in 1964 – and remains a fine expression of the critical humanism that characterised some of the best Russian writing in the broadly Marxist tradition. A second, revised and expanded edition appeared in 1976, followed by an English translation in 1980.[2] This second edition represents the most ingenious and accessible account of the philosophical framework of what in the West has become known as cultural-historical activity theory (or CHAT). Mikhailov was close to many other thinkers associated with that tradition, including E.V. Ilyenkov, V.V. Davydov, A.I. Meshcheryakov and V.A. Lektorsky, who liked and admired his philosophical genius and his irrepressible wit and good humour.[3]

The first part of the chapter takes the form of a personal reminiscence about Felix, his remarkable gifts, and the friendship we enjoyed for more than 25 years. In the second part, I return to the themes of his most famous book, now republished in a third Russian edition,[4] and consider what resonance it has for us today, more than half a century after its first publication.

1. That I met Felix Mikhailov at all was the outcome of extraordinary good fortune. In September 1980, I was an undergraduate at Keele University on a month's visit to Moscow in a bold (and absurdly optimistic) attempt to discover what was happening on the Soviet philosophical scene. My efforts to meet philosophers through official channels had come to nothing and I was about to leave Moscow defeated, when, in the Progress Publishers book shop, I

---

1 Bakhurst 1991.
2 Mikhailov 1964; 1976; 1980.
3 I should note that the revised 1976 version of *Zagadka* is much influenced by Ilyenkov, whom Mikhailov got to know only after the publication of the first edition.
4 Mikhailov 2010.

came across a copy of *Zagadka*, newly translated as *The Riddle of the Self*. When I started to read it, I could not believe how good it was. It was completely free of the doctrinaire tone of most Soviet writing. It treated philosophical problems that were instantly familiar to me – the shortcomings of foundationalist epistemology, the mind–body problem, the elusiveness of the self, the nature of agency – and it did so with great imagination. The tone was conversational, with the author directly addressing the reader and animating the discussion with ingenious literary devices such as dialogues and accounts of dreams. It was exciting stuff. When I returned to my hotel, book in hand, I bumped into someone[5] who told me she knew the translator, Robert Daglish. So, at short notice, we set up a meeting between myself, Mikhailov, Daglish, and Eugene Lampert, the then Chair of the Russian Department at Keele (and translator of Berdyaev), who was also in Moscow at the time. On 11 September 1980, we congregated in Daglish's apartment. Mikhailov and I hit it off immediately, and, thanks to the deft interpreting skills of Lampert, who later became a close friend of the Mikhailov family, we were soon embroiled in a discussion of the errors of 'subject–object dualism'. It was an evening I shall never forget.

I returned to Moscow for the 1982–83 academic year, this time as an exchange student at Moscow University sponsored by the British Council. Mikhailov took me under his wing and helped me find my way into the oral culture that was the vehicle of philosophical thought during the Soviet period. At that time, he was based at the Institute of General and Pedagogical Psychology, to which Davydov, the then Director, had brought a number of philosophers whose styles of thought put them at odds with the academic establishment. Their 'philosophical laboratory' was just a room with samovar. It housed Mikhailov, Vladimir Bibler, Anatoli Arsen'ev and Georgii Shchedrovitsky, among others. This was in the Brezhnev era, at a time that later became known as 'the period of stagnation', and it was true that in academic institutions people rarely seemed to have anything to do (apart from an occasional flurry of activity to complete, or to appear to have completed, their '*plannovaya rabota*'). As a result, I spent many happy hours discussing philosophy with Mikhailov and he introduced me to numerous philosophers and psychologists who gave me accounts of the history of Soviet philosophy that could never have been found in the literature. Moreover, the consideration Mikhailov extended to me was not just academic.

---

5   This was the artist Roxanne Permar, who was in Moscow researching Eisenstein. At that time, it would have been impossible to get a visa to travel to Moscow to do independent research, so I had joined a month-long language class organised by Progressive Tours of London. Permar was one of the group leaders. The other was Eugene Lampert, Professor of Russian at Keele, who is about to enter the story.

He and his wife, Liuda, and daughter, Anya, took me into their family and looked after me with wonderful kindness and generosity. His son from a previous marriage, Igor, became a good friend.

As my Russian language skills improved, Mikhailov organised a series of seminars at which I presented papers to a select group of philosophers and psychologists who were invited to respond. These meetings proved an extraordinary source of valuable material for my work.[6] Mikhailov helped me in all this with no regard for the danger to which his friendship with me might expose him. This was a time, of course, when the consequences of fraternising with foreigners were uncertain: many of my Russian friends and associates were extremely cautious, and some people would not see me at all. Not so Mikhailov. If not for his courage, my work would have foundered.

In later years I saw Mikhailov regularly, in Moscow, and on his various trips to the West.[7] Our lives changed dramatically. Following Davydov's sudden departure from the Institute of Psychology, Mikhailov moved to the Institute of Philosophy. After the collapse of the Soviet Union, he took on further positions, including returning to the Philosophy Department of the 2nd Medical Institute, which he had led with aplomb in the 1960s. He began to write prolifically. I left my native Britain for North America in 1988, spending two years at the University of California, San Diego before moving to my present position at Queen's. Throughout all this, our philosophical discussions continued. Mikhailov was always a delight to talk with, because he was so ingenious and imaginative. He was a terrific speaker, whether in formal academic contexts (where he never worked from notes) or at home with friends in the kitchen ('*na kukhne*', as the Russian has it). He loved weaving complex philosophical arguments – the more paradoxical the better – and he adored telling stories. If he could somehow contrive to do both at once, he would. On numerous occa-

---

6   See Chapter 2 of this volume.

7   These included the following. In 1989 or 1990, when I was an assistant professor at the University of California, San Diego, Mikhailov visited the university with a delegation concerned with the education of the blind-deaf (Alexander Suvorov was also part of the group). In 1991, shortly after I had left San Diego for Queen's University, I invited Mikhailov to Kingston where he gave an extraordinarily impressive colloquium to a large audience at the Queen's Philosophy Department. The talk he gave became 'The Soviet Self: A Personal Reminiscence', his contribution to *The Social Self*, a collection of essays I edited with Christine Sypnowich in 1995 (Mikhailov 1995). A couple of years later we met up in Rochester, New York, which afforded a memorable side-trip to Niagara Falls. And in 1995, while I was on sabbatical in Oxford, Mikhailov was part of a summer school organised by Eureka University that happily took place in Enfield, the town of my birth, making possible an afternoon with Felix and Liuda at my parents' home in North London.

sions I served as his interpreter. We knew each other so well that this came easily, and Mikhailov was extraordinarily good at maintaining the thread of his argument or anecdote despite constantly having to pause while I gave the translation. Interpreting for him, however, was not without its scary moments, as Mikhailov could not resist the temptation to follow a good thought wherever it might lead (and, of course, he always had several good thoughts on the go at once!). So I often felt that I was 'flying blind', unsure of our direction and fearful of what obstacles I might hit. But somehow Mikhailov always ensured that things worked out and our audience went home delighted and invigorated.

Mikhailov and I were philosophical soulmates. From our first meeting, we were always instantly on each other's wavelength. This might seem strange, since our respective styles are so different. Where almost everything I write is cautious, studied and analytical, Mikhailov was a master of free-flowing, dialectical thought. He was as much interested in the process of creating as in the object created, and especially in his later years he wrote with the kind of spontaneity I could only envy. But our differences were superficial. At heart, we were inspired by similar philosophical values and preoccupied with similar issues: the cultural preconditions of psychological development; intersubjectivity and the meeting of minds; the process of education in the broadest sense. And we were not just philosophically like-minded. If we had written lists of the good things in life, they would have been much the same. We enjoyed many enchanting times celebrating those good things with each other in the company of our families.

There was always a great deal of laughter when Mikhailov and I were together, partly because he was extremely witty, and partly because our antics often had an element of farce. I remember once meeting him at a metro station in Moscow on my way to one of our seminars. He broke the (for me disastrous) news that he had to miss the seminar because he was expected at a funeral. 'I've no choice', he cried, 'they've made me Master of Ceremonies'. Mikhailov delivered this news as our paths crossed – he was on the up-escalator while I was on the down! Many years later in Minsk, while we were taking a taxi back to our hotel, Mikhailov contrived to pay the driver in Russian, rather than Belorussian, rubles, thereby blowing a month's salary. The shenanigans that ensued – which included finding and confronting the taxi driver (to no avail, of course) – were situation comedy of the highest quality. Everything worked out well in the end, as it always did, thanks to the generosity of our host in Minsk, but before Mikhailov was gifted back his money, he consoled himself with the thought that the loss was a small price to pay for such a great story. 'I'll be dining out on this one for years', he said. Typical Mikhailov.

Shortly after this meeting in Minsk in Summer 2004, Mikhailov was diagnosed with cancer. He underwent surgery, but decided to forego debilitating treatment so that he could continue work on the book he was writing. In December 2005 I made a trip to see him, Liuda, Anya, and granddaughter, Sasha, in their Moscow apartment in Belyaevo. I found Mikhailov stronger than I had expected and in fine form. We enjoyed several splendid days together. When we parted, we knew that this was likely our last goodbye, though I nurtured the hope that we might have just a little more time. It was not to be. He died two months later. Russia lost a brilliant philosopher, and I lost someone whose influence on me, and on the direction my life has taken, is incalculable. I could not have had a more stimulating, loveable and faithful friend.

2. In 1981, some months after my first meeting with Mikhailov, I discovered a recently published, and rather negative, review of the first edition of *Zagadka* by the philosopher Thomas Nemeth in the journal *Studies in Soviet Thought*.[8] This prompted me to write a response that appeared in the same journal in 1982, my first published article.[9] So it is fitting I should begin this volume by revisiting *Zagadka* and considering how we should assess it today, more than 50 years after its first publication.

What is the riddle that the book is about? *The Riddle of the Self* is a great title, but the literal translation of *Zagadka chelovecheskogo ya* is 'The Riddle of the Human "I"'. (Russian has no easy equivalent of the English word 'self'.) So one way to pose Mikhailov's riddle is to ask what the first-person pronoun refers to. It refers, it would appear, to something that is both an object in the world and a subject aware of the world, and, moreover, aware of itself as an object that is aware of the world and aware of itself as part of the world. The 'I' is a subject–object. It is something that is conscious, but it is also a possible object of conscious awareness and, moreover, of its own self-conscious awareness. What is the nature of such subject–objects and how do they fit into the world? One of the book's principal concerns is to deny that such questions can be answered exclusively by natural-scientific means. We cannot account for mind, consciousness, or self in terms of brain functioning, or computational processes that might be exhaustively described in the terms of cybernetics or information theory.

The possibility of a scientific-naturalist account of mind was a hot topic in the Soviet Union in the 1960s and 1970s, when fascination with the so-

---

8   Nemeth 1981.
9   Bakhurst 1982.

called scientific-technological revolution stimulated considerable excitement about the potential of science to unlock the mysteries of mind. This prompted a humanistic backlash, of which *Zagadka* was a part. Mikhailov argues that human creativity is the rock on which naturalistic theories of mind ultimately come to grief. Human beings respond not just to what *is* but to what *might be*; we can view reality under the aspect of possibility; we set ourselves ends and ideals and act in their light. In thought we commune with the possible, the universal, the infinite, the ideal. There is no prospect of explaining this in the language of natural science. Here is a typical passage:

> Yes, thinking is creativity, and particularly the creating of values, which are not inherent in nature itself, just as the joy in Beethoven's 9th Symphony does not inhere in the physics of sound waves, and the luminous sadness of Levitan's landscapes is not part of the chemistry of the paint on his canvasses. The whole problem of consciousness, the essence of the riddle of the self, lies in understanding how in human life-activity the physical, the chemical and other forms of natural being are transformed into the beautiful, the good; into honour, dignity, truth, and justice; into that which serves as the foundation and the end of human life. Moreover, we need to understand how these great spiritual values can become the foundation of a programme for the transformation of nature carried out in accordance with nature's own laws. This is the way, indeed the only way, to see the question of the identity of thinking and being, which Engels called the great and fundamental question of philosophy.[10]

I think it would be natural for someone reading the book today to come to the following assessment: Considering the time and place in which it was written, *Zagadka* is a fabulous achievement. Its subject matter is just as topical here and now as it was there and then. But, for all its inventiveness and charm, the book is inconclusive, because it really swaps the riddle of the self for another one: the riddle of creativity. Moreover, the argument is outmoded. For instance, Mikhailov's main reason for rejecting the aspirations of artificial intelligence to build a 'thinking machine' is the old assertion that what a computer does is determined by its programme, while human activity exhibits genuine freedom and creativity. But in the twenty-first century we are familiar with computers capable of learning and making novel decisions, so it is much less obvious today

---

10   Mikhailov 2010, p. 342 (1980, p. 255). I cite the 2010 Russian edition and the corresponding page in the 1980 English version. My translation departs in places from Daglish's.

that machines are rule-bound in a way that human beings are not. Surely it would be better to separate the mind–body problem, which concerns the ontological status of mental states and episodes, from questions about imagination and creativity, which are of a different order altogether. So Mikhailov's book is impressive for its time, but it has limited relevance to contemporary debate. Or so it might be argued.

But such a reaction would seriously underestimate the book's achievements. It is true that Mikhailov positively embraces inconclusiveness, creating a mood of open-ended debate and enduring controversy. But he does this, not because he lacks answers, but because he aims to foster a spirit of authentic philosophical inquiry in a philosophical culture so often dominated by dogmatism and a paucity of dialogical imagination. More importantly, I want to suggest that the book does contain a solution to the riddle and, moreover, one of lasting significance.

A crucial theme of the book is what might be called 'the outwardness of mind', the idea that our mental lives are lived in public space, manifest in our interaction with the world and with each other. Mikhailov is determined to attack the Cartesian idea that the individual mind is a kind of self-contained subjective, inner world of thoughts and experiences. The Cartesian inner world is a lonely place. It has one and only one inhabitant – the self – the only subject that has immediate access to its contents. The self is aware of the external world beyond the mind's boundaries only indirectly, via the mediation of mental states; and its awareness of other minds is doubly indirect: it must infer what is going on in other people's minds by observing their behaviour. On this view, mind is a kind of place – an inner space – occupied by special 'subjective' states and episodes. Mikhailov thinks that the scientific naturalist essentially buys into this picture but thinks of the inner world, not as an immaterial substance as Descartes did, but as instantiated in the brain. The brain is portrayed as the organ of thought, the place where thinking happens, and our mental lives are represented as consisting in states and episodes occurring in our brains. And then we have the problem: Where is the self? Is it the brain? Is it *in* the brain? Is it a figment conjured up by the brain?

In contrast, Mikhailov argues that if we want to understand the nature of mind, we should look, not at what is going on inside us, but in our relation to the world. Mind is not a place within; it is present in our life-activity, in our mode of engagement with our surroundings and with each other. Mikhailov's opponents, however, found this difficult to take. To some of them, it seemed that Mikhailov faced a dilemma. If he was saying simply that our minds are manifest in what we do, his claim was true but trivial. Who would deny it?! Alternatively, if he was claiming that mind is not just exhibited by, but somehow *consists in* activity, then his position could only be a form of behaviourism, and behaviourism, as we know, is no good.

Mikhailov is indeed arguing that our mindedness resides in our activity. Activity is not merely the external mode of expression of something, the true nature of which lies elsewhere, in an inner realm no-one but a solitary self can enter. Mind is *immanent in* activity. But his position is not, or is not supposed to be, a form of behaviourism. It is important that the 'inner world' conception of mind is one half of a dualism, the other half being the 'external' world beyond the mind, conceived as a purely physical entity, bereft of mindedness, empty of meaning, normativity, and value. Behaviourism rightly refuses to see mind as an inner world, but it tries to portray mind entirely in terms given by the other side of the dualism: behaviour understood as bodily movement. Mikhailov rejects *both* sides of this 'two-worlds dualism' and the whole inner–outer distinction it brings in its wake.

Critical here is a view, which is central to Mikhailov's philosophy, and to Ilyenkov's. I call this view *personalism*. This is the idea that psychological states and episodes can properly be attributed only to persons. As Ilyenkov would put it: 'The brain does not think; the person thinks with the help of her brain'.[11] A brain cannot think that it is Tuesday, or regret never having been to Kyiv, or wonder whether Tottenham Hotspur could win the Champions League. Such things can only be done by beings that act in the world. This is not because regretting never having been to Kyiv can be reduced to a specifiable set of actual or possible behaviours, but because regretting is intelligible only in light of certain ways of acting, and hence only a being capable of acting can be said to regret. Persons are capable of acting in the appropriate ways, so mental attributes are properties of persons, of *whole persons* but not of their parts. Of course, in order for someone to have a mental life, her brain must be functioning in the right kind of way, but brain functioning enables mind; it does not constitute it.

In my view, this position *is* the solution to the riddle of the self, or rather it shows that there is no riddle because the problem was wrongly posed in the first place, as Mikhailov puts it.[12] We do not have to find a place for a mysterious entity, the self, in the inner world of the mind or in the external world of objects. We just need to recognise that the self is the person, the true subject of thought and experience, a bodily being in the world.

---

11   See Ilyenkov 1974a, p. 183 (2009b, p. 146); 2009a, p. 22 (2014, p. 40); and Arsen'ev, Ilyenkov, and Davydov 1966, p. 265. I discuss personalism at length in Chapter 14 below. It is also a theme in Bakhurst 2011.

12   Mikhailov 2010, p. 339 (1980, p. 253).

Personalism asks us to abandon the 'spatial' logic that represents mental states as entities – representational entities like images or sentences – located in an organ of thought within us. The location of a person's thoughts is not 'in' her brain, but wherever that person is (e.g. in the library, in the pub). But what, then, is thinking? Thinking is moving through the world, navigating reality, in a way that is responsive to reasons. Thinking beings are not just pushed around by causal forces; they mould their activity in accord with reasons for thinking and acting. They are not mere playthings of natural necessity, but rational beings responsible for justifying their thoughts and actions by appeal to the reasons in light of which they think and act. A rational being does not just respond to what is the case, but can think and act in light of what might, could, or will be the case. Such a being can set itself goals. It has the potential to transcend the limitations of its previous conceptions; in other words, to be creative. Now, it is very important that, for Mikhailov, as for most thinkers inspired by Kant and post-Kantian German philosophy, it is our responsiveness to reasons as such that eludes explanation by natural-scientific means, not just our creativity. Once we put the argument this way, it no longer looks like an outmoded appeal to the contrast between creative human activity and the rule-bound stupidity of machines. It is, rather, an appeal to the autonomy of reason, the impossibility of catching rationality in the nomological net of scientific theory, as Donald Davidson once put it.[13]

But how, on such a view, are we to picture mental states like beliefs or sensations? We can think of a belief as an orientation to the world, or as part of such an orientation, since beliefs do not exist in isolation, but are always part of a network. So when we describe someone as believing that it is Tuesday, we are characterising part of her orientation to the world, not describing something inside her. Similarly, when we say that she sees a candle on the table, we are describing her openness to part of reality disclosed to her by her visual field. We are not describing some inner state of hers (a person's visual field is not something inside her; it is that part of the world made perceptually available to her by her sense of sight).

With this, we begin to see the many ways in which Mikhailov portrays our mindedness as immanent in our modes of life-activity. I shall mention one further important connection. The Cartesian conception of the mind typically represents the self as aware of its own mental states in a process of incorrigible inner observation known as introspection. But the idea that each person is aware of her own mental states by observation is profoundly confused. If I

---

13   Davidson 1984a, p. 207.

ask you what you think about some question, you do not arrive at the answer by inspecting your beliefs, like exhibits in a museum, to see which ones you have. Rather, if you do not know what you think on the topic at issue, you have to make up your mind in light of the evidence. A person's relation to her own beliefs and attitudes is a normative, practical, agentive one, not a relation between an observer and objects waiting to be observed in a kind of mental museum.[14]

We must now ask a difficult question: If we reject the Cartesian picture in favour of a view that stresses the outwardness of mind, what sense can we make of the internality, the inwardness of our mental lives? Mikhailov owes us an account of subjectivity, but what resources does he have to provide one? Well, if we construe thinking as a mode of active engagement with the world, we can recognise that activities can be anticipated and rehearsed. Sometimes this involves a different form of 'external' activity, such as working with a model, but sometimes the rehearsal takes place just 'in thought' (though there may be somatic elements to such a mental rehearsal). We can, of course, rehearse, describe and reflect on our orientation to the world in what Vygotsky called 'inner speech', a transmuted form of public discourse. In addition, the very idea of a first-person perspective – a point of view on the world – introduces something unique to a particular agent. Each of us embodies a subjective standpoint, to which we alone are related as responsible agent. These elements can all figure in an account of subjectivity very different from the Cartesian's, and this is precisely what Mikhailov sought to develop over the course of his career.

An important theme in Mikhailov's thinking is that subjectivity is always directed outward toward other people. From the moment of birth, our individual being is addressed to others. Each individual orientation to the world may be unique, but it is never self-contained, insular, self-sufficient. Persons are constantly turned towards each other and their minds meet in their mutual recognition of subjectivity: in joint activity, in discourse, in sympathy, in love.

This talk of intersubjectivity and the meeting of minds introduces another prominent theme in Mikhailov's philosophy: the socio-cultural dimension of mind. Like Vygotsky and Ilyenkov, Mikhailov holds that initiation into culture is a precondition of the emergence of human psychological powers. We become persons, rational agents, only in virtue of our appropriation of forms of social life. This is not just because we need to acquire concepts, learn to reason, and so on. It is because the mode of activity constitutive of rational agency essentially involves inhabiting a world made meaningful by human activity. The

---

14   This is an important theme in Moran 2001, a book Mikhailov would have admired.

life of the mind is lived in a world replete with objects created by people for people, objects that embody human aims and purposes, whose very physical form embodies meaning or 'ideality'. This is a position familiar from Ilyenkov's work on the problem of the ideal, but there is no more poetic statement of it than in *Zagadka*, in which Mikhailov sympathetically expounds Hegel. Let me quote from this discussion:

> A human being lives in a world of things. She is directly surrounded by things created by previous generations. Consider the matter carefully! A person's every movement, every action, is an action with a thing that was previously created by people. The sum totality of these things forms the great 'body of human civilisation', the result of the activity of many generations, the objectified history of humanity. And since every such thing – being a part, a cell, in the totality of the substantialised (*veshchestven-nogo*) body of history – was created in order to satisfy certain desires, needs, or imaginings, and since each such thing is humanity's own spirit objectified and alienated from humanity – then the object-world of civilisation as a whole is the ideal world of mind, of consciousness, inert and settled in its material embodiment.
>
> And it is this 'world' that individual consciousness encounters above all (as something external to it). Encounters? No, we do not simply encounter this world as already fully developed individuals. The individual herself, her needs and the means of satisfying them – that is, the modes of her life-activity, her interaction with other individuals and with the whole world of things – these are not simply given. They emerge, take shape, and develop in the process of assimilating this objectively existing 'body of civilisation'.[15]
>
> The development of individual consciousness represents the gradual initiation of the individual into the spiritual treasure-house of humanity as a whole. An individual may make a contribution to that treasure but only, first, if she acquires sufficient mastery of the accumulated riches and, second, if she is able to resolve the contradictions she finds there – the contradictions of social history.[16]
>
> The universal forms of thought are nothing but super-individual historical 'stages' or forms assumed by the tempestuous flow of human history only to burst out again in a welter of human passions and then flow

---

15   Mikhailov 2010, pp. 141–2 (1980, pp. 88–9).
16   Mikhailov 2010, p. 143 (1980, p. 90).

back into new forms. These are, in fact, the *categories* – the universal forms of humanity's activity and relationship to the world as a whole, the forms in which thought is realised and which guide (determine) the course of our experience. And so far as the individual in the process of her social upbringing and education assimilates human history precisely in the forms in which it has realised itself, they become forms of her reason, the forms (and framework) within which her thinking and sensuous-empirical experience occurs. They are born not of individual experience, but of the 'experience of history' and are its forms. And only thereby are they forms of the individual history of each of us.[17]

There is much to say about these wonderful passages, and the idea of mind and social being contained in them. But I will stop here. And I do this in homage to Mikhailov. He and I discussed philosophy many, many times, usually at his home in Moscow. I would ask him to address some question, but he would typically find some prior question that needed to be considered before we could resolve mine. So we would start on this other question, and never get to my original one, usually because, after a couple of hours, Liuda would call us for dinner. This could sometimes be frustrating, but I quickly consoled myself, because dinner at Mikhailov's was wonderful, and there was always tomorrow to get back to philosophy. Now, of course, there is no tomorrow for our discussions, and I am left thinking about all those topics we might have considered and did not.

Felix Mikhailov is gone, but his many followers remain, and I am sure that discussion of *Zagadka chelovecheskogo ya* will long continue, and that the many writings he produced in his prolific later years will receive the attention they undoubtedly deserve.[18] In the meantime, the reader of the present volume may rest assured that the philosophical themes introduced in this chapter will re-emerge time and again in those that follow.

• •
•

The next chapter presents a transcription of one of the seminars Mikhailov organised on my behalf during my time in Moscow in the early 1980s. It offers the reader the chance to experience the character of discussions among creative and critical Soviet philosophers – to see Mikhailov and his colleagues in

---

17   Mikhailov 2010, pp. 147–8 (1980, pp. 92–3).
18   See, e.g., Mikhailov 1997; 2001; 2003.

action, debating philosophical questions that retain their resonance today. The topic – the nature of personhood and the social preconditions of mind – is one of central importance in both Soviet and Anglo-American philosophical traditions. It therefore allows us to juxtapose their contrasting philosophical styles and methods.

CHAPTER 2

Social Being and the Human Essence: A Dialogue with F.T. Mikhailov, V.S. Bibler, V.A. Lektorsky, and V.V. Davydov

In September 1982, I arrived in Moscow to spend a year exploring the philosophical culture of the Soviet Union. I found it hard to believe that professional philosophy in Russia had been reduced entirely to the stagnant dialectical and historical materialism that represented the public face of Soviet philosophy and the official philosophical 'worldview' of Soviet state ideology. I therefore resolved to work among Soviet philosophers in order to establish how their philosophical culture looked from the inside. It quickly became obvious that Soviet Marxism was by no means monolithic. Among its varieties, I chose to concentrate on a number of critical philosophers of a Hegelian-Marxist persuasion whose work, I felt, deserved scrutiny both for its intrinsic merits and for the light it cast on the tortuous history of philosophy in the USSR. And among these thinkers, I made the contribution of Evald Ilyenkov (1924–1979) my primary focus.

As I recounted in the last chapter, I was fortunate to have excellent contacts among Soviet philosophers thanks to my friend Felix Mikhailov, whose engaging book *The Riddle of the Self*, had first stimulated my interest in Soviet philosophy. Because of Mikhailov's support, many thinkers agreed to talk to me on politically sensitive matters despite the then uncertain consequences of fraternising with inquisitive foreigners. I resolved not just to conduct interviews as a foreign observer, but to engage my Russian hosts in some serious philosophical discussion. This would, I hoped, help to bridge the gulf between our respective backgrounds in philosophy and permit me to appreciate the perspective of a participant in Soviet debate.

It was obviously essential for me to work in Russian. Since that tongue is not my native language, Mikhailov and I decided I would give some seminars, where I could present a written text, carefully constructed in advance. A small group of interested and sympathetic colleagues would be invited to reply to my talks and their responses recorded on tape so that I could reflect upon them later. The result was a number of stimulating discussions that proved an invaluable resource for my research.

What follows is a transcription, translated into English, of a discussion which took place in March 1983. The topic was the concept of a person in Soviet Marxism. In my paper, I considered Ilyenkov's attempt to develop a theory of personhood by developing Marx's claim that the human essence is 'the ensemble of social relations'.[1] I argued that Ilyenkov's stance is ambiguous between two positions, and that while one of them is false, the other is true but trivial. The principal respondents were, apart from Mikhailov himself, the philosophers V.S. Bibler and V.A. Lektorsky, and the psychologist V.V. Davydov. All were friends and colleagues of Ilyenkov. They listened with courtesy to my criticisms, which they interpreted very generously, and proceeded to give considered and illuminating replies. (A number of other people attended some or all of the discussion and made occasional contributions, which are attributed in the text to 'Another'.)

Many years have passed since the discussion took place. The Soviet Union is no more and Soviet philosophy a thing of the past. Nevertheless, the transcription of the debate remains of interest. First, the text is of documentary significance. Philosophy in the Soviet Union was to a significant degree sustained in an oral culture. The published literature is thus only a partial record of Soviet philosophy and often cannot be properly appreciated without an understanding of background debates that may have never fully emerged in print. Despite this, there are few detailed records of Soviet philosophers in debate. This text helps convey something of the style of oral philosophising of one group of thinkers working within the orbit of broadly Marxist conceptions. It also reveals the humanity and charm with which these philosophers engage with ideas.

Second, it is to be hoped that Western readers will find the substance of the discussion philosophically interesting in its own right. Since the seminar took place, there has been a growing interest in the West – stimulated by communitarianism, feminism, post-modernism and other schools – in social constructivist views in general, and in the social constitution of 'persons' and 'selves' in particular. In addition, the participants all work within traditions of Russian thought which have had some influence in the West. The discussion invokes activity theory and Vygotsky's socio-historical psychology, and the influence of Bakhtin's dialogism and his concept of 'answerability' is plain to see.

A note on the participants. Vasili Davydov was a prominent educational psychologist in the Vygotskian tradition, who made his reputation with some significant work on generalisation in learning.[2] In the Spring of 1983, he was Director of the Institute of General and Pedagogical Psychology in Moscow,

---

1   Ilyenkov 1979b.
2   Davydov 1972.

where the present discussion was staged. Davydov had established a theoretical 'laboratory' at the Institute to which he had brought Mikhailov and Vladimir Bibler, whose influential book, *Myshlenie kak tvorchestvo*, had been published in 1975.[3] Also members of the laboratory were A.S. Arsen'ev and G.P. Shchedrovitsky. Shortly after the seminar took place, Davydov was ousted as Director of the Institute and the theoretical laboratory dissolved. Mikhailov moved to the Institute of Philosophy; his later writings include *Obshchestvennoe soznanie i samosoznanie individa* (1990), *Samosoznanie: moë i nashe* (1997) and *Samoopredelenie kul'tury* (2003).[4] Bibler retired from professional academe, but continued to pursue his philosophical concerns, producing in 1991, *Ot naukoucheniya k logike kul'tury*, a substantial book which develops further his idea of the 'philosophical logic of culture', and two further volumes.[5] Thereafter his work attracted quite a following. In 1983, Vladislav Lektorsky was Head of the Sector of the Theory of Knowledge at Moscow's Institute of Philosophy. In 1988, he became editor of *Voprosy filosofii*, a position he held for more than 20 years. He is author of a significant book on epistemology, *Sub"ekt, ob"ekt, poznanie*, which seeks to develop a Marxist epistemology in critical dialogue with Western schools. The book appeared in translation in 1984.[6] As the political climate changed under glasnost and perestroika, so the cloud over Davydov dissipated. He published *Problemy razvivaiushchego obucheniya* in 1986, was elevated to academician, and eventually returned to direct the Institute of General and Pedagogical Psychology.[7] Davydov died in 1998, Bibler in 2000, Mikhailov in 2006. Lektorsky is still very active philosophically. His book *Chelovek i kul'tura*, appeared in 2018.[8]

The discussion proved difficult to render into English. My argument against Ilyenkov trades on the idea that the Russian term *'lichnost''* is ambiguous between what in English is expressed by the words 'person' and 'personality'. The easiest option would have been simply to use the Russian term in the English text, but this created an awkwardness of style at odds with the fluency of my respondents' arguments. I therefore decided to translate *'lichnost''* in different ways according to context (e.g. 'person', 'personhood' and 'personality'), taking care, however, that these contrasting translations do not accentuate

---

3   Bibler 1975.
4   Mikhailov 1990a; 1997; 2003.
5   Bibler 1991a; 1991b; 1991c.
6   Lektorsky 1980. Lektorsky 1984 is an English translation. Bakhurst 1992 presents an interview with Lektorsky.
7   Davydov 1986.
8   Lektorsky 2018. Lektorsky and I remain in touch. I discuss his work in Bakhurst 2002.

the suggestion of ambiguity, or obscure my argument. Similarly, I have translated the difficult concept of *obshchenie* variously, sometimes as 'community', sometimes as 'communion with others'; and the adjective '*predmetnyi*', I have rendered as 'object-orientated', 'objective', or 'reified', according to context. I have tried to make the text gender-neutral, avoiding the general noun 'man', though unfortunately English does not have a term as apt as the Russian '*chelovek*' with its rich etymological associations.

The actual seminar ran over two days. I have collapsed the two discussions into one, and deleted the inevitable repetitions and recapitulations. Apart from this, very little editing was required to produce a polished text, a testimony to the oratorical skills of the Russian participants. Nevertheless, since failures of understanding, either linguistic or conceptual, may have affected my rendition of events, the text is best viewed as my reconstruction of the debate, rather than as a verbatim report. In addition, it should be stressed that the responses were made spontaneously, and should not be taken as representative of the participants' views either before or since the discussion itself. Moreover, as with all conversation, the participants may have said things that subsequent reflection would have led them to withdraw. As for the arguments I presented, they were offered in the spirit of 'devil's advocate'. However, as my respondents detected, I couldn't have played this role unless I had felt, as it were, a certain sympathy for the devil. I admit this with some chagrin, since I now find my former tolerance of such arguments disconcerting.

Whatever else this text may be, it represents some pleasant hours, well spent, in philosophical discussion among friends. I hope above all that the translation conveys the good-natured enthusiasm which characterised this debate.

Bakhurst: In the sixth of the 'Theses on Feuerbach', Marx writes that 'The human essence is no abstraction inherent in each single individual. In its reality it is the ensemble of social relations ...'.[9] Here are three quotations from Evald Ilyenkov's well-known article 'Chto zhe takoe lichnost'?' in which he applies Marx's idea to the concept of personhood:

> Personhood *in general* is the particular (*edinichnoe*) expression of the life-activity of the whole 'ensemble of social relations'. A *given* person is a particular expression of a necessarily restricted sum of these relations (not of all) by which he or she is directly connected with other individu-

---

9   Marx 1968, p. 29.

als (with some and not with all) – that is, with the 'organs' of the 'body' of the community, the body of humanity.[10]

Marxist logic does not locate the 'essence' of separate individuals in their abstract similarity, but, on the contrary, in a concrete totality (*sovokupnost'*), in the 'body' of the real ensemble of their mutual relations, mediated in various ways by things. The 'existence' of each separate individual is understood not as the concrete 'instantiation' of an abstract 'essence' but, quite the reverse, as an abstract and partial realisation of a concrete essence, as a fragment of this essence, as its phenomenon (*yavlenie*), as an incomplete and therefore inadequate (*neadekvatnyi*) embodiment of this essence in the organic body of each individual.

Here personhood is understood along completely materialist lines as something quite substantial and corporeal (*veshchestvenno-telesno*), as the real, corporeal-substantial totality of substantial-corporeal relations connecting a given individual with other such individuals by cultural-historical and not natural (*estestvenno-prirodnyi*) bonds.[11]

In the body of an individual, personhood fulfils and realises itself as a social form (*obrazavanie*) ('essence') which is in principle quite distinct from the body or the brain. What it is exactly is the totality (ensemble) of real, sensuous, object-orientated (*predmetnyi*) relations of a given individual to another individual (or individuals) mediated by things.[12]

Ilyenkov's article makes clear that he takes this view of personhood to have quite general significance. Here, at one fell swoop, is the core of a solution to questions about the nature of the self and self-consciousness, the character of self-knowledge, the development of individuality and the emergence of cultural identity.

There are grounds for scepticism, however, about whether the idea of the human essence as the 'ensemble of social relations' is as explanatory as Ilyenkov supposes. One significant problem is that the Russian term '*lichnost'*', as Ilyenkov uses it, appears to be ambiguous between what in English is denoted by the terms 'person' and 'personality' respectively. As a result, Ilyenkov sometimes seems to conflate metaphysical questions about the nature of persons with psychological and moral questions about the nature of personality. On the one hand, he is concerned with the self as the subject of thought and experi-

---

10   Ilyenkov 1979b, p. 196.

11   Ilyenkov 1979b, pp. 197–8.

12   Ilyenkov 1979b, p. 206.

ence, the criteria of personal identity, and so on. These issues do indeed pertain to the 'essence' of personhood, since they concern those characteristics a being must possess to qualify as a person and to remain the *same* person over time. On the other hand, however, Ilyenkov discusses how human *personality* flourishes or atrophies under certain conditions, and considers the circumstances in which human beings become self-critical individuals in contrast to conformists and self-deceivers. Such issues concern the scope and limits of human *character*, and, while interesting and important, they do not seem to bear on the essence of personhood as such. We understand perfectly well that Felix Mikhailov does not have his particular personality by *necessity*: Felix would have been no less a person had he been moody and foolish in contrast to sweet-tempered and talented.

Thus, in my view, Ilyenkov is trying to answer two distinct sets of questions at once. As a result, conceptual issues about the concept of a person are mixed up with broadly empirical questions about the development of character and personality. In consequence, it is unclear whether Ilyenkov is advancing (1) the *strong* thesis that *identifies* the essence of personhood with the ensemble of social relations, or (2) the *weak* thesis that personality and individuality are *shaped* by social interaction.

Ilyenkov's argument often trades on this unclarity. For example, he suggests that it is possible for a being who possesses personhood to lose it under certain conditions. He writes:

> The death of the person (*lichnost'naya smert'*) not infrequently takes place much earlier than the physical demise of some human being, and the former person, having become a motionless mummy, can bring more grief to people than a natural death.[13]

How is this to be understood? Is Ilyenkov really saying that someone may literally cease to be a person, that she may, as it were, lose her very self? Or is Ilyenkov speaking metaphorically? Is he saying what we all say when we complain that *chinovniki* (petty bureaucrats) are not real persons; that is, when we give metaphorical expression to the familiar thought that *chinovniki* possess no great individuality or character, that they operate more like machines than human beings, and so on? Whichever it is, Ilyenkov's position is in trouble. For while the literal reading (i.e. the strong thesis) looks impossible to defend, the

---

13   Ilyenkov 1979b, p. 235.

metaphorical (i.e. weak) reading merely expresses an uncontentious truth that is philosophically uninteresting. Ilyenkov's position is thus either false or trivially true.

The same dilemma haunts Ilyenkov's discussion of Alexander Suvorov's response to the question 'Where does personhood exist?' Ilyenkov quotes Suvorov, one of the blind-deaf pupils of educationalist Alexander Meshcheryakov:

> Where am I? Not here (touching forehead) and not here (pointing to chest) ... Ah, I understand: I am in the sum of my relations with friends ... and with enemies too. In the totality of my relations with other people, that is where.[14]

Ilyenkov enthusiastically endorses Suvorov's remark. But, again, how is it to be understood? If we are talking about a person's character or personality, and only metaphorically about the person as such, then Suvorov's answer is not really all that remarkable. However, if we take ourselves literally to be describing the location of the person, then the thesis looks obviously false. So once again, Ilyenkov's position appears to be either trivially true, or false.

This problem applies quite generally to the strong and weak theses set out above. The position that the essence of personhood is the ensemble of social relations looks false, and the view that personality is formed in social interaction is a banal and uncontentious thought.

Ilyenkov's article contains an intense treatment of the relation of personhood and self-consciousness (*samosoznanie*). He discusses Descartes's and Fichte's ideas of self-consciousness as an ideal relation of the subject to itself, as an exclusively mental phenomenon exhibited in the act of 'introspection' (*introspektsiya*). According to Ilyenkov, Descartes and Fichte take this special relation of the subject to itself to be central to the concepts of self and person. For them, personhood exists in the form of the self-consciousness of particular individuals (*edinichnoe samosoznanie*). Now, it is quite clear that Descartes's treatment of self-consciousness, in so far as it is relevant to questions of personhood, is entirely metaphysical in orientation: self-consciousness is portrayed as central to the self as a subject of thought, a primary characteristic of the 'I' that thinks and therefore is. Although there is a sense in which, for Descartes, each of us has special knowledge of the contents of our minds, it certainly doesn't follow that each individual has transparent knowledge of the nature

---

14   Ilyenkov 1979b, p. 216. Ilyenkov was much involved in Alexander Meshcheryakov's work on the education of the blind-deaf and wrote a number of papers about its philosophical significance. See Chapter 4 below and Bakhurst 1991, ch. 7.

of his own character or personality. A being self-conscious in Descartes's sense might understand itself very badly. Ilyenkov, however, proceeds to argue against Descartes's invocation of self-consciousness by arguing that people are often poor judges of their own personalities:

> One need not be very well acquainted with psychology to understand that the nature of an individual's personhood (*lichnost'*) in no way coincides with what she says and thinks about herself, with her self-opinion, self-awareness, or verbal self-evaluation, however sincere.[15]

Ilyenkov makes this futile argument because he slides from considerations about self-consciousness as the subject's pure introspective awareness of its own mental states, which is Descartes's focus, to a much richer conception of self-consciousness as self-knowledge or self-understanding, which has nothing to do with Descartes's claims. Once again, metaphysical issues about persons as selves or subjects of thought are conflated with psychological issues about the nature of character and personality.

Ilyenkov's treatment of self-consciousness is strangely ahistorical. He invokes a number of thinkers – Descartes, Fichte, Sartre, Freud, behaviourists, cyberneticians – and writes as if their respective discussions of self-consciousness are all really discussions of the same thing. This is surprising for a philosopher like Ilyenkov, whose Hegelian intuitions usually lead him to emphasise how philosophical conceptions, as products of a complex historically-evolving dialectic, need to be properly contextualised if we are to understand them aright.

But maybe I'm the one who is guilty of being insufficiently historical. Perhaps my background in Anglo-American philosophy makes it hard for me to see the point of Ilyenkov's remarks and my supposed efforts at conceptual clarification are really only expressions of confusion. It might be suggested, for example, that there is no sharp distinction between metaphysical questions about persons and psychological issues about the nature of personality, and hence the supposed ambiguity I find in Ilyenkov's discussion is merely an artefact of my own misunderstanding. So let me offer a thought experiment, adapted from the work of Bernard Williams, designed to illustrate why I think there are genuine metaphysical questions about the identity of persons which Ilyenkov's 'strong thesis' simply fails to address.[16]

---

15   Ilyenkov 1979b, p. 212.
16   See Williams 1973.

Suppose that Felix and I fall into the clutches of a mad scientist, endowed with all kinds of space-age Soviet technology, who wants to carry out the following experiment. First, he plans to hook Felix and myself up to a computer which will record the information stored in our respective brains. Then he will 'erase' the information in our brains: Felix and I will have total amnesia. After this, the scientist will exchange my brain for Felix's and vice versa; that is, he will put my brain in Felix's body and Felix's brain in my body. The computer will then endow Felix's brain with my memories and character, and Felix's memories and character will be given to mine. So, in one place we shall have what is now Felix's body, with my brain, but Felix's character and memories. And in another place we will have what is now my body with Felix's brain but my memories and character. Who will be who? Clearly, it is not all that easy to say. It is tempting, of course, simply to dismiss this as a pseudo-problem. Surely we cannot say in advance what the outcome of such an experiment will be. Perhaps we should declare that there is no determinate answer to the question of who is who.

However, imagine that the scientist tells us that after the operation he will reward one of his guinea pigs with $100,000 and torture the other. Suppose further that he asks me, as one of the unlucky participants, to decide which body should receive the money and which be tortured after the operation. Now, to me at least, the thought that there is no determinate answer to the question of identity in this case looks much less plausible. One and only one question stands before the guinea pig in this situation: When the lights go on after the operation, will I be the subject of consciousness of the body which is going to be tortured? Will I be looking out of the eyes that see the money or the knife? To put it bluntly, the question is: Will it hurt?

Now, were I not so personally involved in this nasty business, I would seek the advice of a sympathetic philosopher like Felix. But what can he, as a Marxist, committed to the 'Sixth Thesis', tell me? If I were to ask advice of a philosopher who holds that the identity of a person over time depends on the continued existence of his or her brain, then I would receive a determinate answer, for since my brain will be in Felix's body, this philosopher will have to say that I will have a new body with a new character and new memories to go with it. And if I consult a philosopher who holds that memory continuity is the key to personal identity, then he will advise me that after the operation I shall have a new brain. A behaviourist would also have an answer up her sleeve. She would say that, despite the physical changes, nothing will happen to the people involved in the operation. But if a Marxist tells me that I must go back to the classics and solve the problem on the basis of the 'Sixth Thesis' then it seems obvious that this is no help at all. The Marxist just gives the wrong kind of answer.

The ineptitude of the Marxist thesis in the face of enduring metaphysical questions about personal identity refutes Ilyenkov's claim that Marxism offers a quite general answer to questions about the human essence. The strong thesis is just false. If the Marxist retreats to the weak thesis and argues that the 'Sixth Thesis' bears only on questions of the development of human personality, then there is a danger his or her position will reduce to no more than the familiar platitude that human beings develop through interaction with other people and the character of that development is influenced, sometimes profoundly, by the social circumstances of their lives.

Let me conclude by mentioning one area where Soviet views of the human essence as 'the ensemble of social relations' seem particularly weak. This is the problem of death. Soviet philosophers are wont to say that there is a sense in which human beings can survive their own deaths, for through her life-activity the individual puts her very life into the world. She takes part in the creation of the very sphere of social relations that represents her essence as a human being. And this contribution survives her own physical death. This 'solution' to the problem of immortality is often presented in optimistic spirit.

Now, maybe I am missing the point, but when a person, suffering terribly in the face of death, asks herself whether she will survive her death, no appeal to the 'Sixth Thesis' will satisfy her. She would surely feel that, once again, the Marxist answer speaks to a different question from the one she is putting. Her question is: Will I continue to exist as a subject of consciousness after my death? Will I be capable of some kind of agency? According to Soviet Marxism, I neither survive as consciousness nor as agent, but only as a fossilised contribution to human history over which I can exercise no control. This is a chilling vision of survival.

I have argued that Ilyenkov's account of the 'human essence' is either false or vacuous. Soviet Marxists must either take full metaphysical responsibility for the claim that personhood is constituted by social relations, or recognise that their position amounts to a collection of platitudes.

Mikhailov: Let met begin with a few remarks about the status of David's paper. In my view, we shouldn't treat David's words simply as a critique, by one particular representative of a foreign philosophical tradition, of one particular article published in the USSR. David's paper raises a number of cardinal, even painful, questions we are forced to face not just in confrontation with Anglo-American philosophy, but also in arguments here at home. I remember how, at a seminar at this Institute, a prominent psychologist gave a paper on personhood (a subject, of course, constantly under discussion) in which he said the following (although he has no relation to analytic philosophy whatsoever!): 'Comrades! Listen! You're always telling us the human essence is the ensemble of social relations. But I'm a *psychologist,* and as such I am concerned with questions about the character of the individual, the explanation of behaviour, and so on. I'm trying, as it were, to define the structure of individuality. What do you offer me in the idea that the human essence is the ensemble of social relations? A general definition of *homo sapiens*; a general answer to the question: What are human beings? Well, taken in that spirit, I agree. Human beings are the ensemble of social relations! Human beings are historically developing beings! Human beings are the culturo-historical environment! But while such definitions are the stuff of philosophical seminars, where I can assent to them with a clear conscience, they don't help me investigate what interests me as an empirical psychologist. I simply cannot *work* with such definitions'. In this we see that, for psychologists, questions of the human essence become questions about the unique, subjective, unrepeatable, individual existence of the individual. Forgive this tautologous formulation, but it's important to emphasise that psychologists typically see problems of the self as problems of the immediate reality of here-and-now-unfolding subjective Being. That's what interests them, that's what they want to focus on.

Now, I agree wholeheartedly with David that personhood *is* intrinsically bound up with the nature of self-consciousness, or what one might call 'reflexion', with the empirical fact expressed in the thought experiment and in the discussion of 'life after life' – of subjective Being, which so captivates psychologists, empiricists, and indeed, writers, artists, and any thinking person at any time. And, in our version of Marxism, this real fact must stand at centre stage. Thus, in my view, the issue is how we can create one approach (and not fall between two, 'weak' and 'strong') which addresses *both* metaphysical questions of the coming into being, development, and the determination of the stream of subjective Being which holds so great a fascination for us, *and* questions about the realisation of the most natural and empirical dimensions of the existence of every human being.

This is especially pressing, because in our work with psychologists the discussion always boils down to this: 'Be concrete', they say, 'We're talking (e.g.) about how the school pupil's developing ability (*umenie*) to solve tasks becomes the foundation of the emergence of her creative capacities (*sposobnosti*)'. But to define the concept of a 'capacity', it's no use lurking in the misty abstraction of the 'ensemble of social relations'. Likewise, naturalistic philosophers, like David Dubrovsky, chide us in the following way: 'While you study the "material development of history", claiming that the human essence is the ensemble of social relations, and so on, I seek a more concrete approach to human beings in science, physiology, medicine, etc. I argue that a human being's brain works in such-and-such a way and therefore he understands so-

and-so. But if you tell me that his understanding, or failure to understand, is connected with whether he has come into contact with clever or stupid people, then that's just *banal*. Such matters pertain to the development of the essence in the external world, but I want to define that essence itself'. And therefore the naturalist doesn't see that essence for what it is. It's not that the naturalist is a fool (I use that undiplomatic expression for the sake of brevity), it's that *we* have not done enough. It is still possible to sail blindly past a proper understanding of Marx's insight. We have not brought this insight face to face with the real issues.

Bibler: Or to put it another way, we have not faced up to the metaphysical responsibility that the 'Sixth Thesis' forces upon us.

Mikhailov: Quite so. Thus, this is the beginning of a conversation about how far this responsibility has been discharged in our works. About what has been achieved and what remains undone. We must identify places where we start to repeat ourselves like a record stuck in the groove.

I want to emphasise that, in my view, the issue here is about a clash of two approaches, two logics. David, in analytic style, urges us not to mix up two sets of questions. But in our tradition, when we make a division between two spheres, the next step is *identification.* We must seek to understand the cause of the split: whether it's logical or historical. In this case, we must ask how a division into, on the one hand, purely metaphysical and, on the other, strictly empirical questions is *possible.* And in our tradition, we must seek a *third* in which neither (A) the metaphysical serves as the basis for the solution of empirical problems, nor (B) the empirical forms the foundation for generalisations masquerading as philosophical truths. The naturalist takes course (B). He wants to define the human essence by considering all the various empirical manifestations of human behaviour, physiology, information processing, and so on. Advocates of course (A), which one could call 'quasi-' or 'feeble-Hegelian' (it's a parody of a truly Hegelian perspective), hold that we can establish general laws of reality – nature, thought, and society – and we may bravely assert that any empirical phenomenon is just a realisation of those laws. All that remains is to provide a justification in the given instance. It was from this perspective that one of our philosophers said that all scientists are like Moliere's character who was told that he'd spoken in prose all his life though he never realised it. Scientists are really all dialecticians. They really all profoundly understand that the quantitative is transformed into the qualitative and so on. They put the laws of the dialectic to work all the time, but they don't know they're doing it. On this view, it's our job as philosophers to say, 'Hey gang, when you're doing an experiment and you notice that after certain quantitative changes there occurs a qualitative change, don't forget that Hegel knew about this too and that Marx also wasn't against this sort of thing'. I want to suggest that these two approaches – naturalist-empiricist and quasi-Hegelian – are identical in logical structure; they're two sides of the same coin. Either we prop up the empirical conception of the person with general concepts that, as it were, decide everything in advance, or we try to draw out the general concepts from the empirical facts. This split manifests itself in other ways too. On the one hand, we talk about 'humanity', and on the other, humanity steps aside and there remain people, individuals. And this is not just a logical contrast between universal and particular concepts: it's easy, for example, to love humanity, but it's difficult to love each individual. Devilishly difficult. (That, of course, is an old thought. We need only mention Dostoevsky.)

So, in my view, David's paper does not just set two national schools at odds with one another, or counterpose two distinct class approaches (though this may not be entirely irrelevant). In the final analysis, the real tension is between two *logics*, two methods, two ways of looking at any phenomenon placed before us. The clash is between, on the one hand, the one-dimensional logic of naturalism and quasi-Hegelianism, and on the other, the genuinely dialectical logic of our own tradition in which humankind and human beings, community and individual, essence and particular, are seen to exist somehow as *one* subject.

I'll return to these themes later.

Bibler: I have a number of detailed observations to make, but for now I'll restrict myself to three points to clarify how I understand David's contribution.

First, in my opinion, we shouldn't see David as simply rehearsing well-trodden moves from the perspective of a particular tradition. The paper clearly expresses some of his own doubts and reflections at a certain stage in his philosophical development. His central point concerns the implicit ambiguity he finds in the assertion that the human essence is the ensemble of social relations, and his principal thought is that without critique, deepening and development, the thesis turns out to be impeachable, since it confuses two distinct assertions of different logical forms: strong and weak. And actually, candidly speaking, in the majority of our work, when we assert that the human essence is the ensemble of social relations, we immediately begin to retreat in the face of rather insignificant challenges. We worry that we can't say straight out that the human essence is the ensemble of social relations, because every person nevertheless changes in those relations, he relates them to himself and, in turn, changes them. He is not simply a manifestation of those relations. If that were so, personhood would simply be a manifestation of an essence existing in (as Ilyenkov has it) 'corporeal-substantial' form as 'corporeal-substantial relations' (this would make personhood more corporeal than even *value*, Ilyenkov's paradigmatic example of an ideal phenomenon that transcends the substantial-corporeal). Moreover, we're nervous about asserting that a person is the ensemble of social relations because of course it's also true that the ensemble of social relations is society itself. It looks like we have a choice between two supposed definitions: (1) Society is the ensemble of social relations; (2) A person is the ensemble of social relations. And if we can't keep them apart our opponents will ridicule us: 'So, persons and society are the same?! What, my dear Marxists, are you talking about? Are you saying that the individual and society are two peas in a pod? After all, you just exchanged the one term for the other!' Faced with this prospect, we weaken our thesis. 'Look', we reply, 'We're not metaphysicians! We don't want you to take us *literally*. Clearly persons and society are not identical. We don't want to overdo the "is" in the thesis that a person is the ensemble of social relations. We really just meant that a human being lives in society, she acts in one way or another in that society and in the course of her life, her personality takes shape as a result of her interaction with the ensemble of social relations'. But now we are asked, not only by analytic philosophers but also by our own Soviet philosophers of an analytical bent, 'Takes shape? What sort of "taking shape" do you have in mind? This now looks like a story about how personality emerges. You have swapped the initial question for another. At best, you're confusing considerations about the emergence of personhood with the definition of its essence. Does the genesis of something define its essence? Obviously not! There's a gap here. Whatever the influence of the ensemble of social relations, it is acting upon *something*'. So when we advance the strong thesis, pretending to be daring, we soon run for cover in the weak thesis when it's demanded we take full metaphysical responsibility for the identity of personhood and the ensemble of social relations. But the weak thesis risks banality.

Taking up David's challenge, I shall not enter into a crude polemic with analytic philosophers, but rather, I want to account for the objections they raise and to assimilate their thoughts into my own logical plan. When I say that personhood arises in the course of social life, then this is a strange, paradoxical combination of the strong and weak variants. Personhood emerges, or better, *arises* only through the action of society, of social relations, on the individual, but it arises as something *irreducible* to that determination by society, as something present only in the individual, quite irreducible to the sum of those interactions from which it emerged. Thus, the strong thesis enters on the back of the weak, and by its sheer strength overshadows the weak and makes it look trivial.

Second, David rightly gestured at the background to the debate. I want to add that I don't think that it's proper to identify the Marxist conception of personhood with the views advanced in Ilyenkov's 'Chto zhe takoe lichnost'?' Of course, it's unimportant whether the view represented by Mikhailov, Lektorsky, Davydov or Bibler is truly *Marxist*. But it's worth pointing out that in this article Ilyenkov does not do justice to his *own* view, to that part of his position which *is* distinctively Marxist.[17] In the *1844 Manuscripts*, Marx said we should never look at human beings simply as the totality of social relations; human beings create those relations and can never be reduced to their influence. This thought, so central to Ilyenkov's philosophical credo, is not sufficiently prominent in this article. Well, I shall not go on about what exactly Marx had in mind, or else we'll get bogged down in tiresome matters of interpretation. I shall restrict myself to Ilyenkov's article in which the central questions are posed very sharply, giving rise to problems which we must solve if we are to proceed. Thus, what I shall say later will be, to an extent, a critique of Ilyenkov, in conjunction with David's own, based on the idea that these problems can be solved in the tradition of the 'High Rationalism' of Hegel and Marx, properly understood. David's paper poses problems from within this tradition, and certainly highlights deficiencies in our position. We will not get very far as Marxists if we criticise at worst Soviet naturalists and at best Descartes. We are Marxists if we are able to criticise ourselves and develop our position by so doing. We must not simply hold up a big stick, moreover one wielded by the state, to beat down traditions which think differently. That is just cheap. We should never even think of such things.

Finally, David is not simply expressing the views of analytic philosophers, nor is he simply giving us *his* views. The point is that two or three central arguments in the paper militate against reducing the problem of the self, of subjective Being – that distinctive view of the world 'from within' of each individual subject – to a pseudo-problem. David is out to reveal the genuinely metaphysical character of the problem. David's style is analytic, but his criticism is really made from the tradition of High Rationalism, albeit in its most Cartesian form. You, David, reveal the reality of the problem and claim that we lack the metaphysical bite to chew on it. That doesn't sound like the words of an analytic philosopher to me.

Mikhailov: Let me make one further point about the relevance of David's paper. We mustn't lose sight of the fact that Ilyenkov's article was written in response to certain concrete philosophical tendencies at work in this coun-

---

17   A more satisfying discussion can be found in Ilyenkov's manuscript 'O suchchnosti chel-oveka' ('On the Human Essence'), first published in Ilyenkov 2018a, pp. 186–92.

try. It is by no means a final statement of an encyclopedic type: 'This is the problem of *lichnost'* and Marxists believe such-and-such ...'. The article is bold, lively, and it has its addressees. If Evald were here today he would urge us to see the piece in the light of a particular controversy. I have in mind not just the fight against naturalism, but a broader battle against the whole logic of 'socio-biological' dualism. This dualism forces us into the following dilemma. *Either* individuality is connected with a certain property (which we might define as 'mind' or 'psyche' or some such, or perhaps we might choose not to define it), and a human being is thought to enter the world with this 'X' which already has a specific form. She enters the world already as *that which must develop*, and the process of individualisation is played out in purely quantitative changes, by degree. Admittedly, there emerge qualities which were not there previously, but the explanation of their emergence takes us back to this 'X'. The main thing is that the subject enters the world as an unrepeatable individual. *Or* the individual is thought to enter the world as a kind of blank, like this freshly minted five kopek piece. The features this coin acquires, which will differentiate it from others, depend on who uses it. All the scratches and erosion are a product of external, social factors. Here the ensemble of social relations does its work. It leads that faceless blank to unrepeatable individuality. These two positions represent *one* logic, the logic of socio-biological dualism. Neither alternative suits me at all, whether in Leontiev's or Rubinshtein's versions (or the version of those contemporary psychologists who claim to be following Rubinshtein, though they are really a long way from that). If we say, as Ilyenkov seems to, that from within *nothing* emerges, then on this logic our view reduces to the banality that each individual differs from others because she was lucky enough to meet A and not B: in these meetings lies her individuality. But this is absurd. Personhood hardly warrants 'stratigraphical' treatment. We recoil from innatism and adopt a view which portrays personhood as acquired in an entirely *external* form. And thus we lose the subject's particular distinctive view on the world that is the key to his or her individuality. Well, it is either one view or the other ... or perhaps, there's room for the impossible 'third'. A question of great significance to which I shall return.

Lektorsky: Let me begin with David's claim that the Russian word '*lichnost''* is ambiguous between, as the English has it, 'person' and 'personality'. He argues that while we may take the Marxist thesis that the human essence is the ensemble of social relations to mean that our personality, or individuality, is formed in the process of our interrelations with others, this fails to speak to questions about the essence of personhood as such. It is clear from what David goes on to say that he takes the essence of the person to be connected with self-consciousness, or the capacity for 'introspection'. Here he invokes Descartes, and also the analytic tradition. This appeal to analytic philosophy strikes me as odd, for this tradition contains many philosophers who see things very differently from David. Indeed, analytic philosophers have, to a far greater degree than Marxists, written off these questions as pseudo-problems. Ryle, for instance, holds that the 'self' is a fiction. So, it is not we Marxists who are dismissing the problem. The dismissal paradoxically comes from within the very tradition in the name of which David reasserts the relevance of the problem.

David's paper is certainly reminiscent of certain writers of the past. Fichte, for example, draws a dichotomy between the 'pure self' and the empirical self or individuality. Where the latter is formed and develops in the actual world – in processes of interaction and interrelation – the analysis of the pure 'I', pure consciousness, pure ego, pure *essence*, leads us simply to self-consciousness. Such dichotomising dominated philosophy for some time. It is not characteristic of contemporary analytic schools, nor, indeed, of contemporary existentialism. But in the 'old philosophical tradition', it was common to draw a fundamental distinction between pure and empirical selves, and I think David is heir to this tradition.

David claims that the strong interpretation of the Marxist thesis is indefensible and that the weak is banal. Against this I want to stress that Marx's approach is by no means trivial. For Marx, the influence of the totality of social relations on a human being makes that being whatever he or she becomes. Thus its influence is far from trivial. Indeed, Marx's distinctive contribution to philosophy consists precisely in the 'detrivialisation' of the status of our social being. It is question-begging to assert the triviality of Marx's position from the point of view of the very tradition from which he is seeking to break away. For me, the crux of Marx's position is precisely the idea that the most essential characteristics of persons cannot be understood without reference to the relations *between* people, for without these relations a person does not develop. By this, I mean, not that persons do not *flourish* outside social relations, but that they do not *come into being*. This is not a trivial claim, but one with far-reaching consequences, not just for the given questions but also for more concrete issues, especially in psychology. The self, for example, is not treated as an object, as a kind of substance to which one might point and which is from the outset open to introspection and self-consciousness. Rather, the self is seen as a system of relations between myself and others. Outside of this system of relations, I simply cannot exist. I am, by my nature, a *dialogical* essence. My self cannot form or function outside mutual relations, outside an *exchange* of relations between myself and others. This approach gives rise to a whole range of questions which simply did not exist for Descartes or Fichte (they begin to emerge with Hegel's *Phenomenology of Spirit*). There is the problem of my Being-for-others, my Being-for-myself and the Being-of-others-for-me. There's the question of the nature of object-orientated activity and its role in the development of the self. And there's the problem of 'reflexion'; that is, of meditative contemplation, of thought directed inward. This relates to that peculiar feature of self-consciousness we call 'introspection', which plays so great a role for Descartes and Fichte. In my view, introspection should not be conceived as a relation of someone to something purely *inside* him- or herself, but as a special way of relating oneself to others. Introspection is really *'extra-spection'*. A human being always lives on the boundary between self and other. These are serious themes which demand serious treatment. Here, I mean only to indicate that the Marxist approach to questions of personhood and self-consciousness is fundamentally different from the classical early modern approach to the subject. I don't mean to suggest that Marxists have all these problems solved. But I do want to say that Marxists take these questions seriously, unlike those who, such as Ryle, treat them as pseudo-problems.

David would no doubt agree that Marxists take the questions seriously and that they approach them differently from other thinkers. Indeed, he suggests that the Marxist approach is *so* different that Ilyenkov's attempt to counterpose Marx to Descartes, Fichte, Freud and so on, is ahistorical because these different thinkers are literally talking about different things. I don't agree with this. It is true that they gave different answers and that the problems were posed for them in different conceptual schemes. But these contrasting 'frames of reference' were just different means to attack the very same problems. I cannot accept the implication that different philosophical systems are, in a certain sense, incommensurable. The incommensurability of theories is implausible even in the natural sciences. It is important to argue with Kuhn's notorious thesis that the discourse of science goes on within paradigms which are in some sense 'closed' to one another. When it comes to philosophy, Kuhn's position is all the more counterintuitive. For, while it is possible to study contemporary physics without taking an interest in Newton, let alone Aristotle, it is impossible to study philosophy in a cultured manner without coming to grips with Aristotle, Descartes, or Kant. In a way, they are our contemporaries. The problems discussed by these philosophers, and the solutions they gave, have not become antiquated. They continue to influence our thought. For me, in a certain sense, all philosophical problems are eternal problems. The problem of truth discussed by contemporary analytic philosophers, is just the same problem that Aristotle attempted to solve. This is perhaps the distinguishing feature of philosophy as a discipline. Thus a truly historical approach must be cognisant of how the same questions have been treated over time. It is talk of incommensurability that is ahistorical for it cannot speak to the question of how theories develop.

David suggests, in his discussion of Descartes and Fichte, that Ilyenkov conflates the notions of self-consciousness and self-cognition (*samopoznanie*) or self-knowledge. This isn't fair. For Descartes, and certainly for Fichte (and others too), self-consciousness was conceived as the premise and foundation of self-knowledge. (It was Kant, by the way, who distinguished these things; for him, self-consciousness and self-cognition are quite different phenomena.) Thus, it is no coincidence that Descartes's ideas not only began endless philosophical discussions about self-consciousness but were also the starting point of classical psychological theories of introspection that treat introspection as a means of self-cognition.

Let me summarise my position. Individuality is formed in the process of interaction with the ensemble of social relations, but so too is the deep structure of personhood itself, for my person is formed in my interaction with others. This interaction is at once both contingent and necessary. It is contingent in the sense that the encounters with others that make me what I am occur contingently. Here there is a considerable factor of chance at work. But it is necessary in that *outside* this system of interaction no person can exist.

Two qualifications are necessary. First, don't think this position underestimates human beings' natural characteristics. Of course, each individual is unique. The natural potentialities of each individual are different, and it is upon them that the ensemble of social relations is laid. Second, persons are not passive products of a system of relations. Nothing of the kind. Marx's point is that human beings are *active*. We make ourselves, but we can do so only in a system of relations with other people. This is a very important feature of the Marxist position which perhaps we do not stress enough.

Now for the problem of death. Of course, I agree that nothing can diminish the fact that, in death, individuality is lost. Death is always tragic. We can't take solace in the ensemble of social relations, but nor can we, in my view, in the strange idea of personhood as something eternal and absolute, a necessary relation to oneself which was, is, and always will be. It's interesting to note, however, that the construal of personhood as individuality in a way which emphasises the uniqueness and dissimilarity of persons is very much a historical product. The majority of cultures, past and present, do not treat personhood in this way. It's a modern Western mode of thought, characteristic neither of Antiquity, nor of the European cultures of the Middle Ages. Take the problem of authorship in the Middle Ages which Bakhtin so beautifully described. When someone painted an icon or created a sculpture, he did not dream of showing *who* had done it. This was not considered important. And Eastern civilisations often reveal different attitudes to death and the self. For modern Western cultures, of course, individuality is a crucial value and our concepts of personhood reflect this.

I must admit, however, that the problem of death is not much discussed in Soviet philosophy ...

Davydov: What about Frolov's recent piece in *Voprosy filosofii*?[18]

Lektorsky: Actually, Frolov approaches the question on the basis of the myth that David attacked. For him, the most important thing is that we somehow survive in our contribution to culture. Frolov has some interesting things to say, but he's hardly the last word on the subject.

Finally, a word about David's thought experiment. Well, it is interesting, but I am reluctant to agree with the conclusions David draws. I am inclined to side with Wittgenstein who disapproves of such procedures in philosophy. The experiment is indeed rather extravagant. The experiment presupposes that, as it were, the body is one thing, the brain another ...

Davydov: What! Never distinguish the brain from the body in that way!

Lektorsky: ... and memory is a third. You imagine the three separated and swapped about among various individuals. But, the whole thing is that, a person – the bearer of this 'I', this self – and his memory are connected with a given body and a given brain. So when you talk about their separation and recombination you destroy the very conditions in which it makes sense to discuss these questions. But if the point of the experiment is just to show that the problems you discuss are real and not pseudo-problems, then I will grant you that. Questions of the interrelation of self, brain and body, and of self and other, are indeed central philosophical questions.

David's paper is essentially a critique of Ilyenkov's 'Chto zhe takoe lichnost'?', although it is also a criticism of Marxist positions on personhood in general. I want to emphasise in conclusion that, although Ilyenkov's article is interesting and provocative and represents our position very well, I do not believe these problems have been entirely solved. However cogent Ilyenkov's position, there is a great deal to add since this whole area is enormously rich in both philosophical and psychological interest.

Davydov: I think that in Ilyenkov's article there are two distinct areas of investigation: on the one hand, a discussion of the human essence, and on the other a treatment of the problem of personhood. Although the book in which the article was published is called *S chego nachinaetsa licnost'*, a significant part

---

18   Frolov 1983.

of the piece is devoted to a cogent, though popular, exposition of the Marxist conception of the human essence. This part of the article wholly fulfils a very significant, and very topical, task. It attacks those naturalistic conceptions of human beings which continue to exist in our philosophy and psychology and, indeed, are growing in strength. In the last years of his life, Ilyenkov fought angrily with Soviet naturalists about questions of the relation between the social and the biological in human development, the genetic pre-conditioning of human abilities, and so on. It is well-known that while the success of genetics strengthens naturalism about human abilities in general, the success, or rather the *imaginary* success of psychophysiology contributes to the survival of naturalism in research into human mental processes. Hence the wealth of naturalistic literature found here. Ilyenkov joined forces with the prominent Soviet geneticist N.I. Dubinin to argue that all human abilities have a socio-communal genesis, and he took on David Dubrovsky in a well-known debate on the status of mental processes.[19] The article under discussion continues these themes; a large part of it is devoted to proving the Marxist thesis that the human essence is the ensemble of social relations, and that from this essence we can derive all aspects of personhood, including emergent individuality.

In my view, although Ilyenkov's article is cogently written (he was able to write clearly and imaginatively), his real contribution to the debate about persons – his way of developing the significance of the Marxist thesis – does not come through here. Well, it was a popular book, written to propagate the views of certain fairly well-known Marxist thinkers.[20] The intention was to block off the stream of all these naturalistic ideas from the consciousness of the general public. But let me not dwell on that. My point is that there is another side of Ilyenkov's contribution which emerges far less clearly in the article. This concerns not the human essence as such, but personhood in particular.

For Ilyenkov, someone is a person (*lichnost'*) if he or she is able to break accepted norms of social practice. To *break* them! And from that perspective, we know that the overwhelming majority of people do not possess personhood, for they are brought up with the souls of conformists and submit themselves to the norms of existence created by others. From this point of view, they are not persons. Indeed, there's very little personhood about. Ilyenkov's image of a person is thus one of a courageous individual, responsible for his or her own actions. He argues further that social life is such that circumstances can arise

---

19   Ilyenkov 1968c. The article appeared in English translation as Ilyenkov 1969.
20   Davydov himself contributed a chapter to the first edition of *S chego nachinaetsa lichnost'*, 'Lichnost' nado "vydelat'sa"' ('Personhood must be "manufactured"'), pp. 109–39. It was cut from the revised and expanded second edition of 1984.

in which someone who possesses the source (*nachalo*) of personhood may lose it and become a *mummy*. They live physically, but they have lost their person-hood. In this sense, someone may die as a person before he or she dies as a social being. In my view, this distinction between the individual and the person represents the strongest aspect of Ilyenkov's article ...

Bibler: But it is not there!

Davydov: It is too ...

Bibler: If it is, then so much the worse for the article.

Davydov: Excuse me, but it is there. For God's sake, it is there in black and white. You just have to read it properly. But I'll tell you for nothing that you don't read everything properly. (*Laughter*)

Why is this important? Today we face the social problem of conformism. This, for Ilyenkov, is the same question as the nature of personhood. How are we to bring up real persons? In the article by Frolov I mentioned above, there's a big quotation from the twenty-sixth volume of Marx and Engels's *Collected Works*, where Marx enthusiastically evaluates Ricardo's position on social develop-ment. Here Marx says something very close to the position I find in Ilyenkov. Marx writes that sometimes the interests of certain individuals coincide with the interests of the development of society. For those whose personal interests, for various reasons, coincide with the interests of a society where real social struggle is taking place, their personal interests coincide with the progressive tendencies of social development as we conventionally express it. On this basis, personhood is born, in all spheres.

When I reproduced this Ilyenkovian thesis at a recent conference on the psy-chology of personhood, there was a scandal! Everyone started to say, 'So, not everyone is a person?!' 'That's right', I replied, 'not everyone'. 'And what about us?!' they bleated. Well, you want to say, 'People who ask such stupid questions aren't even in the running!' (*Laughter*)

It is really rather difficult to say who does and who does not possess person-hood. Fortunately or unfortunately, psychology has not discovered the litmus of personhood. In my view, personhood is not 'chosen', or rather, it is chosen only in the sense in which Marx spoke of special individuals who find themselves situated in a privileged position in terms of the responsibility vested upon them by the social order. Such people are few, but they are present at all levels, from housewives to politicians. However, we see many politicians who are not persons and many housewives who we happily consider are. For example, I consider my own mother to have been a person. She died a long time ago, but she died a person. It's also true that her personhood grew on profoundly religious ground. But, accepting certain Christian precepts, she was a cour-ageous woman because she broke a succession of accepted customs, norms and demands. Moreover, in this she risked a lot. She was a non-conformist. From my mother's point of view, any self-respecting Christian must have the courage to stand up for his or her position against all others. This she identified with the image of Christ. She was, however, by no means a theologian. She never read theological works. So personhood may have many sources, including religious ones.

Wherever there are the roots of non-conformism, we see the beginning of personhood. The idea of fully developed personhood is another matter; the problem of the far-off day when personhood will be fully developed remains unsolved. llyenkov, however, built the foundation for a distinction between the human individual, social by his or her very nature, and personhood.

Ilyenkov's views on personhood have great significance for contemporary psychology, especially educational psychology. It transpires that the school pupil is not a person. Hegel, in his day, wrote very perceptively on this problem, although in rather different terms. For Hegel, young people, spending their time in educational institutions, do not engage in *practice*. They master *ideals*. When they leave these institutions and confront the real practice of civil life, they must either act in accord with their ideals or betray them. By 'practice' here I mean the real productive activity of social reality, in which we confront tasks that demand we take individual responsibility.

Another: But surely a pupil in 5th grade can …

Davydov: Nothing of the sort! They do not have free choice. And here one must freely choose how to act. In the literature on the psychology of custom, we observe that the majority act in conformity with the demands of authority, and thereby they enter a path bereft of personhood. On this score, one should read Tolstoy's magnificent 'Death of Ivan Ilych'.[21] Ivan Ilych, after leaving an institution of higher education, strove to lead a pleasant and respectable life. And what he found pleasant and respectable was what was commanded by authority. Thus Ivan Ilych entered the path bereft of personhood. And with us today similar things occur. Indeed, the majority go that way. That's why the question of how to bring forth personhood is so important to us. Hegel, moreover, thought that a person only acquires personhood if he takes upon himself the responsibility for serious social, moral and political decisions. He must solve such problems himself, and not 'let another man enter his soul'. We find an analogous position in Chernyshevsky, which Lenin quotes approvingly. Thus school only forms the premise or ground of personhood, which finds its syn-

---

21   Tolstoy 1960.

thesis only when the individual confronts social reality, civil society. If you're looking for a 'strong thesis' to read into Ilyenkov then look no further.

Now to the question of self-consciousness. Ilyenkov did not really study the phenomenon of self-consciousness. Well, thank God for that. In Russian literature you can find anything you like on self-consciousness, amongst all the waffling and religious searchings, and spread much thicker than in Dostoevsky or Tolstoy. Ilyenkov was simply advancing the old Marxist idea that, just as an epoch should not be judged by the way it represents itself, so a person should not be judged by his or her words. Ilyenkov prettifies this thought (which is also in Hegel and Lenin): someone is a person to the extent to which she is a socially significant individual who establishes herself by her deeds in the complex system of social interrelations, and not to the extent that she wallows in herself and so on. Ilyenkov once wrote that a person is an individual who is able to bear the tension of all social contradictions. The tension of these contradictions is often reflected in personal suffering, in doubts and searchings, for one often gets slapped in the face in the process. But personhood is not to be found in endless self-reflection. That's only to dig one's own grave.

Issues of self-consciousness and self-knowledge are not much discussed in our philosophical literature, but they do feature in our artistic literature to a considerable extent. It seems to me that (despite my joking remarks just now) Russian Literature, both classical and contemporary, provides enormous insight into questions of personhood and self-consciousness. On this topic, we should stay away from both philosophers and psychologists, for neither have much of interest to say. Equally, science is a poor way to study people. When people talk about 'scientific philosophy' I reach for my gun. Of course, we must understand the term 'science' historically. When I attack science, I attack the methodology of the Enlightenment, of science, naturalistic and objectivist, and focused entirely on causal relations. To understand persons, we must go beyond the boundaries of science to literature, works of art, ethics and religion. A scientific approach, be it Marxist or some other, cannot grasp the *whole* human being. I suppose it may capture the human essence, but from essence to reality is a distance of enormous proportions. Ilyenkov knew this, because he was not only a philosopher, but also an artist, and to a certain extent, he was a moralist in the best sense of the term.

Now for your 'experiment', David. My dear friends, whoever got it into their heads that the brain can be distinguished from the other parts of the body in the integral life-activity of the individual? The *whole* body is the carrier of a grandiose idiomotoric code. So you can't talk of brain transplants for a brain simply could not work in another body ...

Bibler: But look, that's just irrelevant ...

Davydov: Not so, for what I am challenging is whether the experiment *can* be represented in thought. David himself will admit there's a problem about whether imaginability is the test of possibility. The issues that David seeks to raise with this thought experiment – say, about the relation of consciousness, self-consciousness, and personhood – have to be raised another way.

Mikhailov! Come here, you're in charge of all this ...

Mikhailov: Let me invite Vladimir Solomonovich to take the floor again.

Bibler: As I said earlier, the serious challenge posed by David's paper lies in his claim that, when we assert that the human essence is 'the ensemble of social relations', what we say is ambiguous between strong and weak interpretations. Let's have the thesis in Ilyenkov's own inimitable style:

> Personhood is to be understood as something substantive and corpor-eal [notice that Ilyenkov has 'personhood' here and not 'a human being' or 'the human essence'], as the real corporeal-substantial totality of sub-stantial-corporeal relations which link a given individual to other indi-viduals ... Personhood, in general, is the particular expression of the life-activity of the ensemble of social relations in general.[22]

Now, David argues, if we take this to mean that personhood in some sense *just is* the ensemble of social relations, then we have a proposition that is essentially impossible to defend. But if we say that personhood takes shape in the process of social relations, then this is obviously true but rather trivial. Moreover, it invites the objection that the ensemble of social relations, conceived as a kind of universal totality of relations binding together a given society, is identical for all its members, and this fact cannot explain the emergence of individual differences in people.

Davydov: But it is not identical at all!

Another: And Ilyenkov argues against just such a conception, by the way.

Mikhailov: There's no need to interrupt.

Bibler: So, the first thesis is impossible to defend and the second isn't worth it because it's banal.

Davydov: I don't understand. What is impossible to defend? That the essence of personhood is the ensemble of social relations? Only Ilyenkov stressed that we are talking about *internalised* social relations.

Bibler: He did nothing of the kind!

---

22   Ilyenkov 1979b, pp. 196, 197–8.

Davydov: But tell me Volodya, why is it impossible to defend this position?

Bibler: Well, once again, the strong thesis is impossible to defend because we seem committed to two mutually exclusive claims: first, that personhood is the ensemble of social relations, and second, that society is the ensemble of social relations. Consequently, when I attempt to make the strong thesis intelligible, I find I can't take logical responsibility for it. And if we assert simply that, in the process of social life, persons are formed (as you like to say, Vasa, upon leaving university, or even at the very end of life itself), then that can, of course, be defended, but there arises an important question. In what way is the part formed that is *not* reducible to those social relations? What is the origin of that part which the ensemble of social relations influences and which is therefore irreducible to those relations?

In order to show that the strong thesis is impossible to defend, David produced his thought experiment. Clearly, he does not advance it as a real possibility. He simply wants to press the point that those philosophers who have asserted that individuality is seated in the structure of the brain can answer for their words. If it turns out that Felix's brain is transplanted into my body, then supporters of this position will say that, in the given case, Bibler's body acquires the personhood of Mikhailov. They know what to say. We are not talking about whether they've guessed right or not. Others, who believe personhood is identical with memory and character will say that, in the case where my body has Mikhailov's brain but *my* memory and character, that Bibler has a new brain. But what can those who hold that personhood is the ensemble of social relations say? In the face of such an experiment they simply have no answer. Well, we can laugh this off so long as we see the matter purely theoretically, but if we imagine that there is something at stake here if it transpires that we must decide who is who on pain of death – then it is clear we have a problem that demands an answer, and furthermore, a problem that focuses on the nature of self-consciousness. That is the sense of David's thought experiment, so it's a waste of time to tell him that the brain cannot be removed from the body, and so on. He will no doubt agree, but that's not the point.

So, the first point I want to develop is this. I think the Marxist tradition, and, before it, the tradition of High Rationalism, which includes not only Hegel, but also Leibniz and Descartes, would say that the strong thesis (that the human essence *is* the ensemble of social relations) cannot be separated from the weak thesis (that the ensemble of social relations represents, at best, the essence of the process in which personhood is formed). They turn out to be, in some paradoxical way, *two sides of the same thesis*. And a representative of this tradition should turn to David and say (we can argue about whether what they say is correct, but we ought first to understand it): So, a person is 'the ensemble of social relations', as Marx says. But now one must ask what is meant by the terms 'is', 'totality' and 'relation'. On no account should one take these concepts for granted. In this case, if I say that personhood 'is' the ensemble of social relations, then I am by no means asserting a formal equality. 'Is', in the logic of Hegel, is inseparable from *becoming*. Existence, Being, acts in unity with non-Being. Thus, when I, as an educated Marxist, assert that personhood is the ensemble of social relations, I am speaking within a philosophical position with a definite logic of its own. The concept of identity here is not abstract identity. Personhood *is* and *is not* the ensemble of social relations. Therefore, the weak thesis, through the window if not through the door, enters the strong thesis. We must consider what 'is' means here. A person cannot simply be; all the time he is *becoming*. And all the time, the ensemble of social relations in which he acts is focused in him. It transpires that these relations must be transformed, and so they are with every act. Is this kind of individuality banal? No. Everyone is confronted by the problems of his or her own life. They are focused in each person and transformed by his or her individuality. And in this, *being* and *becoming* are inseparable.

Furthermore, you must think about what is meant by the idea of 'totality' (*sovokupnost'*). This is not simply a 'collection', but a kind of *integration* of social relations in which there emerges 'n + the unit'. The unification, or 'copulation' (if you will forgive the intended ambiguity) of these relations leads to the birth of that which did not previously exist in the given totality. So, it is not serious to criticise some assertion while ignoring its real historico-logical meaning. I aim this remark not so much at you, David, but at analytic philosophers in general. Moreover, our philosophers are no better. For ten years philosophers here have been discussing whether it is possible to represent the qualities of miniature particles as an ensemble of relations, but some understand 'ensemble' simply as a summation of qualities, a potpourri of attributes, while others work with a more integral conception. They thus spend a lot of time talking past one another. So my point is that we can take responsibility for Ilyenkov's words only if we are prepared to answer for the whole philosophical context in which they make sense. An isolated phrase can neither be strong nor weak; it just lacks meaning altogether. My second main point is this. It's crucial that, for Marx, the thesis that the human essence – the essence of individuality – is the ensemble of social relations, does not simply reduce to the assertion that human beings are *nothing* more than the ensemble of social relations. That would simply mean the identification of the individual, or individuality, with society. Marx deciphers the paradoxical sense of his thesis many times. Let's take the following passage from 'On James Mill':

> Since human nature is the true communal nature of man, men create
> and produce their communal nature by their natural action; they produce
> their social being which is no abstract, universal power over against single
> individuals, but the nature of each individual, his own activity, his own
> life, his own enjoyment, his own wealth.[23]

So you see, it is not only that the human essence lies in our connection with
each other, but that the essence of social connectedness is individuality. Social
relations are focused in individuals, and do not exist outside them, as some
kind of abstract, universal force. This is fundamental.

When we say that certain external relations in which an individual acts are
an essence, we must take into account that here a process of *internalisation*,
of transformation, takes place. But just using the word 'internalisation' doesn't
make everything right, for it is too easy to hold that internalisation means that
social relations are simply transplanted into the individual and act there in a
kind of diminished form. But in this process, social relations are transformed
in some fundamental way, becoming a form of psychological, not sociological,
determination ...

Davydov: Even *breaking* the sociological determinants.

Bibler: *Transforming* them fundamentally from within. I prefer to put it this
way because 'breaking' is a somewhat mechanical notion. I have said this many
times before, but I am simply amazed when I read in the psychological literature that 'such-and-such an external process or activity is internalised', full stop.
But can that really be all there is to it? Are social relations somehow simply
transplanted into the soul?

As Vygotsky never tired of repeating, internalisation is a process of *transformation*: the logic of reference is transformed into the logic of meaning, the
syntax and semantics of external speech are fundamentally transformed so
that inner speech has quite a different syntax and semantics, where things
temporally distinct act simultaneously, where a distinct system of relations is
condensed to a point, a subjective phenomenon, and where there emerges 'n +
the unit', irreducible, as always, to that focal point. The psychologists have heard
all that, they've read Vygotsky, and yet they throw away the texts and begin to
babble: 'So, Vygotsky showed that in the beginning there are social relations
which are then transplanted into the soul by internalisation, and ...' Where is
this in Vygotsky? Where is it in Marx? Nothing of the kind is to be found, but
we are used to reading what we want to see. That's a psychological law too. We

---

23   Marx 1971, pp. 193–4. (I have amended the punctuation in the translation.)

project views upon a text and then, depending on our preference, either attack the author or pat him or her on the back.

The idea of Being as transformation (the 'is' of transformation), as a focusing in the individual from which the irreducible emerges, is a crucial notion. For Marx, the notion of activity possesses from the very beginning a strange character, this is the idea of the individual *not coinciding with the activity itself*. If this were not so, activity would be senseless. Marx says that activity is always a *self-striving*. Activity, even the most basic form of labour, is connected with *change* by definition. For example, an agent must isolate the object (*predmet*) of activity *as* the object of his activity, and not simply, as for the animal, as that which must coincide with him. The object which I work upon cannot enter into me and be assimilated by me. The very reproduction of the object in consciousness and in action, necessary in the simplest process, represents the object as not assimilable to me. In this lies the separation of myself as a *subject*, as that which does not coincide with my thingishness, which is not identical to myself as thing. Activity thus presupposes that I do not coincide with my activity, I change it. Therefore, I am not identical with the way in which that activity defines me.

Consider tools, for tools mediate activity, and are developed and changed over time. Tools are a continuation of my own organs which are nevertheless distinguishable from me. Thus, in my use of tools, I, as it were, work *upon myself*, or 'strive after myself'. And Marx, in distinction from Hegel, writes that self-consciousness is not the definition of the human essence, for activity itself has a *self-striving* character and therefore, in this character, we find a prior definition of self-consciousness. Thus, it is not that we have activity, labour, social relations, and then, as the result of these relations, persons are formed as the effect of economic relations existing outside them (as the textbooks of '*istmat*' write to this day). That is not what this is all about. In the course of activity, personhood and individuality are formed (let's ignore whether they are identical; for present purposes we may suppose they are), but the principal question is to what degree the agent, participating in social relations and social activity, is formed as something irreducible to that activity.

This is not just the issue of the formation of a psychological subject as something irreducible to sociological determinants, but also the question of the degree to which the agent is identical with his or her role in the ensemble, and with his or her actions. For instance, Ilyenkov takes Lenin's words about judging people by their deeds and throws them into a new context. And this invites the response that, equally, if we are going to judge someone only by his deeds then we can *only* judge him partially, *only* externally, for a person as a psychological being cannot be reduced to his deeds for one simple reason. Suppose

I am a machine operator. My business is with metal rather than, say, with land. Here, not only is the character of my work impressed upon me, but also *the fact that this is metal*, and I can't work with metal in the way that I can with earth. The nature (*zakonomernost'*) of this metal, this material, this substance, leaves its mark on my action. Therefore to judge me purely by my actions is unserious, for my activity does not depend wholly upon me, but upon the part of the ensemble of social relations in which I find myself, on those bonds in which I take part. I may break them, change them, or simply passively enter into them. The actions will be mine, but will be determined not only by my individual singularity, but by those relations in which my singularity is transformed.

Forgive me, Vasa (Davydov), for taking myself to be a grown-up, but from childhood, from the kindergarten, there arises the necessity to participate, to be included, and at the same time the necessity to revolt. The feeling of revolt – 'I want things to be different' – of 'non coincidence with things', arises from the very beginning. This does not simply come down to the fact that one child, due to the disposition of his genes, is prone to revolt, while another is a conformist. It depends, of course, on the child's upbringing and the degree to which the relations we impose on him are allowed to become simply a set of external norms and standards. They should rather take the form of real problems, of 'life disparities'. That is, when I enter into relations, into *what* do I enter? Not surely into some kind of standardised sphere of activity, but into a mass of questions that are posed for me, into difficulties I must resolve. I see a little chair. I want to sit on it. But then I shall be too small. I want to be the same height as the others. I start to put something on the chair ... That is, it is necessary to *change* relations, because those relations, do not coincide with each other: lives are different, contradictory, problematic, and not standardised by their very essence. So when we speak of the role of the ensemble of social relations, we mean that the human spirit (*dusha*) is formed in the necessity to solve these emerging problems from the very first moment of existence, problems which the person can solve only if he or she does not coincide with the relations which bring these problems to life.

For this reason, personhood cannot coincide with the norms set by external relations. On this score, Ilyenkov's article contains a most unfortunate passage. He writes: 'Personhood arises when the individual begins to act independently as a subject ... [very good, but he continues] ... to realise external actions by norms and standards given from without'.[24] Disaster! Well, I know, Vasa, that this isn't the real Ilyenkov, but I draw attention to it because we must improve

---

24   Ilyenkov 1979b, p. 205.

our way of putting these points. There are many such problematic assertions. I pointed out before that social relations are reduced to substantial-corporeal relations, where for Marx even economic value is super-corporeal, supersensuous. There is much such stuff. I don't think, David, you should dwell on Ilyenkov's articles on this theme, or indeed, forgive me Felix, on Mikhailov's or Bibler's, but you should try to get to grips with the essence of the concepts, to get 'to the heart of the matter', as Ilyenkov loved to say. Each of us here has his peculiar approach, each with its manifest flaws and failings, its unhappy moments. To judge a tradition's ideas on the basis of a few articles is not appropriate.

David spoke about self-consciousness. To be sure, the problem of self-consciousness has received little serious attention from Soviet philosophers. Typically self-consciousness is treated in either of two ways. On the one hand, it is reduced to the philosophical concept of 'reflexion' (and here, though there is a genuine psychological problematic, the philosophical discussions rarely capture what psychologists are after). On the other hand, self-consciousness is reduced in a way that sometimes occurs in the articles of Ilyenkov. He rightly argues that we must get away from the crude naturalism on which the nature and essence of human life can only be explained in terms of the relation between physical bodies. Further, he argues that we must understand self-consciousness as the relation of a person to him- or herself. This would hardly appear worth arguing, for it seems so obviously true, but some have wished to argue against, say, the possibility of solipsism, by holding that the subject cannot relate to him- or herself but only to another. Now, the idea of a pure relation of the subject to him- or herself is deemed problematic, so Ilyenkov picks up this famous remark of Marx's:

> In a certain sense, a man is in the same situation as a commodity. As he neither enters into the world in possession of a mirror, nor as a Fichtean philosopher who can say 'I am I', a man first sees and recognizes himself in another man. Peter only relates to himself as a man through his relation to another man, Paul, in whom he recognizes his likeness. With this, however, Paul also becomes from head to toe, in his physical form as Paul, the form of appearance of the species man for Peter.[25]

This is an interesting and instructive remark, but it is often developed quite wrongly. Does the sum of relations between these bodies comprise an answer

---

25   Marx 1982, p. 144n.

to the question of the nature of self-consciousness? This is just no good. What Marx points to is significant, but we must not sink to the depths where we say things like, 'Your opinion about me constitutes *my* self-consciousness'.

Another: But there's no need to overdo this. Ilyenkov clearly says that self-consciousness is formed when the subject can relate to herself *as to another*, that is, she relates to herself by occupying the point of view of others.

Bibler: But genuine self-consciousness is absent there too. There are just three dots in its place, for the contrary assertion is missing, and this is most important as far as the psychological definition of personhood is concerned. Personhood is formed when the subject comes to relate to him- or herself as to another. Very good. But personhood, self-consciousness, the self, is formed just where you left those three dots ... where the subject comes to relate to *another as to him- or herself*. Without that inversion, no moral or logical consciousness is possible. Unless we turn this thesis around, and turn oneself around to confront oneself as another and oneself as oneself-in-another, all truly human sensibilities cannot be.

In the light of phenomena such as self-consciousness, which define personhood and bring out the significance of the idea of 'non-coincidence with oneself', it seems wrongheaded to construe personhood as the ability to alter, or to break with, surrounding reality. Well, there were those who tried to smash the Weimar Republic, but this was no great mark of personhood. The mere striving to destroy does not display personhood. So here I disagree with Vasa.

In my view, the problem of self-consciousness represents a crucial starting point for understanding personhood. Personhood begins in the moment of dissatisfaction with oneself. This is not simply a psychological point. It is clear that the child manipulating his tiny chair, of whom I spoke of earlier, does not coincide with himself. He does not coincide with his activity: he is not equal to that which he seeks. At the very foundation of the formation of personhood lies that non-coincidence with self, and with it, the necessity that all my actions should be understood as *one deed*, so that the whole of my fate should be understood, and should have actually become, not simply the result of forces acting upon me, but my unitary deed, played out from birth to death. Here considerations of self-consciousness are important, and indeed, self-consciousness conceived as self-knowledge.

The idea of a life as a unity emerges in different ways in different historical epochs. In antiquity, the point or focus of the whole of a man's life, understood as a single manifestation of his fate, is expressed in the idea of *acme*: the point of culmination or blossoming. In the course of forty years of heroic deeds, a man's life comes to a focus and is seen as the manifestation of him as one. The Middle Ages introduced a very important idea that is seemingly readily rejected today. This is the idea of death as a kind of summation of life. Here, the moment before death is conceived as the collection of a person into *one*, so that the whole of his life can be understood as one deed for which he is responsible.

Modernity brings with it a very complicated conception of the focus of an individual life, where the external – that in a person's activity which is connected with his non-coincidence with him- or herself – can be understood as the manifestation of the subject as an integral, and most importantly, an atemporal, being.

But this is not the place to embark on a discussion of these ideas. Here's a different, but equally important, point. Ilyenkov says that language is of secondary significance for philosophical investigation. There are all sorts of other manifestations of mind in human activity. This point should be taken seriously, but at the same time, we should observe the following. In contrast to passive sensory modalities such as sight, where objects act upon the perceiver, speech and hearing are extremely important in the material expression of self-consciousness. In speech I begin to hear myself. Aspects of speech are always connected with the dialectics of outer and inner speech, with the 'immersion' of outer speech in inner speech, and the non-coincidence of the latter with the former. This is immensely important: it reflects what Heidegger expressed when he said that in speech man hears his own Being and is non-coincident with it. My speech is not simply important because *you* hear it, but because I hear it myself.

Lektorsky: Moreover, I hear myself quite differently from how others hear me.

Bibler: Exactly so.

Mikhailov: In the purely physical sense or in terms of meaning?

All (save Mikhailov): In terms of meaning too.

Davydov: You hear yourself on tape saying things you simply did not realise were there when you were speaking.

Bibler: The most important thing is this. You hear *only* my outer speech, but I hear it against a background of intension that illuminates what I am saying. At the level of meaning, in the structure of meaning, my non-coincidence with myself in speech is displayed quite differently than it is in what others hear from me. On the one hand, I 'say' many things which, thank goodness, you cannot hear, and on the other, the follies of what I am saying are understood far better by others than by myself. These factors are essentially connected with the idea of self-consciousness. If we take into account, in light of what was said by Vygotsky and others, that outer speech immersed in inner speech takes on a new syntax and semantics, then this 'introversion' of speech into thought has great significance for the understanding of the nature of thought itself.

Davydov: But Ilyenkov didn't belittle the role of speech as such. He just stressed that behind the word lies a reified meaning-reference.

Bibler: Okay, so the idea is that we must look to human activity and practice to understand meaning and thought. But in thought, human practice is somehow 'rolled into a ball' and is transformed. Action pertains to the done. Machines can act. But words, in a certain sense, relate to that which cannot be done. In this, the word, the unity of thought and speech, is the essential feature of self-consciousness.

In conclusion, let me say that I think the subject David has raised is most important and I have tried to speak to it by raising a few provocative ideas from the tradition of High Rationalism. Well, everyone dances to his own tune, which is called by his tradition. I have my existence as part of this tradition, and without it I could not think. It is fashionable today either to extricate oneself from this tradition and attempt to reveal its deep Freudian basis or to treat it as a big stick with which to beat down schools which think differently, turning Marx into a prophet who said infallible things that fall to us to interpret. I am not, of course, one to follow fashion.

While I adopt a serious attitude to my own philosophical universe of discourse, I should like to say the following to analytical philosophers. Although they often subtly lay out the logical essence of an argument, the trouble with analytic philosophers is that they reduce theoretical concepts to sets of atomic sentences. And if they decide to work outside their tradition, in a scheme where primary concepts such as 'is', 'totality' and 'relation' have a different logical significance from their role within the analytic tradition, they immediately go over to some kind of phenomenological definition of the subject under study (here, personhood, individuality) and treat the conceptual scheme as some kind of formally given, immovable, data. But these concepts are also in the process of transformation. One must analyse how these seemingly immutable concepts are formed and transformed. Analytic philosophers do not pay attention to this. For example, we must take the very concept of the relation of essence and phenomenon by the hand and lead it out into the sunlight of historico-logical and culturo-logical meaning, and only then with it be possible to speak about strong or weak interpretations of Marx's, and Ilyenkov's, thesis.

Mikhailov: As I mentioned earlier, it seems to me that David's paper gives refined expression to an objection to the 'Marxist thesis' we commonly hear, not so much from philosophers, but psychologists (though they don't invoke David's distinction between strong and weak interpretations): 'Very well', they say, 'we are agreed that a human being lives in society, in a "social environment", that he or she enters into various relations with other people and that his or her character and moral sense are formed in the context of all this ...'.

Davydov: Banality!

Mikhailov: 'But (so they go on) you are aspiring to something more. You claim to be revealing the *essence* of all those processes with which we are concerned as psychologists studying specific aspects of human existence; that is, language acquisition, cognitive processes, the nature of learning, and so on. But vague talk about social relations scarcely gets us to the essence of these phenomena'.

This objection reflects one side of a clash of two approaches, two logics, two ways of constructing the object of discussion. I think that Bibler expressed this conflict quite brilliantly in what he said about the copula 'is'. On the one hand, there is the naturalistic, or 'object' logic, on the basis of which the above objection is posed. This takes the object given as an objective, present, structured totality of various qualities and properties. In contrast, we can see the object of inquiry quite differently, as a self-negating, developing formation, directed against or onto itself, as a process which is a unity at its base but is at the same time multivarious in its manifestations.

If we work within the latter logic, it seems to me we should take the weak, empirical thesis about human needs and abilities in all their diverse manifestations, and show how, through it, we can see that origin, or *arche*, by which we can define the very essence of all these disparate phenomena. That is, speaking lyrically, we must aim to make the weak variant one with the strong. We should object to David's position like this: You think that the strong thesis cannot be defended, but we'll do just that precisely by considering it through the weak thesis, through the idea of *becoming* or *movement*. Bibler has expressed the logical side of the matter very well. I don't want to repeat it, I simply want to try to show it empirically.

I believe that, if we try to describe empirically the human essence and its various manifestations within the terms of the first, naturalistic, logic, and then to reduce the manifestations to the essence or to derive the essence from its appearances and so on, we shall always be prone to fall into one of two extreme positions. As I tried to show in my last article, these two extremes are represented in psychology by, on the one hand, Rubinshtein's school, and on the other, Leontiev's.[26] Rubinshtein treats the human essence as *given* prior to communion with other people (*obshchenie*) and the influence of the ensemble of social relations. The essence is a distinct and prior thing. Thus Rubinshtein (and I have followed this closely in his works) attributes to each human being an individual source or *arche*. That is, a human being enters the world with a particular prop-

---

26   Mikhailov 1981.

erty. Rubinshtein calls it mind (psyche), others have called it 'the power to act', and some may choose to call it something else, but, in any case, the essence is defined as something *given* by nature.

Lektorsky: Does Rubinshtein really hold such a view?

Mikhailov: Yes. For Rubinshtein, 'the inner' is given as a manifestation of life (*zhizenost'*) in general. Mind is always there in us somehow and somewhere; we are born with it and it develops from conception to death. *How* it develops depends on the ensemble of social relations, on activity, and so on. Here, Rubinshtein's famous 'dual determination' manifests itself: the influence of the external through the internal. It is all very wholesome and pretty but nevertheless the 'inner' is given and, with that, lies somehow beyond the bounds of investigation.

Davydov: Brushlinsky writes straight out that, according to Rubinshtein, the psyche is formed in activity but is not created.

Mikhailov: It is a kind of moulding. Formation as moulding, so to speak. And the essence itself lies somewhere beyond the modelling process. The plasticine is, as it were, already given to us and which figures will be made out of it depends on the ensemble of social relations, or whatever else you care to name. But then it becomes legitimate to ask: what represents the essence of *this* special quality with which we enter the world? It will be quite impossible to reduce *that* to the ensemble of social relations, to object-orientated activity, or to any other concept in the Marxist repertoire. So we have to concede that Marx really occupied himself with *subsequent* questions about the development of the human person and not the essence of personhood itself ...

Davydov: Banality, of course.

Mikhailov: And then we really have David's weak thesis thrust upon us as the tired repetition of trivial truths.

How did Leontiev approach this question? I want to stress that I'm not aiming to *criticise* these views, but to bring out the characteristic lines of thought that divide the two positions. Leontiev makes a very strong attempt to put the question differently. How successful it is is another matter. For Leontiev, there is no special 'quality' which we can describe as the genuine, specifically human essence until a human being is included in the ensemble of social relations ...

Bibler: Nor after ... (*Laughter*)

Mikhailov: Quite so, but that's not really the point. All I'm doing here is trying to outline the characteristic shape of these two positions ...

Davydov: The point is not that the mind is *formed*. Any evolutionist will agree with that. Even Piaget will agree.

Mikhailov: Of course. The whole problem is that if we are to answer for that logical tradition which Bibler calls 'High Rationalism', and which I prefer to call the tradition of genuine philosophy (philosophy in the true sense of the term, for today 'philosophical thinking' includes any project of generalisation, everyday thinking, naturalism, and the logic of the natural sciences), then we must see these approaches as two sides of the same coin and seek to put the question another way. Really, how are we to define the human essence? And now I shall come out with my favourite and, in the context of the present discussion, rather surprising view. The human essence should be defined as the source or *arche* of personhood (*lichnost'noe nachalo*). Human beings are *born* persons – that's my favourite view.

Bibler: Personhood exists even prior to kindergarten?

Mikhailov: Yes, before kindergarten. Human beings are born persons. That is the human essence. Here, however strange it may seem, I am not really contesting what Vasa said ...

Bibler: That shows remarkable cunning.

Mikhailov: Well, in general I am rather cunning, but in the given case my cunning is simple. I understand very well the impetus behind the position Davydov expresses and which motivates the views of, not only Ilyenkov, but also Hegel. Nonetheless, this is not merely a terminological dispute between me and Ilyenkov; I want to urge a change in the very foundation of our position. In my view (and, though others may agree with me, I want to underline that this is *my* view so that I am not thought to be expounding Hegel or Marx or Ilyenkov), human beings live in a very beguiling way. They can exist *physically* only by transcending themselves, only by distinguishing themselves from themselves, and, through that internal, reflexive relation of non-coincidence with themselves (as Bibler loves to put it), *change themselves* (and not simply the 'objects' of their activity). Only then can they survive physically as individuals.

It is not that a human being is born a particular entity, acquires individuality and then grows up to be a person. One can talk like this *only* if one conceives of personhood in a very narrow sense: as a quality of a particular member of the ensemble of social relations, responsible for him- or herself and capable of non-conformism. But that conception, and that reality, is only one historical development of the genuine human essence, only one way in which it has found historical expression. It is one of the congealed (*stavshykh*) forms placed before us, and we should never attempt to define an essence on the basis of what is immediately given to us.

Here we must consider the phylogenetic and ontogenetic unfolding of the *arche* or source of personhood as such. Human beings came down from the trees and developed their own essence only because that essence, from the very beginning, had been *given* to them. *How* it was so is quite another matter. That essence was that they had to distinguish themselves from themselves. They were forced not to coincide with themselves.

Bibler: It was not that they were 'forced' not to coincide with themselves, but that from the very beginning they *did not* coincide with themselves.

Mikhailov: Quite right and ...

Davydov: Look, excuse me, human beings did not coincide with themselves from the beginning of their history because they were placed as individuals *into the collective*, as individuals in a totality of other people.

Mikhailov: Quite right, and I will show just that. And with this the concept of the ensemble of social relations really does become the definition of the human essence. Here I am defending the *strong* thesis. I believe it is not only possible but also necessary to defend it. Therefore, in that phylogenetic, or for clarity's sake let's say *historical*, enfolding of the human essence, we see how a human being undergoes 'individualisation', how he finds the form, the objective (*predmetnyi*) form, of the means to change himself by reflecting upon himself, by orientating himself on himself. We see how the various forms of the social division of labour arise and how, in that 'alienation from his essential powers', a human being comes to see himself from outside of himself and thereby comes to change himself on the strength of that vision. This is certainly a massive problem, which I can scarcely address, even schematically. I shall rather attempt to make clear just one simple thing: the origins of anthropogenesis.

Davydov: How brave can you get?

Mikhailov: But what else is to be done? If I can't define that source, that *arche*, even logically, then later, when we come to talk about the formation of developed forms of consciousness and complex human abilities, we shall be in a position where the beard takes itself to be the person on which it is growing. Our very way of setting up the problem has to confront the mechanism by which human beings overcome their own thinginess (*predmetnost'*), their own objectuality. When we assert that a human being is *formed* as a human being, becomes a human being – really *becomes* and is not stamped out by some machine – when we say that he or she becomes a human being by overcoming his or her own reity, or animal essence, we are immediately drawn into the sphere of community (*obshchenie*). We confront the *form* of communion with others and its symbolic representation in means of communication that are at first external and become internal.

Here, I should say in parenthesis that I happily agree with the view that, in the final analysis, the symbolism of speech in all its internal 'discreteness' is the most immediate, the most reified-immediate form of the social essence of human beings, that is, of self-expression, self-consciousness. I like this idea and return to it in my writings over and over. I don't want to repeat what Bibler said, though I should like to take issue with him on one point. The edifice of language, in its historical development, is connected not so much with the vibrations of air from which the signal system is formed (not the 'second signal system', of course!), but with the fact that, from the very beginning, it is a means of entering into community. Marx is right when he talks about 'the language of real life'. It is a form of sociality (*obshchestvennost'*), an expression of the reified essence of my own relation to myself. That very sociality is represented, not as a developed norm as such, but in what is really possible to call 'the language of real life': it is represented in the thingishness of the symbolic means that maintain our mode of communion with others. What we call 'ritual', and all the ritualistic symbolism passed on so painstakingly from one generation to the next in communities with an indigenous division of labour (some call this a 'natural' division, but in my view it is certainly genuinely human and therefore *social* in kind), is the root of this form of communion with others. This basic form then begins to divide and develop and becomes the most fundamental means through which a person is split into herself *as* herself and herself as another. Here, of course, it has become language proper. But its source, its essence, is the thingishness, the objectuality, of that communion with others, where another person, or the ritual mask that person wears, stands as a symbol which reconstructs the unitary wholeness of the form of communion with others ...

Bibler: In so far as you have already digressed from your theme, may I ask whether, when we define personhood in terms of a human being's non-coincidence with him- or herself, it is really necessary, from a logical point of view, to talk about anthropogenesis at all, for the schism of this essence is such that human beings are *every moment* in the process of becoming themselves. This is the whole point of talk about non-coincidence, and this is just in what the singularity of the human person consists. It is our special feature. There is no reason to take anthropogenesis back to some dim point in history, for it is just as real right now. We never *are* people, we always only have the possibility to *become* people.

Davydov: You know what? Your idea of 'communion with others', Felix, contains something which Ilyenkov attacked. The Marxist tradition primarily focuses upon 'object-mediated, material communion with others' – Marx often used this kind of phrase – and the most important thought is that material, object-mediated communion persists always. The forms of linguistic communication of course attain autonomy and go off according to their own laws, but at the basis of their autonomy lies material communion with others. When you, Mikhailov, for all your cleverness, propagandise this stuff about community, you *abstract* to a considerable degree from this initial basis: object-mediated, material communion with others. Evald perceived this trend in many thinkers and never hesitated to protest. This was most clearly expressed in his 1974 article on hermeneutics which I recommend you read.[27]

Mikhailov: I know that article very well.

Davydov: You know it, but you've never read it! (*Laughter*)

Mikhailov: Nevertheless, I shall continue with what I am saying ...

Davydov: We wouldn't expect you to do anything else!

Mikhailov: Assuming that the present misunderstanding has been settled, all that remains is for me to explain one important fact. Please excuse that digression. I was forced into it. But pay attention to the fact that when my colleagues spoke we maintained an air of decorum, but I see these problems ...

Bibler: ... more sharply than they do ...

Mikhailov: ... and so they interrupt out of jealousy! (*Laughter*)

Another: It's obvious why you're interrupted. In speaking about the birth of personhood, you speak as if the individual human being is isolated, alone.

Mikhailov: Although this objection is obviously unfair, there is a grain of truth in it, and thank goodness for that! I do speak of human beings as individuals, and will continue to do so, for it is precisely the essence of human individuals that I wish to define. I refuse to reduce human beings to the community. A company of people is a very good thing when there's something to drink, but when we are talking about the human essence we'd better make sure that what we say pertains to the nature of persons as particular individuals.

Okay, on the question of communion and community. I completely agree with Ilyenkov's hostility to the exaggeration of the concept of communion with others. The notion of community, now sometimes invoked as a theoretical alternative to the concept of object-orientated activity, is so often seen as some kind of social phenomenon hanging above human beings, connecting and uniting them. It is impossible to express this clearly, for in principle there is simply no reity, no objectuality about community thus conceived. This is a very serious problem which amounts, in its logical essence, to a kind of Hegelian panlogical interpretation of the universal, a view that is Hegelian in the worst sense of the term. On such a position, the universal is portrayed as something instantiated in community, relating to each person as a power hovering above and determining him or her.

Bibler: That very 'abstract power' of which Hegel speaks.

---

27   Ilyenkov 1974b. An English translation appears in Ilyenkov 2018b, pp. 98–114.

Mikhailov: Yes. Now, when I say that true collectivity finds objective form in 'communion with others', I am of course reminded of Marx, who spoke of objectification, not just in objects, but in the objective form of community with others. It was not for nothing that he called communism the truth of the process of 'the production of forms of community', and not, excuse me, the production of pieces of iron. This is important because many advocates of the theory of object-orientated activity are wont to invoke Ilyenkov without understanding the essence of the matter at all. There is a tendency to say: the subject takes the pure object, dances about with it, and bang, the object takes on a special essence which is 'objectified' in the object ...

Another: No, the object is a reified action ...

Mikhailov: So much the worse!

Bibler: Any human object (*predmet*) represents a form of communion with others. Otherwise it has no meaning at all.

Davydov: Who are you criticising?

Mikhailov: Vasa, let he who has ears hear the target of my criticism.

Lektorsky: The behaviourists?

Mikhailov: Of course the behaviourists are included. So, I have finished my digression. Allow me to explain my position ...

Davydov: We mustn't interrupt any more, or else you won't finish your paper.

Mikhailov: Exactly. And you interrupt to tell me that! Marvellous! (*Laughter*)

So, I want to underline that when I speak about the symbolic means (without question objectified in character) by which human beings in so-called 'primitive' societies fixed and relayed the subjective reality of their lives as culture, as their selfhood and *subjectivity*, I mean that here lies the fundamental definition of the linguistic essence of the system of the collectivity, immersed into human beings' inner world. Otherwise, I agree with what Bibler said.

So, now for the question of ontogenesis. Leontiev's work arrives at the following thought. Human beings are born as individuals with certain needs (*nuzhdy*): for air, nutrition, and so on. That is, they have basic needs of a physical nature which, when they encounter the already encultured or humanised world, acquire the character of genuinely human desires (*potrebnosti*). In order to return to the strong Marxist thesis, I want to exchange this line of thought for another. The fact is that the human child, by her birth, by her bodily, morphophysiological organisation represents the continuation of the life of her parents, of their corporeality, their objectuality, of their bodiliness (this is crucial to the nature of *human* inheritance, the continuation of the physical existence of what Hegel so appropriately called the symbol, or rather the 'mark', of individuality, the human body). That objective, reified mark of the child's individuality, that reified singularity (which is just as much an individual particular as that cup, or any other product of human culture and history, only it is expressed through the *life-arche* of a corporeal organism) comes into being, comes to life, and *cannot live*. Here we confront a substantial contradiction. The child cannot live because that corporeality does not carry within itself the most important thing: it does not have the means of life (*sposob zhizni*).

Davydov: It has instincts.

Mikhailov: You can call them 'instincts', or 'needs', or whatever, but in the final analysis it makes little difference because the child does not have the ability to live. If that ability is to emerge in that tiny body it is absolutely necessary that there be *another person*. We have a strange relation to birth. When the child is in the mother's womb we confidently say that the child is part of the life-activity of the mother's organism. And we see the whole of the mother's organism as an organ of the life-activity of that tiny child. But when the umbilical cord is severed, we, like good naturalists, immediately see the individual as isolated and solitary. We look at him and say, 'Ah, he has come into the world and all around him are other people'. Exactly that: *other* people ... the group, the company, the community, the environment, nature, the sun, the air, ..., and he is alone, tiny and alone. And supposedly all this 'external' environment provides nourishment of various kinds, he internalises it, and ...

Davydov: Alright, don't drag it out! We've understood.

Mikhailov: The whole thing is that the reality of his being is tied to the continuity of symbiosis, not in the physical sense of the term, or rather, *not only* in the physical sense of the term, but in the necessity for there to be an organ of the child's life-activity which is another person. The adult, the grownup, is the physical organ of his life-activity. And in this we see an expression of David's strong thesis; we see the strong thesis immediately given before us. Why? Because the adults, the other people, are effective organs of child's life-activity only when they take a particular path: when they live their own life, when they see the child as an organ of the life-activity of their *own* organisms, when the child's arrival and the joys of motherhood and fatherhood change *them* as persons, human beings, individuals (in the given case, the distinctions are not important). The more they are themselves *outside* the child, representing through themselves the totality of the history and culture of the community into which the child has been born, the more effective they will be as the organ of the development of that tiny body, of even its physical needs, its breathing and feeding.

Thus it transpires that it is neither the teat nor the spoon, as objects, that the child must come to 'possess' as objects of 'object-orientated activity', but rather the *subjectivity* of another person that is so crucial. I must stress this. And that subjectivity is one side of what we call the identity of subjectivity and reified objectivity in the process of human life-activity. That very subjectivity of the adult, in relation to the child, becomes the child's own organ which brings him or her to life. But nevertheless the contradiction is still present. And to transcend it the child has but one way. To deny it. To bring forth his or her own selfhood, as yet unformed. There is nothing terrible in this. The child cannot simply adopt the point of view of the adult. She cannot 'internalise' actions. She can't take up the mother's position. Bibler mentioned this but I want to make it a little more concrete. The child is simply unable just to pick up the character of 'object-orientated' actions. She cannot simply internalise the mother's activity, as a determinate repertoire of actions. Can you imagine what it would be for a child to be able to wash her nappies before she can even see them? The whole thing is that her *becoming*, her distinguishing herself from herself, takes place first of all because her own organ of life-activity is represented for her as *counterposed to her*. Her own organ of life-activity, another person, acts not only as a mirror in which she looks at another and therefore becomes able to relate to herself. This is a very one-sided assertion, as Bibler was not slow to point out. He turned it upside down, as it were, and in so doing, put everything back in its place. One must relate equally to oneself as another and to another as oneself. At one and the same time; it is the same process.

So what do I conclude here? It is that very *not* taking up the position of a grown-up, that ingenious caprice, that refraction of those canons in which one is included through oneself, that is so important. We are creatures forced to solve one and the same contradiction from the moment of birth to the moment of death. The contradiction comes to this: here is a canon of life-norms, but I can only accept it by *changing* it, by transforming it through myself, making it mine not by simply accepting it, but by creating a relation to it and thereby transforming it, because I am included in that activity *in my own way*. And here it will do no good to appeal to the fact that I have different genes, or a different 'nature' ...

Another: Then what is it? Why does the child protest?

Bibler: Because he cannot breastfeed himself.

Mikhailov: I've said that already, really I have.

Another: And isn't it really because, up to his birth, others relate to him as to another?

Mikhailov: That's mysticism. If I say that the child can relate to himself because before birth people related to him as to another, then it seems I'm committed to some ridiculous view of the transmission of consciousness ...

Another: What 'transmission of consciousness'? They relate to him as another, and when he is born he also relates to himself as another.

Mikhailov: That's mechanism. You must see the subtlety here. They don't relate to him as another. This is the great egoism of parenthood. They relate to him as themselves beyond or outside of themselves ...

Another: And as another, at the same time.

Lektorsky: As their *own* other.

Mikhailov: Yes, as their own other. But let's stop this digression and return to the position of the child. For her, the most essential contradiction she is forced continually to solve, first by her physical actions and then also in thought, is her relation to the ensemble of social relations. And here we must speak out against the idea of the ensemble of social relations, or community, as that which somehow hovers above the individual, determining his or her actions, as an external force which forms and educates us all ...

Bibler: Such a view reflects terribly on the present state of Soviet theory.

Mikhailov: Yes, it is a terrible and dangerous thing if the ensemble of social relations is portrayed as a system which simply *produces* us. This idea has already been put to the test and there is no need to return to it either in theory or, especially, in practice. Therefore, the strongest possible Marxist thesis begins from the same premise as that which opens the *German Ideology*: the premise of the *individual*.

Davydov: We begin from the individual and not the collective.

Mikhailov: Thus, only if we see collectivity as a contradiction posed and solved by the individual do we stand on a Marxist position. Then the strong thesis will completely coincide with the weak. And the weak will not be as banal as it appears when we approached things from a naturalistic position.

Davydov: The individual solves his own contradictions from the moment of his birth by means of tools presented by other people.

Mikhailov: For me, the most important consideration is the interpretation of the human essence as a *contradiction*: as a contradiction lying at the basis of the process of human life-activity. If this contradiction is formulated as an abstract *arche*, a source, and if we see in it *not* physical relations between people, but interpersonal relations, expressed through the subjective and its Being, through the ideal above all, through the sensuous and super-sensuous, through symbolism and so on, then this contradiction will be – in its unfolding, its evolution, and in the process of its solution – the coming into being of the Marxist thesis that, in its reality, the human essence is not an abstract thing present in each individual, but the ensemble of social relations.

Bibler: Just as the essence of these relations is the individual.

Mikhailov: Quite so.

Davydov: Besides the individual there is nothing at all.

Mikhailov: Nothing at all. It is only in the individual that the whole thing exists. So here we are all of one voice. My very last point concerns David's thought experiment and the considerations about death at the end of his paper. Here we see the logic of empiricism in its existential and phenomenological variants (and in its analytical form too). The problem is formulated very naturalistically, very existentially: 'It is *I* who am dying'. Ah – so Soviet philosophers say – what the dying person does not take into account is that because of what she has done for society, for people, for humanity, she shall remain here forever, like an Egyptian pyramid, or at least for a remarkably long time ...

Davydov: But it was surely part of the fascination of those pyramids for their creators that their creation gave them immortality, or at least the pyramids were symbols of immortality. And do you know what? I don't like that damned thought experiment. It is quite senseless. You see a logic in it that's simply not there. You've just thought it up yourself. You're so clever, Felix, you've just dreamt it up!

Mikhailov: Well, I like it. The crucial thing is that the question of self-consciousness in the issue of 'life-after-life' is the question of whether the subject will be able to *relate to himself* and not just to exist in some or other way. It is this relation we are anxious to preserve. Human beings are, unfortunately, mortal ...

Davydov: What a discovery! All men are mortal, Socrates is a man ... (*Laughter*)

Mikhailov: That is of course not the point! I just want to say that in death the strong thesis is verified. A human being is the ensemble of social relations because the ability to relate to oneself before, during and after life can be lost *only* if it is possible to lose it during life as well. During life, if a person stops changing himself, stops relating to himself as himself and takes the form of a fossilised, self-satisfied fool for whom everything seems fine from his armchair, then, despite the fact that he is both physically and spiritually before us, there is a sense in which he is already at the edge of the grave. He is a disappearing essence. Maybe his conscience will reawaken someday. Certainly, Tolstoy's 'Death of Ivan Ilych' is very pointed psychologically in this regard. But I can't agree with Vasa that only imaginative fiction treats such questions seriously.

Bakhurst: Can you give an example of such a person?

Mikhailov: Well, of course I'm not so much speaking theoretically as emotionally. Unfortunately, there are very many examples of people whose conscience is no longer awake, who die during life. They turn into that sort of machine which is only able to ... Well, on the other hand, it is very complicated psychologically. They perhaps begin to drink, or to take it out on their spouses, but in any case the human essence ...

Bibler: A fine artist would say that there really were no such people.

Mikhailov: Well, of course, it cannot be personhood which dies during life. It is terrible and shameful for us to suggest that personhood can die during life because we so desperately want to see it in an individual. And here I go, arguing against myself, but we demand of everyone, even the most fossilised, that they should be persons. We say, 'Look, you're now no more than an excuse for a person. But understand that and *be* a person!' It is terrible if we declare of someone that they either are or are not a person, as if this verdict were a closed book.

I remember how a former Director of this Institute once told me the story of a little girl. Sometime ago, somewhere in Minsk, a group of pedagogical scientists (neuropathologists, teachers, psychologists) turned up and began to give the children tests. On the basis of these tests, one little girl was sent to a remedial school. A teacher from another school who happened to live on the same square as the little girl had known her from early childhood. She went to the local department of education to try to show that the child was quite able, and could do well in a normal school. But science had given its verdict. One surely cannot pick a fight with the highest instantiation of human consciousness. Science had said that the little girl was an idiot. So the teacher went higher – to the Ministry – but everywhere that piece of paper sealed the girl's fate. Finally, the teacher appealed to the then Director of this Institute. When he got involved, the child was moved to another school, just the one in fact where the concerned teacher was working. And the Director followed the case for seven years. He thought it was interesting as a former geneticist. And the result is, as you have already guessed, very simple. She didn't become a genius but a normal, active child and did very well. It is the most terrible thing if educationalists relate to children of any age, not as developing persons, but as finite and finished products, as the bearers of some kind of quality which determines their fate: 'This one is able, this one not', 'This one is clever, this one stupid', 'This one has a certain pedigree, his genes are of such-and-such a type'. The teacher looks at the child and immediately knows what kind of person stands before him. But the child's human essence consists in that she relates to herself as to a developing being. It is the mark of a true teacher to appreciate this.

This problem is dramatically posed in the education of blind-deaf pupils. What is so awful now that Meshcheryakov has died? The basic problem is that a stagnant system of evaluation is applied to them, 'You're blind. You're deaf. By the way, you're also a bit retarded'. They talk such rubbish because they evaluate the special subjectivity of blind-deaf children by normal criteria. 'Therefore (so they go on), apart from sticking down envelopes the future holds nothing for you'. And the blind-deaf are sent off to work in a special organisation. And if the organisation churns them out for that kind of work it is deemed to be doing its job. 'What a wonderful thing! Blind-deaf people are sitting and sticking down envelopes! They are still alive! They haven't died! Science at work. Wonderful!' But it's a *nightmare* because these little boys and girls could be just the same as our own. The very same. That is the human essence, to put it simply.

I've gone on a bit, excuse me.

Lektorsky: So Felix and Vasa occupy quite different positions. Davydov has it that personhood develops fairly late, if it develops at all, so that it is wrong to consider the schoolchild a person. And Felix holds that personhood is born with the child, but that it may subsequently be lost. Absolutely counterposed positions.

Bakhurst: When I asked for an example of someone who had ceased to be a person, I did so not merely out of curiosity but because I'm interested in what you take the moral status of such an individual to be. If the possession of personhood is a condition of the development of the moral subject (or maybe the emergence of personhood coincides with, or perhaps just is, the emergence of the moral subject, the moral self), then is it possible for someone to lose or to abdicate from their status as a moral subject? And how does morality dictate we treat such people?

Bibler: The most important question here is how to understand the claim that, at a certain time, someone can stop being a person.

Mikhailov: I was speaking metaphorically, of course.

Bibler: If we put the question differently, it may become clearer. Is there ever a point in a person's life where he may claim that he is not responsible for his actions? When he can point to society, or to the orders of the Fuhrer, or to the fact that he is determined by the environment or his genes? No. Never. From birth to death we may never appeal to these things. The heart of the matter is that there is always that 'gap', that non-coincidence with self, thanks to which an individual always answers for his own activity. He becomes himself, and not just a product of the ensemble of social relations.

Mikhailov: Moral questions are concrete-historical, socially created problems, yet we are always inclined to place above them some kind of suprahistorical moral scheme and talk about the subject's eternal right to life, and so on. In this sense we establish a very strong contradiction between two spheres, which some have tried to capture in a distinction between the ethical and the moral. Anatoli Arsen'ev, for example, has it that there is the sphere of concrete, historically developing moral problems, which find their solutions in particular communities, and an ethical sphere of eternal, transcendent moral principles. I think this view is misguided. We cannot go into this enormous issue now, but the creation of the moral law from human collective practice – its objectification in the form of a code, its alienation from human practice so that it confronts us as an autonomous entity dictating our actions – is just part of a general theory of objectification, of alienation. Our gross confusion in the face of morality is evidenced by the fact that those who claim that abortion is the killing of a real human being, notoriously hold that we can justify the execution of a criminal by saying that he is 'already finished', that he has lost his personhood, by, say, murdering another person. In my view, the question of the convicted murderer is very interesting. I am strongly against the death penalty, but not because I feel it transgresses some transcendent moral law. If I sentence this man to death, then, in the name of society, I put limits on his development as a person. I have said, 'He's a person no longer. He is alive. He breathes. In principle he relates to himself, critically or uncritically. But for breaking certain laws laid down by society I do not consider him a person and I will obliterate him'. How can we seriously justify such an approach? Is personhood some property, conjured up by the influence of the ensemble of social relations, which then goes off on its own, as it were, until one day it disappears, leaving us with a dehumanised shell we can just throw away? Bibler was right to insist that the formation of personhood, of the self, is a continual process. A person cannot lose her essence, that *arche*, that contradiction which stands before her, however much she may capitulate. It is for the community to try to bring that person forth anew. This is the principal business of the community after all. So, to say that one can give up being a person is just a joke, but a very black one in societies which are expert in suppressing personhood and weak at re-engendering it, in calling it back to life.

This would seem a good place to stop.

.·.

'Social Being and the Human Essence' seeks to preserve a sense of the oral culture that sustained so much Soviet philosophy. This oral culture was a vehicle of the collective memory of the Soviet philosophical tradition, since it was the primary means by which the contributions of many Soviet thinkers were sustained, debated, assessed and passed on. The social character of memory is a fascinating topic, and this I take up in the next chapter, which focuses on the ideas of a thinker mentioned more than once in the above discussion, the psychologist L.S. Vygotsky. In 1989, David Middleton asked me to contribute a chapter on Vygotsky to a book on collective remembering that he was editing with his colleague Derek Edwards. Though Vygotsky did not write on collective memory as such, his work offers exciting insights about the social mediation of individual memory, so I proposed that I would address that aspect of his legacy. However, as I tried to reconstruct Vygotsky's conception of the mind, I found myself forced to confront issues about how his contribution has itself been remembered. As a result, rather than side-stepping the issue as I had originally intended, I found myself writing a kind of case study of the complexities of collective remembering.

CHAPTER 3

Social Memory in Soviet Thought

1   Remembering Soviet Conceptions of Memory

The recent literature on collective or social memory contains two principal themes. The first emphasises the significance of 'group remembering', of those social practices by which the members of a community preserve a conception of their past. Such practices, it is argued, must be brought from the periphery to the centre of social theory, for within them a community's very identity is sustained and the continuity of social life made possible. The second theme is the social constitution of individual memory. Here we find a radical challenge to the orthodox view that memory is located solely within the head, a challenge which suggests that the nature of individual memory cannot be analysed without essential reference to notions such as 'society', 'community' and 'history'.

This chapter is devoted primarily to the second of these themes. Any argument that memory is an essentially social phenomenon flies in the face of the individualist conceptions of mind dominant in Western philosophy and psychology and provokes a range of predictable, yet worrisome, objections. Thus, for example, it will be argued that memories are undeniably states of the brain, or at least of 'the mind', and to admit this is surely to locate memories in the individual head. Moreover, since 'remembering' is just an operation on memories, it is natural to hold that it too goes on in the head. Of course, the objection continues, we are certainly often caused to (mis)remember events by 'social interaction', but that is no more grounds to believe that memory is essentially social than my Siamese cat's reminding me of days spent in Toronto is grounds to believe that memory is essentially feline!

I propose to examine whether such objections can be met by arguments in the writings of certain Soviet thinkers, in particular the psychologist L.S. Vygotsky (1896–1934). Vygotsky is well known to have advanced a theory of the social genesis of the mental, and work on memory was central to the development of his position. Vygotsky's legacy is thus an obvious place to look for an argument that memory, at least in its 'higher', human manifestations, is a capacity of social origin. Furthermore, other like-minded Soviet thinkers seem to offer ways to strengthen and develop Vygotsky's position. In the work of his contemporary, V.N. Voloshinov (1895–1936), for example, we find the suggestion that, since remembering involves giving a *reading* of the past, our memories are the products of interpretative skills that are social in both nature and origin. In addition, the philosopher E.V. Ilyenkov (1924–79) offers a vision of how human social activity serves to preserve the past in the present, thereby constituting a form of memory irreducible to happenings in any individual mind. The Soviet tradition, then, seems rich in resources for defending a strong reading of the social foundation of individual memory, and one which represents a marked departure from the prevailing orthodoxy in the West.

However, as we construct the argument we shall find ourselves drawn inexorably into a discussion of the first of the two themes, into cultural issues of collective remembering and forgetting. The writings of these Soviet thinkers are often complex and inaccessible; to use them as a resource requires much interpretative work. In this, the socio-political context in which they were produced is inescapable. It determines both the agenda and the mode of expression of these thinkers' contributions. Especially significant is that social and political circumstances have greatly determined how this Soviet work has been remembered, commemorated and (in some cases) forgotten by subsequent generations. The way in which it is read today is the outcome of a long and sometimes mysterious process of collective remembering.

Consider Vygotsky, a thinker with an explicit political commitment to founding a 'Marxist psychology', whose views took shape in the intense intellectual milieu of the Soviet Union in the 1920s. He was immediately recognised as a leading figure within Soviet psychology, a discipline charged with making a significant contribution to the success of the new regime. Accordingly, Vygotsky often addressed questions with immediate consequences for Soviet educational, clinical and academic policy, and spoke on them to audiences with established political commitments. This role must have called for considerable sensitivity to the political situation, and as the climate darkened with the rise of Stalinism, a number of his followers moved the base of their activities from Moscow to Ukraine. Nonetheless, soon after his premature death in 1934 his works were suppressed. For twenty years his thought was preserved by his former collaborators, largely within an oral culture which itself was influenced greatly by changing social and political circumstances. After Vygotsky's rehabilitation in 1956, his works were gradually republished in the USSR and he was celebrated (in some circles) as the founder of Soviet psychology, though the issues to which his views were read as contributions had changed since the time he was writing. Vygotsky's brilliance was also recognised in the West, though for a long time, many who cited him knew his work only from a small number of translations, some highly edited.[1]

---

1   This situation was improved, though not entirely remedied, by the publication, between 1987

This history makes clear that the path leading from Vygotsky's contribution to our present ways of representing it is an extremely tortuous one. It is therefore significant that the political context of his work has often been ignored by modern scholars concerned to recover it. Vygotsky is portrayed not so much as a Marxist theorist who negotiated a tense political environment and whose work was a victim of Stalin's purges, but as a thinker whose genius 'transcend[s] historical, social and cultural barriers'.[2] It is easy to understand why this is so. The very political climate that so influenced how Vygotsky was remembered also served to inhibit discussion of its influence. There was therefore no tradition in the USSR of scholars writing serious histories of their disciplines. The situation was scarcely easier for the few Western scholars in the area, for those who mastered the Soviet tradition did so by entering the oral culture which sustained it, and were thereby themselves subject to the constraints and responsibilities such participation entails.[3]

Vygotsky has been our example, though similar stories could be told about Voloshinov and Ilyenkov, as we shall see. It is clear that anyone who would seek to draw on their insights must be aware that their work was preserved in a collective memory under extraordinary constraints and pressures, paramount among which was that the nature of the process of remembering could never be explicit in the memories it yielded. The memory of their tradition suffered from amnesia about its own history. This cannot be irrelevant to the interpretation of the substance of their theories.

Thus, issues from both the themes identified above will be interwoven in what follows. We shall explore how a strong reading of the social nature of memory can be defended by appeal to these Soviet thinkers, but we shall do so in a way which reveals the collective memory of their contributions to be an exceedingly relevant factor in the construction of that defence.

---

and 1998, of an English translation of Vygotsky's *Collected Works*, a six-volume edition that had appeared in Russia in the 1980s, though note that, as van der Veer and Yasnitsky point out, the Russian texts 'were heavily edited and censored by the editorial team' (van der Veer and Yasnitsky 2016, p. 74). Van der Veer and Valsiner's *The Vygotsky Reader* (1994) is a good single-volume collection of Vygotsky's writings.

2 Wertsch 1985, p. 231. See Levitin 1982 (2009), ch. 1; Luria 1979, ch. 3.

3 It is notable that during the Soviet era those scholars who offered the most detailed picture of the political setting of Vygotsky's work were the émigrés Alex Kozulin (1984; 1986; 1990) and Jaan Valsiner (1988).

2   Vygotsky's Conception of Mind and Memory

I begin with an exposition of Vygotsky's basic theoretical stance – faithful,
I hope, to the way it is usually remembered. I shall then present Vygotsky's
account of memory.[4]

Vygotsky made his entrance on the Soviet psychological stage in 1924, when
he presented his 'Methods of Reflexological and Psychological Investigation'
to the 2nd All-Russian Psychoneurological Congress in Leningrad. In this and
other early works, his main concern was to identify what he called the 'crisis in
contemporary psychology'. Vygotsky argued that, like most young disciplines,
psychology was a battleground of warring schools. Gestalt psychology, psychoanalysis, behaviourism and Stern's personalism, for example, all seemed to offer
insightful suggestions for a theory of mind. Yet since each school employed an
explanatory framework incommensurable with the others, it was impossible
to integrate their separate findings. It therefore seemed that psychology would
become a unified science only if one of the competing schools defeated its
rivals. But, Vygotsky argued, none of the existing frameworks had sufficient
explanatory power to ground a science embracing all psychological phenomena. Each offered insights in its own limited domain but threatened to become
vacuous when its principles were applied more widely.

The weakness of the prevailing schools was clearest in their failure to make
good sense of *consciousness*, the phenomenon Vygotsky saw as the principal
subject of psychological inquiry. Psychologists, he argued, adopted either one
of two strategies to its analysis: either (a) a subjectivism which treated consciousness as a *sui generis*, non-physical phenomenon occurring in a self-
contained, 'inner' world of thought and accessible to the investigator only
through 'non-scientific' modes of inquiry (for example, through the introspective reports of the subject or phenomenological analysis); or (b) an objectivism
which held that consciousness is reducible to a set of objectively observable

----

4 For accounts of Vygotsky's theory, see Leontiev and Luria 1968; Bakhurst 1986 (1991, ch. 3);
   Wertsch 1985; Kozulin 1986; 1990; Minnik 1987; Valsiner 1988; van der Veer and Valsiner 1991.
   My treatment in this section draws on Vygotsky 1997g [ss 1, pp. 43–62]; 1997b [ss 1, pp. 78–
   98]; 1997d [ss 1, pp. 291–436]; 1987d [ss 2, pp. 1–361]; and those writings which deal explicitly
   with memory Vygotsky 1929; 1997i [ss 1, pp. 149–55]; 1997e, ch. 10 [ss 3, ch. 10]; 1987b, lec. 2
   [ss 2, lec. 2]; and 1978. Note that where I refer to writings of Vygotsky's that appear in the six-
   volume *Collected Works of L.S. Vygotsky*, I cite the English translation and give the reference
   to the appropriate volume of the original Russian edition in square brackets (e.g. [ss 3, p. 32]
   = *Sobranie sochinenie*, vol. 3, p. 32). Note that the numbering of the volumes in the English
   version differs from the Russian original (Vygotsky 1982a; 1982b; 1983b; 1983c; 1984a; 1984b).

physical happenings governed by a specifiable set of physical laws (of which laws relating 'stimuli' to 'responses' seemed the most likely candidates).[5]

For Vygotsky, the debate between these positions was structured by two widely held beliefs: first, that the two strategies exhausted the possible alternatives for a theory of consciousness; and secondly, that psychology could be scientific only by adopting a reductionist approach. Neither belief could be true, Vygotsky argued, since both subjectivism and objectivism were untenable. While the former transformed the mind into an occult entity beyond the reach of scientific investigation, the latter brought the mental into the ambit of science only by doing violence to the higher forms of human psychological functioning. Thus, if the Soviets were to establish a scientific psychology, their task was to carve a path between subjectivism and objectivism.

Vygotsky's proposals for this project invoked a sharp distinction (drawn from Marx and 'German classical philosophy') between 'elementary' and 'higher' mental functions. The elementary functions are said to be characteristic of purely animal, in contrast to distinctively human, psychological functioning. They include non-verbal thought (simple problem-solving activity), involuntary memory and primitive forms of attention, perception and desire. Vygotsky held that an organism possesses such elementary functions purely in virtue of its physical organisation, and that they develop and mature as the organism develops physically. The character of a creature's elementary mental functioning is thus determined exclusively by natural or biological considerations, and *can* therefore be explained in reductionist terms.

In the case of the human child, however, psychological development is not limited to the natural evolution of the elementary mental functions with which it is endowed by nature. On the contrary, the child comes to develop 'higher' mental functions which are distinctively human in kind. These include verbal thought, intellectual speech, voluntary or 'logical' memory and attention, and rational volition. The higher mental functions form a system or totality of psychological capacities said to be 'interfunctionally' related; that is, the character of each is determined by the developing relations it bears to the others. On a Vygotskian perspective, consciousness is portrayed not as one among other

---

5 Both strategies were represented in Russian psychology at the beginning of the twentieth century, the first by Chelpanov and other advocates of 'subjective psychology' who formed the psychological orthodoxy prior to 1917, the second by Pavlov, Kornilov, Bekhterev and the 'reflexologists' who sought an account of all psychological phenomena in stimulus-response terms. The latter approach won institutional supremacy immediately after the Revolution as most consonant with the Bolsheviks' call for a Marxist psychology built on scientific materialist foundations.

higher mental functions, but as the system of interrelated functions itself. As the child develops this system, so its innate, elementary functions are totally restructured or cease to exist altogether.

Crucial to Vygotsky's position is the claim that higher mental functions are qualitatively distinct from, and hence irreducible to, their primitive antecedents. This is so, he argues, because higher mental functions represent *mediated* forms of psychological activity. Vygotsky's elusive notion of mediation underwent significant development as his work progressed. It first emerged as a response to stimulus-response (S-R) theory. Vygotsky held that in analysing psychological states in terms of behavioural responses caused by specific stimuli, the S-R model was unduly unidirectional. It concerned itself with the effect of the world on the psychological subject without considering the subject's effect upon the world. Vygotsky demanded that psychology be concerned with the consequences of human action as well as its causes, arguing that the distinguishing feature of human behaviour is that human beings actively change their environment so as to create new stimuli. We fashion special artefacts, tools, solely for the purpose of manipulating the world and, thereby, the behaviour the world elicits from us. And we create signs, a class of artificial stimuli that act as means to control behaviour (by tying a knot in a handkerchief we create the cause of our own later remembering). Hence the relation between world and subject is never simply unidirectional, but is constantly mediated by tool and sign. The linear connection between stimulus and response is replaced by a triangular interrelation between stimulus, response and 'mediational means'.

From the outset, Vygotsky stressed how the creation of the sign vastly broadens the horizons of the human mind. Just as the tool helps us master nature, so the sign enables us to master our own psychological functioning (hence Vygotsky calls signs 'psychological tools'). We employ signs to draw attention, to aid recall, to represent problems in a way that facilitates their solution and so on. Hence, Vygotsky concluded, the key to the nature of higher psychological functioning lies in the mediating role of the sign.

As Vygotsky explored this role, so he became fascinated with the notion of *meaning* and, with this, his account of mediation underwent an important change. While earlier he had portrayed signs as a class of special, artificial stimuli, operating alongside other 'natural' stimuli, he now came to focus on our ability to create elaborate symbolic systems, such as natural language and mathematics, which mediate our relation to the world through the power of representation. For the later Vygotsky, the introduction of such semiotic systems of mediation completely transforms our psychological relation with reality. We now stand in relation not just to a brute, physical world, but to an *inter-*

preted environment, an environment conceived as being *of a certain kind.* This being so, our behaviour can never be simply 'called forth' by the world in itself. Rather, we act in the light of some reading of reality, a reading that renders our behaviour an appropriate response to the perceived situation. On this view, our actions are more like conclusions to arguments than effects of physical causes. Such a position places the semiotic at the very heart of the relation between psychological subject and reality; the world is an environment endowed with significance, and the trajectory of the subject's behaviour is determined by the meaning he or she takes from the world.

While Vygotsky's early account of mediation may seem a variation on the stimulus-response theme, the later 'semiotic' approach represents a radical departure from that framework. The attraction of the S-R model derived from its promise to establish law-like relations between stimuli and responses described in purely physical terms. However, on this Vygotskian position, the subject's acts, and the situation in which they are undertaken, are described not in a purely physical vocabulary, but in words which render those actions meaningful in the light of the subject's interpretation of the situation. Moreover, the project of establishing laws which relate world and action described in such meaning-laden terms is hopeless. Thus, when Vygotsky recognised semiotic analysis to be 'the only adequate method for analyzing human consciousness',[6] he strengthened his conviction that a scientific psychology cannot be achieved by treating human mental capacities on the model of physical phenomena governed by natural laws.

Thus, for Vygotsky, for psychology to be scientific it must employ, not a reductionist method, but one adequate to the specific character of semiotic mediation. To this end, he urged that psychology become a 'socio-historical' discipline. The systems of mediation which form the fundamental basis of human mental functioning are, he argued, cultural creations. They are products of social history and are preserved in human activity, in what might be called the 'interpretative practices' of the community. The development of the child's higher mental functions must therefore be seen, not as the outcome of some process of natural evolution, but as the consequence of the child's appropriation, or 'internalisation', of such interpretative practices, in particular, natural language. Psychology must therefore make systematic sense of the child's assimilation into its culture and of the qualitative transformations in mental functioning that this precipitates. These transformations will be captured,

---

6 Quoted in Wertsch 1985, p. 79, from Vygotsky 1977. See Vygotsky 2018, p. 292 (where the translation has 'semic analysis').

Vygotsky believed, only by a 'genetic' account which reveals the history of the developing system.

The Vygotskian model, then, is this. The human child enters the world endowed by nature with only elementary mental capacities. The higher mental functions constitutive of human consciousness are, however, embodied in the social practices of the child's community. Just as the child's physical functions are at first maintained only through connection with an autonomous system beyond the child, so his or her psychological life is created only through inauguration into a set of external practices. Only as the child internalises or masters those practices is he or she transformed into a conscious subject of thought and experience.

The distinction between 'elementary' and 'higher' mental functioning is central to Vygotsky's research on memory. Vygotsky describes 'natural' memory as 'mechanistic' or 'instinctive'. This is purely involuntary recall, evoked spontaneously by some state of affairs in the world. The infant may be caused to remember his or her last meal by the smell of the next, or that it is bath time by the sound of water running, but these are cases of remembering over which he or she exercises no control. In contrast, the higher mental function of memory permits us to search at will for an image or an account of the past. In such voluntary or 'logical' memory, it is not that the mind is just prompted to 'go and get' an image by some encounter in the present; rather, the past is deliberately recalled for a determinate reason. Vygotsky argues that logical memory is made possible by the mediating power of signs. By using signs as aids to memory human beings are able deliberately to control the conditions of their future remembering. He writes:

> The very essence of human memory is that human beings actively remember with the help of signs. It is a general truth that the special character of human behaviour is that human beings actively manipulate their relation to the environment, and through the environment they change their own behaviour, subjugating it to their control. As one psychologist has said [Dewey], the very essence of civilisation consists in the fact that we deliberately build monuments so as not to forget. In the knotted handkerchief and the monument we see the most profound, most characteristic and most important feature which distinguishes human from animal memory.[7]

---

7   See Vygotsky 1983a, p. 86; 1978, p. 51. I have revised the translation.

In the late 1920s and early 1930s, Vygotsky and his colleagues designed a series of experiments to explore the influence of mediational means on children's remembering. These experiments used cases of simple memorisation and recall. Children were asked to remember lists of words, the members of which bore no special relation to one another. Vygotsky compared the children's performance in cases (a) where they were required to recall the list 'by heart', and (b) where they were offered symbolic devices in conjunction with the list as an aid to recall. (From the various accounts of these experiments, it seems that these symbolic aids were usually schematic representations, pictographs, of objects which, when suitably interpreted, could be linked with the word to be recalled; thus a picture of a jug of milk might be employed to help remember 'cat', and so on.) Vygotsky found that, after the age of four, children were able actively to employ the pictographs as memory aids and that their performance was significantly improved as a result. Conducting similar experiments with adolescents and adults, however, revealed that for these groups the availability of symbolic aids caused a less significant improvement in their ability to remember, and sometimes even inhibited their performance. Vygotsky concluded that the adolescents and adults were indeed employing symbolic devices as aids to memory, only now their techniques had become *internalised*; they worked with various mnemonic systems which they had silently invented in thought, and which could easily be disrupted if they were forced to use external aids.

Vygotsky consistently maintained that these findings confirmed his general theory of the mind. His interpretation of their significance, however, altered in a way which reflects the shift in his understanding of mediation. At first, Vygotsky argued that the use of signs as memory aids can be understood on the stimulus-response framework: signs figure as artificial stimuli which we consciously employ to cause ourselves to respond in the desired way. Thus in 1929 he wrote that mediated ('mnemotechnical') memory can 'be divided without remainder into the same conditional reflexes as natural memorizing'.[8] However, as he began to consider exactly how signs facilitate remembering, Vygotsky came to recognise that the character of semiotic mediation could not be explained by extending the S-R model.

In some versions of the experiment, the children had been allowed to choose which pictures to use as memory aids. The experimenters noticed some unexpected choices and asked the children to explain how these signs had helped them remember. Thus, for example, one child who had chosen a sketch of a

---

8 Vygotsky 1929, p. 420.

camel to remember the word 'death' explained that the camel was in a desert where its rider was dying of thirst. Another, who had taken a picture of a crab on the beach to remind him of the word 'theatre', replied that the crab spends all day looking at a beautiful stone (also represented in the picture) as if it were at the theatre.[9] Faced with such accounts, Vygotsky moved to the position that the sign could not be represented as simply an extra, artificial link in a causal chain. Rather, it seemed that the sign facilitated remembering as part of an argument in which the word to be recalled figured as the conclusion. It was as if the child used the picture to construct a story which led to the required word as its punchline. This suggests that the structure of mediated memory must be seen as *narrative*, delivering its results in virtue of the meaning of the employed mediational means, and not as straightforwardly causal. We remember by constructing narratives which require the recall of past events for their intelligible completion.

I believe that as Vygotsky came to appreciate this insight, he began to regret that the memory research he and his collaborators had so far conducted had not explored in more depth the semiotic dimension of mediation.[10] In 1932, he wrote that while their research had successfully set the debate on memory into motion, it had not produced definitive conclusions. 'Moreover', he continued, 'I am inclined to think that it represents a colossal oversimplification, even though at first it was often criticised as unduly complex [because of its rejection of a linear S-R model]'.[11] Sadly, Vygotsky's life was cut short before he could take this work further.

What, then, does this work contribute to our understanding of the claim that individual memory is a social phenomenon? Vygotsky, it appears, would endorse a very strong reading of that claim. Throughout his career he held that the distinctive character of human memory is that it is mediated by symbolic means which are cultural phenomena; the human child thus only acquires the higher mental function of memory in so far as he or she is led to appropriate those cultural means by adult members of the community. Moreover, towards the end of his life Vygotsky began to develop a distinctive view of symbolic mediation which introduced a yet richer conception of the social basis of memory. On this view, to possess 'logical memory' involves more than a sens-

---

9   Vygotsky 1997d, p. 181 [*ss* 3, p. 242].
10   It might be better in this context to speak of the semantic plane of consciousness rather than of semiotic mediation. See Yasnitsky and van der Veer 2016a, p. 238.
11   Vygotsky 1987b, p. 308 [*ss* 2, p. 392] (I have adjusted the translation); see also Leontiev and Luria 1968, p. 345.

itivity to the instrumental use of cultural artefacts; it requires the ability to engage in the specific practice, social in origin, of the production and interpretation of narrative forms constructed in that most powerful of socially forged symbol systems, natural language. Furthermore, Vygotsky holds that the genesis of logical memory entails the complete reorganisation of the elementary forms of memory the child is given by nature. Thus, it seems that, for Vygotsky, no form of adult memory can be rendered intelligible without essential reference to the concepts of 'society', 'community' and 'culture'.

Yet, however attractive Vygotsky's conclusions may be, his writings fail to provide arguments which would make them truly compelling. The experimental research, though often novel and ingenious, remains underdeveloped, relying heavily on Vygotsky's theoretical framework for its interpretation. In turn, while I have argued elsewhere that Vygotsky's theoretical vision can be developed and defended,[12] it remains that much of it consists of pregnant insights in need of further elaboration. This is particularly true of his later ideas about semiotic mediation, the development of which would appear so central to the defence of his mature position.

Thus, if Vygotsky's legacy is to provide the basis for a theory of social memory we must find ways to strengthen and develop his insights. A natural place to look is the work of his students and followers, Soviet and Western, who see themselves as members of a 'socio-historical' school of psychology with its roots in Vygotsky's thought. Such a project, however, draws us inevitably into a discussion of how Vygotsky's thought has been preserved in the complex collective memory of the Soviet psychological tradition.

3   Vygotsky Remembered

Two crucial elements of Vygotsky's insights about memory which need further clarification are, first, his conception of the relation of 'the cultural' and 'the natural' which lies behind his distinction between 'higher' and 'elementary' mental functions; and secondly, his understanding of the nature of semiotic mediation. I want to argue now that the way these features of Vygotsky's thought are presently remembered has been significantly influenced by events largely forgotten in accounts of his contribution – namely, the suppression of his writings in the 1930s. This will prove relevant to how Vygotsky's position should be defended and strengthened.

---

12   See Bakhurst 1986 (1991, ch. 3); and Chapter 10 below.

The Soviet intellectual climate at the beginning of the 1930s was dominated by the 'Great Break', a period of massive cultural revolution in which groups of young Party activists in several fields called for the 'bolshevisation' of their disciplines and accused the first generation of Soviet scholars of a multitude of sins. These included 'formalism', a failure to produce theories responding to the practical needs of the Soviet state, inadequate 'party spirit' (*partiinost'*) and a betrayal of the 'Leninist stage' in Soviet thought. Although these criticisms were mostly without substance, they were forcefully endorsed by the Party leadership and precipitated a wave of persecution throughout the Soviet academic world.

Little has been written about the bolshevisation of Soviet psychology in 1931.[13] It seems, however, to have drawn inspiration from the assault on philosophy of the previous year.[14] In this, Abram Deborin's school of Hegelian Marxism, which had dominated Soviet philosophy for several years, was accused of 'menshevising idealism', an epithet apparently coined by Stalin himself. The same heresy was soon detected among psychologists, including Konstantin Kornilov, the influential 'reactologist' who directed the institute where Vygotsky and his collaborators pursued their research. Menshevising idealism in psychology, it was asserted, was 'rotten at its roots and contributed nothing to the practice of socialism, but rather slowed down socialist development with the help of its objectively reactionary, pessimistic theories'.[15] The currency of such dangerous nonsense in the capital must, at least in part, explain why in 1931 some of Vygotsky's collaborators, including Luria and Leontiev, moved their activities from Moscow to Kharkov (Kharkiv), at that time capital of Ukraine, where P. Ya. Galperin and P.I. Zinchenko were already based.[16] As the mythology around menshevising idealism grew, to remain under Kornilov's patronage was to risk not only the preservation of the group's research, but the very lives of its members. Several philosophers perished in the prison camps, and there was no reason to believe that psychologists guilty of 'ideological deviation' would not suffer a similar fate.

Although the move to Ukraine helped secure the survival of the group's research, Vygotsky's legacy remained under threat. After his death in 1934,

---

13   See Joravsky 1978, pp. 20–23; Kozulin 1984; Valsiner 1988, pp. 95–8.

14   See, for example, Bakhurst 1991, ch. 2; Joravsky 1961; Valsiner 1988, pp. 89–95.

15   Zalkind 1931, p. 19, quoted in Kozulin 1984, p. 20.

16   Vygotsky himself did not move to Kharkov, but continued to work with colleagues in Moscow and Leningrad. Luria and Leontiev remained in Kharkov until 1934. On the Kharkov School, see Yasnitsky 2008; Yasnitsky and Ferrari 2008.

his work suffered a barrage of criticisms.[17] First, he was attacked for 'cosmopolitanism'; that is, for showing respect for the work of 'bourgeois' authors. Secondly, despite his well-known critique of conventional intelligence tests, his interest in psychological testing was dismissed as reactionary. Such testing, it was argued, always serves to preserve the status quo, representing the less educated as the intellectually inferior. Finally, a third criticism zeroed in on just those elements of his work we have found central to his views on memory. He was argued to have emphasised semiotic and cultural phenomena at the expense of practical activity in his account of the development of consciousness, thereby implying that the mind is formed not in 'material production' (that is, in the process of object-orientated activity with material objects), but through interpersonal relations (that is, participation in communicative and representational practices). He was thus held to have misrepresented the relation between the 'natural' and 'cultural' forces in development, overemphasising the significance of enculturation, while ignoring the (purportedly) natural process of the child's material interaction with the physical environment.

The second of these criticisms is usually cited as most significant. When the Central Committee's 1936 decree outlawed 'pedology', a form of child psychology which emphasised testing, his work was withdrawn from public consumption for the remainder of the Stalin era. However, the effect of the third criticism's assault on Vygotsky's semiotic and cultural emphasis should not be underestimated. With Vygotsky's writings suppressed, his legacy could only be preserved in an oral culture sustained by his followers.[18] I shall argue that this third criticism significantly shaped how his disciples came to represent and remember his contribution.

Despite its more scholarly tone, the third criticism is no less ideologically motivated than the others. In this period, Soviet polemicists would typically seek to discredit their opponents by associating their work with some form of philosophical idealism. This is precisely the criticism's implication: Vygotsky's recognition of the fundamental explanatory importance of 'ideal'

---

17   Translations of a number of essays attacking Vygotsky appear in *Journal of Russian and East European Psychology* (38.6); see especially those by Razmyslov (2000) and Rudneva (2000).

18   In a provocative recent essay, Fraser and Yasnitsky (2016) challenge the idea that Vygotsky's writings were subject to any kind of official ban, and even go so far as to suggest that some of his followers, including Leontiev, were responsible for inhibiting the publication of his works. Yasnitsky is the leading figure in the recent 'revisionist revolution in Vygotsky studies' that questions the traditional presentations of Vygotsky's life and work (see Yasnitsky and van der Veer 2016a and Yasnitsky 2018). Yasnitsky's approach is vigorously challenged by Andrey Maidansky (2020b).

phenomena such as meaning and communication is perceived as an idealist departure from the orthodox dialectical materialism of the founders of Marxism, with its emphasis on human beings' material transformation of nature. In the Stalin period, no one would have made such a critique without realising its implications; the third criticism is certainly a charge of ideological heresy in academic guise. It is therefore interesting that those who raised this criticism included members of the Kharkov group itself, such as Alexei Leontiev, and Peter Zinchenko, who explicitly attacked Vygotsky's account of memory.

To be fair, the Kharkovites may initially have made this criticism in self-defence. With Vygotsky in disgrace, they surely had little choice but to distance themselves from his views. Since they could not avoid an ideological pronouncement, it would have made sense to produce a critique with some theoretical content, for this at least required them to give voice to Vygotsky's position in the course of 'refuting' it. Nonetheless, whatever the Kharkovites' intentions, the criticism quickly became a habitual feature of their presentation of Vygotsky's work. Indeed, they began to define their research programmes in response to these supposed weaknesses of their teacher's contribution. A good illustration is Leontiev's 'activity theory', an approach which has proved very influential in both the USSR and the West.[19] The initial rationale for this theory, which identifies object-orientated activity (*predmetnaya deyatel'nost'*) as the developmental root of human consciousness, was precisely to replace Vygotsky's cultural-semiotic orientation with an account on which psychological operations 'are determined by the actual [that is, physical, material] relations between child and reality'.[20] Thus, it seems that the scholars responsible for keeping Vygotsky's thought alive through the Stalin period internalised an image of his work which, paradoxically, had its origins in the Stalinist attempts to suppress it.

This image endured long after Vygotsky's rehabilitation. In 1968, for example, in an article introducing Vygotsky's work to a Western audience, Leontiev and Luria still maintain that his 'cultural-historical' theory of the mind 'has serious shortcomings, related to an insufficient regard for the formative role of man's practical activity in the evolution of his own consciousness. Thus it has counterposed too sharply the various forms of conscious activity of social origin

---

19   The concept of activity, which was profoundly important to Ilyenkov, is discussed in many
      subsequent of the chapters below. Activity Theory specifically is the focus of Chapters 15–
      17.
20   Leontiev 1980, p. 14.

with "naturally formed" mental processes'.[21] These remarks reproduce almost exactly the case Peter Zinchenko made against Vygotsky some thirty years earlier.[22]

Since the Kharkov school was the guardian of the oral culture which preserved Vygotsky's memory, it is natural that its representation of his contribution should have had enormous influence on how it is presently interpreted and assessed. An excellent example of this influence is found in James Wertsch's exposition of Vygotsky's views in his influential *Vygotsky and the Social Formation of Mind*. Wertsch's text was the first high-quality book-length treatment of its subject, Western or Soviet. One of the reasons for its excellence is its author's ability to speak with the authority of a participant in the debate; Wertsch absorbed himself in the Soviet tradition and arrived at his interpretation through discussions with many of Vygotsky's former collaborators.[23] A consequence of this, however, is that Wertsch's presentation reproduces the Kharkovites' critique. Despite his admiration for many of Vygotsky's ideas on meaning, Wertsch argues that Vygotsky was wrong to take a semiotic category, 'word meaning', as the basic unit of analysis of consciousness in his classic *Thought and Language*. Wertsch proposes the notion of 'tool-mediated action' as an alternative unit, which he draws from the work of Vladimir Zinchenko (Peter Zinchenko's son).[24] Moreover, like the Kharkovites, Wertsch maintains that Vygotsky's work is flawed for its opposition of the natural and the cultural, which, he suggests, is so radical that it precludes a proper explanation of their interaction.[25] Again like the Kharkovites, Wertsch argues that this weakness is 'directly tied' to Vygotsky's account of meaning.[26] Thus, we find that our contemporary reading of Vygotsky bears the mark of a critique forged in the political machinations of the Stalin era.

At the opening of this section, two elements of Vygotsky's thought were identified that need further elaboration if his suggestions about the social essence of memory are to be developed into a theory: namely, his conception of semiotic mediation and his view of the relation between the natural and the cultural. We now know it is unlikely we shall find the inspiration for this project in the work of those psychologists to whom we owe the preservation of Vygotsky's legacy. On the contrary, since the Stalinist attempt to suppress Vygotsky, the collective

---

21   Leontiev and Luria 1968, p. 342.
22   Zinchenko 1983–84; see Kozulin 1986, pp. xlv–lii.
23   Wertsch 1985, p. xiii.
24   Zinchenko 1985; see Wertsch 1985, pp. 196–7, 205–8.
25   Wertsch 1985, pp. 197–8.
26   Wertsch 1985, p. 197.

memory of his thought has consistently marginalised its semiotic orientation and sought to reshape his view of the natural and the cultural.

We have no choice, then, but to look beyond the mainstream of Soviet psychology. We turn first to a theorist of language also working in the 1920s, V.N. Voloshinov, whose ideas have been argued to complement Vygotsky's.[27] In Voloshinov, I believe, we find the means to develop the semiotic dimension of Vygotsky's stance. As expected, the result is a radical view of the cultural constitution of mind in general, and memory in particular.

4   Voloshinov and the Textuality of the Mental

Our present understanding of Voloshinov's work is a legacy of collective remembering every bit as intriguing as the processes which have preserved Vygotsky's thought. Little is known of Voloshinov's life. He was born in 1895 in St. Petersburg, where he began studying law some twenty years later. By 1918 he had moved to the provincial town of Nevel where he became a member of the circle of thinkers surrounding the now famous scholar Mikhail Bakhtin. He followed Bakhtin to Vitebsk and eventually back to Leningrad in 1924, where he re-enrolled at the University. His interests included not only philosophy of language and psychology, but also musicology and composition. He died in 1936 from tuberculosis. During his life, he published two books, a critique of Freud, *Freudism*,[28] and his seminal work on language, *Marxism and the Philosophy of Language*.[29] He also produced several scholarly articles.

The controversy around Voloshinov's legacy began when, at the commemoration of Bakhtin's 75th birthday in 1970, the Soviet linguist Vyacheslav Ivanov declared that Bakhtin was the author of the major works published under Voloshinov's name. Ivanov's claim was neither confirmed nor denied by Bakhtin himself and, as the evidence remains inconclusive, scholars have taken contrasting views of its authenticity. In the West, Bakhtin's biographers, Katerina Clark and Michael Holquist, are adamant that he is the true creator of these works, while Voloshinov's translator, I.R. Titunik, maintains that Voloshinov

---

27   Emerson 1983; Wertsch 1985, pp. 224–6.
28   Voloshinov 1987. Zavershneva (2016, p. 272n6) observes that Vygotsky referred to Voloshinov in one manuscript (Vygotsky 1997k, pp. 120 [*ss* 1, p. 148], where Voloshinov is listed among 'several of Freud's critics'), though the reference was excised from the text as it appears in the *Collected Works*. It is not known whether Vygotsky ever cited Bakhtin or knew him personally.
29   Voloshinov 1986.

should be regarded as their sole author. Still others, such as Tzvetan Todorov, treat Voloshinov's writings as one voice among many in a Bakhtinian discourse and call their author 'Voloshinov/Bakhtin'.[30]

This puzzle is significant because the different solutions invite different readings of the Voloshinov texts. Those who treat Bakhtin as their author must somehow account for the Marxist idiom, conspicuously absent in Bakhtin's other writings. Clark and Holquist, for example, suggest that references to Marxism were added to the already completed texts to get them past the censor.[31] From such a perspective, the Voloshinov texts are read primarily as stages in the development of Bakhtin's theory of language, 'ventriloquated' through the persona of an orthodox Marxist.[32]

However, once Voloshinov is restored as author, it becomes possible to treat the professed Marxism of these writings as central to their concerns. We can read Voloshinov as setting out, like Vygotsky, to re-establish his discipline on a Marxist foundation. Indeed, there are many interesting parallels between the way in which Voloshinov and Vygotsky conceived their respective projects. For example, Voloshinov shares Vygotsky's conviction that a Marxist approach must carve a path between subjectivism and objectivism. Hence, in the philosophy of language, Voloshinov seeks an account which neither treats the individual mind as the sole source of meaning, nor construes meaning as a property of language conceived as a purely formal system.[33] Moreover also like Vygotsky, Voloshinov argues that an alternative to subjectivism and objectivism is possible only by recognising the essentially social nature of the phenomenon under study. For Voloshinov, the linguistic act (the utterance) 'is born, lives, and dies in the process of social interaction ... Its form and meaning are determined basically by the form and character of this interaction'.[34] Finally, despite his emphatic appeal to the social, Voloshinov is as anxious as Vygotsky to avoid a crude social reductionism. He denies the claim of some Soviet Marxists that the content and character of a discourse is exhaustively explained merely by citing the socio-economic situation of its participants. Rather, he advances a subtler position where the voices we may choose to speak in, and the ways in which we shall be understood, can be rendered intelligible only in light of the specific character of the communicative practices of our culture, which, in turn, cannot be explained without essential reference to socio-economic factors.

---

30   Todorov 1984, p. 11.
31   See, for example, Clark and Holquist 1984, p. 159.
32   Holquist 1983, p. 6.
33   Voloshinov 1986, part II, ch. 1.
34   Voloshinov 1987, p. 105.

On this reading, Voloshinov's texts appear as part of a developing Soviet Marxism, rather than as a contribution to another intellectual tradition dressed up in Marxist attire. I find such an interpretation more plausible than that of Clark and Holquist. The parallels with Vygotsky – whose professions of Marxism are now generally regarded as sincere – are only one example of how Voloshinov's work is indeed characteristic of (good) Soviet Marxist writing in the 1920s. Although Bakhtin was certainly clever enough to write in this idiom, had he done so he would in fact have been making a contribution to Soviet Marxism. Thus, in so far as the argument for Bakhtin's authorship of the Voloshinov texts falsely implies that their Marxism is a deceit (or alternatively that Bakhtin was a Marxist), we should continue to consider Voloshinov to be their author.

Voloshinov offers an argument to strengthen Vygotsky's account of the social nature of memory. The first step is Voloshinov's claim that conscious psychological states are essentially semiotic phenomena. They are all forms of *utterance* (or 'verbal reaction'). This is true, he argues, not only of those mental states which are clearly propositional in content (such as beliefs, desires, intentions and so on), but also of the human subject's conscious experiences.

'*Experience exists*', he writes, '*even for the person undergoing it only in the material of signs*'.[35] Hence, for Voloshinov, there is no pure experience of reality to which we later give words; rather, the world we confront is one already organised by our modes of representation. There is no access to reality which is not an interpretation or reading, and hence the world our minds encounter is always a read or interpreted world.[36] Hence, he concludes, '*consciousness itself can arise and become viable only in the material embodiment of signs*';[37] if we deprive consciousness of its semiotic content, there would be 'absolutely nothing left'.[38]

It follows that the content of our mental states is determined by the meaning of the signs which comprise them. However, Voloshinov maintains that signs do not possess meaning in virtue of their intrinsic properties, but take on meaning only in the context of communicative practices in which they are interpreted. And as we have seen, Voloshinov argues that these practices are essentially social in nature. Thus, just as the author's intentions do not fix the meaning of his or her work, so the individual subject does not occupy a logically privileged position in the interpretation of his or her own thoughts. He writes:

---

35   Voloshinov 1986, p. 28; his emphasis.
36   Voloshinov 1986, p. 26.
37   Voloshinov 1986, p. 11; his emphasis. I have modified the translation.
38   Voloshinov 1986, p. 13.

The verbal component of behaviour is determined in all fundamentals and essentials of its content by objective-social factors.

The social environment is what has given a person words and what has joined words with specific meanings and value judgements; the same environment continues ceaselessly to determine and control a person's verbal reactions throughout his entire life.

Therefore, nothing verbal in human behaviour (inner and outward equally) can under any circumstances be reckoned to the account of the individual subject in isolation; the verbal is not his property but the property of his *social group*.[39]

Thus, if 'the reality of the inner psyche is the same reality as that of the sign', and the sign derives its meaning from the interpretative practices of the speech community rather than the fiat of the individual,[40] then psychological states are, in a very strong sense, socially constituted phenomena. 'The logic of consciousness', it transpires, 'is the logic of ideological communication, of the semiotic interaction of the social group'.[41]

What, then, of memory? For Voloshinov, the social essence of individual memory follows simply from the social constitution of all mental states. On this position, to remember is always to give a reading of the past, a reading which requires linguistic skills derived from the traditions of explanation and story-telling within a culture, and which issues in a narrative that owes its meaning ultimately to the interpretative practices of a community of speakers. This is true even when what is remembered is one's own past experience.[42] For Voloshinov, memory can never be understood as an immediate relation between the thinking subject and some private mental image of the past. The image, he argues, becomes a phenomenon of consciousness only when clothed with words, and these owe their meaning to social practices of communication.

Voloshinov's argument greatly strengthens Vygotsky's position. First, while Vygotsky's studies focus narrowly on a specific species of remembering (recall of lists mediated by the use of mnemonic devices), Voloshinov's conclusions are quite general in kind, stressing the social constitution of all forms of individual memory. Secondly, Voloshinov's account is consonant with Vygotsky's account of higher mental functioning in general and of the role of semiotic mediation in particular. Moreover, Voloshinov's writings contain material that

---

39 Voloshinov 1987, p. 86; his emphasis.
40 Voloshinov 1986, p. 26 (see also 1986, p. 86; 1987, pp. 79, 105).
41 Voloshinov 1986, p. 13.
42 Voloshinov 1987, p. 87.

suggests how a Vygotskian theory of semiotic mediation might be developed; they are a rich resource for any theory which represents consciousness as a developmental achievement precipitated by the internalisation of communicative practices broadly understood.

Significantly, if we enrich Vygotsky's account of semiotic mediation by appeal to Voloshinov, we find further support for the former's radical opposition of the 'cultural' and the 'natural'. Like Vygotsky, Voloshinov insists that the human mind cannot be treated as a natural phenomenon intelligible by appeal to natural laws. Mind is 'a socioideological fact and, as such, beyond the scope of physiological methods or the methods of any other of the natural sciences'.[43] We are not born conscious persons, but *become* them after 'a second birth, a *social* birth' when we 'enter into history'.[44] Such Vygotskian thoughts abound in Voloshinov's writings. However, Voloshinov's position suggests a way to defend them not articulated by Vygotsky himself. For Voloshinov the relation between the contents of consciousness and the physical states of the thinking subject's body or brain is analogous to the relation between the meaning of a text and the physical form in which it is inscribed, or (to use a more dynamic model) between the content of a drama and the physical states of the medium (for example, television) in which it is presented. Just as it would be hopeless to look for law-like relations between the physical states of a television and the semantic content of the programmes it transmits, so the search for laws relating the states of mind and brain is, for Voloshinov, equally in vain.

As the Kharkovites would have predicted, taking the notion of semiotic mediation seriously leads to a very radical opposition between 'the natural' and 'the cultural', and to the view that human psychological phenomena are essentially cultural, and hence non-natural, phenomena. Such a view was too radical for many of the Kharkov group, and may be too much for Vygotsky's Western followers. If Vygotsky's thought is developed in this way, there seems little prospect of reconstructing it as an 'emergent interactionism',[45] where the mental development is traced as the outcome of an interplay between biological and cultural forces. For while Vygotsky and Voloshinov hold that mind emerges in the transformation of the child's biological being through the appropriation of culture, they both invoke quite different principles of explanation for the natural and cultural realms. It thus seems unclear how there could be a systematic *theory* of their interaction.[46]

---

43   Voloshinov 1986, p. 25.
44   Voloshinov 1987, p. 15; his emphasis.
45   Wertsch 1985, pp. 43–7.
46   Since writing this essay, I have come to reject the strong view of the social constitution

5 Ilyenkov, Ideality and Memory

Now that we have used Voloshinov's writings to strengthen Vygotsky's position we should briefly return to the Kharkovites' critique of it. We observed that, since the 1930s, the mainstream of Soviet psychology has tended to marginalise the semiotic dimension of Vygotsky's legacy. The theories of his best-known followers (Leontiev, Luria, Zaporozhets, Galperin, Meshcheryakov, V. Zinchenko and Davydov) have all taken 'object-orientated activity', rather than a semiotic category, as the basis of the genesis of consciousness. It would seem that there are two conflicting trends within Soviet Marxist philosophy of mind; one, seen in the contributions of Vygotsky and Voloshinov, which treats semiotic mediation as the foundation of consciousness, and another, dominant since the 1930s, which adopts the 'activity approach'.

It would be wrong, however, to take the conflict between the two camps at face value. The judgement that there is necessarily a theoretical incompatibility between them, itself a product of the 1930s, may owe more to the political shadowboxing of orthodoxy and heresy than to genuine argument.

This can be seen, I think, if we consider the work of Evald Ilyenkov, one of the most interesting Soviet philosophers of the modern period. In his work of the early 1960s Ilyenkov sought to revitalise Soviet philosophy after the stagnant years of Stalinism. Though he never referred in his published works to the thinkers of the 1920s, he reintroduced many issues and ideas which had been prominent in their debates. It is interesting, therefore, that despite his constant emphasis on activity as the foundation of the mental (which endeared him to Leontiev), Ilyenkov seems to share Vygotsky's and Voloshinov's presupposition that there need be no grand opposition between the practical and the semiotic in a Marxist theory of the mind.

Consider, for example, Ilyenkov's theory of 'the ideal'.[47] This theory is an attempt to explain the nature and possibility of ideal (that is, non-material) phenomena (for example, values, reasons, psychological processes and states) in the material world. Ilyenkov turns to the concept of activity for his explan-

---

of mental states I here attribute to Voloshinov (see Bakhurst 2011, ch. 2, especially pp. 37–42). I also prefer to think of human psychological phenomena, not as 'non-natural', but as aspects of our 'second nature' (see Chapter 18 below), thereby softening the apparent opposition between the natural and the cultural, in a way perhaps more faithful to Vygotsky's own aspirations.

47 See Ilyenkov 1962 (revised as ch. 8 of Ilyenkov 1974a [2009b, pp. 147–67]); Ilyenkov 1977b (reprinted in Ilyenkov 2009b, pp. 253–84); 2014. I discuss Ilyenkov's work in detail in Part 2 of this volume and in Bakhurst 1991.

ation. A Marxist form of materialism, he argues, must hold that ideal phenomena are genuine constituents of objective reality that ultimately have their source in human activity. On this view, the natural world comes to embody non-material properties as objectified forms of social activity. Ilyenkov's argument presupposes, however, that the act of transforming nature is itself a semiotic act: by acting on the world, human beings endow their natural environment with meaning, with the significance which is its 'ideal form'. This is illustrated by appeal to a concept important to Vygotsky: the tool. An inanimate lump of matter is elevated into a tool through the significance with which it is invested by activity. It stands as an embodiment of human purpose in virtue of the way it is fashioned and employed by human agents. And the artefact created through the manipulation of matter by tools is, Ilyenkov argues, more than merely material because of the meaning it derives from incorporation into human practice.

Ilyenkov takes his theory of the idealisation of the natural world very seriously, arguing that his account of the ideality of the tool and the artefact may be generalised into a wholesale theory of the relation of culture and mind. For Ilyenkov, 'humanity's spiritual culture', the total structure of normative demands objectively confronting each individual member of the community (including the demands of logic, language and morality), must be conceived not as a realm of super-material phenomena, but as patterns of meaning embodied in the form of our material environment through the influence of our activity. In turn, Ilyenkov argues that the capacity to think is just the ability to inhabit such a meaning-laden environment. For him, the higher mental functions must be seen primarily as capacities to engage in a certain species of activity: the negotiation of ideal properties and relations.

Like Vygotsky and Voloshinov, Ilyenkov argues that the human child does not possess the capacity to inhabit an idealised environment from birth, but is inaugurated into the relevant species of activity by adult members of the community. As the child masters or 'internalises' these activities, so he or she becomes a thinking subject. Ilyenkov, again like Vygotsky, conceives of internalisation as the appropriation of patterns of social meaning, as the assimilation of a culture, and he would accord language learning a special place in this process. But Ilyenkov would certainly not claim that the internalisation of these patterns of meaning should be contrasted with engaging in 'real, practical activity', since, for him, to assimilate a culture is to appropriate the forms of social activity which sustain it. To learn a language, for example, is to learn to manipulate a special class of artefacts, words.

Thus, for Ilyenkov, activity is the root of consciousness. It is so, however, only because in activity the natural world is invested with enduring patterns of meaning, the negotiation of which constitutes thought. In Ilyenkov's work, the practical and semiotic orientations in Soviet theory live in harmony.

Ilyenkov's contribution, however, offers more to the present discussion than the suggestion that there need not be a theoretical impasse between those trends of Soviet thought which take semiotic mediation as the unit of analysis of consciousness and those which adopt an 'activity approach'. His theory of the ideal offers another dimension to our account of social memory. Ilyenkov holds that the socially significant practices of the community represent thought made objective. Each human child enters the world to find the forms of activity which constitute thinking embodied in the community's activities and expressed in the shape impressed upon the physical environment by human labour. Just as our status as conscious subjects requires that we master these activities, so the continuity of our mental lives over time depends on the preservation of the world of shared significance the activities sustain. Thus, this idealised world of 'humanity's spiritual culture' can itself be seen as a form of memory, and one which is essentially collective in kind.

6   Conclusion

I have argued that a distinctive theory of the social nature of memory may be drawn from the work of three distinguished Soviet thinkers, Vygotsky, Voloshinov and Ilyenkov. This theory holds, first, that memory is a psychological function which is essentially social in origin; secondly, that memories are socially constituted states; and thirdly, that certain forms of collective activity represent a form of social memory, irreducible to the happenings in any individual mind, yet essential to the continuity of the mental life of each individual.

Our discussion revealed that the contributions on which we sought to draw have themselves been preserved by complex processes of collective remembering that have influenced how they are interpreted and commemorated today. In particular, we found that two ideas central to Vygotsky's conceptions of social memory have been marginalised in the Soviet tradition since the Stalin era – namely, the notion of semiotic mediation and the specific distinction between 'the cultural' and 'the natural' which follows from it. I have tried to tell a story which restores these ideas to the centre of discussion. Such a strategy does not, I believe, compromise the Vygotskian tradition in psychology, despite the way it has perceived itself since the 1930s. It does, however, have some radical consequences. The account of social memory we have constructed is no self-contained theory but follows from a general conception of the social constitution of the thinking individual. This idea, which may seem wild and unscientific from the perspective of much contemporary cognitive science, remains enigmatic and undeveloped. It is to be hoped that a greater understanding of this idea's Soviet past will lead to its fruitful elaboration in the future.

∴

The next chapter explores a remarkable episode in the history of Soviet special education: Alexander Meshcheryakov's work on the education of blind-deaf children. This work, conducted in the 1960s and 70s, was much celebrated by thinkers in the broadly Vygotskian tradition, including both Ilyenkov and Mikhailov, who knew Meshcheryakov well and befriended his pupils, especially Alexander Suvorov. Suvorov was one of the famous quartet of blind-deaf students who graduated from Moscow University in the 1970s; he went on to do work in psychology and philosophy. The story of Meshcheryakov and his charges is undoubtedly fascinating and inspiring. However, the philosophical significance of his legacy is controversial and Ilyenkov's interpretation of, and involvement in, Meshcheryakov's work was attacked in the late 1980s by some of his longstanding critics. While that incident was a rather sorry episode, it does cast 'the Meshcheryakov experiment' as another absorbing example of collective remembering during the Soviet era.

CHAPTER 4

The Meshcheryakov Experiment: Soviet Work on the Education of Blind-Deaf Children

Co-authored with Carol Padden

1 Introduction

In 1929, Lev Vygotsky wrote of the responsibility facing the new community of Soviet psychologists:

> A sense of the enormity of the tasks facing contemporary psychology ... is my most basic feeling. And that places an *infinite* responsibility – a most serious, almost tragic (in the finest, most genuine sense of the word) burden on the shoulders of those few who are conducting research in any new branch of science – and especially the science of the person.[1]

This chapter focuses on one of Vygotsky's successors – Alexander Meshcheryakov (1923–74) – who rose to this responsibility in a remarkable way. Meshcheryakov was what in Russian is called a *tiflosurdopedagog*, that is, a psychologist concerned with the upbringing of individuals who are both blind and deaf. He set the sights of his pupils' development far beyond the basic vocational training typical of programmes for the 'multi-sensory deprived'. In 1977, his four eldest charges – Alexander Suvorov, Sergei Sirotkin, Natalia Korneeva (later Krylatova), and Yuri Lerner – graduated from Moscow University with degrees in psychology. Each has subsequently been involved in research or teaching. Suvorov, for instance, described in Meshcheryakov's field notes as one of the slowest safety-pin makers in history,[2] has published a number of accomplished articles in Soviet philosophy and psychology journals. He also wrote and codirected a powerful short television film.[3]

---

1 Quoted in Levitin 1982, p. 322. (This book has been republished as Levitin 2009. The new edition contains some additional material. Most notably, much of the chapter on Meshcheryakov has been replaced by the article 'The Best Path to Man' (Levitin 1979), which is essentially an expanded version of the material originally included.)

2 Meshcheryakov 1979, p. 271. (This book has been republished as Meshcheryakov 2009.)

3 See Suvorov 1983, 1988, and Sirotkin 1979. (Note that the translation of Suvorov 1983 [Suvorov

Meshcheryakov's work thus represents a remarkable Soviet experiment in education. The experiment is interesting, however, not only for the quality of its results; it is also striking for its relation to *theory*. Meshcheryakov's ideas are steeped in the theoretical framework of the 'socio-historical' school of Soviet psychology, the tradition founded in the 1920s by Vygotsky and developed by thinkers such as Leontiev, Luria, Zaporozhets, Galperin, Davydov and V.P. Zinchenko. The tradition has enjoyed a growing influence in the West since the first English translations of Vygotsky's appeared in the 1960s. Meshcheryakov wrote that his work was made possible by the insights of this tradition[4] and, in return, a number of prominent Soviet psychologists and philosophers maintained that Meshcheryakov's achievements demonstrate the validity of the socio-historical approach.[5] Both the practical success and the theoretical sophistication of Meshcheryakov's work suggest that it deserves detailed scrutiny.

This chapter will first present Meshcheryakov's account of the condition of the blind-deaf child prior to systematic instruction. We shall then turn to Meshcheryakov's theoretical perspective and explore how it influenced his pedagogical methods. Finally, we shall examine how Meshcheryakov's work was received in the Soviet Union.

2   The Initial Condition of The Blind-Deaf Child

Blind-deafness may be a consequence of a number of different conditions, including prenatal insult caused by rubella, other congenital disorders such as Usher's syndrome, or childhood diseases such as tuberculous meningitis. The variety of causes, and the complexity of their effects, mean that the profile of each blind-deaf child's condition may be unique in significant ways, depending on the time of onset of blind-deafness and the presence or absence of other physical and cognitive disabilities. This demands that any educa-

---

1983–84], which is devoted to the concept of imagination, is eccentric. Throughout, the Russian 'voobrazhenie' is translated not as 'imagination' but as 'representation'. Although this helps convey the richness of the Russian word not shared by its usual English equivalent, it obscures an important polemical point. One of Surovov's aims is to argue that the formation of *any* image or representation of reality involves the creative exercise of imagination, and hence that the blind-deaf individual's conception of the world is not *qualitatively* distinct from that of the sighted and hearing person in virtue of its reliance on imagination.) Apart from such theoretical works, each of the four wrote insightful biographical pieces. See, for example, those included in Meshcheryakov 1979, pp. 327–44 and Gurgenidze and Ilyenkov 1975, pp. 73–84. See also Suvorov 1989 and Alexander Rozhkov's 2017 film *Ilyenkov*.

4   Meshcheryakov 1979, pp. 31–2.
5   See, e.g., Gurgenidze and Ilyenkov 1975; Ilyenkov 1970; 1977c.

tional programme devised for a blind-deaf child must be tailored to the specific character of the child's abilities and needs.[6] In consequence, any account of the education of blind-deaf children must find some way to reconcile the particularity of individual cases with the need to present a coherent general picture of the blind-deaf child's predicament. Meshcheryakov's approach is to attempt a general account of the theory and practice of the education of children who are 'pedagogically blind and deaf', but without significant cognitive impairment, and who have been blind and deaf since birth or early childhood. To say that a child is 'pedagogically blind-deaf' is to say that whatever hearing and sight they possess is insufficient to permit them to be educated in a way which relies on the exercise of those faculties.[7] Not all Meshcheryakov's pupils were blind and deaf from birth or infancy. This was not true, for example, of three of the four graduates of Moscow University.[8] Meshcheryakov's account is essentially a 'worst case scenario' embodying a general educative framework which he believed applicable to less severe cases. At all times in his writings, Meshcheryakov takes pains to illustrate this framework with extracts from particular case histories.

The starting point of Meshcheryakov's account is a description of the blind-deaf child's 'initial state', i.e., his or her condition prior to systematic instruction.[9] 'All those who have observed such children', he writes, 'describe them as absolutely helpless and deprived of the capacities of human behaviour and thought'.[10] In the words of one of Meshcheryakov's predecessors, Avgusta Yarmolenko:

> These 'inert masses' or 'frenzied animals', as they appear to the outside observer, are shut out from ordinary life by the absence of aural and visual impressions. Passive and immobile, they would sit in the same spot for hours at a stretch, sometimes even in the same pose. They do not use the faculty of touch to investigate spatial relationships or to familiarise themselves with new objects: even the process of eating, dressing and undressing and the satisfaction of their most basic physiological needs are only carried out after external stimulus, without which the processes concerned might be postponed in time until an extreme degree of need be reached, which in its turn would produce an outbreak

6   Meshcheryakov 1970, p. 81.

7   For a more technical definition see Meshcheryakov 1979, pp. 70–71.

8   See Meshcheryakov 1979, pp. 267–71.

9   See, for example, Meshcheryakov 1979, pp. 79–84.

10   Meshcheryakov 1979, p. 79.

of fury. They do not manifest even the most elementary urge for contact with other people.[11]

A similar description is offered by Meshcheryakov's friend and colleague, philosopher Evald Ilyenkov:

> [The blind-deaf child] is a creature which, as a rule, is immobile and reminds one rather of a plant, of some kind of cactus or ficus, which lives only so long as it is in direct contact with food and water … and dies without uttering a sound if one forgets to feed, water and protect it from the cold. It makes no attempt to reach for food, even if that food is half a meter away from its mouth. It utters not a squeak when it is hungry, will not cover itself from the draught with a warm blanket … It is a human plant in the full sense of the term.[12]

In the Soviet literature, the blind-deaf child's 'initial condition' is almost always drawn in such rhetorical terms. To put it more prosaically, prior to intervention, blind-deaf children are either *hyperactive* or (as emphasised by Ilyenkov) *hypoactive*, i.e., they are passive and immobile apart from occasional anarchic discharges of energy. Crucial here is that blind-deaf children do not engage in end-orientated activity. Indeed, according to Meshcheryakov, they fail to exhibit many of the unconditional reflexes which, on the Pavlovian or 'reactological' framework Meshcheryakov rejects, form the innate basis of animal behaviour. For example, Meshcheryakov contends that blind-deaf children do not display the so-called 'search-orientation' reflex, showing no interest in finding or manipulating objects, or in orientating themselves with respect to them.[13] Finally, Meshcheryakov argues that, in spite of their total dependence on other people, blind-deaf children show no propensity to communicate. Indeed, they fail to exhibit those facial expressions we deem most 'natural': these are children who must even be taught to smile.[14]

Meshcheryakov draws this picture on the basis of his own work with blind-deaf children (see the numerous case histories cited in *Awakening to Life*) and that of his Soviet predecessors, Sokolyansky and Yarmolenko, particularly the latter's studies of blind-deaf children who have suffered 'pedagogical neglect'.[15]

---

11   Yarmolenko 1961, p. 82, cited in Meshcheryakov 1979, p. 80.
12   Ilyenkov 1977c, p. 23.
13   Meshcheryakov 1979, p. 87.
14   Meshcheryakov 1970, p. 80.
15   Yarmolenko 1941; 1961.

The picture is difficult to assess because the cited data is fragmentary and anecdotal, drawing, for example, on parents' accounts of their child's development before he or she was delivered into the pedagogue's hands. Nonetheless, such Western literature as exists tends to confirm Meshcheryakov's story.[16] We should observe, however, that such a description of the 'classical' condition of the blind-deaf child prior to instruction is a theoretical construction. Few of the children Meshcheryakov describes had not encountered some kind of amateur training within the family which modified the classical picture to a degree, sometimes even for the worse.[17] Crucial to Meshcheryakov's stance, however, is the claim that there is little pedagogically relevant difference between the predicament of a child born deaf and blind, and one who loses sight and hearing in infancy or early childhood. In the latter case, he claims, with the onset of blind-deafness the child regresses to the 'initial condition', in spite of prior developmental achievements he or she may have made.[18] The initial condition thus expresses the raw material with which the *tiflosurdopedagog* must begin.

3   Meshcheryakov's Position Contrasted

How, then, may the blind-deaf child be rescued from this condition? Significantly, this question cannot be answered without a commitment to one or other psychological theory, be it a 'folk' or a 'scientific' theory. The educator must operate with a conception of what remains of the child's psychological

---

16   See, e.g., McInnes and Treffrey 1982, ch. 1.

17   See, e.g., the discussion of Lena G., who came into Meshcheryakov's care at the age of two. Until this time, she had been carried around by adults to such a degree that she appeared to have lost the capacity to regulate her own body temperature (Meshcheryakov 1979, p. 111). For a case where training in the home yielded some progress in the child's development see the case history for Valya P. (pp. 146–9).

Sandomirskaja (2008, p. 328) suggests that Soviet *tiflosurdopedagogika* disdained education within the family and insisted that appropriate intervention could only take place within dedicated, residential institutions, and she ventures that blind-deaf children's 'initial condition' – 'half-animal, half-plant', in Sokolyansky's expression – may have issued from the trauma of being withdrawn from the family and institutionalised. Note, however, that Vasilova (2013) describes Sokolyansky working with blind-deaf children in their homes and Suvorov (2016, pp. 659–61) writes approvingly about A.V. Apraushev's conception of a *guvernator* (from the English 'governess'), who would work with blind-deaf children at home in a way that involves family members in the educational process. Apraushev was director of the Zagorsk School for 18 years.

18   Meshcheryakov 1979, p. 83.

functioning and of how it might best be harnessed and developed. No such conception is possible without indulging, explicitly or tacitly, in philosophical psychology.

To appreciate Meshcheryakov's contribution, it helps to understand the position he rejects. This approach has its roots in the philosophy of mind of the seventeenth and eighteenth centuries and informs many of the 'classical' Western descriptions of blind-deaf children, such as Helen Keller and Laura Bridgman. Important components of the picture are implicit in the following passage from one of the first modern authors to consider blind-deafness, Denis Diderot:

> We have arranged that ... signs should be common property and serve, as it were, for the staple in the exchange of our ideas. We have made them for our eyes in the alphabet, and for our ears in articulate sounds; but we have none for the sense of touch, although there is a way of speaking to this sense and obtaining its responses. For the lack of this language, there is no communication between us and those born deaf, blind, and mute. They grow, but they remain in a condition of mental imbecility. Perhaps they would have ideas, if we were to communicate with them in a definite and uniform manner from their infancy; for instance, if we were to trace on their hands the same letters we trace on paper, and associated always the same meaning with them.
>
> Is not this language ... as good as another? Is it not ready to hand, and would you dare to say that you have never been communicated with by this method? Nothing remains but to fix it, and make its grammar and dictionaries, if it is found that the expression by the common characters of writing is too slow for the sense of touch. Knowledge has three entrances by which it reaches our mind, and we keep one barricaded for want of signs ... We have to lose one sense before we realise the advantage of symbols given to the remainder, and people who have the misfortune to be born deaf, blind, and mute, or who have lost these three senses by some accident, would be delighted if there existed a clear and precise language of touch.[19]

This remarkably advanced passage – written 120 years before the adoption of braille – conveys the idea that a blind-deaf individual is a being imprisoned in a dark, noiseless and impenetrable world of solitude, into which no other being may intrude and beyond which he or she cannot reach, for want of a

---

19   Diderot 1916, pp. 89–90.

channel of communication. Meshcheryakov would find much to agree with in Diderot's remarks. He would concur that the child's ultimate disadvantage is his or her enforced isolation for want of communication, and that the primary task is to give the child the kind of 'language of touch' Diderot describes. What Meshcheryakov would resist, however, is the reasons for which Diderot privileges language. These reasons derive ultimately from Diderot's general picture of the mind, a picture which owes its origin to Descartes. According to this view, each human mind constitutes its own self-contained 'internal' world of thoughts and experiences, which are directly revealed only to the thinking subject itself. We are all, on this picture, prisoners within our own minds. Language, however, permits each subject to reveal the contents of his or her private mental world to others. It forms a medium through which we may compare our conception of the world with those of others and receive ideas from them.

On this picture, the blind-deaf child is, like any other, a thinking self at the centre of a world of mental events. The child's predicament, however, is twofold. First, the child's disability prevents him or her from learning a language from elders and peers, and without language the child cannot name such sensations as he or she has and is unable to convey thoughts and experiences to others. Second, and more significantly, on Diderot's empiricist framework, the absence of the two primary senses means that the child has insufficient sensory material to form the basis of a coherent mental life. The child can think but is unable to make anything the object of thought. Hence, in virtue of this sensory deprivation, the child's psychological faculties fall into a dormant state. For this reason, Diderot looks to communication as an alternative *source* of sensory information for the child. Language is to provide an artificial channel which is to compensate for the child's lack of sight and hearing.

This image of the blind-deaf child as a dormant mind or 'soul' (as the nineteenth century literature often has it), asleep for want of things to think, leads naturally to a compelling idea of the education of a blind-deaf child as a process of the *awakening* of a mind imprisoned in the body.[20] Interestingly, it is language once again that is presented as the key to this process. The child's mind

---

[20]   The image of the awakening of an imprisoned soul dominates discussion of the two most famous Western cases of the education of blind-deaf children: Laura Bridgman's education in the 1830s and '40s by Samuel Howe – the founder of the Perkins Institute for the Blind, and the more successful and better known case of Helen Keller and her tutor Anne Sullivan, who was a graduate of Howe's Institute. Take, for example, Charles Dickens's description of Laura Bridgman: 'There she was before me; built up, as it were, in a marble cell, impervious to any ray of light, or particle of sound; with her poor white hand peeping through a chink in the wall, beckoning to some good man for help, that an immortal soul might be awakened' (quoted in Levitin 1982, p. 223).

awakens at the moment the child grasps the idea of *meaning*, that some con-figuration of physical movements may serve as a sign which *represents*. Since this awakening is precipitated by a single leap of intuition on the child's part – the grasping of the idea of *reference* – it is taken to occur not gradually, but in a moment of revelation, a sudden dawning which, as it were, casts light across the whole terrain of the child's mind.[21]

Thus, on this 'classical' picture, the crucial moment in the development of the blind-deaf child is the *awakening* of the child's mind through the *revelation* of *language*. This idea, and the philosophy of mind at its heart, is Meshch-eryakov's principal target.[22]

4   Meshcheryakov's Theoretical Alternative

Meshcheryakov was not a 'professional theorist' by inclination, preferring to commit most of his career to 'hands on' work with blind-deaf children. He engaged in little theoretical research, and his writings contain few purely theoretical discussions. Nonetheless, circumstances were such that Meshch-eryakov's approach became steeped in theory. Meshcheryakov studied psycho-logy at Moscow University in the immediately post-war years. At that time, there was no independent department of psychology at the University; psycho-logy was taught in the philosophy department. This brought Meshcheryakov into contact with a fellow student who was to have a great influence over his work, the philosopher Evald Ilyenkov (1924–79). By 1952, when Meshcheryakov entered the laboratory of one of the founders of the socio-historical school of psychology, Alexander Luria, he was well versed in the Marxist philosophical idiom which had so influenced the school.

Three years later, Meshcheryakov encountered another figure who was to be an important source of his theoretical perspective, Ivan Sokolyansky (1889–1960), the man from whom he learnt his basic educational techniques. Sokoly-ansky, the 'father' of Russian *tiflosurdopedagogika*, had worked with blind-deaf children since the Revolution, basing himself in Kharkov, Ukraine until 1939,

---

21   Hence, in the folkloric accounts of Helen Keller's education, the crucial moment in her development is taken to be the appearance of her first word. For example, the well-known 1959 play *The Miracle Worker* (Gibson 2008) concludes with the famous scene at the pump, when Helen grasps the word 'water'.

22   It is thus ironic that Meshcheryakov's book, prosaically entitled in Russian *Slepoglukho-nemie deti* (*Blind-Deaf Children*) was translated into English as *Awakening to Life*.

and afterwards in Moscow. Sokolyansky's work was a victim of the tempestuous times in which he lived. He was twice arrested, in 1933 and 1937, the second arrest resulting in a prison term of 20 months, and in 1938, his special clinic was closed by the Ukrainian government on the grounds that blind-deaf children should be classified as severely mentally retarded and uneducable. In this process, most of Sokolyansky's equipment and materials were lost. Of the ten children in the clinic's care, four were moved to Leningrad, where three perished during the war, and all but two who remained in Ukraine were killed during the Nazi occupation.[23] But Sokolyansky's career had one stunning success: the education of Olga Skorokhodova, who survived the war to become, like Helen Keller, a distinguished woman of letters. Sokolyanksy was even less a professional theorist than Meshcheryakov. Nonetheless, the fact that he was based in Kharkov between 1930 and 1939 brought him into contact with leading representatives of the socio-historical school. Vygotsky, Luria, Zaporozhets and Galperin all took an interest in Sokolyansky's work[24] and their ideas influenced his pedagogy, which in turn was passed on to Meshcheryakov.

How may we characterise the socio-historical perspective Meshcheryakov inherited? The perspective is best captured by the following four tenets:

(1)   The mental life of the human individual exists in the forms of its expression; that is, certain species of activity constitute the exercise of mental functions. These activities share, among other things, the fact that they are socially significant. Linguistic or, more generally, communicative activity is thus a central example of mental activity;

(2)   Language is an essentially social phenomenon, in at least the sense that the possibility of language presupposes the existence of a socially forged communicative medium: a set of shared social meanings against which any communicative act has its reality;

(3)   This set of shared social meanings represents a culture. Cultures are real phenomena constituted by socially significant forms of activity of a community: cultures objectively exist in the form of social practices;

---

23   It is difficult to assemble the facts of Sokolyanksy's career for it has only recently come to light that the Ukrainian government, as well as the Nazis, contributed to the destruction of his Ukrainian base (see Vasilova 1989; 2013; Levitin 1982, pp. 266–7). Note that some archival materials of Sokolyansky's are available at the Archive of the Institute of Corrective Pedagogy in Moscow (formerly the Institute of Defectology) and the Joint Archives of the Russian Academy of Education in Gorki Leninskie (see Sandomirskaja 2008, p. 329n8).

24   See Vasilova 1989, p. 73; 2013. Vygotsky briefly discusses Sokolyansky's work in Vygotsky 1993b, pp. 60–2 [ss 5, pp. 43–5], and considers the education of blind-deaf children on p. 181 [p. 185].

(4)   It is only through the appropriation, or internalisation, of such socially
      significant forms of activity that the child becomes a conscious being. The
      child's mind comes to be his or her inauguration into a culture.

How does allegiance to these tenets affect Meshcheryakov's approach to the
education of blind-deaf children? First, this perspective dictates that the educator has less material to work with than the 'classical' model implies. According to (4), prior to the child's appropriating certain forms of social activity, he or
she is less than a conscious being. The blind-deaf child thus cannot be seen as
a mind imprisoned in a body for want of communication. The educator's task
is therefore not to 'awaken' the child's dormant mind, but to bring that mind
into being. Second, we know that if (4) is true, this will be achieved only if the
child can be made to appropriate certain socially significant forms of activity.[25]
Third, we can suppose that this process of appropriation is unlikely to be rev-
elatory (there is, after all, not yet a subject to experience revelation!), but will
be drawn out in time as the child gradually internalises particular activities.
Fourth, we may also suppose that the appropriation of language will be crucial
to the development of the child's mind; however, on this view, language practices are just one of the relevant forms of socially significant activity, and by no
means the most fundamental. Language, according to (2), presupposes shared
social meanings; we may therefore surmise that before we can even begin to
teach the child language, we must first get the child to orientate him or herself
in a socially significant environment. Finally, fifth, the socio-historical idiom
leads us to reconsider how we should describe the blind-deaf child's disability.
The child's primary impairment, inhibiting the development of psychological
functions, is conceived not simply as the absence of sensory information from
the primary senses but as access to what Russian calls *obshchenie* (i.e., interpersonal relations), and the principal task is not to compensate for the technical
deficiency of his or her impaired sense-organs, but to inaugurate the child
into the social environment. This is an important reorientation, for while it is
impossible ever to compensate entirely for the absence of sight and hearing,
nothing in the child's condition makes him or her in principle unable to enter
into relations with others.

---

25   See Meshcheryakov 1979, pp. 84–94.

5   Meshcheryakov's Methods

Meshcheryakov's theoretical framework leads him to the first principle of his pedagogy: the first stage in the education of the blind-deaf child is to engage the child in basic forms of meaningful activity. The activities on which Meshcheryakov focuses are self-care skills. The child's mental life first begins in the process of learning how to dress him- or herself, to use the toilet, to make a bed, to eat with a spoon, and so on. It is important to note that Meshcheryakov's strategy differs from approaches which see such skills as important primarily because, once the child has basic self-care skills, caretakers need not squander valuable time on menial activities. For Meshcheryakov, in contrast, these 'menial' activities are valued as the very basis of future intellectual development for the reason, as we shall discuss below, that they are activities carried out *jointly* with others.

However, if the educator is to involve the child in these self-care activities, the child must be capable of participating. But as we saw, the classical blind-deaf child lacks, not only higher mental states, but many of the basic behaviours taken for granted in sighted and hearing children: an exploratory interest in a world of objects and people. So, before any interaction between child and educator can begin, 'orientating-investigatory' activity must be engendered in the child.

The teacher begins by exploiting the child's primitive unstructured and uncognised needs. In particular, the bridge between adult and blind-deaf child is the latter's need for food:

> We used special methods to encourage [Nina (aged at least 4) to take] a more active approach to food. A teaspoon was used to feed her. Only the first spoonful was poured into the child's mouth, while she remained completely passive. The second spoonful would then be placed in the child's mouth, but the food not poured in immediately, only after she had taken hold of the food with her top teeth and top lip, after which the spoon would be drawn out, while the food gripped by the upper lip would remain in her mouth. This constituted the manifestation of the child's first active response to food, and it was vital, come what might, not to overlook that activity and let it die out. It was essential that the next spoonful of food should not simply be poured into her mouth; that it should be taken by the child actively moving her lips. This way, gradually and in measured doses, holding back the moment when food would actually be poured into the child's mouth, we encouraged her to make an active movement with her upper lip, and later to carry out a more diffi-

cult movement – that of sucking in food ... The child's active movements during feeding gradually and slowly increased ...[26]

Several weeks, perhaps months of patient training are condensed into that paragraph, and the subsequent programme Meshcheryakov describes is no less painstaking – getting the child to respond when the spoon was placed on her lower lip, getting her to respond 'at a distance' to the smell or warmth of the food, and so on.

Once the child has the wherewithal to engage in simple activities, Meshcheryakov's programme of 'primary humanisation' (*pervonachal'noe ochelovechivanie*) commences. In this, the motor of the child's development is a form of interaction between child and caretaker very different from the almost Skinnerian conditioning employed to encourage the child to enter a reactive relation to the environment. The programme of primary humanisation is based on the notion of joint activity (*sovmestnaya deyatel'nost'*) between child and adult. The child is encouraged to engage in simple self-care activities jointly with his or her adult helpmate. At first, the child is simply led through the activity by the adult: for instance, as the adult dresses the child, she simultaneously leads the child through the appropriate movements. Eventually, however, the child comes to take an active part in these movements, so that the task is fulfilled jointly by adult and child. This joint activity is the seed 'from which sprouts the whole "body" of human behaviour and mentality'.[27]

In time, the adult need only initiate the activity to cause the child to begin the appropriate behaviour. This is a very significant moment, for though the child is prompted to begin the activity by the adult's initiation, typically he or she cannot complete it without the latter's help. The child gets stuck on the difficult bits! Thus, a simple division of labour develops between adult and child: now the activity is joint, but it is 'joint, separate activity' (i.e., both participants make their own contribution to the task). Now, crucially, such a division of labour requires co-ordination, and co-ordination can only be achieved if adult and child communicate with each other: joint activity generates a need for communication.[28]

---

26   Meshcheryakov 1979, pp. 97–8. I have slightly modified the translation.
27   Meshcheryakov 1979, p. 307.
28   It is artificial to drive a hard wedge between the initial stage in which the child is trained to enter a reactive relation with the environment and the later programme of primary humanisation based on joint activity. For example, as Meshcheryakov's description of Nina's training continues (1979, pp. 98–9, 101–2), we come to see that the caretaker's purpose is not only to cause Nina to react in a certain way to food, but also to encourage her to negotiate a socially significant object: the spoon. Meshcheryakov earlier establishes that

Significantly, Meshcheryakov argues that this form of joint activity engenders not only the need for communication, but also the means with which to satisfy that need. The germ of language is to be found in the interaction in which these simple activities are realised. This is so in two respects. First, as we described, the adult initiates the activity and invites the child to attempt to proceed with it, and in so doing provides the basis of *gesture*. The adult's movements have the *meaning* 'action so-and-so', or perhaps the command 'do such-and-such'. Second, the fact that the child actively participates in an aim-orientated activity means that he or she comes to stand in a special relation both to the object of his or her actions and to the actions themselves. The task is identified as the *thing-which-has-to-be-done*, and the child's movements as *that-by-which-the-thing-gets-done*. As such, both object and activity become the kinds of things which could have names, which could be the object of a gesture.

The 'primary gestures' with which child and adult co-ordinate their joint activity take their form from the movements that compose the activities in which they originate and which they denote. A primary gesture may directly reproduce the physical movement at the core of some activity (e.g. raising a cupped hand to the mouth for 'drink', moving hands upwards from ankle to waist for 'putting on trousers'), or may be based on the actions which precipitate an activity (e.g. movements as of putting on a coat to indicate 'going outside'). Such gestures become the foundation for the development of more advanced communicative skills.[29] First, the primary gestures are simplified, stylised, and 'decontextualised' (i.e., the child must learn that one can refer to an activity without actually going on to do it). Second, the primary gestures are then accompanied by exposure to dactylic Russian: cyrillic alphabetic handshapes spelled out into the palm of the child's hand.[30] As the child

---

initially Nina displayed no interest in objects, failing even to hold them when placed in her hand. In the feeding activity, she at first displays only incidental interest in the spoon, but gradually, through selective changes on the part of the teacher, she grows not only to take in food, but to interact with her teacher and the object she proffers. Here, of course, the spoon plays an instrumental role in the child's new-found ability to participate in feeding. But the spoon is not merely an instrument, a technical device. It also serves as a socially meaningful medium of interaction, for to come to interact with a physical object *as* a spoon is to appropriate a small part of human culture, to master something about the way *we* eat. (See Suvorov 2016, pp. 655–7, for further discussion of the significance of learning to eat with a spoon. See also Ilyenkov's 'Poema o lozhke' ('A Poem about a Spoon') in Ilyenkov 2018a, pp. 249–54. Heed also Mikhailov's comments on pp. 57–8 above.)

29   See Sirotkin 1979.

30   For an excellent account of the details and principles of dactylic Russian see Krylatov 1988. As Diderot foresaw, the principal disadvantage of dactylic languages is the speed at which

appropriates the Russian language, so he or she is able to participate in a structured programme of schooling.[31]

Meshcheryakov, like Sokolyansky before him,[32] was adamant that blind-deaf individuals' developmental potential crucially depends on the extent to which they can master a spoken language, for only through such a language can they appropriate the legacy of 'world culture' and become participating members of society. Thus, for Meshcheryakov, the development of speech skills, mastery of braille, and competence in foreign languages are essential skills for literate blind-deaf individuals, and should figure prominently in any school curriculum for blind-deaf children.

6   Acclaim and Adversity

With four of his eldest pupils at Moscow University, Meshcheryakov's work began to receive considerable acclaim. All the major living exponents of the socio-historical school, Luria, Leontiev, Davydov, Zaporozhets, Galperin and, of course, Ilyenkov, gave voice to their admiration. For these thinkers, Meshcheryakov's work made an important contribution to their paradigm for two reasons. First, they argued that Meshcheryakov had produced an '*experimentum crusis*' demonstrating the validity of the socio-historical tradition's conception of the mind. As Zaporozhets wrote in the foreword to the English translation of Meshcheryakov's book:

> Dr Meshcheryakov's practical work has provided experimental substantiation, more convincing than anything yielded by research into the development and instruction of normal children, of the main tenets of the dialectical-materialist theory of knowledge and psychology to the effect that the subject's ideal, mental activity takes shape on the basis of his practical material activity and emerges as a result of the infinitely complex process of internalising external activity.[33]

---

speech may be conveyed. In response to this problem, Yuri and Natalia Krylatov proposed to develop a cyrillic version of the dactylic alphabet devised by Lorm in the nineteenth century and later deployed in West Germany. This alphabet is much faster to use since it indicates letters, not by whole hand-shapes, but by a system of points and lines which the speaker describes on the listener's palm.

31   A very basic sketch of a school curriculum for the blind-deaf is included in Meshcheryakov 1979, pp. 211–27.
32   See Vasilova 1989.
33   Meshcheryakov 1979, p. 9.

Second, Meshcheryakov's work makes available a gold mine of data with which to give the Vygotskian framework empirical content. In Leontiev's words, Meshcheryakov's work reveals:

> The conditions in which the key events in the process of the formation of the person and (just think of it!) the coming-to-be of human consciousness become *visible* – one wants even to say touchable, and moreover drawn out in time as if in slow motion – the conditions which, as it were, open a window on the depths of consciousness' hidden nature.[34]

In light of these two claims, the philosopher B.M. Kedrov called for a major research initiative to explore in full the educational, psychological and philosophical implications of Meshcheryakov's work.[35]

It would be wrong, however, to close our presentation of Meshcheryakov's contribution on this celebratory note. The research programme Kedrov proposed was never undertaken, and no empirical research has been conducted with Meshcheryakov's materials that promises to unlock 'the hidden nature of consciousness'.

The only thinker to attempt to argue that the socio-historical perspective is vindicated by Meshcheryakov's work was Ilyenkov. But the case, as he develops it, is problematic.[36] Ilyenkov treats the blind-deaf child as a modern-day *enfant sauvage*. He argues that the child's initial state represents the condition of any human child prior to the influence of society. This shows, he maintains, (a) that the human mind is not a gift of nature, and (b) that our mental capacities do not develop spontaneously according to some biological programme. He concludes, therefore, that Meshcheryakov's work confirms that:

> All the specifically human mental functions without exception ... are in their genesis and in their essence 'internalised' modes and forms of external, sensuous-objective activity of man as a social subject ... [and therefore] *that in the composition of man's higher mental functions neither*

---

34   Reported in Gurgenidze and Ilyenkov 1975, p. 63.
35   See Levitin 1982, p. 238.
36   See Ilyenkov 1970; 1977c. Ilyenkov 2018a contains important archival material including the text of a 1975 lecture by Ilyenkov to Moscow University's Faculty of Psychology (pp. 240–49; see also Ilyenkov 2007a for another paper from the same year) and the transcript of a presentation to the Scientific Council of the Institute of Philosophy in 1977 (pp. 381–97). The discussion at the latter event vividly displays the degree to which Ilyenkov's colleagues were oblivious to the philosophical significance of Meshcheryakov's work.

*is there nor can there be absolutely anything innate or genetically inher-
ited,* that the human mind in its entirety is the result of up-bringing in
the broadest sense of the term – that is, it is passed from generation to
generation not by a natural, but by an entirely artificial route.[37]

It should be clear, however, that Meshcheryakov's work cannot be presented
as 'experimental proof' of such a position. As Ilyenkov's opponents immediately pointed out, Meshcheryakov's achievements are perfectly consistent with
nativism about mental development and with empiricism about concept formation.[38] For where Ilyenkov takes the 'initial condition' of the blind-deaf child
to reveal the biological endowment of the normal human mind, his nativist
opponent sees there a paradigm case of abnormality, wherein the mind's innate
faculties are suppressed due to sensory deprivation. To make good Ilyenkov's
case would take a great deal more argument than he provides in his brief writings on Meshcheryakov.

However, anyone familiar with Ilyenkov's major writings will wonder why
a thinker who usually makes a sophisticated philosophical case against innatism and empiricism resorts to such primitive 'knock down' arguments in this
context? The answer is that much of what was written in support of Meshcheryakov's work, particularly in the years immediately following his death, has
a political function. Meshcheryakov never received the support he deserved.[39]
Throughout his career his work was beset by bureaucratic obstacles, generated
in part by objections to the substantial cost of his methods and in part by his
theoretical allegiances. He was never in charge of the Zagorsk children's home
where he conducted his principal work. He always worked there on secondment from his principal position, which was head of a laboratory at Moscow's
Institute of Defectology. It seems, however, that he was not entirely comfort-
able at either place. The ideology of the Institute was closer to Diderot's than
to Vygotsky's idiom, and Meshcheryakov constantly clashed with its Director.
And at Zagorsk, Meshcheryakov sometimes found himself in the position of
the intruding academic, whose concern with issues of high science disrupted
routines and distracted teachers and children from their prescribed duties. It
was thus Meshcheryakov's dream that a scientific research centre might be

---

37   Ilyenkov 1970, p. 89, my emphasis.
38   See, e.g., Malinovsky 1970. Interestingly, Malinovsky was the son of A.A. Bogdanov, the
      philosopher-scientist who was once Lenin's rival for the leadership of the Bolshevik fac-
      tion, whose 'empiromonism' Ilyenkov attacks in Ilyenkov 1980 [1982b; 2009b, pp. 285–391].
39   See Mareev in Dubrovsky 1989, pp. 32–4.

established at which he and other researchers could pursue their work for the benefit of both science and their pupils. For this reason, he and his friends, particularly Ilyenkov, did their best to popularise his work in the 'party press' and the mass media.[40] This explains, therefore, the rather simple-minded nature of the enthusiastic treatments of Meshcheryakov's work. Ilyenkov's strategy, however, did not work: resources remained unavailable and, hence, none of the promised research materialised.

Meshcheryakov's bad fortune was bequeathed to his four most famous students. When they graduated from Moscow University in 1977, their future was unclear. On Ilyenkov's instigation, however, they were brought to the Institute of General and Pedagogical Psychology, then under the directorship of Davydov, where they were installed in the laboratory of Felix Mikhailov, who had long been involved with both Meshcheryakov's and Ilyenkov's work. This remarkable arrangement – four blind-deaf researchers working together! – was disturbed in 1983, when Davydov lost his position as director of the Institute and Mikhailov moved to the Institute of Philosophy. The new directorship proved less willing to fund this research and, though Sirotkin found support elsewhere, only Suvorov remained on the staff of the Institute as a 'Junior Scientific Worker'. A few years later, Suvorov published a moving tribute to his mentor Ilyenkov, which can be read as a masked appeal for the means to continue the work Meshcheryakov began.[41] At that time, the Zagorsk school, which had been the principal centre of blind-deaf education in the Soviet Union since its foundation in 1963, had moved to a new site, but appeared to be badly in need of equipment in order to function effectively as a teaching institution, let alone as a research centre.[42]

Moreover, in the late 1980s, Meshcheryakov's legacy came under attack from a group of long-standing critics of the socio-historical approach, including David Dubrovsky, Igor Narsky and Andrei Brushlinsky. Together with Sirotkin, Meshcheryakov's former pupil, and a number of disgruntled teachers of the blind-deaf, the group subjected Meshcheryakov's work to severe public criticism. A disturbing feature of this assault is that it was by no means restricted to matters of science but included accusations of unethical conduct and falsification of data. These accusations were directed not so much at Meshcheryakov himself as to those who propagandised his work, especially Ilyenkov. As the published symposium reveals, this is a debate charged with personal anim-

---

40   See Goncharova in Dubrovsky 1989, pp. 55–7.
41   Suvorov 1988.
42   See Goncharova's and Kondratov's contributions to Dubrovsky 1989, pp. 55–7, 61–3.

osity.[43] Western observers are in a poor position to adjudicate the more *ad hominum* of the accusations. Nonetheless, Ilyenkov can be defended from the central charge against him.

Dubrovsky, Narsky, and Brushlinsky all, curiously, seem to endorse the weakest part of Ilyenkov's argument for the significance of Meshcheryakov's work: namely, the conditional that if individuals who are totally blind-deaf from birth could attain high levels of psychological development, this would show that human mental functions are not gifts of nature, but are socially-constituted phenomena. Ilyenkov's detractors accept this argument is valid, and then object that in none of the most successful cases of the education of the blind-deaf have the individuals in question been totally blind-deaf from birth. They then accuse Ilyenkov of unethically distorting the facts of these case histories in his writings. In order to vindicate his own theory of the socially-constituted subject, it is argued, Ilyenkov exploited the party press and lied to the public, pretending Meshcheryakov's pupils were profoundly blind-deaf from birth.[44] Finally, Ilyenkov's critics try to turn the argument they attribute to him on its head, arguing that those blind-deaf children who have been successfully educated in the Soviet Union have triumphed in virtue of their 'innate gifts'. 'After all', Narsky surmises, 'not everyone with normal sight and hearing is capable of going to university, let alone passing with flying colours'.[45]

The great irony of this attack on Ilyenkov was that it was conducted under the banner of perestroika. Dubrovsky calls for a 'battle for truth in *tiflosurdopedagogika*' and portrays Ilyenkov as the Lysenko of the Brezhnev era, manipulating the party press to ensure that his own views are unchallenged.[46] Yet for all its rhetoric of glasnost, the case against Ilyenkov ignores the constraints

---

43   Dubrovsky 1989. There was some 'history' between Dubrovsky, Narsky and Ilyenkov. Dubrovsky and Ilyenkov were involved in a famous exchange about the mind-body problem on the pages of *Voprosy filosofii* in 1968, and Ilyenkov was critical of both Dubrovsky and Narsky in his later work on the problem of the ideal (see Dubrovsky 1968; Ilyenkov 1968c; Ilyenkov 1979a, 2009a, 2014).

44   See Dubrovsky 1989, pp. 3–6, 30–31, 47–50, 79–84.

45   Narksy in Dubrovsky 1989, p. 50.

46   Dubrovsky 1989, p. 3. Ilyenkov's opponents even go so far as to claim that Ilyenkov was himself a Lysenkoite (see Sirotkin and Shakenova in Dubrovsky 1989, pp. 92–4). This charge is absurd, since where Lysenko advanced a theory of genetics on which characteristics organisms acquire through environmental influences might be passed on genetically to the next generation, Ilyenkov's theory of mind gives no substantial role to genetic inheritance, however understood, in the explanation of individual psychological functioning. For Ilyenkov, psychological capacities are transmitted across generations by a process of cultural, and not biological, inheritance.

under which he was writing. His opponents conveniently forget that, in the Soviet Union, no popular or party publication in the 1970s would have carried an article on 'defectology' unless it grandly advertised Soviet educational practices and heralded the victories of Soviet science. If he was to publicise Meshcheryakov's work, Ilyenkov could not permit himself the luxury of rigorous case histories and subtle theoretical arguments. True advocates of glasnost, however, would ask themselves how the political conditions under which Ilyenkov was writing might have influenced his choice of arguments. Instead, Ilyenkov's opponents remain faithful to traditional Soviet methods of argumentation, presenting their target as an opportunist whose actions are out of keeping with the present 'party line'.

More ironic still was that Ilyenkov's opponents take the case he makes in his popularisation of Meshcheryakov at face value, and then argue against it by advancing a position Ilyenkov himself deemed unethical. For Ilyenkov, the idea that individuals are predisposed to different developmental paths in virtue of the genetically determined characteristics of their brains was simply a rationale for dividing individuals between the talented and the talentless, the intellectual and the practical, between those who are able and those who are not. As such, Ilyenkov believed that such a view served as an excuse to place what was ultimately the responsibility of the education system onto the shoulders of biological chance. For Ilyenkov, the experience of Meshcheryakov's blind-deaf students indicated that even individuals for whom the vagaries of nature had had the harshest consequences might come to lead flourishing intellectual lives in a society prepared to take full and proper responsibility for the education of its citizens.

Ilyenkov's reputation has survived this assault on his integrity. However, the discussion certainly had damaging consequences if only because its bitter tone obscured a number of potentially constructive criticisms of Meshcheryakov's work. For example, Sergei Sirotkin and E.K. Shakenova challenged Meshcheryakov's account of language acquisition, arguing that the emphasis traditionally placed on the assimilation of Russian has led to a neglect of the significance of gesture. Indeed, Sokolyansky, Meshcheryakov and many of their followers had a dismissive attitude to gesture as a mode of communication, mistakenly treating sign languages of deaf communities as primitive analogs of spoken language. In consequence, scant attention had been paid, Sirotkin argues, to the spontaneous gestures that blind-deaf children develop to converse among themselves. These gestures, he argued, might profitably be made the basis of further language development. Such objections raise profound issues, the exploration of which might advance both the theory and practice of blind-deaf education. It is a shame, therefore, that the polemical mood of the case against Meshcheryakov was an impediment to productive discussion of this and other theoretical issues.[47]

Two years after this controversy broke out, the Soviet Union collapsed. Zagorsk was renamed Sergiev Posad in 1991 and the famous children's home now continues its work as the 'Sergievo-Posadskii Home for Blind-Deaf Children', operating under the auspices of the Ministry of Labour and Social Support of the Russian Federation. Non-governmental initiatives include the creation in 1992 the Elvira Foundation for the support of blind-deaf people, by Sirotkin and Shakenova, an organisation that by 2013 had established eleven regional centres, and the creation in 2014 of the Soedinenie Deaf-Blind Support Foundation. In a recent paper, Surovov expresses the hope that the Foundation will help 'revive the almost forgotten legacy' of Sokolyansky and Meshcheryakov, and indeed the Foundation is committed as part of its Education and Science Programme, to collecting archive materials, digitising the records of the 'Zagorsk experiment', and preparing editions of the works of Sokolyansky, Meshcheryakov and Yarmolenko.[48] It is very much to be hoped that this project comes to fruition.

It seems, then, that the spirit of the Meshcheryakov experiment has not been entirely extinguished. Of course, some might regret this, taking the word 'experiment' to imply the kind of authoritarian project of social engineering associated with the Stalin era – an experiment conducted *on* people with the aim of engineering new kinds of persons.[49] But it is unfair to impose this interpretation on Meshcheryakov, whose work, whatever else it may be, is really an experiment in radical hope, guided by the idea that educators must strive so that all their charges, notwithstanding their disabilities, are enabled, so far as humanly possible, to lead autonomous, flourishing lives in meaningful communion with other human beings. The Meshcheryakov experiment is a testimony to the power and value of education, and for that reason alone, it should never be forgotten.

∴

In Part 2, we will explore in detail the legacy of Evald Ilyenkov, a thinker whose name has already figured prominently in the opening chapters of this book. Ily-

---

47   See Andrey Maidansky's insightful essay on the 'Lessons of the Zagorsk Experiment', in Ilyenkov 2018a, pp. 413–34. For a less sympathetic assessment, see Pushchaev 2017.

48   Suvorov 2016, pp. 671–2. The Society's website is at: https://so-edinenie.org. Unfortunately, the link to its 'Archive of Research on Deafblindness', which was working in January 2020, is now broken (6 February 2023).

49   See the discussion in Sandomirskaja 2008, pp. 325–9.

enkov was the most significant Russian Marxist philosopher of the Soviet era. In the years that followed Stalin's death – the period known as 'the thaw' – Ilyenkov produced remarkably original writings on Marx's method and on 'the problem of the ideal'. Throughout the 1960s and 70s, he advanced a view of philosophy as dialectical logic, the science of thinking, and offered a broadly humanistic vision in response to Soviet optimism about the scientific-technological revolution. He also wrote on aesthetics and education, including of course his collaboration with Meshcheryakov. A celebrated and influential figure among critical and creative Marxists, Ilyenkov was at odds with the Soviet philosophical establishment throughout his career, from the bitter controversy in the mid-1950s over the heretical 'Theses on Philosophy' to the suppression of his late essay, 'The Dialectics of the Ideal', which contributed to his tragic suicide in 1979. Although it is now more than 40 years since his death, interest in his work has not diminished. Indeed, in the last few years, it has only increased thanks to the publication of fascinating archival material by his daughter Elena Illesh and the making of Alexander Rozhkov's engaging documentary film, *Ilyenkov*, which explores his life, work and legacy.

Ilyenkov was born in Smolensk on 18 February 1924. Four years later, his family moved to Moscow, where they were fortunate to take up residence in a writers' co-operative apartment on Gorky Street. His father, Vasili Pavlovich, was an author later to achieve fame with such socialist realist novels as *Sunny Town, Driving Axle*, and *The Great Road* (which won the Stalin Prize in 1950), and young Evald grew up in the company of writers and artists. He developed an affection and appreciation for art and culture. In 1941, after completing his secondary education at School No. 170, Ilyenkov became a student at the prestigious Moscow Institute for Philosophy and Literature (MIFLI). After only a month, the war necessitated the evacuation of students and faculty, and the institute was absorbed into Moscow State University (MGU), which moved first to Ashkhabad in Turkmenia (now Ashgabat, Turkmenistan) and then to Sverdlovsk (Yekaterinburg). Yet despite this chaotic beginning, Ilyenkov threw himself into his studies. He was fortunate to encounter Boris Chernyshev, an expert on Ancient thought and a distinguished Hegel scholar, and by the time Ilyenkov was conscripted into the army in August 1942 he had developed a passionate interest in philosophy.

Ilyenkov first fought on the Western front in Belorussia as an artillery lieutenant. In 1945, he commanded a platoon in the battle for Berlin and later served in the occupying forces in Germany. His experiences had a profound effect on him, and when he was posted back to Moscow in 1945 to work on the army newspaper, *Krasnaya zvezda (Red Star)*, he returned a changed man, his youthful hopefulness tempered by his encounter with the awfulness of war, its heroism, horror and brutality. Back in Moscow, Ilyenkov was uncertain how to proceed with his education. It was unclear what the University had to offer. His mentor Chernyshev had died in 1944, and the philosophical faculty was now dominated by hacks and time-servers. As a result, Ilyenkov decided to forsake philosophy for art, but his realistic sketches of battle were not in keeping with the romantic images preferred by the establishment and he was denied admission to art school. He therefore chose to return to philosophy at MGU. Despite the inhospitable climate, his studies progressed well and, in 1950, he became a graduate student in the 'Kafedra' of the History of Foreign Philosophy, a liberal department which encouraged its students to engage with original texts rather than parrot Marxist-Leninist primers. Under the supervision of T.I. Oizerman, he began the research on Marx's method that formed the basis of his Candidate's dissertation, which he defended successfully in 1953. In the same year, he became a research fellow at Moscow's Institute of Philosophy. The following chapter tells the story of what happened next – the battle over the infamous Theses on Philosophy. The tale reveals a great deal about Ilyenkov's brilliance and the peculiar circumstances of Soviet intellectual life.

PART 2

Ilyenkov

∴

CHAPTER 5

Punks versus Zombies: Evald Ilyenkov and the Battle for Soviet Philosophy

1. This chapter focuses on an incident that occurred at the very beginning of Ilyenkov's career, about which relatively little was known until recently. In April 1954, Ilyenkov and his friend Valentin Korovikov, both junior lecturers at Moscow State University (MGU), wrote a set of 'theses on philosophy'.[1] The following month, the theses were the subject of an open discussion, attended by some 200 people, at a meeting of their department, the Kafedra of the History of Foreign Philosophy. The subsequent furor pitched Ilyenkov and Korovikov against the Soviet philosophical establishment, controlled by philosophers who had come to prominence at the height of Stalinism and whose conception of philosophy was defined, to a greater or lesser extent, by the rigid form of Marxism-Leninism that had been codified during that period, and which found its most definitive, and most primitive, expression in 1938 in the notorious fourth chapter of *The History of the Communist Party of the Soviet Union (Bolshevik): Short Course*. The establishment cast Ilyenkov and Korovikov as 'punks', or in the Russian idiom of the day, *stilyagi*, disrespectful of authority, contemptuous of orthodoxy and indifferent to the 'class character' of philosophy.[2] In turn, Ilyenkov, Korovikov and the students they inspired, saw the old guard as brain-dead automata, empty shells moved around by ideological dictates rather than the deliverances of free thought – the zombies of my title. The controversy – the ensuing confrontation between Punks and Zombies – was a formative moment in Ilyenkov's philosophical development. Moreover, it influenced an entire generation and through them the subsequent course of Soviet philosophy, or so it has been claimed.[3]

Though the incident was known to have occurred, the theses themselves were lost and no record of events were available until the publication in 2016

---

1   The full title was 'Theses on the Question of the Interrelation of Philosophy and Knowledge of Nature and Society in the Process of their Historical Development'.

2   *Stilyagi*, in the words of novelist Francis Spufford (2010, p. 402n), were 'quaffed, music-loving members of the Soviet Union's first distinctive teenage tribe. Associated with delinquency, and therefore conveniently blamable for all ills, and not just by the Russians: Anthony Burgess claimed that it was a violent encounter with *stilyagi* outside a Leningrad nightclub that inspired him to create Alex and his droogs in *A Clockwork Orange*'.

3   For example, by Lektorsky, in Ilyenkov and Korovikov 2016, p. 236n1.

of a book, edited by Ilyenkov's daughter, Elena Illesh, which contains fascinating archival material, including transcripts of Faculty and Party meetings and
various unpublished writings of Ilyenkov's.[4] This material helps us understand
exactly what happened and why, and gives unprecedented insight into Ilyenkov's mind and character at the time.

In what follows, I recount the story of the theses and evaluate its significance.
The story is a tortuous one, and before we begin, I must note a further twist that
occurred only after the publication of Illesh's book. In the book, Illesh attempts
a partial reconstruction of the theses.[5] After the book's completion, however,
Illesh discovered a complete text of the theses in the Archives of the Russian
Academy of Sciences in materials pertaining to the Institute of Philosophy.[6]
If Illesh had had the complete text available to her earlier, she might have
composed her book differently. Nevertheless, the need to scour the archives
for clues about the content of the theses forced her to take an interest in the
detail of discussions that might otherwise have been overlooked. It may be that
the almost Gogolian elusiveness of the manuscript, turning up only after its
story had been told, enriched rather than hindered scholarship into the circumstances of its reception. Time will tell. Now to the story itself.

2. Let's begin with the furor. It was intense and protracted. On 29 March 1955,
eleven months after the theses were first presented, the Scientific Council of
the Philosophy Faculty of Moscow University passed six resolutions after two

---

4   Ilyenkov and Korovikov 2016. The title of the book, *Strasti po tezisam*, is hard to translate.
    '*Strasti*' can mean 'horrors', but I prefer 'passion' because it preserves the religious connota-
    tions of the original ('*Strasti po Matfeiu*' for example, is the St. Matthew Passion). Thus, I
    propose *The Passion of the Theses*. The archival material is supplemented by valuable com-
    mentary by Illesh herself, Ilya Raskin and Vladislav Lektorsky, who was an eyewitness to the
    events (and who features in the seminar transcribed in Chapter 2, above). I should stress that I
    played no part whatsoever in the archival research. My role here is simply to make the history
    known to a wider audience than might be expected to become acquainted with the book.
5   Ilyenkov and Korovikov 2016, pp. 143–7. For an English translation, see Bakhurst 2019a, Ap-
    pendix I, pp. 66–8.
6   The archival reference is: АРАН. Ф. 1922. Оп. 1. Д. 767. Л. 109–19. For an English translation of
    the complete text of theses, see Bakhurst 2019a, Appendix II, pp. 68–75. There are some differ-
    ences between the passages in the reconstruction and the original theses. For example, Illesh's
    extract from Thesis 1, appears in Thesis 3 in the original; part of Illesh's Thesis 3 does not
    appear at all in the original. The cause of these discrepancies may be human error, possibly
    by those who recorded the meetings where the theses were discussed (e.g. misinterpreting a
    paraphrase as a direct quotation). But it may also have been the case that different versions
    of the theses were in circulation.

days of impassioned discussion before a large audience.[7] The first resolution was an act of self-criticism, admitting that the Council had not acted soon enough to prevent the propagation of Ilyenkov and Korovikov's supposedly 'anti-Marxist' views. Thereafter the Council lays into Ilyenkov and Korovikov. The second resolution castigates their stance as a pernicious idealist deviation. The third reproaches Ilyenkov and Korovikov for 'insincerity', for hypocritically making as to acknowledge their mistakes in public while continuing privately to hold fast to their heretical views. The fourth instructs faculty members to set students right about the philosophy of Marxism, particularly on those matters wrongly interpreted by Ilyenkov and Korovikov. The fifth enjoins the Dean to take decisive measures to prevent the further dissemination within the Faculty of anti-Marxist ideas connected with the theses. Finally, the sixth resolution charges the Presidium of the Faculty Council with reevaluating Ilyenkov's Candidate's dissertation, which he had defended, apparently successfully, in 1953.

To contemporary Western eyes, such resolutions appear almost comic, so remote do they seem from the realities of academic life as we tend to know it, but it is important to remember that in Moscow in 1955, such charges put one's livelihood, and possibly one's liberty, at risk. This was serious, scary stuff. And the criticism was to become even more intense over the next several months. What, then, had Ilyenkov and Korovikov done to provoke this response?

3. The central issue posed in the theses is 'What is philosophy?', or rather, 'What ought philosophy to be?', and the principal contention is the rejection of the orthodox Soviet view, usually attributed to Engels, that philosophy is the science of 'the world as a whole', or of the most general laws of nature, society and thought. This orthodox view was very widely embraced in the USSR, even among philosophers who had not been entirely zombified. In Ilyenkov's *Philosophical Notebook*, included in Illesh's volume, he quotes his supervisor T.I. Oizerman, writing with V.I. Svetlov, saying that '[t]he world as a whole, the world in its material unity, in its movement, change and development – such is the subject of Marxist philosophy'; and comments that on the next page they add that philosophy studies the most general laws of nature, society and consciousness.[8] Ilyenkov and Korovikov propose to overturn this view.

Anyone who has taught first-year philosophy classes knows it can be difficult to say what philosophy is. It is not uncommon to suggest that philosophy oper-

---

7   Ilyenkov and Korovikov 2016, p. 61.

8   Ilyenkov and Korovikov 2016, p. 182; Oizerman and Svetlov 1948.

ates at a higher level of generality than natural science, that in studying being *qua* being philosophy has pretensions to understanding 'things as a whole'. In Wilfrid Sellars's famous phrase: 'The aim of philosophy, abstractly formulated, is to understand how things in the broadest possible sense of the term hang together in the broadest possible sense of the term'.[9] Not so contentious a definition. So why do Ilyenkov and Korovikov protest so vigorously about the standard Soviet characterisation?

I think there are three principal reasons. Note that, in articulating them, I draw on the archival materials in Illesh's volume, as well as the theses themselves. This is essential, since the accusations made against Ilyenkov and Korovikov go far beyond the claims made in the theses – this is very clear now that we have the complete text – to engage with views that Ilyenkov and Korovikov defended in discussion, taught in seminars, and so on.

(i) The first is that Ilyenkov argues that the orthodox view makes for bad philosophy. Part of the problem resides in the notion of *law*. What are these 'most general laws' that philosophy is supposed to study? Leaving aside the problem of how one evaluates degrees of generality,[10] Soviet philosophers appeared to mean either basic laws of particular fundamental sciences (cosmology, physics, political economy ...), or they had in mind broad philosophical claims of the kind that appeared in textbooks of dialectical materialism, such as the principle of the primacy of matter over spirit, the dialectical law of the unity of opposites, and so on. Ilyenkov argues that natural-scientific laws are not the province of philosophy, but of the sciences in question, and that philosophical claims dressed up as universal laws become empty slogans without explanatory power. In his *Notebook*, Ilyenkov scorns the law of the transformation of quantity into quality, and back again, as 'philosophical twaddle' (*pustozvonstvo*)[11] and complains that the orthodox view of philosophy 'opens up infinite possibilities for dialectical games – for exploring the interpenetrations of the general and the particular and such like – but all that is about as far as you can get from a well-formed question'.[12] It thus

> directs the powers of philosophy towards fruitless reflection of a foolish kind, discrediting the philosophy of dialectical materialism in the eyes of practitioners of other sciences, and inevitably reducing philosophy itself

9   Sellars 1963, p. 1.
10   Ilyenkov and Korovikov 2016, p. 206.
11   Ilyenkov and Korovikov 2016, p. 195. Compare Mikhailov's remarks about 'quasi-Hegelianism' in Chapter 2 above (p. 28).
12   Ilyenkov and Korovikov 2016, p. 206.

to a parade of examples illustrating things long known. That this is so is incontrovertibly borne out by the way we have practiced philosophy in recent years.[13]

Ilyenkov argues that all positive knowledge about nature, society, and thought, however particular or general in kind, is to be established by natural science, and there is no further 'more general' knowledge for philosophy to lay claim to.[14] Nor can philosophy play a synthesising role, reconciling the approaches of particular sciences and integrating them into a vision of reality as a whole. No philosophy (not even Marxism-Leninism) is equipped to do this.[15] It is for the sciences themselves to represent the world as a materially developing whole.[16] There is no place for a 'science of sciences', subsuming scientific laws under somehow yet more universal laws.[17]

So, if the orthodox view is wrong, what is the alternative? Ilyenkov and Korovikov argue that the subject matter of philosophy is *thought*, or the apprehension of reality in or by thought. Philosophy elucidates the forms in which we think the world, the character of the movement of scientific thought,[18] or the logic of theoretical thought.[19] This is consistent, they argue, with Lenin's famous identification of dialectics, logic and the theory of knowledge. Only by embracing this task does philosophy itself become a science[20] with a well-defined subject matter: 'the order (*zakonomernost'*) of cognising thought'.[21]

(ii) The second reason to challenge the orthodox view is that it is in fact wrongly attributed to Engels. Ilyenkov and Korovikov argue in a short paper[22]

---

13   Ilyenkov and Korovikov 2016, p. 230.

14   See Thesis 12, where Ilyenkov and Korovikov praise Marx for applying philosophical insights to concrete issues of political economy, and conclude: 'This is the best proof of the proposition that positive knowledge is itself able to reach, and is obliged to reach, that very final essence of the object of research, beyond, above and below which there is nothing to find for the reason that there is nothing more'.

15   Ilyenkov and Korovikov 2016, p. 183.

16   See Theses 12 and 13, and Ilyenkov and Korovikov 2016, p. 187.

17   Ilyenkov and Korovikov 2016, pp. 213–14. The critique of the idea of philosophy as 'the science of sciences' is a constant theme throughout the complete text of the theses.

18   See Theses 13 and 14.

19   Ilyenkov and Korovikov 2016, p. 193.

20   Ilyenkov and Korovikov 2016, p. 180.

21   Ilyenkov and Korovikov 2016, pp. 185, 202–3. The term *zakonomernost'*, akin to the German *Regelmäßigkeit*, is difficult to translate. 'Regularity' does not capture the sense of necessitation implicit in the Russian term; 'lawfulness' is too legal in connotation; 'law-governedness' is barely English. In this context, I use 'order', but this will not suffice for many uses of *zakonomernost'*.

22   The paper, entitled 'With Regard to the Question of the Subject of Philosophy as a Science',

that Engels, in *Anti-Dühring*, 'Ludwig Feuerbach and the End of German Classical Philosophy' and *Dialectics of Nature*, explicitly claims that, with the emergence of dialectical materialism, philosophy loses its status as the science of sciences.[23] Engels makes it clear that what natural science leaves to philosophy is thought ('the study of the laws of the process of thought itself, logic and dialectics').[24]

Of course, Ilyenkov and Korovikov continue, there is a sense in which that view can be reconciled with the idea that philosophy's business is the most general laws of nature, society and thought, properly understood. A philosophical exploration of our modes of thought will disclose the most fundamental forms in which we think reality, and if we hold that those forms of thought capture the nature of things (if we endorse what Ilyenkov calls the identity of thinking and being, which he holds a materialist conception of logic demands[25]), then philosophy does disclose the general form of reality, and so a version of the Engelsian claim stands. As Ilyenkov puts it: 'Thought itself, if it correctly apprehends/cognises the world, realises in its development objective laws – and in that sense, of course, philosophy discloses the objective laws of reality, the so-called most general relations ... of nature, society and thought'.[26]

Many subjects study thought (psychology, cognitive science, neurophysiology, linguistics) but philosophy studies thought in its relation to being, as truth, as knowledge (in this sense, the basic question of philosophy *is* the relation of thinking and being). And thus it falls to philosophy to study how thought brings reality into view, and that includes exploring the nature of theoretical thinking and scientific method in a way that answers the question how rigorous scientific understanding of the world is possible. This is the real province of philosophy.

---

        is either a preparatory study for the theses, or a subsequent attempt to defend them. It is
        included in Ilyenkov and Korovikov 2016, pp. 229–34.

23   Ilyenkov and Korovikov 2016, pp. 229–30; see also pp. 202–3.

24   Engels 1968, p. 621; cf. Thesis 13.

25   At this early stage, Ilyenkov is not great at characterising the nature of this identity: 'The
        laws of thought are nothing other than the laws of objective reality itself transplanted into
        the human head and transformed therein' (echoing Marx on the ideal in the Afterword to
        the second edition of *Capital*). This is not a happy way of seeing things, and Ilyenkov con-
        tinued to work on this theme, producing a notable paper in 1964.

26   Ilyenkov and Korovikov 2016, p. 222 (Ilyenkov's ellipses). See also Thesis 14 and Ilyenkov
        and Korovikov 2016, p. 189, 'Insofar as the historically-sedimented order (*zakonomernost'*)
        of theoretical thought is the analog of the objective order, it remains correct to give the
        most general definition of philosophy as the science of the most general order of nature,
        society and thought' and p. 207, 'the laws of cognising thought cannot in principle contra-
        dict the laws of nature and society in so far as thought is objective, object-orientated'.

(iii) Finally, the orthodox view distorts the revolutionary character of Marxist philosophy. Soviet Marxism-Leninism declared Marxist philosophy a *worldview*; indeed, the first truly scientific worldview. This idea embodied two different senses of 'worldview'. The first was the idea of a complete conception of the nature of reality (from which it seemed to follow that philosophy had to embody the most general laws of reality). The second was the idea of a political or ideological identity. Marxist philosophy, it was argued, was the worldview of the revolutionary proletariat engaged in class struggle against the bourgeoisie, which embraced a contrary worldview, idealist in character and politically reactionary. Philosophy is therefore essentially partisan (*partiinyi*).

Ilyenkov allows that Marxist philosophy embodies a worldview, but not in the sense that it has a monopoly on the question 'What is the world?'.[27] Philosophy cannot answer empirical questions or disclose facts. Its worldview significance lies in its status as *method*.[28] Philosophy 'is first a method, and thereby, penetrating all the other sciences, directing their development, enriching them, it represents a worldview'.[29] There *is* a close relation between philosophy and politics, in that philosophy can establish methodological insights of value in political inquiry, but we should not politicise the problems of epistemology – seeing them as expressions of the class war.[30] Political issues cannot be addressed by throwing around philosophical phrases, but demand the application of concrete political methods, albeit informed by philosophical frameworks (which themselves are deepened and refined in the process).

The revolutionary character of Marxist philosophy lies, not in its interest in class war, the dictatorship of the proletariat, etc., but in its invocation of the concept of practice, *activity*, in its understanding of the relation of thinking and being, mind and world. It may be true that the emergence of the proletariat is a precondition of this philosophical insight, but that doesn't mean the struggle of the revolutionary proletariat is a genuine subject of philosophy.[31]

It is important that, when he speaks of philosophy as method, Ilyenkov does not see method as a set of a priori principles to be applied to any concrete subject matter. Method must change and adapt in relation to the material under

---

27 Ilyenkov and Korovikov 2016, p. 205.
28 This issue is not developed in the theses, but is prominent in Ilyenkov's *Notebook*.
29 Ilyenkov and Korovikov 2016, p. 207.
30 Ilyenkov and Korovikov 2016, pp. 218–19.
31 As even Oizerman maintains (see Ilyenkov and Korovikov 2016, p. 193). Ilyenkov writes that we need to create 'a never-before-existing dialectico-materialist theory of knowledge, which incorporates *partiinost'* together with practice, and makes it not an external stimulus to thinking, but its internal essential character' (p. 195).

consideration[32] and thus can be understood only in application to concrete material.[33] We need to understand the movement of thought in the object, the objectuality (*predmetnost'*) of thought.[34] So the deep question is how to characterise method if it must be understood in its concrete particularity.[35] We need to adjust our conception of the appropriate modes of inquiry in light of our emerging conception of the object, just as we adjust our conception of the object itself in light of the deliverances of our methods of inquiry. The picture he offers seems broadly Neurathian.[36] And, of course, we gain insight into such methodological issues by carefully studying successful cases of scientific inquiry in order to disclose just how, in those particular cases, thought captures the logic of the object under scrutiny.

Needless to say, this picture is a long way from orthodox Soviet views of Marxist philosophy as a weapon in the class war.

4. Although these three reasons probe deep into Soviet philosophy's conception of itself, and although the third has clear political resonance, one may yet wonder why the controversy gained such momentum. And indeed, when it first broke, there was little to suggest that things might get out of hand. We have the minutes of the Party Organisation of the MGU Philosophy Faculty from 16 October 1954, five months after the theses were first presented.[37] At this meeting some colleagues complain that Ilyenkov and Korovikov are creating a clique of students interested in their unconventional views and this is dampening students' interest in other parts of the curriculum (especially History of Russian Philosophy). But others recognise the importance of the questions Ilyenkov and Korovikov are addressing, and treat the enthusiasm generated among the students as a positive thing. Oizerman even sug-

---

32   Ilyenkov and Korovikov 2016, p. 197.
33   Ilyenkov and Korovikov 2016, p. 216.
34   Ilyenkov and Korovikov 2016, p. 196.
35   Ilyenkov and Korovikov 2016, pp. 198–9.
36   Otto Neurath's famously likened reforming the body of knowledge to repairing a boat at sea: any part of the boat can be modified or fixed but only by relying on some other part of the boat. When it comes to knowledge there is no dry dock. Consider: '... these principles, these laws (*zakonomernosti*), characteristic of the present stage of theoretical thought, must not be turned into blinkers, into categorical limits to the further development of thought. No – if the material convinces the researcher that certain laws, till now considered the *sine qua non* of cognising thought, need to be reconsidered, broadened, clarified, then that is a completely normal and justified phenomenon. Dialectic as a method changes and develops together with the development of theoretical thought, wh ... [manuscript breaks off]' (Ilyenkov and Korovikov 2016, pp. 199–200).
37   Ilyenkov and Korovikov 2016, pp. 24–7.

gests that Korovikov should publish a paper on the subject of philosophy. Admittedly, Kosichev, deputy dean of the faculty, pronounces that Korovikov 'practically rejects Marxist Philosophy'.[38] But at that time, this does not ruffle Korovikov himself, and over the next several months he is bold, confident and defiant. He resists those who would cast things as an intergenerational battle between young upstarts and established professors, arguing that the debate concerns serious questions about the nature of philosophy that obviously warrant discussion, and he complains it is deplorable if some of his colleagues are too ignorant even to see this, let alone to contribute to the discussion.

Ilyenkov does not figure in these minutes because his primary position was at Moscow's Institute of Philosophy, which was, as it is today, a research institute under the auspices of the Soviet (now Russian) Academy of Sciences and independent of the University. He taught at MGU on secondment, so his party affiliation was at the Institute. But he became very much involved as the controversy heated up. And by the end of March 1955, when the Scientific Council of MGU's Philosophy Faculty passed the resolutions described above, the temperature had risen considerably. The atmosphere at that meeting was one of a trial, and in true Russian fashion, a trial in which the outcome is a foregone conclusion. In his opening statement, Dean Molodtsov reads the charges, or rather, the verdict: Ilyenkov and Korovikov (i) reject the Bolshevik principle of the party-character of philosophy; (ii) deny that dialectical materialism is a worldview; (iii) deny that Marxist-Leninist dialectics are the science of the most general laws of nature, society and thought and reduce Marxist-Leninist dialectics to the science of thought; and (iv) deny the historical materialism is an inextricable part of Marxist-Leninist philosophy.[39] Korovikov and Ilyenkov are then permitted lengthy statements. Now Korovikov's attitude has changed. He is conciliatory, admitting that the theses contain significant mistakes and 'any number of unclear, slipshod and incorrect formulations'.[40] He pledges to heed his colleagues' wise criticisms in future. He denies that anything in the theses was meant to be inconsistent with Marxist philosophy's status as a worldview or with its class character. He apologises for discussing the theses with students – this, he now sees, was inappropriate. Throughout his speech, however, Korovikov tries to maintain that the issue is primarily a scholarly one – What is Philosophy? – and accordingly, he volunteers to run a seminar among young

---

38   Ilyenkov and Korovikov 2016, pp. 26. Though, as Illesh notes (pp. 26–7), Kosichev paints a rather different picture in his 2007 memoir.

39   Ilyenkov and Korovikov 2016, pp. 29–30.

40   Ilyenkov and Korovikov 2016, p. 32.

faculty members to clarify the issues (a proposal that suggests he did not quite appreciate the seriousness of his situation).

Ilyenkov, for his part, is cool.[41] He immediately concedes he is in complete agreement with the contrite Korovikov, and he plays down the significance of the whole affair. The theses were a working document, written to stimulate discussion. They have no definite form, having evolved in various ways over the course of many debates, so much so that he cannot remember exactly what is in them. No doubt they are full of mistakes, so he has no problem with people challenging whatever version of the theses they care to address. But anyway, what *he* thinks on the subject ought not to be the issue. All that is important is that the nature of Marxist philosophy is seriously discussed. The one thing he cannot accept is the accusation that he has behaved 'insincerely' or 'duplicitously'. That is unfair. Otherwise, Ilyenkov avers, let the Council pass whatever resolutions it likes.

Ilyenkov's strategy was to defuse the debate over orthodoxy while defending his academic integrity. But he was only prepared to compromise so far. When asked by Molodstov, 'Do you deny that philosophy has developed during the Soviet period?', he replies, 'My view is that Marx, Engels, Lenin and Stalin did a service to philosophy, but there's no way that's true of our philosophy'.[42] This remark caused a stir in the room, and was met by applause from the groundlings.[43]

On day two, Korovikov and Ilyenkov are not permitted to speak and the case for the prosecution becomes increasingly hysterical, in both senses of the word. Prof. Gagarin (no relation to the astronaut) announces that the nature of philosophy is no longer in dispute, having been settled by Stalin in Chapter 4 of the *Short Course*.[44] Prof. Kosichev responds to Ilyenkov's scepticism about the achievements of Soviet philosophy by asking: 'Could the successes of Michurinist biology really have been gained without the application of dialectical materialism? Could the battle against Morganism-Weismannism really have been successful without dialectical materialism?'[45] This was, of course, the time when the USSR was committed to the pseudo-scientific biology of Trofim Lysenko. And Molodstov causes laughter in the auditorium

41   Ilyenkov and Korovikov 2016, pp. 39–44.
42   Ilyenkov and Korovikov 2016, p. 41. Lektorsky comments on how strange it is to see Ilyenkov referring to Stalin, and even Zhdanov, while making arguments that were utterly heretical (Ilyenkov and Korovikov 2016, p. 236n).
43   It is interesting that the protocol of these meetings contains notes on audience reactions.
44   Ilyenkov and Korovikov 2016, p. 47.
45   Ilyenkov and Korovikov 2016, p. 57.

when he rebukes Comrades Korovikov and Ilyenkov for 'dragging us into the realm of thinking'.[46] Ilyenkov and Korovikov are variously accused of positivism, Trotskyism, deborinism, and menshevising idealism. They are said to be self-appointed innovators, evangelising their heretical views, and cast as hypocritical and duplicitous, philosophically dissolute, depraved, and debauched.

Many of these terms of abuse recall Soviet controversies in the 1920s between the positivist 'mechanists' and the Hegelian 'dialecticians', led by Abram Deborin, a controversy in which the deborinites were briefly victorious, before both camps were swept aside by a young generation of Party-activists which Stalin himself established on the 'philosophical front'.[47] Many of the old guard in Ilyenkov's time owed their careers to the rout of the deborinites, and so in defending themselves against Ilyenkov they reached for the old insults, though by the 1950s, these terms had lost any content at all and were used entirely indiscriminately.

5. So why the growing hysteria? There is no doubt that the old guard felt threatened by Ilyenkov and Korovikov. The orthodox Soviet interpretation of philosophy made it possible for the majority of Soviet philosophers to do philosophy without knowing anything about its history (except as the history of previous error terminating in Marxism-Leninism) or about science (insofar as the project of establishing the most general laws operated at an entirely abstract and vacuous level). The conception of philosophy recommended by the theses, in contrast, required real knowledge of the history of philosophy, knowledge of natural science, and a willingness to engage critically with the classics of Marxism, thought to contain methodological insights not yet fully understood. This was therefore extremely intimidating, since the old guard could not do philosophy as Ilyenkov and Korovikov understood it. And it was no surprise that the punks' position was attractive to students, some of whom were well versed in the content of Ilyenkov's dissertation, a circumstance that was potentially humiliating to the senior faculty, who could not cope with the questions the students were now putting to them.

So even seen as a merely scholarly issue, as Ilyenkov and Korovikov tried to cast it, this was not just an arcane debate about orthodoxy, but a battle for hearts and minds, and one that threatened to leave the philosophical establishment in the doldrums while the Soviet philosophy took a new course. That is one reason for the severity of the reaction.

---

46   Ilyenkov and Korovikov 2016, p. 59.
47   See Bakhurst 1991, ch. 2.

But the controversy had also acquired a new political dimension that contributed to the rising temperature. On 15 March 1955 (beware the Ides of March), at a party meeting in the Philosophy Faculty that was supposed to unanimously affirm the resolutions of the January Plenary of the CP USSR, a number of students had made critical objections, arguing that the resolutions should be merely 'taken under advisement', and calling for electoral reform, greater transparency, and moves against corruption in the Party. This was a scandal. One philosopher, I. Ya. Shchipanov, head of the Sector of the History of Russian Philosophy, immediately tried to lay the blame for this at Ilyenkov and Korovikov's door. We know this because there is a statement in Ilyenkov's archive, dated 22 March, in which he defends himself from the charge, arguing that he had never had anything to do with the students in question. But it is clear that the stakes had now been raised, for the implicit suggestion is that Ilyenkov and Korovikov, by cultivating a group of like-minded students, were involved in sedition. That was a very dangerous accusation indeed.

Moreover, the Central Committee had become aware of the student discontent and had accordingly initiated a review of the Faculty. The old guard was therefore anxious to find a scapegoat for student unrest, and Ilyenkov and Korovikov were the perfect targets. After all, whether or not the students in question had in any way been influenced by them directly, there was no doubt that Ilyenkov and Korovikov stood for a climate of independent thought. Few among the old guard would go as far as Shchipanov and all but accuse Ilyenkov and Korovikov of sedition, but most were happy to offer them to the Central Committee in sacrifice. A few figures dissented, but no-one would now dare openly defend the philosophical integrity of the theses, so those friendly to Ilyenkov, such as Oizerman, were reduced to endorsing the charge of heresy, but suggesting that blame lay with the Faculty's Scientific Council for failing expeditiously to prevent such revisionist views from gaining momentum.[48] The strategy was to give the University an incentive to downplay or bury the controversy, for fear of being burnt along with the heretics.

Unfortunately, the strategy did not work. At the end of April 1955, the Central Committee concluded that, while it was true that the quality of teaching in the Faculty had been lamentable for years, and hence had caused students to lose interest in orthodox Marxism-Leninism, Ilyenkov, Korovikov, and a number of other young faculty, were to blame for irresponsibly teaching revisionist doc-

---

48   To some extent Korovikov and Ilyenkov deployed the same tactic themselves; see Korovikov arguing that he was a child of the Faculty of Philosophy ('I didn't fall from the sky') and that his views, whatever their (no doubt many) errors, are a product of the poor climate of research and teaching (Ilyenkov and Korovikov 2016, p. 75).

trines. Accordingly, the review recommended that they should be relieved of their duties.[49] Korovikov was suspended from teaching; he received a strong rebuke and warning from the Faculty's Party organisation; and he was fired from MGU on 28 June. This was not as bad as it could have been. In May, the Faculty's Party organisation apparently voted for his exclusion from the Communist Party, but for some reason this did not proceed. Moreover, though dismissed from MGU, he was given a reference and offered a position at the Stalingrad Pedagogical Institute.[50] Korovikov chose instead to quit academe and eventually became a journalist, serving as a foreign correspondent for *Pravda* for many years, principally in Africa. The British and Americans apparently thought he was a Soviet spy and had him under surveillance. In any case, he seems to have lived a happy life, and died in 2010.[51]

Ilyenkov was also suspended from teaching at MGU, but since his primary appointment was at the Institute of Philosophy, he was not in danger of losing his job and the Faculty's Party organisation had no power over him. The only real danger was that he would be stripped of his Candidate's dissertation, but Oizerman contrived that the committee established to reassess the work included M.M. Rozental', a philosopher, not of the old guard, but of the old school – one of the few figures at MGU who was genuinely respected for his intellectual contribution. Oizerman was sure Rozental' could be trusted to affirm the merits of Ilyenkov's dissertation and stare down know-nothing opposition, and that, it seems, is what happened.

6. I had previously thought that the Institute of Philosophy was a calmer, more scholarly institution than the University, where Ilyenkov was protected by figures with integrity, such as B.M. Kedrov.[52] But Illesh's book reveals that this view is quite wrong. The Institute was in just as big a mess as the University. In fact, it was a worse mess. For one thing, figures who had enjoyed a distinguished career in some or other avenue of Soviet life – be it engineering, agriculture, state security, or whatever (the more hands-on the better) – would sometimes be put out to pasture at the Institute. So the faculty complement included people, now expected to write books on philosophy, who had no qualifications, let alone expertise. Some, such as ex-KGB operative Elena Modrzhinskaya, relished the chance to put their previous expertise to work in this new area, but most were

---

49   See the finding of A. Rumiantsev, Head of the Central Committee's Department for Science and Culture, dated 29 April 1955 (Ilyenkov and Korovikov 2016, pp. 85–90).

50   Ilyenkov and Korovikov 2016, p. 90.

51   Ilyenkov and Korovikov 2016, pp. 141–2.

52   See Chapter 9 below.

simply at sea and lingered as '*bezdel'niki*' (loafers). Moreover, in Spring-Summer 1955, the former director of the Institute, G.F. Aleksandrov, who had stepped down in 1954, was under a storm of criticism and embroiled in a scandal of some kind, which led to his being exiled to Belorussia to head the sector of dialectical and historical materialism at the Institute of Philosophy and Law in Minsk.[53]

From Illesh's narrative, one might surmise that the general shenanigans at the Institute distracted people's attention from the controversy going on over at the University, but this is not so. On 6 and 7 April 1955, on the heels of the trial-like proceedings at MGU, similar meetings were held at the Institute's Sector of Dialectical Materialism.[54] Eighty-one people were present at meetings where the principal agenda item was 'The Theoretical Mistakes of Comrade Ilyenkov, E.V.'. And once again the outcome was resolutions condemning Ilyenkov for his antiscientific, revisionist reading of Marxism – which, so it was stated, amounts to an idealist form of neopositivism – and removing him from the role of leader of the graduate special seminar. Ilyenkov was also much criticised for his hubris and arrogance.

And that was by no means the end of the matter. By the autumn of 1955 the situation had worsened still. Now the Institute was under scrutiny from above: questions were being asked about its role, and about the quality of work coming out of it. And, as at MGU, members of the establishment sought a scapegoat in Ilyenkov. Throughout the autumn, the Institute hosted a (protracted) conference on the nature of philosophy, at which many figures, including Ilyenkov, gave presentations. Since Ilyenkov was continuing to develop the ideas first expressed in the theses 18 months previously (notwithstanding his public retractions of his errors), he became the target of familiar accusations of revisionism. These accusations were now supplemented, however, by charges pertaining to Ilyenkov's behaviour, which is variously described as politically 'tactless', 'disgraceful', and 'criminal'.

What had he done now? First, Ilyenkov had asked that Korovikov be permitted to address the conference, which many considered inappropriate. But second, Ilyenkov had requested that a letter from Todor Pavlov be read out at the conference. Pavlov was a Bulgarian philosopher, President of the Bulgarian

---

53   Ilyenkov and Korovikov 2016, p. 258.

54   These meetings are not mentioned in Ilyenkov and Korovikov 2016. They are documented in the archives of the Russian Academy of Sciences (АРАН. Ф.1922. Оп. 1. Д. 767. Л. 40–106). It was among these materials that a complete text of the theses was found. See P.E. Fokin's posting from 27 December 2016 at: http://russophile.ru/2016/12/27/тезисы-к-вопросу-о-взаимосвязи-филосо/#_ftnref2 (retrieved 3 August 2020).

Academy of Sciences. The Ilyenkov-Korovikov theses had found their way to him, conveyed by Bulgarian students studying in Moscow, and Pavlov had written a letter to the Directorship of the Institute. It seems that Ilyenkov did not know what was in the letter, but he wanted its contents made public. The Directorship did not want that to happen. Pavlov was no free thinker, but he was interested in epistemology, and so one might surmise that he would at least have endorsed Ilyenkov's efforts to get Marxist philosophy to take epistemological issues seriously. In addition, Ilyenkov and Korovikov had also written to Palmiro Togliatti, leader of the Italian Communist Party, whose article, 'From Hegel to Marx', had appeared in the April 1955 issue of *Voprosy filosofii*. In the letter, Ilyenkov and Korovikov pointed out that they had been accused of revisionism for advancing a reading of Engels not dissimilar to Togliatti's own.[55]

In the disputes at MGU, Ilyenkov and Korovikov were often criticised for involving students in the debate, and they drew special criticism for involving foreign students. Corrupting the youth was bad, but corrupting foreign youth was especially malevolent. Now Ilyenkov was under fire for attempting to draw foreign Marxists into the discussion. This was considered outrageous. Ilyenkov, it was argued, was either amazingly naïve or incredibly arrogant (or both) to think that he could do this, and at a time when Khrushchev was counselling all to avoid confrontation with their foreign friends in the socialist brotherhood. On 2 November, a motion was passed at the Party organisation giving Ilyenkov a severe warning and reprimand for his behaviour.[56]

This panic-stricken concern over the involvement of foreigners was prompted by fear on the part of the establishment – fear of losing control of the debate, fear of being seen to wash dirty linen in public, fear of making tactical errors which would draw the ire of the Central Committee, fear of appearing to be no longer the vanguard of Marxist thought, and fear of being exposed as ignorant of the issues. No-one in the academic establishment took an interest in the *ideas* of thinkers like Pavlov or Togliatti. If their work was published in Russia, the reason was intellectual diplomacy, not debate. The last thing anyone wanted was to address the question of the plausibility or otherwise of the philosophical content of what was said (unless it proved expedient to criticise it as heretical). By trying to force that, Ilyenkov was playing with fire.

The seemingly inevitable conflagration, however, never happened. For although the controversy continued till the end of December, when a closed Party meeting at the Institute of Philosophy condemned the 'rejection of Marxist philosophy in the articles and speeches of E.V. Ilyenkov', it was eventually

---

55   Ilyenkov and Korovikov 2016, pp. 95–6.
56   Ilyenkov and Korovikov 2016, p. 121.

overtaken by the 20th Party Congress in February 1956, where Khrushchev gave his 'secret speech', denouncing Stalin's crimes and the cult of personality.[57] Thereafter, the Ilyenkov-Korovikov theses were no longer the subject of discussion.

7. The abstract of Illesh's book describes it as a '*filosofskii detektiv*',[58] a crime thriller or 'whodunit'. It certainly took detective work on her part to collect and interpret the archival material on which the story is based, but one might question whether '*detektiv*' is an apt description. In a whodunit, there is always at least one body, but so far we don't have one. True, we have witnessed an internecine struggle between, on the one hand, the zombies of the Soviet philosophical establishment, and on the other, the critical Marxists or philosophical *stilyagi*, exemplified by the young Ilyenkov. But this is not so much a tale of murder, but of survival, even rebirth. For the message of Illesh's book is that a new generation of Soviet philosophers drew encouragement from Ilyenkov, from the range of philosophical issues his thinking opened up to them. Moreover, Ilyenkov was an inspiration for his independence of mind. Few were prepared to stand up for him during the original controversy, but it is interesting to read the words of one who did, Elena Basova of the Institute of Philosophy, who came to his defense as a party meeting. She said:

> We all know that Ilyenkov is a young philosopher. He has passion, but he is also very observant. He has a lot of life-experience, erudition in philosophy, and importantly, he has a love of science. He works incredibly hard. He has what is most important of all, independence (*samostoyatel'nost'*), inner independence (*nezavisimost'*); he learns from everyone, but follows no one. He listens hard to all the advice he is given, but does things his way, as his scientific conscience dictates ...[59]

It must have taken great courage to say these words – indeed Basova's speech breaks off as she is shouted down. They give us insight into Ilyenkov's status as an inspirational figure.

It is worth noting that Ilyenkov has sometimes been portrayed as a rather weak, beleaguered, even cowardly figure.[60] But the transcripts published in

57   Ilyenkov and Korovikov 2016, p. 141.
58   Ilyenkov and Korovikov 2016, p. 2.
59   Ilyenkov and Korovikov 2016, p. 124.
60   Mikhailov confirms that such criticisms were made by Ilyenkov's contemporaries (though Mikhailov does not agree with them, of course): 'During his life, and after his death, bad

Illesh's book show otherwise. He always behaves with poise and is resolute in his insistence that what is at issue is a theoretical matter of great importance – the nature of philosophy – and that all eyes should be on that and that alone. He is never cowed by the institutional power of his adversaries, and he never concedes that the sword is mightier than the pen, telling V.I. Chertkov, head of the Institute's Party organisation, that Chertkov was in no position to comment on the philosophical quality of the work produced by those in Ilyenkov's department, since he took no interest in it. You had to be very brave in Soviet Russia to stand up to authority in that way.[61]

The story is also one of the birth of Ilyenkov's own philosophical career. It may have been a long and painful labour, but Ilyenkov went on to do important work, and all of it can be seen as originating in the ideas sketched in his *Notebook* and propounded in the theses. His study of Marx's method, begun in his Candidate's dissertation, was developed into an influential book, *The Dialectics of the Abstract and the Concrete in Marx's 'Capital'* (1960). He took up the nature of thought in his seminal 1962 paper on 'The Ideal', written for the five-volume *Philosophical Encyclopedia*, a work symbolic of the Krushchev thaw. As we have noted, Ilyenkov argues that our most fundamental forms of thought should be seen, not as pure a priori categories, but as essentially embodied in forms of collective human activity (a kind of 'cultural a priori'). Accordingly, he maintains that human beings become thinking things, acquire powers of reason, as they are initiated into collectively-instantiated modes of activity, objectified both in the practices of the community and in the form of the humanised environment. It is precisely in this, he maintains, that the revolutionary philosophical significance of the concept of activity resides, a theme signaled in his earliest writings but substantiated only later. The idea of the social formation of mind brought Ilyenkov into dialogue with the Vygotskian tradition and also inspired his writings on education, in which he at once stressed the social (i.e. state) responsibility to create the conditions in which human minds can flourish and extolled the importance of intellectual creativity and independence of mind. These and other prominent themes in his work – such as the nature of dialectical logic, the identity of thinking and being, and the defense of humanism

---

things were said of him. For example, that he was not a very brave person, that he was frightened of the apparatus of oppression and therefore did not always write what he thought' (Mikhailov 1990b, p. 60).

61 Of course, the Illesh volume is selective in what it presents to us, and Illesh is Ilyenkov's daughter, so she might be expected to paint as rosy a picture as possible. However, she makes no attempt to edit out her father's favourable references to Stalin and Zhdanov, from which we can conclude that her editorial policy took fidelity to the truth very seriously.

against technocracy – all have their seeds in his writings from the time of the theses.

So isn't this a story of renaissance, rather than a whodunnit? Well, in fact this is one of those zombie stories when, just when you think the world restored to order and the hero safe, he turns a corner and ...

Sadly, there is a corpse in the story. Ilyenkov's own. Although the 20th Party Congress put a stop to the controversy over the theses, and the subsequent 'thaw' made it possible for Ilyenkov to proceed with his work, the Zombies that almost got him in 1955 were not vanquished. Far from it. They all maintained their positions of power and influence within the Soviet academic world[62] and many continued in their animosity to Ilyenkov, whose career lurched from one controversy and to the next. Eventually the stress wore him down, the last straw coming when a substantial paper he had written on the problem of the ideal was refused publication. That event reputedly that led to his suicide. The story of the end of his life is tortuous and much detail remains unknown.[63] But it is very much the conclusion, perhaps the natural conclusion, of the tale this chapter has told: the story of one young punk, Ilyenkov, in a strange and surreal land, who unlike his friend Korovikov, chose to be a zombie fighter till the end, and who, despite many noble victories, was eventually torn apart.

∴

In the next chapter, we begin to evaluate the substance of Ilyenkov's mature philosophy, focusing on what is widely regarded as the most creative part of his legacy – his work on 'the dialectics of the ideal'. Here we see Ilyenkov deploying the concept of activity to explain and illuminate the relation of thinking and being, mind and world. In my writing, I have always sought to do justice to Ilyenkov's ideas in a way cognisant of the thinkers who inspired him and the social and political context in which he was working. At the same time, I have striven to bring his ideas into dialogue with thinkers from other philosophical traditions. Here, I defend Ilyenkov's position from objections by drawing on Kant and Wittgenstein, and noting parallels between Ilyenkov's ideas and the thought of John McDowell, whose pathbreaking *Mind and World* was published in 1994, shortly before the original version of this chapter was written. I explore these parallels further in several works, notably *The Formation of Reason* (2011) and Chapters 14 and 18 of the present volume.

---

62   Illesh's volume includes helpful biographical sketches of the *dramatis personae* (pp. 258–68). Not one was a 'victim' of de-Stalinisation.

63   I present my version of events in Chapter 9 of this volume.

CHAPTER 6

Meaning, Normativity and the Life of the Mind

1 Introduction

In 1991 I published *Consciousness and Revolution in Soviet Philosophy*, a critical history of the philosophical culture of the USSR, focused on the work of Evald Ilyenkov. Western writers on Soviet philosophy typically approached their subject matter from the perspective of external observers, chronicling the state's official Marxism-Leninism or giving a panoramic survey of Soviet philosophical discussions.[1] In contrast, my book aspired to a more ethnographic approach, aiming to convey what it was like to be a participant in Soviet philosophical culture and to give a sense of the internal dynamic of Soviet debates. To this end, I encouraged my readers to engage in an enterprise of 'sympathetic identification', working their way into the positions of Ilyenkov and others, engaging with their ideas rather than simply noting them.

No sooner was *Consciousness and Revolution* published than the collapse of the Soviet Union transformed the book from an account of a contemporary tradition into a historical monograph. This immediately posed the question of what interest remains in that tradition and, in particular, in the work of Ilyenkov. It had been claimed, by myself and others,[2] that the ideas of Ilyenkov and other like-minded contemporaries, such as Felix Mikhailov and Vladislav Lektorsky, cast important light on the philosophical framework which informed influential schools in Russian psychology, such as the socio-historical psychology of Lev Vygotsky and the 'activity theory' of Alexei Leontiev. But many would argue that this philosophical framework is intellectually bankrupt, and so much the worse for any psychological schools that draw upon it. Thomas Nemeth, for example, maintains that Ilyenkov was a dogmatic Marxist-Leninist, an apologist for Soviet ideology incapable of critically confronting deep philosophical questions. Nemeth wonders why I deemed Ilyenkov worthy of a book.[3]

---

1 Works of the former kind include Wetter 1958 and Bochenski 1963; examples of the latter variety are Scanlan 1985 and Graham 1987. Of course, there are works about the Soviet tradition that do not fit these models, such as Joravsky 1961 (a particularly fine account of Soviet debates in the 1920s and early 1930s) and Joravsky 1989.
2 See Tolman 1993; Jones 1994.
3 Nemeth 1995.

In this chapter, I explain why I think Ilyenkov is a serious philosopher whose ideas are of enduring significance. Ilyenkov offers an intriguing vision of the relation of mind and world, which, I shall argue, has radical implications for conceptions of thought, language and human communication. Of course, this is not an apology for Soviet philosophy or Russian Marxism as such; I seek only to show that one thinker in that tradition had creative and challenging ideas about meaning, consciousness and the life of the mind.[4]

2   Some Important Background

As a prelude to my argument, let me put Ilyenkov's contribution in context and explain some of the complexities involved in interpreting Russian philosophy of the Soviet period.

The tortuous political context of Soviet academic life was such that philosophers who sought to challenge the philosophical establishment, and its role in the legitimation of the Soviet state, often had to express themselves in terms dictated by orthodoxy. It is not just that critical philosophers were sometimes compelled to speak in an idiom they did not endorse (though this is true). Rather, the very resources they had to frame their positions, perhaps even to themselves, were partially defined by the dominant philosophical ideology. Furthermore, despite their avowed historicism, Soviet philosophers could not publicly reflect on the history of their own tradition or the character of their intellectual culture. Such considerations reveal the difficulty in reading the Soviet philosophical literature, a task already complicated by more ordinary instances of censorship. This is a body of writing intelligible only in light of the

---

4 Although Nemeth was not my only critic (Zakydalsky 1993 raises similar objections), I had a special reason for wanting to respond to his criticisms. Soon after my first meeting with Felix Mikhailov – described in Chaper 1 above – I came across Nemeth's recently published, but very belated review of the 1964 edition of Mikhailov's *Zagadka chelovecheskogo ya* (Nemeth 1981). I penned a reply, exploring parallels between the concept of activity, as it features in Mikhailov's epistemology, and Wittgenstein's conception of a practice (Bakhurst 1982). In addition, I sought to defend Mikhailov by invoking a theory of action inspired by John McDowell, where the world is pictured, not as a motivationally neutral setting for human agency, but as embodying objective reasons for action, genuine affordances for activity, which are objects of belief rather than projections of passion. Subsequently, of course, I returned to Moscow, where with Mikhailov's aid, I conducted the 'field work' which eventually issued in *Consciousness and Revolution*. In view of this history, I felt I could not leave Nemeth's criticisms of my book unanswered.

oral culture that was a significant, though concealed, dimension of the Soviet philosophical tradition. This is why I stressed in *Consciousness and Revolution* the importance of developing a feel for the participant perspective on Soviet philosophy. Indeed, I could have argued that it is impossible to understand the Soviet tradition without having actually participated in it or engaged seriously with those who had.[5]

I chose Ilyenkov as my focus because of the situation of his work in the Soviet tradition as a whole. As we saw in the last chapter, Ilyenkov was an important and controversial figure in the revival of Russian Marxist philosophy after the dark days of Stalinism. In the 1950s and early 1960s, he produced significant work in two main areas. First, he wrote at length on Marx's dialectical method, the subject of his Candidate's Dissertation and his first book, *Dialektika abstraktnogo i konkretnogo v "Kapitale" Marksa* [*The Dialectics of the Abstract and the Concrete in Marx's 'Capital'*].[6] This work, though it can now seem obscure, has an important political sub-text: it contains a critique of empiricism aimed at the positivism and scientism that Ilyenkov thought prevalent in Soviet political and intellectual culture.[7] Second, Ilyenkov developed

---

5 Nemeth is puzzled by my idea that 'sympathetic identification' is needed to understand fully the pronouncements of Soviet philosophers and regrets that I 'spend so little time enunciating' my method in *Consciousness and Revolution* (Nemeth 1995, pp. 146–7). Why, he asks, must we sympathise with a culture if we are to understand it? My so-called 'method' rests on the following commonplace. If you wish to understand a culture you must understand how things look to its members; you must be able to put yourself 'in their shoes'. Hence the desirability of 'sympathetic identification'. But this does not require you to sympathise with the beliefs and values dominant in the culture in the sense that you take them to be justified or estimable. To understand a serial killer, it may be necessary to grasp, as far as possible, how the world looks to such a person, but such an exercise in identification will likely intensify one's horror rather than diminish it. I could have substantiated this approach by appeal to hermeneutics or action theory, but I was anxious not to overtheorise a simple point.

6 Ilyenkov 1960 (1982a). Note that this book – which appeared in English translation in 1982 – is an abbreviated and censored version of Ilyenkov's text (the circumstances of its publication are discussed in Chapter 9 of this volume; see also Ilyenkov 2017). The complete manuscript had to wait a further 37 years until its publication (Ilyenkov 1997a).

7 *Dialektika* is a work of epistemology, broadly conceived. Ilyenkov's subject is the nature and possibility of cognition and his purpose is to develop the so-called method of ascent from the abstract to the concrete sketched by Marx in his 'Introduction to a Critique of Political Economy'. In both natural- and social-scientific inquiry, Ilyenkov argues, our objects of cognition are complex, 'organic' wholes (indeed, Ilyenkov suggests that all substantial objects of cognition are organic wholes). Such wholes consist of parts standing in relations of mutual determination, and they develop through the tensions, or dialectical contradictions, between those parts. In such cases, Ilyenkov maintains, cognition must proceed by isolating the 'prin-

a distinctive solution to what he called 'the problem of the ideal'; that is, the problem of the place of the non-material in the natural world.[8] The latter – on which we will dwell in the sections that follow – involves a resolute

---

ciple of development' of the whole. This phenomenon – the 'cell', or 'unit' – represents some part of the whole, the evolution of which necessitates the development and mutual determination of the other parts. The 'unit' is the 'concrete universal' of the whole: it explains the whole's development through the necessary interrelations of its developing parts. Cognition thus represents a movement from the *abstract* – from the individuation (abstraction) of the unit – to the *concrete*, a conception of the whole as a 'unity in diversity' of essentially related components. In this process, historical and logical analyses are said to coincide, for to represent the history of the object correctly is to chart the necessary logic of its evolution. Ilyenkov argues that Marx's analysis of capitalism in *Capital* best illustrates the method in action. By isolating the concept of *commodity* and tracing its development, so Marx reconstructs the logic of capitalism, the principles of its existence and necessary transformation.

When today we read Ilyenkov reflecting on the nature of dialectical contradiction or the relation of the logical and the historical, it is hard to appreciate why someone seeking to reanimate Soviet philosophy should be drawn to such seemingly abstruse topics. One reason Marx's method was an important theme for Ilyenkov, and for other Eastern European philosophers in this period (such as Alexander Zinoviev or Jindřich Zelený (1980)), was that the analysis of the logic of Marx's thought demanded that Marx be treated, not as an authoritative source of State ideology, but as one philosopher among others, whose ideas were to be criticised and developed and could be understood properly only against the history of Western traditions in philosophy. Presenting Marx this way showed the virtues of scholarship, rather than partisanship. Moreover, as I have observed, Ilyenkov's work on method had an important political subtext. Ilyenkov draws a sharp contrast between Marx's approach and empiricism. The latter typically construes the knowing subject as arriving at a conception of the world by a movement from concrete to abstract: the subject makes sense of the chaotic data of perception through the formation and application of abstract concepts and general laws that facilitate the organisation and prediction of experience. Ilyenkov was convinced that empiricist conceptions, often ill-conceived and poorly articulated, were prevalent in the Soviet academy. Moreover, he believed they contributed to an unhealthy positivism that construed natural science as a promethean force, able ultimately to solve any problem, theoretical or practical. Ilyenkov's work on method thus represents a critique of empiricism in Soviet thought and scientism in Soviet culture. This made his ideas especially relevant and controversial. (See Bakhurst 1991, ch. 5, for a fuller discussion.)

8 See Ilyenkov 1962. A version of this article appears as ch. 8 of Ilyenkov 1974a (2009b, pp. 146–67). As I mentioned at the end of the last chapter, Ilyenkov returned to the topic in the mid-1970s, writing a long paper that was initially refused publication in Russia and appeared in *Voprosy filosofii* as 'Problema ideal'nogo' ('The Problem of the Ideal') shortly after Ilyenkov's death in 1979 (Ilyenkov 1979a). (An abridged version had appeared in English as Ilyenkov 1977a; reprinted in Ilyenkov 2009b.) 'Problema ideal'nogo' was reprinted under its original title, 'Dialektika ideal'nogo' ('The Dialectics of the Ideal'), in Ilyenkov 1984c, pp. 8–77; 1991b, pp. 229–70. An unexpurgated version appeared in the journal *Logos* in 2009 (Ilyenkov 2009a) and is reprinted in Ilyenkov 2018a. The definitive English translation, by Alex Levant, appears

defence of the objectivity of ideal phenomena, which are said to exist as aspects of our spiritual culture, embodied in our environment. These works, which were extremely influential, cannot be properly appreciated without considering the Stalinist climate to which Ilyenkov was reacting and the Khrushchev 'thaw' which made them possible. Moreover, there are important continuities between Ilyenkov's ideas and controversies in Soviet philosophy and psychology in the 1920s and '30s, particularly, as often noted, with Vygotsky's sociohistorical psychology. The subsequent fate of Ilyenkov's career is also interesting. After the insightful writings of his early period, his inspiration gradually diminished as the political climate became more oppressive. Though he wrote extensively, engaging in polemical assaults on scientism and reductionist theories of mind, and taking up questions in aesthetics and philosophy of education,[9] he did not break much new ground. He died in 1979, by his own hand. Under glasnost, his work enjoyed renewed attention and was acclaimed as embodying humanistic ideas in keeping with the ethos of perestroika. Ilyenkov is thus a prism through which many aspects of the Soviet tradition are refracted. In the post-Soviet period, it seemed likely that interest in his work would wane, but this is not so: an annual conference, The Ilyenkov Readings, is held every Spring, many of his writings have been reprinted, important archival material has been published (as should be evident from the last chapter) and a multi-volume edition of his works is in preparation.[10]

Ilyenkov was a Marxist and he certainly admired Lenin. However, since the doctrine of 'Marxism-Leninism' was very much the ideological construction of Stalinism, Ilyenkov was hardly an orthodox Marxist-Leninist.[11] On the contrary, he was an important critic of that doctrine.[12]

So much for background. It remains to show that Ilyenkov's ideas are worth taking seriously as philosophy.

in Ilyenkov 2014. I cite here the 1991 version in my translation, in keeping with the original version of this chapter, but add references to the 2009 Russian version and Levant's translation.

9   See Chapters 7 and 8 above.

10   Six volumes have so far appeared: Ilyenkov 2019; 2020a; 2020b; 2020c; 2021; 2022.

11   See Bakhurst 1991, ch. 4.

12   See Mikhailov 1990b; 1995; Korovikov 1990; Novokhat'ko 1991, 1997; Sadovskii 1993. Further reminiscences of Ilyenkov are collected in Lobastov 2004.

3   Ilyenkov on Culture, Meaning and Mind

We shall focus on what is widely regarded as the most significant part of Ilyen-kov's legacy: his solution to 'the problem of the ideal'. This is the linchpin of his philosophy, the key to his distinctive view of the relation of mind and world.

Conceived at its broadest, the 'problem of the ideal' is the problem of the status of non-material phenomena in the material world. Most philosophers would construe this problem primarily as one about the existence of the mental, but Ilyenkov takes a different approach, arguing that if we want to comprehend our mental powers, we must understand the nature of *normativity*. The distinctive character of human mentality is that our thoughts, utterances and actions are, at least sometimes, governed by *reasons*. Our behaviour issues, not just from the causal influence of the world upon us, but from the recognition that we *ought* to believe such-and-such, that we *should* say or do so-and-so. Reasons objectively weigh with us. Ilyenkov maintains that we cannot understand this normative dimension of human activity unless we suppose that ideal phenomena may exist objectively as aspects of the world independent of individual human consciousness. To appreciate the nature of our status as minded beings we have to look beyond the human head.

Ilyenkov's position might seem like a kind of platonism. However, he does not intend the objective existence of the ideal to represent a metaphysical extravagance. To give content to the reality of ideal forms, Ilyenkov introduces the idea that many of the normative constraints on human thought and action are borne by social, rather than individual, consciousness. Sympathetically expounding Hegel, he writes:

> ... social consciousness is not simply the sum of many individual con-sciousnesses, just as the social organism in general is not the sum of many individual organisms. Social consciousness represents a historic-ally formed and historically developing system of 'objective representa-tions', of forms and schemes of the 'objective spirit', the 'collective reason' of humanity (or more directly of 'a people' with their distinctive spir-itual culture). This system comprises the general moral norms regulating people's daily life, legal structures, forms of governmental and political organisation, ritually established patterns of activity of all kinds, rules of life which must be obeyed by everyone ... up to and including the gram-matical and syntactical structures of speech and language and the logical norms of reasoning.[13]

---

13   Ilyenkov 1991a, p. 247 (2009a, pp. 29–30; 2014, pp. 47–8).

This idea of social consciousness is importantly qualified in two significant ways. First, it and the ideal forms it embodies exist only in their expression in *culture*, which in turn exists only in and through the activity of the community:

> [Ideality] represents forms of human social culture embodied (objectified, substantialised, reified) in matter, that is, [a quality] of the historically formed modes of the life-activity of social beings, modes of activity which confront individual consciousness and will as a special nonnatural [*sverkhprirodnaya*] objective reality, as a special object, on a par with material reality, and situated in one and the same space as it (and hence often confused with it).[14]

Second, culture is materially embodied not just in the form of practice: activity transforms the material world itself, endowing it with significance and value. Through the objectification of activity, the material world comes genuinely to embody ideal properties. Our environment is transformed into one rich with meaning. Cultural phenomena reside not just in the heads of individuals, nor in some ethereal collective consciousness, but in the practices of human communities and in the very character of the world as it is transformed by those practices:

> 'Ideality' is like a peculiar stamp impressed on the substance of nature by social human life-activity; it is the form of the functioning of physical things in the process of social human life-activity...[15]
> ...Ideality is a characteristic of things, but not as they are defined by nature, but by labour, the transforming, form-creating activity of social beings, their aim-mediated, sensuously objective activity.
> The ideal form is the form of a thing created by social human labour. Or, conversely, it is the form of labour expressed in the substance of nature, 'embodied' in it, 'alienated' in it, 'realised' in it, and thereby confronting its very creator as the form of a thing or as a relation between things, which are placed in this relation (which they otherwise would not have entered) by human beings, by their labour.[16]

The idea here is not just that some objects – artefacts, for example – possess special significance as embodiments of human activity. Ilyenkov holds that all

14   Ilyenkov 1991a, p. 249 (2009a, p. 32; 2014, p. 50).
15   Ilyenkov 1991a, p. 256 (2009a, p. 41; 2014, p. 58).
16   Ilyenkov 1991a, p. 268 (2009a, pp. 59–60; 2014, p. 76).

objects which are brought into the sphere of 'human spiritual culture', incorporated in whatever way into human ends and purposes, acquire 'a new form of existence that is not included in their physical nature and differs from it completely: an ideal form'.[17]

Thus, for Ilyenkov, we inhabit a world made significant, or 'idealised', by human agency, and the objects of nature speak to us in so far as they are incorporated into this domain of meaning. He writes:

> Outside the individual and independently of his consciousness and will exists not only *nature*, but also the socio-historical environment, the world of things, created by human labour, and the system of human relations, formed in the process of labour. In other words, outside the individual lies not only nature as such ('in itself'), but also *humanised* nature, nature re-made by human labour. From the point of view of the individual, 'nature' and 'humanised nature' merge together into the surrounding world.
>
> To this we must add one more consideration: nature 'as such' is given to the individual only in so far as it is transformed into an object, into the material or means of production of material life. Even the heavens, where human labour directly changes nothing, became an object of attention (and contemplation) only when transformed into a natural 'clock', 'calender' and 'compass'; that is, a means and 'instrument' of our orientation in time and space.[18]

So, on Ilyenkov's view, what Wilfrid Sellars pointedly called 'the logical space of reasons' is not situated in a purely mental domain; for the environment we inhabit as human agents is properly conceived as such a space. Our very 'external' environment, as a domain of meaning, offers us reasons for belief and action. It is cognitively and motivationally animating.[19]

All this profoundly affects the starting points of psychology. For Ilyenkov, our status as minded beings is manifest, even constituted, by our ability to navigate the space of reasons. Historicising Spinoza, Ilyenkov argues that a 'thinking body' is one which shapes its activity to the culturally forged ideal forms that comprise our humanised environment. Thus, the leading metaphor

---

17   Ilyenkov 1991a, p. 256 (1977a, p. 86; 2009a, p. 41; 2014, p. 58).

18   Ilyenkov 1964, pp. 41–2; Ilyenkov 1997b, p. 33.

19   My appropriation of Sellarsian talk of 'the space of reasons' is inspired by McDowell 1994. I discuss McDowell's work and its relation to Ilyenkov in the concluding section of this chapter, in Bakhurst 2011, ch. 5, and in Chapters 13, 14 and 18 below.

in our understanding of mind shifts from the notion of *depiction* to *movement*. Thought is in the first instance conceived, not as the ability to picture or mirror the environment, but as the capacity to conform to and manipulate meanings as they are formed and transformed in the flux of social being.[20]

Ilyenkov takes his position to undermine the idea that human higher psychological capacities are innate. Through the objectification of activity, our forms of thought are written into the structure of the environment, and as children we 'assimilate these forms ready-made as [we] are assimilated into a culture'.[21] This process is one in which the human child becomes a thinking being, an inhabitant in the space of reasons.

Ilyenkov sees the acquisition of language as crucial to the child's inauguration into the space of reasons and the emergence of her distinctively human mental powers. Nevertheless, Ilyenkov sees language as just one – albeit sublime – example of the idealisation of the material. Words and signs are not the only meaningful entities in the child's environment and their appropriation is but one way that she learns to relate to, and to master, the meaning in her world. Indeed, the child's first discovery of meaning lies in her ability to manipulate socially meaningful objects in the course of joint activity. The manipulation of sounds is a further stage in this appropriation of significance, another dimension of our commerce with the ideal. For Ilyenkov, no theory of language and its acquisition will be adequate unless it sees linguistic meaning, with all its specificity, in the context of the general phenomenon of the idealisation of nature.[22] Moreover, Ilyenkov advances the speculative hypothesis that the secret of the deep structure of language lies not in some innate universal grammar, but in the form of fundamental human activities at the root of the idealisation of nature. We can see Ilyenkov as supplementing the Wittgensteinian maxim that the life of the sign is its use with the claim that the systematic character of language reflects (albeit in an obscure way) the structure of human practice.[23]

---

20   Ilyenkov 1991d, p. 274.
21   Ilyenkov 1974a, p. 208 (2009b, p. 164).
22   Ilyenkov 1991d.
23   Ilyenkov's views of language reflect the fact that Russian philosophy underwent no 'linguistic turn'. In keeping with the German classical tradition that informed so much Russian Marxism, Ilyenkov charts conceptual space in terms of 'forms of thought', which he sees as grounded in activity. Although this facilitates insights about language as one among other modes of the ideal, and allows issues to emerge that are obscured by Anglo-American philosophy's obsession with the linguistic, it has its costs. Ilyenkov is not much interested in matters of formal logic or the study of syntax, supposing these

It follows from all this that our capacity to think and speak is as socially constituted as the idealised environment the thinking thing inhabits: 'the contemplating individual and the world contemplated are products of history'.[24] Ilyenkov writes:

> [T]he subject of thought becomes the individual in the nexus of social relations, the socially-defined individual, whose every form of life-activity is given not by nature, but by history, by the process of the coming-to-be of human culture.[25]

4   Assessing Ilyenkov's Position

I argue in *Consciousness and Revolution* that Ilyenkov's position is best understood as a response to the conceptual opposition between mind and world which has haunted philosophy since Descartes. Descartes is famous for his metaphysical dualism of mind and body as distinct substances, but his philosophy also includes a familiar epistemological dualism in which each thinking thing is in cognitive contact with the external world only via the mediation of mental representations (ideas). Each mind can reach out only as far as representations of reality, not directly to reality itself. This picture yields an atomistic conception of the mind, where each mind constitutes a kind of self-contained world of thoughts and experiences; it encourages a view of language as a device for naming the contents of this mental world so that they may be conveyed to other, equally atomistic, selves; and it generates a host of sceptical puzzles about our knowledge of other minds and the external world. (Indeed, the very idea that the world is 'external' gets its sense from this picture.) The picture presupposes that representations constitute not so much a boundary as a barrier between mind and world.

Just as metaphysical dualism derives from puzzlement about how the natural world could contain things which have states of the kind minds have (i.e. states that are subjective, intentional, conscious, and so on), so epistemological dualism issues from a failure to see how minds could engage directly with things like physical objects. A brutally physical object is not the sort of thing a mind can manipulate, as it were; the mind can entertain such an object

---

pursuits to foster mechanistic visions of thought and to detract from what really matters – a (dialectical) logic of content.

24   Ilyenkov 1974a, p. 207 (2009b, p. 165).
25   Ilyenkov 1974a, pp. 207–8 (2009b, p. 165).

only when it is presented via an intermediary, a mental representation. On the Cartesian picture, there is a sense in which mind and world are not made for one another. We have dealings with the world only via its representatives.

Ilyenkov seeks to resist this picture. Mind and world *are* made for one another because the world itself contains meaning, through the objectification of ideality, and to engage with that world as meaningful (to move through the world in light of the meaning it contains) is what it is to be a thinking thing. The story of the idealisation of the world in activity is thus the story of the world's coming to be a world-for-us-in-thought. To put it differently, mind and world are not two separate domains: the former, the domain of the rational, the ideal, the conceptual, where representational states move under the sway of reasons; the latter, the realm of the causal, the natural, the pre-conceptual, where brutally material things are influenced by physical forces. If this is how we see it, we shall forever face intractable problems about the interface and interpenetration of the two domains. But we are not forced into this problematic picture, for we can think of the world as objectively embodying the kinds of properties which make it a possible object of thought.

Of course, in the present climate, it is no particular distinction to be critical of Descartes and the representationalism he fostered. But the manner of Ilyenkov's critique is novel and must be distinguished from two familiar styles of anti-Cartesianism. The first consists in varieties of naturalism that aspire to explain the relation of mind and world by employing only explanatory resources compatible with the natural sciences. In the philosophy of mind, the most extreme version of naturalism is eliminative materialism, which declares that our familiar ways of describing psychological phenomena (in terms of beliefs and desires, etc.) constitute a mistaken 'folk psychological' theory of the mental destined to be replaced by a scientifically more respectable theory cast in neuroscientific terms. In epistemology, the extreme is occupied by evolutionary approaches to knowledge that construe matters of the justification of belief purely in terms of an organism's strategies for adaptation to its environment. Both these approaches are exercises in revisionary metaphysics in the name of science, in that they seek to engineer fundamental changes in our present conception of ourselves.

The second kind of anti-Cartesianism consists in forms of radical constructivism. Constructivists typically argue that it is a mistake to suppose that our representations genuinely depict an objective world. To say that a belief is true is just to say that it is deeply entrenched in our theories, but those theories are rationally unconstrained by reality itself: for what is real is just what shows up in our best theories (where 'best' does not mean, 'best at mirroring an independent reality'). There are numerous different ways of developing such a position.

Indeed, some are compatible with naturalism, since one might suppose (with positivists and some pragmatists) that scientific theories are always best. But in keeping with the ethos of the era, many contemporary constructivists are hostile to scientism and view reality as a construction of many discourses, not just one. Thus we see a resurgence of interest in conceptual relativism[26] and the emergence within psychology of 'discursive' approaches that portray mind and self as constructions of our modes of talk and explanation.

I mention these extremes because I want to suggest that both continue to labour under Cartesian conceptual oppositions. In my view, many constructivists are too impressed by sceptical arguments of a Cartesian kind. Convinced that we cannot reach beyond representation to reality itself (for that would involve 'climbing out of our minds' as Rorty puts it), they conclude that we are inevitably confined within our representational scheme. This move is often made in a spirit of humility that eschews the idea that our conceptions are warranted by the authority of Reality with a capital 'R'. But in fact the modesty is false, for the idea that our conception of things is rationally unconstrained by reality itself often involves a certain hubris: the world-text may be a litany of disasters but at least it is written by us.

Constructivism seems much less compelling if we do not start from the idea of a boundary between mind and world that we cannot see beyond. But the crucial task is to remove the appearance of such a boundary without losing sight of our distinctive nature as minded beings, as occupants in a domain of reasons. This is what naturalism fails to do when it proposes to collapse the rational into the causal. The interest in Ilyenkov's work is that he aspires to reconcile the space of reasons and the space of causes, to portray us as minded beings who are inhabitants in a natural world, but whose distinctiveness resides in the

---

26   Not all constructivists are keen on conceptual relativism; some invoke Donald Davidson's arguments that attack the coherence of the relativist's position. The idea that we might recognise other beings as operating with a conceptual scheme incommensurable with our own presupposes that we can translate their language. However, Davidson (1984b) argues it is a precondition of the possibility of translation that we assume that, for the most part, we share beliefs with those whom we are translating and that most of what we and they believe is true. Thus, the presumption of translatability undermines the threat of incommensurability. This, Davidson maintains, removes the whole motivation for talk of conceptual schemes at all, since the idea gets its point from the possibility of a plurality of schemes. Davidson's arguments are much cited, but I am convinced neither of their success, nor that their orientation is in fact compatible with the broadly irrealist views of many who invoke them. Davidson, after all, thinks his argument helps us recapture the idea of unmediated contact with reality itself (though in his later work it appears that this unmediated contact is merely causal, an assumption too weak for Ilyenkov).

fact that our mode of interaction with our environment cannot be exhaustively explained in causal terms. This is why Ilyenkov is important.

5   Objections to Ilyenkov

It is one thing to argue that Ilyenkov's aspirations are admirable, another to show his philosophy plausible. Let us begin by considering what exactly Ilyenkov is trying to do.

Ilyenkov's position represents a spirited defence of the reality of culture against the positivistic view that the natural sciences are the exclusive arbiters of what really exists. For though Ilyenkov concedes a sense in which all that exists is 'matter in motion', human agency endows nature with a cultural reality that confronts individuals as part of their objective world. Ilyenkov maintains that this insight is crucial to any adequate philosophical anthropology, for human beings create themselves through the creation of culture. This is so, first, because the mental powers of human individuals develop through their assimilation of culture, and second, because human history involves an on-going dialectic of transformation and development. The world acquires significance through human activity; this significance calls forth further activity which changes the world, thereby endowing it with new meaning and bringing about the necessity of further changes, and so on. In this process, we must constantly adapt to our changing environment, acquiring the skills necessary to orientate ourselves within it.

No doubt we should grant Ilyenkov that considerations about the nature of our 'humanised' environment must figure in any remotely adequate account of the human condition and our powers of mind and language. This is something much philosophy, particularly of the analytic stripe, has failed to appreciate, relegating such considerations to the contingent context of thought and language, rather than the very medium of the mental.

However, there seems to be a further dimension to Ilyenkov's position, and one which is more obviously problematic. At first sight, Ilyenkov's insights about human activity seem broadly empirical in kind – they are claims about the character of the world we know. But Ilyenkov, in an effort to articulate a substantive philosophical alternative to the Cartesian tradition he despises, endows these claims with a speculative significance. Activity is made a precondition of the possibility of knowledge, and not just in the ordinary sense that to acquire knowledge human beings have to act. Ilyenkov seems to be venturing a transcendental argument which invokes activity to explain the very possibility of the relation between subject and object. Activity is depicted as a force which transforms brute nature into a possible object of thought. Activity lays meaning upon the world, turning nature from a formless, pre-conceptual chaos into something which can be for us a world of objects. The 'idealisation of nature' is a precondition of the possibility of the commerce with the world that constitutes the manifestation of thought.

Read this way, Ilyenkov's position seems beset by problems similar to those which dogged Kant. First, we want to know about the character of the process by which activity transforms brute nature. But illumination is surely impossible, for since this process is a precondition of the possibility of experience, it is not itself a possible object of representation. Moreover, the world-constituting power of activity cannot be taken as straightforwardly causal (as the power of the potter or carpenter is). Activity consequently appears as a force with strange, even magical, propensities.

Second, Ilyenkov offers us a kind of speculative anthropology, a philosophical account of anthropogenesis, of 'the transition from ape to man'. At the level of the human race, we are asked to believe that the emergence of certain modes of activity constitutes the genesis of the relation between thinking beings and the world as an object of their thoughts. And each human child is said to become a subject of thought only through the appropriation of culture, only by assimilating the modes of norm-mediated activity that manifest thought. Is it not the case, however, that such speculative accounts encroach too much on matters empirical? As we noted above, it is inviting to supplement Vygotskian socio-historical psychology with Ilyenkovian arguments that compel us to conceive the mind in socio-historical terms, thereby buttressing Vygotsky's anti-innatism. But how human beings evolved, and how child development occurs, seem to be matters of empirical discovery not philosophical legislation. Vygotsky, who had a profound appreciation of the interplay of the conceptual and the empirical, would not have wished to achieve so much by *a priori* means.

A third and yet more damning problem is that the transcendental argument we are here attributing to Ilyenkov threatens to make his position self-defeating. If our access to reality is always via the mediation of the ideal (that is, of our spiritual culture in the broadest sense), are we not denied access to reality as it is prior to its infusion with culturally established modes of meaning? I argued above that the point of Ilyenkov's position is to express a harmony or identity between thinking and being, not to drive a wedge between reality as we conceive it and as it really is. But now it looks as if Ilyenkov also makes us prisoners of our conceptual scheme, or rather, that his philosophy affords us only a limited access to reality – to reality as far as it is humanised or idealised, and that we are denied cognitive access to the world as it is out of all relation to activity. Ilyenkov seems stuck with Kantian problems about 'things in themselves'. If so, he can hardly claim to have erased the barrier between mind and world.[27]

6   Re-reading Ilyenkov

In *Consciousness and Revolution*, I suggested that Ilyenkov's view of ideality might be developed and defended in two contrasting ways, the first broadly Kantian in orientation, the second Wittgensteinian.[28] However, in that work I resisted giving Ilyenkov's position either interpretation, preferring to anticipate objections of the kind just cited by stressing important differences between his position and Kant's.[29]

For instance, Kant argues that since experience necessarily presupposes the exercise of certain conceptual capacities, those capacities cannot themselves be acquired from experience. The way we represent the world is thus the product of an interplay between two factors: a scheme of concepts and the material on which the scheme goes to work. These two factors cannot intelligibly be imagined apart: the concepts have application only to possible objects of experience and nothing pre-conceptualised can be present to the mind. It follows from this picture that we cannot know things as they are 'in themselves'; that is, as they are out of all relation to our modes of representation. Kant proceeds to contrast the phenomenal world – the world we experience – with the noumenal world. The existence of the latter may be acknowledged by reason, though we cannot think contentful thoughts about it.

Read this way, Kant's account of the preconditions of the possibility of experience clearly invites objections of a kind outlined in the previous section. Ilyenkov's position is, however, significantly different. His account of how the world

---

27   Some Russian critics argue that 'activity-centred' approaches to psychology face a yet more fundamental problem. How can we explain the concept of the thinking subject by appeal to the concept of activity, when the former concept presupposes the latter? Human activity just is the characteristic activity of thinking subjects (see Brushlinskii 1994). This objection is inconclusive. Ilyenkov's point is that the possibility of the relation between subject and object rests on the emergence of a certain mode of active interchange between human beings and their world. This activity is constitutive of a thinking engagement with the world, it does not presuppose the exercise of antecedently existing (or even antecedently intelligible) mental powers. For further discussion of the activity approach, see Chapters 15–17 below.

28   Bakhurst 1991, pp. 210n12.

29   Bakhurst 1991, pp. 207–12.

becomes an object of thought does not invoke a special class of intermediary mental objects – representations – forged by the mutual interplay of understanding and sensibility, objects which intervene between subjects and 'things in themselves'. For Ilyenkov, it is the physical world which is lent meaning by activity and it is this world which the thinking thing is thereby empowered to navigate.

Nevertheless, despite this difference between Ilyenkov and Kant, the whole point of Ilyenkov's stance is that idealisation *changes* brute nature in some important sense. It lends significance to nature, thereby making it something that a mind can entertain. Does it not therefore follow that a mind cannot in principle describe and explain the character of that change, since the world prior to the influence of activity cannot be represented at all?

In *Consciousness and Revolution*, I shrugged off this objection, maintaining that there is no real problem envisaging the character of the world prior to activity's influence.[30] On Ilyenkov's view, it is not that there is some shadowy noumenal world existing behind or beyond the boundary constituted by our representations. The question of the world as it is prior to human agency is a historical question and we can characterise that world by exercises of the imagination and by building theories.

Such an account, however, is not likely to diminish the puzzlement of Ilyenkov's critics. The stories we tell about the nature of the world prior to human agency (e.g. about the world prior to the 'dawn of humanity') are essentially empirical stories. But if Ilyenkov's appeal to activity is to have transcendental significance – if activity somehow lends form to reality – then these empirical stories are not all there is to tell. Moreover, our empirical accounts seem to stand in tension with the transcendental view of the structuring of reality by activity, since our empirical stories of the world prior to humanity's emergence attribute to that world a form which, if the philosophical story is right, it could not possess independently of human agency.

Let us therefore explore the alternative readings of Ilyenkov's position.

6.1   *The Kantian Reading*

The first approach accepts that Ilyenkov is offering some kind of substantive transcendental argument, but argues that his critics' concerns are misplaced.[31] Let us reconsider Kant's own position. Kant thought that his transcendental idealism was compatible with 'empirical realism'. The objects of the material

---

30   Bakhurst 1991, p. 210.

31   This reading builds on the approach taken in Bakhurst 1995a, pp. 169–71.

world, *as we encounter them in experience*, are not mind-dependent entities or constructions of reason. They are independently existing entities, the antics of which do not, for the most part, depend on human agency or thought. It might seem, however, that Kant's transcendentalism compromises this realism. Yet although Kant's view that we have no pre-conceptual access to reality does set limits to thought, these limits may not be as serious as they seem. The Kantian need only admit that we cannot represent objects without deploying concepts. It follows that we cannot depict this tree in thought as a material object without representing it as a spatio-temporally situated configuration of substance. But the idea that it might, in its true nature, be something else, is a thought that represents the mere expression of an abstract possibility, a possibility which cannot be given real content and cannot be supported by grounds. It is not that the tree has, like the moon, a dark side that we can never bring into view from our earthly perspective. Nor is the tree 'in itself' really a shadowy entity situated in a never-to-be-encountered noumenal reality, while the tree we confront is a mere creation, an artefact of human representation. Both thoughts rest on the mistake of conflating transcendental with empirical conceptions, the error of allowing the story of how experience is possible to influence our view of what it is we experience. Once our concepts are in place, we have no choice but to recognise the tree as a wholly real, independently existing object.

Kant certainly fosters misleading talk of the noumenal. He sometimes writes as if there are two perspectives: one from within our conceptual scheme, and one from beyond it. The latter perspective is one we cannot occupy, but if we were to occupy it, we would glimpse the nature of things in themselves and the interplay of such objects with our conceptual scheme to yield our conception of the world. We are 'empirical' or 'internal' realists when we view reality from within our conceptual scheme, but that realism must be circumscribed by the haunting presence of an unoccupiable transcendent perspective. It seems to me, however, that we should simply deny the coherence of the transcendent perspective and of the noumenal world that goes with it. We should conclude from Kant's philosophy that there is no sense to the idea of a view of reality *sub specie aeternitatis*, not that there is such a view only it is denied to us. Kant cannot draw this conclusion, because speculation about the noumenal world is crucial to his vision of how freedom and rationality can coexist with the natural order. But we need not follow him in this. Once there is no longer a contrast between how things look from within our conceptual scheme and some unattainable transcendent perspective, then empirical realism is no longer 'merely internal'. It expands to fill all the available space, which is all the space there is.

Can we construct a similar argument for Ilyenkov? Ilyenkov agrees with Kant that we have no pre-conceptual access to reality, though he differs in his understanding of the nature of conceptualisation:

> All the schemas Kant defined as 'transcendentally inborn' forms of the work of particular minds, as the 'internal mechanisms' present *a priori* in each mind, in fact represent forms of the self-consciousness of social beings (understood as the historically developing 'ensemble of social relations'), assimilated from without (and confronting them from the very beginning as 'external' patterns of the movement of culture, independent of their consciousness and will).[32]

For Ilyenkov, it is not that the mind imposes conceptual structure on material 'given' in perception. We are given a world already conceptualised by the historical agency of our fellows. This position, like Kant's, sets limits to thought. We should not, however, overreact to these limits. Ilyenkov is clearly committed to empirical realism – the world as we encounter it is replete with mind-independent entities and properties – and there is no meaningful philosophical contrast between the world as experience presents it to us and the world as it is. The world as it is is something our concepts disclose to us.

There does remain in Ilyenkov's view some transcendental sense in which activity lends form to reality. One might say (as Barry Allen puts it) that nothing constitutes a self-identical object out of relation to human practice.[33] But it is crucial not to let this transcendental thought prompt us to adopt a quasi-empirical story about the primordial structuring of reality by human practice, where a kind of formless mass is moulded by the world-constituting power of activity. Such ideas cannot be given content since they transcend the limits to thought established by Ilyenkov's philosophy itself. They thus must not be allowed to infiltrate our view of empirical reality, leading us to conclude that objects are 'really' constructions of human practice and that everything is artefactual. Once again, such claims rest on a conflation of the transcendental and empirical.

6.2   *The Wittgensteinian Reading*

Ilyenkov's critics may be sceptical about whether it is possible to neutralise the speculative, metaphysical dimensions of transcendental philosophy in a way

---

32   Ilyenkov 1991a, p. 250 (2009b, p. 33; 2014, p. 51).

33   See Allen 1994 (though I am now inclined to think one should resist the temptation to say anything like this; see Bakhurst 2011, ch. 2).

that renders his position unproblematic. There is, however, another strategy open to the Ilyenkovian.

The core of Ilyenkov's insistence on the objectivity of the ideal is an injunction not to think of objective reality as disenchanted in Weber's sense. Rather, the world we confront is alive with significance; it embodies meaning, value and reasons. To this, Ilyenkov adds a stronger idea: in virtue of the objective existence of such properties, the world is a possible object of thought. We have seen how this latter claim entails that what we confront in experience is not pre-conceptualised raw material which the mind proceeds to organise, but something laden with conceptual significance prior to its apprehension by the individual mind. Hence, the world we experience exercises a rational influence over us; the significance it embodies offers us objective reasons – reasons for belief and action. The world's influence over us is normative as well as causal. This is the core of the attractive, but vague, thought that our environment is laden with meaning, for to engage with an environment so conceived is to inhabit a space where one's movements can be assessed as appropriate to the significance of the objects that space contains, and such assessment is normative in kind.

In the Kantian reading of the previous section, we sought to establish this position by transcendental argument. We might, however, deny that we need to win the right to these thoughts at all. Perhaps we should just resist the temptation to offer a speculative theory of how human activity lends meaning to nature. We need not respond to the image of reality as disenchanted with a theory of how a disenchanted world is somehow re-enchanted by human agency. We can adopt a more defensive strategy. Ilyenkov's view would have us take appearances at face value: we seem to be inhabitants in a world laden with meaning, value and reasons; Ilyenkov tells us things are as they seem. The task is to defend these appearances against those who would challenge them. (Note that this strategy represents a defence of 'folk psychological conceptions' in the broad sense in which Jerome Bruner uses that idea.)[34]

Such a reading preserves a significant place for the concept of activity in Ilyenkov's position. The objective norms Ilyenkov envisages cannot be rendered intelligible without appeal to the kind of responses they make appropriate, just as the responses themselves are, in particular cases, rendered intelligible by appeal to the norms. This circle is not vicious. It is just that norms and the activities they license or require are mutually intelligible phenomena. As Ilyenkov might have put it, each is the other's other-being.

---

34   See Bruner 1990, esp. ch. 1. In Chapter 14 below, I consider whether Ilyenkovian ideas might strengthen Bruner's call for a 'cultural psychology'.

So, the Ilyenkovian's task is to defend the objectivity of the normative against sceptical attack. Here we might enlist Wittgenstein's help. Saul Kripke has argued that Wittgenstein's famous remarks on rule following can be seen as raising the spectre of rule or meaning scepticism.[35] Wittgenstein discusses how rules guide or dictate behaviour. What is the nature of the necessity with which a rule (of logic, mathematics or language) tells us what to do? When we know a rule – say the mathematical rule for addition – we know something that tells us what to do in an infinite number of cases. Imagine that I write on a blackboard the command, 'Follow the rule "add 2!" Begin, "2, 4, 6, 8 ..." and continue like that until I return!' The command legislates what you must do *forever*. But how can writing a few marks on a blackboard achieve that? This is the question of the nature of normativity in a finite, physical world. The rule tells us what we *ought* to do (if we are to be consistent, rational, etc.), but what is the character of this *ought?*

Wittgenstein invents puzzles to explore these issues. He compares a rule to a sign-post.[36] How does a sign-post direct us? It just stands there! It is natural to say: The sign-post itself cannot direct us, we need an *interpretation* of it. But if we need an interpretation to understand the rule, we will surely need a further interpretation to understand the interpretation. An infinite regress looms.

It is tempting to recoil from these puzzles into a traditional form of platonism. When we learn a rule, it is as if the steps the rule dictates are already taken; the rule somehow contains its extension wrapped up inside it. So we might imagine that there is, in fact, an ideal world in which all the steps have been already taken, in which all the solutions to mathematical problems and the extensions of all mathematical series are laid out like rails along which our thoughts can run.

Wittgenstein, in contrast, dispels the threat of scepticism in a way congenial to an Ilyenkovian. He stops the regress of interpretations by appeal to activity or practice. The regress shows that there must be 'a way of grasping a rule which is *not* an *interpretation*, but which is exhibited in what we call "obeying the rule" and "going against it" in actual cases'.[37]

Explanation stops with action: 'In the beginning was the deed'. That we treat the sign-post as pointing one way rather than another, that we extend a series this way rather than that, that we deploy a word thus and so, is wholly manifest in what we do. These customs or practices comprise our 'form of life'. If someone does not follow rules as we do, they are not missing some definitive

---

35   Kripke 1982.
36   Wittgenstein 1953, § 85.
37   Wittgenstein 1953, § 201.

interpretation or failing to glimpse a platonic realm; they are simply somehow out of kilter with our form of life.

The extent to which these Wittgensteinian ideas can be deployed in Ilyenkov's defence depends on how they are construed. The interpretation of Wittgenstein's later philosophy is of course a matter of lively controversy. In my view, Wittgenstein's appeal to activity has an almost entirely *negative* function. He does not respond to rule scepticism with a substantive behaviourism or conventionalism which defines mental states, truth and objectivity in terms of specific human practices. Wittgenstein does not hold truth to be a matter of convention. What is true, what is real, are matters decided within our 'language games' and the criteria we deploy do not, for the most part, resolve matters of truth or reality into questions of agreement. It is when we try to reflect on the foundation of our language games themselves that we see they rest on nothing more or less than that we play them as we do. But that recognition should not be allowed to affect how things look from within our language practices. Wittgenstein is not out to give us substantive philosophical insight into the nature of reality.[38]

Despite the differences in style between Ilyenkov and Wittgenstein as philosophers, I think Wittgenstein's appeal to practice is a valuable complement to Ilyenkov's thought. The picture which results is devoid of metaphysical pretensions. It does, however, retain a minimal transcendental dimension in that it takes seriously the idea that we can reflect on the preconditions of the possibility of experience (conceived very broadly). Nevertheless, it should now be clear that such reflection need not yearn for a perspective beyond experience. The attempt to explain how the relation of mind and world is possible leads us to considerations about our form of life, about the kinds of beings that we are. If we seek to look beyond ourselves and our conceptions, we are brought back in the end to our own reflection. Ilyenkov would no doubt have found this degree of anthropocentrism agreeable.

Anthropocentrism, like transcendentalism, is problematic where it invades our attitude to the world we encounter, where we find ourselves saying that reality is just what we take to be real. But on this Wittgensteinian reading there is no reason to hold that Ilyenkov's position is incompatible with a natural realism, for nothing has been said that is, or need be, in conflict with the idea that our concepts enable us to make contact with an independent world, that thought can harmonise with the facts.

---

38   See Bakhurst 1995c, pp. 37–8.

The fact that we cannot underwrite our practices by philosophical argument should not drive us from one overdrawn philosophical theory (metaphysical realism) to another (scepticism, conventionalism or constructivism). Wittgenstein's famous remark that 'philosophy leaves everything where it is' is not an assertion of intellectual conservatism, but the recognition that philosophy's task is to cast light on the nature of our practices, not to engineer their revision. We must rest content with the realism that is the presumption of everything we think and do when we are not in the spell of high theory.

How faithful is the resulting position to Ilyenkov? By diminishing the Kantian dimensions of Ilyenkov's thought to make better sense of the identity of thinking and being, we are probably moving closer to the real Ilyenkov, whose primary influence, Hegel, took a similar path. The resulting picture obviously does not contain Hegel's extravagant metaphysics or teleological vision of history. While Ilyenkov would not miss the former, he certainly admired the latter, in its form if not its content. Moreover, much of the Marxist context of Ilyenkov's philosophy does not surface on this reading. Ilyenkov's fondness for dialectics is also muted. Nevertheless, the position emerges naturally enough from Ilyenkov's thought and represents a plausible interpretation of central themes within it.

One prominent feature of Ilyenkov's philosophy preserved in the Wittgensteinian reading is the significance of enculturation in the development of the individual mind. We must continue to think of the child's appropriation of the community's practices as her entrance to the space of reasons, as the coming-to-be of the powers that make her a thinking being. However, the details of the child's journey are an empirical matter, as is the question of to what extent she is predisposed by nature to undertake it. Ilyenkov's philosophy, like Wittgenstein's, certainly sets constraints on cognitive science; it defines a framework for empirical inquiry, but it need not decree what that inquiry must find.

7   Conclusion

I have contrasted two possible readings of Ilyenkov. The first takes Ilyenkov as engaged in an exercise in transcendental philosophy, appealing to the concept of activity as part of a substantive philosophical theory of the nature and possibility of the relation between subject and object. I contrasted this 'Kantian' reading with a more modest approach, inspired in part by Wittgenstein, in which the task is to defend the reality of the normative, and the perspective from which normative requirements are visible, against sceptical attack. Although this latter position finds an important place for the concept of activity, it has no grand philosophical ambitions. It aspires neither to a speculative theory of the genesis of subject and object in activity, nor to undermine the basic realism that is a feature of our practices as we live them. Both readings offer responses to the objections raised in section 5. I leave it to the reader to decide which, if either, is successful.

It is tempting to counterpose the two readings sharply, arguing that where the first preserves faith with philosophical argument, the second is overtly post-philosophical. Such a contrast is superficial. In my view, for all their differences, Kant and Wittgenstein's respective contributions represent dimensions of the same dialectic. Both Kant and the early Wittgenstein set out to give substantive philosophical accounts of the very possibility of representation. It is true that where Kant's philosophy is dominated by the aim of establishing genuinely metaphysical insights into philosophical problems, Wittgenstein's later thought is preoccupied with the idea that the problems themselves are unreal. Nevertheless, on the one hand, as I tried to show, Kant's view can evolve to lose much of its metaphysical excesses so that 'empirical realism', uninhibited by incursions of transcendent flights of reason, expands to encompass all our world and the only world there is. And on the other, Wittgenstein's later philosophy shows a constant recognition that philosophical puzzles are not foolish in nature. Someone who could not see the allure of these puzzles would be missing something important about the human condition, and the only path to a dissolution of the problems is through a morass of misplaced philosophical solutions. Thus, when we engage with the legacy of both Kant and Wittgenstein, we are led in different ways from a preoccupation with metaphysical puzzles, through philosophical theories that aim to resolve them, to a gradual awareness of the emptiness of philosophical theorising. This awareness, however, ought to engender, not a penchant for constructivist ontology (a philosophical excess), but a return home to the world as we know it. In my view, Ilyenkov's philosophy should be seen in the same light.

I hope I have shown that Ilyenkov warrants attention as a philosopher. He is important because he has interesting things to say about the life of the mind which engage in illuminating ways with issues of enduring significance. Nemeth's view that Ilyenkov said nothing 'that cannot be found in ... the analytic tradition with far greater rigor and insight' is myopic.[39]

Paradoxically, if we take such a view we will miss interesting parallels between certain Ilyenkovian ideas and recent work in the analytic tradition. I

---

39   Nemeth 1995, p. 146.

have in mind John McDowell's book, *Mind and World*.[40] McDowell's ideas were among the inspiration for my first study of Soviet thought in 1982, focused on the work of Felix Mikhailov, but the parallels are more visible today, partly because we know more about the Russian tradition of which Ilyenkov and Mikhailov are members, and partly because McDowell's own work is now more explicitly informed by Kant and Hegel.

McDowell aspires to find an alternative to two prominent views of the mind's relation to reality. The first is the 'myth of the given', the idea that experience presents us with pre-conceptualised perceptual presences which the mind somehow conceptualises. The second is a kind of coherentism which recoils from the idea of Givenness and maintains that mental states cannot stand in rational relations to anything which is not itself a mental state. Our beliefs, though they may be caused by external influences, can therefore be justified only by other beliefs. While the myth of the given places experience beyond the space of reasons, coherentism denies our conception of reality any rational warrant in reality itself. McDowell's solution is to combine the idea that experience represents the impingement of the external world upon the mind with the idea that experiences are states in which our conceptual capacities are already engaged. In this way, we can think of the world as exerting a rational influence over perceivers and view perception as warranting, rather than just causing, belief.

There is an obvious affinity between McDowell's and Ilyenkov's positions. Both seek to erode the opposition between mind and world by portraying the world we encounter in experience as 'made for' the exercise of our conceptual powers, and both effect this harmony of thinking and being by presenting our human environment as constituting a space of reasons. Moreover, both see the child's emerging capacity to inhabit this space as a product of enculturation, or *Bildung*, as McDowell puts it. I shall end by sketching three points of contact between their positions which would be fruitful to explore.

The first concerns the role of language in enculturation. McDowell and Ilyenkov agree that human beings 'are born mere animals, and they are transformed into thinkers and intentional agents in the course of coming to maturity'.[41] As I mentioned above, Ilyenkov does not give language acquisition as central a role in this transformation as it often enjoys in the work of Western thinkers who see mind as a cultural product. McDowell, however, offers a clear rationale for the emphasis on language. He argues that the idea that

---

40   McDowell 1994.
41   McDowell 1994, p. 125.

children are transformed into thinking beings through initiation into the space of reasons can seem profoundly mysterious. However, it is not hard to see the child's appropriation of her first language – an entirely normal and 'natural' process – as an entrance into a conceptual realm that pre-exists her being. Language, sustained by the child's community, 'stands over against [her] as a prior embodiment of mindedness, of the possibility of an orientation to the world'.[42] The emphasis on language, then, helps make tangible the idea of the space of reasons.

I think Ilyenkov could grant that the focus on language acquisition helps bring out how a human being can, as McDowell puts it, be initiated into 'something that already embodies putatively rational linkages between concepts, putatively constitutive of the layout of the space of reasons, before she comes on the scene'.[43] Ilyenkov would, however, argue that McDowell's picture needs supplementation. This is so, first, because a full appreciation of the child's entrance into the space of reasons must countenance the myriad of other, perhaps more obscure, ways that her environment is an embodiment of meaning, of 'mindedness'. And second, we need to understand how it is that there are such things as 'languages' that serve as embodiments of meaning in the requisite sense or senses. We dissolve the mystery of the transition from 'merely animal' to thinking being only in so far as we describe the process in terms which are not themselves mysterious. McDowell's position threatens to transfer the mystery from the idea of *Bildung* to the notion of a language itself. Ilyenkov's concept of the ideal is an attempt, if only a sketchy one, to provide a framework in which these two issues can be addressed.

The second point of contact concerns the nature of animal mentality. For Ilyenkov, our ability to commune with the ideal sets us apart from the beasts, facilitating human capacities for self-transcendence unknown to animals, who are 'identical with themselves', defined by the dictates of biology. Such a view naturally strikes many contemporary thinkers as profoundly counter-intuitive. It is interesting, therefore, that McDowell is drawn to a similar position, arguing that while humans and animals share a perceptual sensitivity to their environment, animals lack the conceptual resources which inform human modes of thought and experience. For McDowell, our conceptual capacities entirely transform our mode of apprehension of the world. It is not that we share with animals experience of the world but can do so much more with it. The charac-

---

42 McDowell 1994, p. 125.
43 McDowell 1994, p. 125.

ter of human experience is fundamentally different, precisely because we are inhabitants of the space of reasons in the way that animals are not.

McDowell cites Gadamer's account of 'how a merely animal life, lived in an environment, differs from a properly human life, lived in the world' and notes a parallel between this view and Marx's position in the *1844 Manuscripts*.[44] Interestingly, Ilyenkov builds on the same passages in Marx to conclude that

> even in the sphere of sensory-motor development, human development differs in principle from the development of animal 'thought'. The sensory-motor schemes of human activity emerge as schemes of activity *with things created by human beings for each other*, and reproduce the logic of reason, of social-human thought, 'reified' in them. From the very beginning the child confronts not just an environment, but an environment essentially humanised, where all things and their relations have a socio-historical and not just biological significance.[45]

McDowell's and Ilyenkov's emphases are different here. Ilyenkov stresses the human character of the environment to which the child must adapt. In contrast, McDowell's Gadamerian point introduces an element of holism: the space we inhabit is not defined by that which immediately impinges on us; rather, we situate ourselves, and everything that happens, in the broader whole which comprises the world. It would be fruitful to explore the extent to which these different points are complementary.

Third, and finally, an interesting aspect of McDowell's philosophy is his commitment to a form of moral realism, where moral properties are construed as genuine constituents of reality. Although morality is not theorised in Ilyenkov's work, it is fitting that an Ilyenkovian position should incorporate a conception of moral requirements. Ilyenkov was in many respects a moralist. His hostility to scientism, his view of individuals as socially constituted beings, his interest in education, were all ethical concerns. As I said above, the aspiration of Ilyenkov's philosophy is to show how we are, or can be, at home in the world. Ilyenkov fully understood that no treatment of this topic can remain content with unmasking philosophical confusions but must address the question of the nature of a meaningful life. This Ilyenkov sought to do with his teleological vision of history, culminating in the emergence of communism. However, there is no reason why Ilyenkovian insights cannot be combined with alternative understandings of the nature of human flourishing, and the 'neo-Aristotelian'

44   McDowell 1994, p. 117.
45   Ilyenkov 1991d, p. 273–4, Ilyenkov's emphasis.

position advanced by McDowell, and other like-minded thinkers, is an attractive place to begin an exploration of how Ilyenkov's philosophy might be complemented by an articulate meta-ethical position.[46]

These and other points of contact with McDowell are certainly worth exploring. However, I do not want to suggest that continued study of Ilyenkov's thought will yield a boundless source of insights that will further advance our understanding of the relation of mind and world. I, for one, think it is also important to explore ways to address these issues by other means. But Ilyenkov will always remain for me a singular influence. Whatever his faults, he was a man of vision, whose ideas illuminated the intellectual terrain for many others. And he was a philosopher who had something deep and valuable to say.

∴

The next chapter explores Ilyenkov's thinking about education. From the outset of his career, Ilyenkov saw himself as an educator, seeking to reform and renew Soviet philosophy's conception of philosophical inquiry and its role in the building of communism. But at first, he did not theorise education. He held, contrary to Soviet orthodoxy, that philosophy is the science of thought, but in his early writings he embraced a conception of logic that treats thought quite impersonally, focusing on the forms of thought, its movement, and the logic of scientific inquiry. In this, thought is understood as a socio-historical reality, but the focus is not on individual thinkers. This begins to change with Ilyenkov's famous writing on the ideal, which opens up space for a conception of individual formation (*Bildung*), a conception that came to play an important role in the creative, humanistic Marxism so often associated with his name. The chapter considers the reasons – various and complex – behind this change of emphasis, and examines its expression in Ilyenkov's statements on education, from his participation in the ill-fated *Komsomol'skaya Pravda* roundtable in 1967 to his passionate defense of education as 'learning to think'. The chapter shows how both the theory and the practice of education were central to Ilyenkov's life and work.

---

46   See e.g. McDowell 1979.

CHAPTER 7

Ilyenkov, Education and Philosophy

1   Introduction

This essay is devoted to an often-overlooked part of Ilyenkov's legacy: his work on education. Ilyenkov was someone who thought hard about education, and who conceived of himself as an educator. Yet this is not how he is usually seen. Instead, the relation between his philosophy, on the one hand, and his educational and psychological interests, on the other, is often taken to be external and contingent.[1] Such readings fail to appreciate, not just the significance of Ilyenkov's own writings on education, but the extent to which both the concept and the practice of education were central to his life and work.

2   The Courage of Thought

Let us begin with an unusual source: the article, 'The Courage of Thought', which appeared in *Komsomol'skaya Pravda* on 8 December 1967,[2] reporting on a roundtable the newspaper had organised on the nature and purpose of philosophy. The article, written by Alexander Tsipko and Igor Klyamkin,[3] begins by quoting a letter from a schoolgirl to the editors: 'If all the laws of being are known, as the textbooks tell us, what use is philosophy?' That question is then debated by Ilyenkov and seven other philosophers, A.S. Arsen'ev, G.S. Batishchev, V.S. Bibler, I.S. Narsky, F.T. Mikhailov, T.V. Samsonova and V.V. Sokolov. Ilyenkov's participation not only reveals his interest in education but helps put it in context.

---

1   So far as I know, the only Western article devoted directly to Ilyenkov's views on education is Bakhurst 2005b. The present chapter provides a more substantive discussion than was possible in that earlier paper.

2   Klyamkin and Tsipko 1967.

3   In 1967 Alexander Tsipko and Igor Klyamkin were philosophy students at Moscow State University, working also in the propaganda department of *Komsomol'skaya Pravda*. They graduated in 1968. Both later became influential political thinkers under glasnost and perestroika and in the 1990s held fellowships at the Wilson Center in Washington D.C. At the time of writing, both continue to produce political commentary. Tsipko is affiliated with the Institute of International Economic and Political Research of the Russian Academy of Sciences and Klyamkin with the National Research University Higher School of Economics in Moscow.

The article meanders, interweaving quotation and commentary, touching on such questions as the nature and extent of young people's interest in philosophy, how philosophy is taught in the USSR, whether philosophy should be approached through its history, and whether philosophical ideas should be popularised. The discussion is noteworthy for its lively, argumentative character. The participants voice disagreement and contradict one another. It might appear that no coherent position emerges from this diversity of opinion, except that artificially imposed by the journalists who put the article together. It is important, however, that five of the participants form a cohort of like-minded thinkers. In the mid-1960s, Arsen'ev, Batishchev, Bibler and Mikhailov were all much influenced by Ilyenkov.[4] It is therefore illuminating to read their respective remarks as contributions to a common cause. And if one does that, the following picture emerges.

The cultivation of philosophical consciousness is critical to the future of humanity (Mikhailov). Soviet citizens, however, can be forgiven for doubting this because philosophy in the USSR is so badly taught. Marxist philosophy – indeed, philosophy as such – is a unity, but the orthodoxy is to divide the dis-

---

4 As I described in Chapter 1 above, Mikhailov was my friend and mentor, without whom my work on Ilyenkov would have been impossible. He introduced me to Arsen'ev and Bibler in the early 1980s and I had several opportunities to discuss Ilyenkov's life and work with them. Arsen'ev had collaborated with Ilyenkov on a critique of the philosophical significance of cybernetics (Arsen'ev, Ilyenkov, and Davydov 1966). Bibler and Mikhailov's admiration for Ilyenkov is evident in the symposium transcribed in Chapter 2 above. I met Batishchev in 1986. At the time of the roundtable, he was Ilyenkov's colleague in the Sector of Dialectical Materialism at the Institute of Philosophy and much inspired by Ilyenkov's conception of activity. Arsen'ev, Batishchev, Bibler and Mikhailov were all highly creative, independent thinkers and over the years their philosophies grew apart from each other's and from Ilyenkov's, particularly Batishchev (see Chapter 16 below) and Arsen'ev (the only known recording of Ilyenkov's voice is the tape of a lecture in which Ilyenkov responds critically to a talk of Arsen'ev's; the text is published as 'Istorizm v psikhologii' ('Historicism in Psychology') in Ilyenkov 2018a, pp. 219–39). Lektorsky specifically mentions Arsen'ev and Batishchev when he comments that Ilyenkov 'could not but have suffered as those who in the recent past had been close to his ideas began to move away from them' (in Ilyenkov 2018a, p. 445). In December 1967, however, all five thinkers were brothers-in-arms.

  As for the other participants, I.S. Narsky (1920–93) was a longstanding opponent of Ilyenkov's philosophy. Ilyenkov openly criticises Narsky's work in Ilyenkov 2009a; 2014. I met with Narsky in 1983, when he was editor of the journal *Filosofskie nauki*. I remember him saying that he couldn't understand why young people would be remotely interested in Ilyenkov. V.V. Sokolov was a specialist in the history of Western philosophy, especially Spinoza. He died recently at the age of 99. T.V. Samsonova was a specialist in moral philosophy. She and her husband, the philosopher Petr Markovich Abovin-Egides (1917–97) (editor of the *samizdat* journal *Poiski*), were expelled from the Soviet Union in 1980 and thereafter lived principally in Paris until their deaths in the 1990s. (I am grateful to Vladislav Lektorsky for information on Sokolov and Samsonova.)

cipline into dialectical and historical materialism. Students are thus offered two dismembered parts of a living whole. In the first, they get reality without humanity; in the second, humanity without reality (Mikhailov). Moreover, philosophy is represented as merely generalising or synthesising the findings of the other sciences. And so dialectical materialism (*diamat*) is reduced to a set of abstract and ultimately vacuous 'laws' that students are told to commit to memory. Thus, philosophy becomes ossified doctrine, rather than spirited thinking, and students pass philosophy courses by 'cramming' rather than by exercising their powers of thought (Mikhailov). But this is not real philosophy, for philosophy is method, not doctrine. Its history is a history of *searchings* (Batishchev). It makes progress, not by deciding issues once and for all, but by raising its problems to a new level of understanding (in this, of course, it is just like any other science) (Arsen'ev). These problems reflect its distinctive subject matter: Philosophy is *the science of thought* (Ilyenkov).

Philosophy does not just study thought 'sideways-on', it cultivates critical thinking. As Bibler puts it, '*philosophy begins where stereotypical thinking stops, where critical self-consciousness begins, where the self-evident begins to call forth doubt*'. The proper study of philosophy exposes students to a treasure trove of ideas in a way that encourages independent and autonomous thought (Ilyenkov, Batishchev). In their commentary, Klyamkin and Tsipko continue this line of argument, affirming that such thinking is essential to human flourishing, and a necessary condition for instituting reform and realising a socialist future. The unity of philosophy as a discipline – its interest in knowledge as such – is an antidote to a technocratic cult of narrow specialisation. Philosophy reminds us that socialism concerns the all-round development of the individual. Its task therefore is to cultivate our humanity – to make human beings of us – so that we become authors of our destiny. The article concludes: 'A person whose brain is loaded, like never before, with tons of complex, diverse and contradictory information, needs a profoundly moral, general-humanitarian orientation, which Marxist philosophy is called upon to give. From it we draw critical self-consciousness, the demand for truth, the courage of thought'.

Although this summary is a composite, the views expressed can all be associated with Ilyenkov. As we saw in Chapter 5, the Ilyenkov-Korovikov theses, and other writings from the early to mid-1950s, argue for the unity of Marxist philosophy and for the claim that philosophy's true subject matter is thought. Accordingly, Ilyenkov rejects the idea that philosophy's role is to generalise the finding of other sciences into a 'worldview' articulating the most general laws of nature, society and thought. Philosophy practiced in that way produces only vacuous generalisations, supposedly universal truths that are, at best, commonsensical platitudes and, at worst, empty nonsense. Ilyenkov's reverence for the history of philosophy, and his recognition that philosophical progress consists in the insights gleaned through the dialectical transformation of its problems, is evident in many of his writings in the 1960s, particularly his doctoral dissertation,[5] parts of which were published in his *Dialectical Logic*.[6] Finally, the cultivation of critical thinking as a power of self-determination is a theme in *Of Idols and Ideals*,[7] a book on which Ilyenkov was working at the time of the roundtable, as is philosophy's responsibility to uphold humanistic ideals in the face of the positivist and technocratic conceptions that were gathering momentum in Soviet culture in the mid-1960s.

The humanistic character of this position was very much in harmony with the spirit of the times – the Prague Spring, with its advocacy of 'socialism with a human face', was in the making at the time the *Komsomol'skaya Pravda* article was published. This, together with the disputatious character of the discussion and the open criticism of the teaching of philosophy in the Soviet Union, provoked an angry response from the philosophical establishment and many of the participants suffered as a result. Worst affected were Mikhailov, who lost his job as Head of the Philosophy Faculty at the 2nd Medical Institute, and Arsen'ev. Ilyenkov himself emerged relatively unscathed, though his (and Batishchev's) participation did not go unnoticed at the Institute of Philosophy.[8] The incident contributed to his denigration and persecution as a 'revisionist', which intensified after the Soviet intervention in Prague in August 1968 and continued till his death in 1979.[9]

Thus the '*Kosomolka*' article is more than an intriguing intellectual curio. The document illuminates the importance of education for Ilyenkov and some of his like-minded colleagues, and the reaction it provoked reveals just how much was at stake in the debate. At the dawn of 1968, Ilyenkov saw the purpose of Marxist philosophy, and of the communist project as such, as the flourishing, not only of a class or a party, but of real human individuals, engaged together in autonomous critical activity. Socialism must create conditions in which truly self-determining activity becomes possible, and possible for all. Since such

---

5   Ilyenkov 1968a.
6   Ilyenkov 1974a (translated in 2009b).
7   Ilyenkov 1968b.
8   It was not only the Ilyenkovians who provoked controversy. Perhaps the most incendiary remark of all was Sokolov's rejection of the Marxist-Leninist orthodoxy that the history of philosophy should be seen as a struggle between materialism and idealism, dialectics and metaphysics. Alexander Tsipko tells me (personal communication) that the publication of this comment very nearly brought him and Klyamkin an official reprimand from the Party Bureau of MGU's Philosophy Faculty.
9   See Chapter 9 below; Ilyenkov 2018a, p. 340; Maidansky 2018.

activity is the mark of the human – of our 'species being' – then socialism creates the conditions in which we can 'become human'. Philosophy therefore has a vital educative and moral role in engendering critical self-consciousness and addressing the forms of alienation that stifle and distort it. Of course, this responsibility lies not just with philosophy, for the entire education system must be harnessed to cultivate and sustain powers of critical thought central to the nature and possibility of human flourishing. This theme figures in many of Ilyenkov's writings devoted specifically to questions of education.

3   Ilyenkov's Humanism in Development

From the outset of his career, Ilyenkov conceived of himself as an educator and recognised the educational importance of philosophy in the communist project. The Ilyenkov-Korovikov theses were written with a view to transforming Soviet philosophy's conception of itself. Moreover, both Ilyenkov and Korovikov, in their teaching at Moscow University, saw their mission as to reform and renew the way philosophy was taught and learnt. This is why they and their ideas provoked such an enthusiastic response from their students and peers and a correspondingly hostile reaction from the older faculty members, whose credibility was threatened by this new vision of philosophy. Despite his sacking from MGU and the efforts to discredit him at the Institute of Philosophy, Ilyenkov remained undaunted, and as soon as the 20th Party Congress in 1956 had taken the wind from his critics' sails, he was busy writing to Anastas Mikoyan, deploring the philistinism of the philosophical establishment and urging the transformation of Soviet philosophy.[10] On Ilyenkov's view, dialectics is a method for the concrete analysis of concrete reality. Philosophy as the science of thought must therefore understand and illuminate the logic of creative, critical thinking as it grapples with, discloses and illuminates the nature of things. An education in philosophy is an education in the history, logic and application of such thinking. This is critical to understanding the founders of Marxism and to furthering their legacy. Ilyenkov's faith in this conviction never wavered,[11] even if his optimism about the possibility of reform, and his appetite for a fight, diminished in his later years.

---

10   See Ilyenkov 2017, pp. 26–36.

11   See, e.g., 'O polozhenii c filosofiei [Pismo v TsK Partii]' ('On the Situation with Philosophy [letter to the Central Committee]'), available at: http://caute.ru/ilyenkov/texts.html; last retrieved 15 February 2023.

There was, however, a gradual change in the orientation of Ilyenkov's philosophy. Although Ilyenkov's early work *exemplifies* critical self-consciousness – and thereby teaches by example – he does not explicitly theorise it, at least in relation to the individual. Although Ilyenkov portrays philosophy as *the science of thinking*, his early writings treat thought quite impersonally. His is not a psychological inquiry, but a *logical* one. Philosophy concerns the norms of thinking – how we ought to think, not how particular people happen to think. Of course, Ilyenkov does not treat logic as a purely formal discipline. His is a logic of *content* that unifies epistemology – understood as the theory of inquiry or scientific method – and dialectics, the theory of thought's movement towards insight, truth, and self-understanding.[12] Thus the *reality* of human thinking must be in view, but Ilyenkov's emphasis is on thought as a socio-historical reality, not on individual minds.

The emphasis begins to change with Ilyenkov's famous encyclopedia article, 'The Ideal', published in 1962.[13] Here Ilyenkov explores how a materialist is to understand the nature of non-material phenomena and their place in objective reality. As we saw in the previous chapter, the orthodoxy among Soviet philosophers was to naturalise the ideal by a two-step reduction. They first identified the ideal with the mental, and then reduced the mental to brain-functioning. The ideal was thereby construed as a 'subjective reality', which, though emerging from and dependent upon material processes, was ultimately confined to the human skull. Ilyenkov takes a very different approach, rejecting the reduction of the ideal to the mental and arguing that at least some ideal phenomena exist objectively. Artefacts, for example, have an ideal dimension because they are embodiments of purpose. Artefacts cannot be understood merely in terms of their physical constitution; we must grasp their function and use. Similarly, economic value is treated by Marx as a real property of certain material entities, understood as an objectification of human labour rather than a projection of merely subjective mental states. Marx's appeal to labour is the key to understanding the ideal, enabling us to see that objectively existing ideality is neither occult nor supernatural; rather, its source lies in human activity, which becomes objectified in the form it imposes on material reality.

Ilyenkov argues that the human world is laden with ideality. We inhabit surroundings structured by objectively existing ideal phenomena that reside in the activity of the community and in the form the world takes on as a result.

---

12   Ilyenkov never tires of quoting Lenin on the unity of logic, dialectics and the theory of knowledge.

13   Ilyenkov 1962, reprinted in modified form as chapter 8 of Ilyenkov 1974a (2009b, pp. 146–67).

Notwithstanding the preoccupations of empiricist epistemology, human individuals do not create a conception of the world from scratch. On the contrary, we inherit forms of thinking and reasoning as we are initiated into 'humanity's spiritual culture' and internalise the community's practices, including its language practices. Thereby we acquire the conceptual resources constitutive of our powers of reason. Thus, on Ilyenkov's view, the nature and possibility of individual human minds is explained by appeal to the nature and existence of the ideal, and not the other way around.

With this, the individual enters Ilyenkov's philosophy. Admittedly, at this point, individual minds are represented as vehicles of culture, conceived as the living embodiment of human mindedness. The individual is seen, not quite as a *product* of culture, but as its agent. Ilyenkov writes: '[T]he subject of thought becomes the individual in the nexus of social relations, the socially-defined individual, whose every form of life-activity is given not by nature, but by history, by the process of the coming-to-be of human culture'.[14] However, here space emerges for a theory of personal formation, and soon Ilyenkov came to focus more and more on the thinking individual.[15]

4   Explaining the Change

What accounts for this change of emphasis? When he returned from the liberation of Berlin in 1945, Ilyenkov saw the Soviet project principally in world-historical (indeed, cosmic) terms, and he continued to think that way in the immediately post-Stalin era. But the failings of de-Stalinisation put things in a different light. The dispute over the Ilyenkov-Korovikov theses was a battle for hearts and minds between the old guard of the Soviet philosophical establishment and a younger generation which sought to create a culture of crit-

---

14   Ilyenkov 1974a, pp. 207–8 (2009b, p. 165).

15   Ilyenkov's view of the ideal is consistent with, and anticipated in, his writings on method from the second half of the 1950s. However, the latter treat thought as 'above all a "natural process", the subject of which is not the individual considered alone, but humanity in its development, in all its rich and complex relations to the surrounding world. The laws and forms of logic are the universal forms of the historical process of the development of humanity's objective knowledge of the surrounding world' (Ilyenkov 1997a, p. 71). Logic concerns itself with the categories of reason, conceived as a socio-historical reality, in their dialectical engagement with the world, rather than with individual minds (see, e.g., the section on the distinction between *rassudok* and *razum* in Ilyenkov 1997a, pp. 59–70). Ilyenkov's writings on the ideal maintain this conception of logic, yet they countenance a *Bildungstheorie* in a way his more strictly logical inquiries do not.

ical, independent thought. Ilyenkov and Korovikov soon realised that although history had to be on their side, it was not obvious that it actually was. Notwithstanding de-Stalinisation, the members of the philosophical old guard retained their positions of power and, with various adaptations to credo and vocabulary, continued as they were. This made it clear that reform – whether in the Party, academia, or society at large – presupposed a cultural transformation that would foster self-critical, independent and, in the words of the roundtable, *courageous* thought that would embrace change and confront dogmatism. This was not a small or local problem. On the contrary, it concerned the politics of mass education. And so, in 1964, Ilyenkov started writing pieces on education, targeting a wide audience. Their message is captured in their titles, which became Ilyenkovian slogans: 'Schools must teach how to think!' and 'Learn to think while you are young!'.

Another important factor was Ilyenkov's involvement in Alexander Meshcheryakov's work with blind-deaf individuals, which began in 1967.[16] Meshcheryakov had had remarkable success, particularly with four blind-deaf students who were successfully completing secondary education and about to enter Moscow University. Ilyenkov was fascinated, seeing Meshcheryakov's work as illuminating the social preconditions of mind. This made questions of individual formation very real for Ilyenkov. But more than this, Ilyenkov came to care deeply about Meshcheryakov's students, whom he befriended and mentored, and this both drew him deeper into education's role in psychological development and intensified his conviction that socialism was to be measured by its power to enable the flourishing of all human individuals, however disadvantaged.

A further component was the growing influence in the mid-1960s of the concept of the 'scientific-technological revolution', prompted by speculation about the potential of advances in computing, information technology and robotics rapidly to transform socio-economic life. Such issues are, of course, back at the centre of attention today as we ponder the likely consequences of innovations in automation and artificial intelligence. And, as today, reaction ranged along a spectrum with heady optimists at one end and gloomy pessimists at the other. The optimists among Eastern-European socialists saw the revolution as transforming the forces of production in a way that would enable a communist future. Innovation would increase productivity, creating wealth and abundance. Automation would free workers from monotonous, dangerous and otherwise unpleasant jobs, creating leisure time on an unpreceden-

---

16   See Chapter 4 above.

ted scale. Cybernetics would eradicate the notorious inefficiencies that beset planned economies, by enabling the flow of information (which market economies achieved spontaneously) and eliminating the human factor – i.e. error and corruption – in middle-management and bureaucracy. Reformists among the optimists saw the revolution as a catalyst that would sweep away ossified Marxist-Leninist dogma and stimulate the renewal of socialist theory.

Ilyenkov was more pessimistic. Of course, he had nothing against cybernetics itself, or against liberating workers from meaningless labour. But he was concerned about the idolatry of technology – which, he argued, had a long history in Soviet Marxism, notably in the philosophy of Lenin's rival Alexander Bogdanov.[17] He feared the dehumanisation of economic life. The technophiles, he argued, fantasise about the Soviet economy as a self-organising machine. But we know what a self-organising economic machine looks like – capitalism is just such a thing. We must never to forget that machines are artefacts of our making. Speculation about the creation of machines more intelligent than human beings rests on a mistake. Of course, machines can often do tasks better than human beings – that's why we invent them. But so what? Many animals can navigate long distances better than human beings. That doesn't make them more intelligent.

Human reason is universal in character. Our minds can hold the world in view as a totality. We can commune with the infinite, the ideal; we can contemplate the possible, the unreal, and the not-yet real. This power is manifest, not just in our heads, but in our form of life, in our life-activity, played out in the world, in historical reality. Thinking is thus qualitatively different from a machine function. For this reason, philosophers who reduce thinking to brain functioning simply fail to understand what thinking is. If we portray human beings as machines, then we must ask: What are human beings for? (We can always ask 'What's it for?' of a machine.) But that is a question that shouldn't be answered because it shouldn't be put. Socialism is the rejection of that question. The question we should be asking is: Who should we be? And we can answer that only if we understand what a non-alienated mode of life is like. Ilyenkov attacks the pretension that alienation is impossible under socialism and argues that faith in the scientific-technological revolution only promises to make things worse. Such themes run through many of his writings in the mid-1960s.[18]

---

17   Ilyenkov 1980; the 1982 English translation (Ilyenkov 1982b) is included in Ilyenkov 2009b, pp. 285–391.

18   See, especially, Arsen'ev, Ilyenkov, and Davydov 1966; Ilyenkov 1967; 1968a; 1968b; 1968c. Richta 1969, a multi-authored interdisciplinary analysis of scientific-technological revolu-

These three factors help explain the shift of emphasis in Ilyenkov's perspective, leading him to speak not just in general-philosophical terms about the cultural formation of the thinking subject, but to consider more concrete questions of the upbringing and education of human children. I turn now to his writings on education.

5   Education and the Social Formation of Personhood

It follows from Ilyenkov's work on the ideal that the environment into which the human child is born is not simply a physical environment. She enters a world of meanings, norms, rules, traditions, practices, reasons, values, and so on – the ideal realm of culture. Ilyenkov argues that, unlike other animals, nature does not provide human children with the means to orientate themselves in such an ideal space. This facility they can acquire only through upbringing and education, for '...it is not a matter of the child's adjusting ready-made patterns of behaviour, but of the child's assimilation of forms of life-activity that bear no relation to the biologically necessary ways in which the child's organism reacts to things and situations'.[19] The realm of the ideal has its own laws of evolution – cultural-historical evolution – and the child can inhabit it only insofar as she becomes a thinking subject, a person. With this, she attains a new form of existence – a mode of life no longer confined by the demands of her immediate environment, one open to the world, to the universal, the infinite, the ideal.

Thus, for Ilyenkov, to be a thinking thing is to navigate the ideal forms objectified in human activity and in the form that human activity has lent the world. This is not an ability that is innate in us. We are not born thinking beings; we become such as we enter culture, and we depend upon the agency of others to lead us inside. Ilyenkov sometimes puts his conception of the socio-cultural formation of mind in extremely strong terms:

All the specifically human forms of mind ... are determined socially and not biologically by innate structures of the brain and body of the individual member of the species *Homo sapiens*.[20]

---

tion by a team of Czechoslovakian scholars, provides fascinating insight into the spirit of the times. The optimistic mood is often tempered in ways with which Ilyenkov would have been sympathetic.

19   Ilyenkov 2018a, p. 72; 2014, p. 70; 2009a, p. 53.

20   Ilyenkov 2002b, p. 102; 2007c, p. 91.

Everything human in human beings – that is, all that specifically distinguishes human beings from animals – is 100 percent (not 90 percent or even 99 percent) the result of the social development of human society, and any ability of the individual is an individually-exercised function of the social and not the natural organism, although, of course, it is always exercised by the natural, biologically innate organs of the human body – in particular, the brain.[21]

Nature gives to human beings only the natural preconditions of the emergence of mind, but not mind itself. It gives them brains, but not the ability to use the brain as the organ of thought, as the organ of a specifically human mindedness – intellect, imagination, consciousness, will, self-consciousness. Human beings owe that entirely to themselves, to their own labour, to their own activity, to their own history. These remarkable psychological functions, possessed by no [other] animal, are not just 'trained' in society (as Kant supposed), but for the first time are born, emerge, and are formed in society, and only then do they attain the higher forms of their development – the stage of personhood, the stage of talent.[22]

The contemporary reader might find this difficult to swallow. Ilyenkov seems committed to an extreme environmentalism that pays lip-service to the 'natural preconditions' of mind while casting the thinking individual as entirely a social product. It might therefore be argued that, for all his supposed hostility to Soviet authoritarianism, his view betrays an affinity with Stalinist ideas of social engineering centred on the creation of the 'New Soviet Man'. We might also wonder how this view can be reconciled with a commitment to autonomy as an end of education. It is paradoxical to represent autonomy as acquired through teaching or training, for how could a being that lacked autonomy be gifted it through the agency of others?[23]

Ilyenkov invites such objections because, as he admits,[24] he often states his position rather sharply. But when he does so, his target is usually the prejudice that a person's educational potential is genetically fixed: that the abilities on which education goes to work are limited by factors not subject to change. Educationalists are too quick, Ilyenkov complains, to invoke innate factors to

---

21   Ilyenkov 2002b, p. 75; 2007c, p. 67.

22   Ilyenkov 1991c, p. 27.

23   For a contemporary discussion see Rödl 2016 (responding to Bakhurst 2011), Bakhurst 2015a; 2019, pp. 238–41.

24   Ilyenkov 2002b, p. 102; 2007c, p. 91.

explain why one child succeeds and another fails. It is a convenient excuse to blame a child's natural inability instead of our ineptitude as teachers.[25] Better that Marxists reject naturalistic explanations of psychological differences and focus on creating conditions that will promote the all-round flourishing of everyone, which is, as Ilyenkov puts it, 'the main task of communist transformation'.[26] This is why he found Meshcheryakov's work so inspirational.

In less polemical mood, Ilyenkov offers a more thoughtful take on the issue. Consider his essay 'On the Nature of Ability', responding to the debate between psychologists A.N. Leontiev and S.L. Rubinshtein. Leontiev, Ilyenkov contends, represents human abilities as determined entirely from without. Although individuals must possess the biological preconditions for the formation of an ability, these preconditions are not constitutive of the ability itself, which comes to exist only through the individual's 'assimilation' or 'internalisation' of socio-culturally inscribed forms of activity.[27] Rubinshtein complains that Leontiev offers a causal-mechanistic view of the external conditioning of mind, which fails to countenance the reciprocal – indeed dialectical – interrelation of external and internal factors, of 'the social and the natural'. As a result, we lose a sense of the person as the *subject* of their own development. This has a disastrous effect on our conception of education, transforming 'the student into a creature of the pedagogue, into a person who knows how to live only by his cribs and accomplish only those things that his teacher has "programmed" into him'.[28] For Rubinshtein, the exercise of a psychological ability is not just a matter of reproducing some 'internalised' pattern of behaviour; it is the expression of the agency of a subject who understands herself to be acting as the situation dictates and who can modify her activity as circumstances change. Human abilities are self-conscious and have marks of autonomy and creativity built into their very nature. But this goes missing in Leontiev's theory.

Ilyenkov expresses sympathy with Rubinshtein's complaint, and calls his arguments 'incontrovertible'.[29] Yet he is dissatisfied with Rubinshtein's solution to the problem he diagnoses. Rubinshtein interprets the 'internal core' of an ability as a fundamentally biological, 'anatomical and physiological' phenomenon. But if that is so, then we have merely exchanged one form of causal determination (external) for another (internal), where what we wanted was a vision of the child as *author* (or at least co-author) of her own development.

25   Ilyenkov 2002b, pp. 75–6; 2007c, pp. 67–8.
26   Ilyenkov 2002b, p. 77; 2007c, p. 68.
27   Ilyenkov 2002b, p. 63; 2007c, p. 57.
28   Rubinshtein quoted in Ilyenkov 2002b, pp. 64–5; 2007c, p. 58.
29   Ilyenkov 2002b, p. 66; 2007c, p. 59.

Moreover, Ilyenkov argues, Rubinshtein does not really want to think of the child's abilities as 'given' and merely triggered by social factors. But he thinks this is the only alternative to Leontiev. Ilyenkov suggests there is another way. We can see the child's development as a thinking subject as a process of self-development, self-becoming, but recognise that this is possible only through the appropriation of culture, precisely because culture is the vehicle of the conceptual resources, the forms of thought and knowledge, through which the child's mental powers realise themselves. The child is not merely a passive recipient, 'stamped' by social practice. On the contrary, she internalises social forms of activity only in so far as she makes them her own, the means by which her life-activity is expressed. In this, she is agent, not patient; subject, not object. For Ilyenkov, human beings are self-creating animals, defined neither by God nor by nature, but by their own powers of self-transformation. The individual becomes what she is through her own agency, but that agency is in turn possible only through her appropriation of a cultural legacy, and that in turn depends on the agency of others who teach and mentor her.

6   Learning to Think

Ilyenkov's distinctive way of combining his conception of the social formation of mind with a commitment to the cultivation of autonomy is expressed in a theme that runs throughout his pedagogical writings: *learning to think*. Ilyenkov portrays the power of thought as a social gift, not just because the child acquires it though initiation into culture, but because she learns how to exercise it in consort with others. The concept of thinking is a normative notion: it contains within itself a standard of excellence. To understand the concept is to know what it is to think well or poorly.

What, then, does excellence in thinking amount to? For Ilyenkov, a good thinker is resolute in her intellectual commitments, but she is never dogmatic. She has a sceptical disposition, not in the sense that she questions for questioning's sake, but because she is open to entertaining well-motivated doubts about her beliefs, however entrenched those beliefs may be. A good thinker has a range of intellectual virtues. She is imaginative, able to see problems and to find creative solutions. She is a good listener and a thoughtful interpreter, who finds sympathetic readings of texts or utterances. She is an able communicator, who makes her thinking transparent to others.

Such intellectual virtues cannot be codified into a set of rules or principles. A talented thinker has *good judgement*: she is able carefully to discern the factors relevant to belief or action in the case at hand, weigh them up judiciously, and

come to a decision about what to think or do. Such discernment is akin to perception – to seeing what matters and how. It is not a question of following
procedures.[30]

The non-codifiability of intellectual virtue leads some philosophers of education to wonder whether it even makes sense to speak of teaching people
to think.[31] But Ilyenkov argues that we cultivate good judgement, not by giving students abstract rules and principles, but by putting them in situations
in which the objective character of the problem they confront calls forth from
them a solution. Only then can they appreciate the principle that grounds their
solution and internalise it as a living guide to thinking. If you start by giving
them a rule, then it will be just one more object to deal with, and a lifeless one
at that, because, as Wittgenstein teaches us, the rule cannot contain the conditions of its own application – that must be seen in the particular cases the
student confronts.[32]

Ilyenkov stresses the dialectical character of inquiry. Dialectics is the theory of the movement of thought through the resolution of contradiction.[33]
Ilyenkov, in a way reminiscent of Dewey and the pragmatists, represents all
thinking as stimulated by contradiction: 'To acquire the culture of thinking
means, therefore, to learn to "bear the burden" of contradiction'.[34] Thinking
critically requires an ability, not just to respond to contradictions when they
present themselves, but to find contradictions that might otherwise go unre-

---

30   See Ilyenkov 2002b, pp. 7–8, 81–2; 2007c, pp. 10–1, 72–4. Ilyenkov warns that the uncodifi-
      ability of the power of judgement leads people wrongly to assume it is innate.

31   See Fairfield 2016. It is sometimes argued that no one can be taught to think because only
      something that can already think can be taught at all. This circularity objection is not very
      impressive. Even someone, like Ilyenkov, who thinks that powers of thought emerge in the
      individual does not think that their first appearance is the consequence of explicit teach-
      ing. What is at issue is learning to think well – learning to think in a way that befits the
      norms contained in the concepts *thinking being, rational animal.*

32   See Wittgenstein 1953, §§ 138–242. Ilyenkov writes that 'the trick lies *not* in training the
      individual to act in accordance with a memorized schema, activated by an "indicator" of
      its applicability given in advance, but in placing the child in a situation within which he
      will be compelled to act as "himself", as a subject ... The art of teaching, the pedagogical
      tact, acquired "by experience", consists precisely in always knowing how to place the child
      in a situation such that its "resolution" is within his reach ... [but] is possible by only one
      means – through the child's independent "discovery" of the operation that is required and
      that gives a "way out" of the difficulty' (Ilyenkov 2002b, p. 69; 2007c, pp. 61–2).

33   See Ilyenkov 2002b, pp. 20–9; 2007c, pp. 21–8. In his writings on dialectics, Ilyenkov sub-
      scribes to the view that there are 'objective contradictions', or contradictions in reality, as
      well as within the realm of thought. Fortunately, we do not need to address this contro-
      versial view in this context. See Bakhurst 1991, ch. 5.

34   Ilyenkov 2002b, p. 27; 2007c, p. 27.

cognised, and address them with imagination and creativity. Again, there is no recipe for this. However, we can teach students not to fear contradiction, but to seek it out, and this requires they develop the kind of sceptical temperament Ilyenkov applauds. Moreover, we can guide students in the diagnosis and transcendence of contradiction in a way that fosters the intellectual virtues described above, by putting them into situations that engender critical and creative thinking and giving them confidence to think for themselves. All this has implications for curriculum design, and for the ethos of the classroom, which must value and reward creativity, imagination and talent, and encourage students to challenge received wisdom and see the world anew.

7   Abstract and Concrete

Ilyenkov's writings on the dialectics of the abstract and the concrete were a significant influence on his friend, the educational psychologist Vasili Davydov, who, together with Daniil Elkonin, developed an influential elementary mathematics curriculum.[35] Ilyenkov himself explores some of the educational dimensions of the method of ascent from the abstract to the concrete in his paper 'Schools Must Teach How to Think!'

On Ilyenkov's account, teaching students to think is not just a matter of cultivating intellectual virtues. It also requires that we equip students with concepts that are appropriate tools for thinking. It is common to think of education beginning from encounters with the concrete – from the deliverances of experience – and proceeding therefrom to more abstract theoretical representations of reality. So the kindergarten is the domain of concrete representations, while students in high school operate in the realm of abstraction. Ilyenkov, thinks this is superficial. Scientific concepts, he argues, may appear remote from everyday reality, and hence abstract, but in fact they enable us to understand the world in its concrete particularity. Scientific concepts enable you to determine not just that, say, this animal is a tiger, but exactly why this life form is as it is, thereby providing a framework to explain why this particular tiger behaves as it does. Scientific concepts aspire to unlock the essence of the matter, as Ilyenkov puts it. They are intelligible only when situated in the context of a theory and related holistically to other concepts, and hence they require powers of abstraction to develop and integrate into a conceptual framework, but the understanding they facilitate can be supremely concrete, enabling us to see just

---

35   El'konin and Davydov 1966; Davydov 1972.

why these particular events happened as they did.[36] By the same token, the seemingly concrete deliverances of experience can yield a highly abstract conception of reality. Drawing on Hegel's essay 'Who Thinks Abstractly?', Ilyenkov maintains that simple empirical concepts and everyday verbal definitions offer a merely superficial rendering of the world that is abstract in being partial and one-sided.[37]

It is a mistake, therefore, to think of the child's conception of the world as more concrete than the scientist's. On the contrary, it is more abstract. And this has pedagogical consequences. Citing Davydov and Elkonin, Ilyenkov argues that, in mathematics, we assume that counting is the most concrete operation that forms the foundation of all mathematical thought. In this, we fail to see that counting presupposes commensurability: the child must identify the units that are to be counted. This requires powers of abstraction – the child must count the three cats in the picture, but not the cushion on which one of the cats is sitting, or the sky, etc. More fundamental are basic algebraic relations of quantity – greater than, less than, equal to – working with which in practical contexts motivates the arithmetical notions needed to address the question: 'Exactly how much greater?' In this way, Ilyenkov speculates, the development of a child's mathematical concepts follows the same path, and is motivated by the same necessities, that characterised the historical evolution of the concepts in question.[38]

Ilyenkov's focus on scientific concepts might suggest a narrow preoccupation with natural-scientific forms of understanding. But this is far from the truth. First, Ilyenkov's conception of 'science' is broader than natural science; the Russian term *nauka*, like the German *Wissenschaft*, embraces all forms of world-disclosing systematic inquiry, not just natural science. Second, Ilyenkov is an advocate of a broad education that equips students to gain familiarity with many dimensions of 'humanity's spiritual culture'. Though he recognises that modern societies call for experts who are specialists in particular knowledge domains, he nevertheless makes a plea for education orientated towards the all-round development of the individual. The mutual interplay of diverse conceptions and idioms is an important source of novelty and insight, and thus Ilyenkov was a fierce critic of educational systems that preached early spe-

---

36   Ilyenkov 2002b, pp. 37–8; 2007c, p. 35.

37   Ilyenkov was much enamored of Hegel's essay, praising it at the roundtable, and publishing Russian translations of it, in 1956, 1972 and 1973 (available at: http://caute.ru/ilyenkov/texts.html; last retrieved 15 February 2023). There are affinities between Ilyenkov's and Vygotsky's views on concepts and abstraction; see Chapter 10 and Derry 2013.

38   See Ilyenkov 2002b, pp. 39–55; 2007c, pp. 36–49.

cialisation. This, he believed, only served to reproduce the societal division of labour, when communism ought to seek the all-round, multi-dimensional flourishing of all citizens. Moreover, a worthwhile education is an education in *what matters*, and since this can be apprehended only in living engagement with things of value, students must experience a diverse range of disciplines and subject matters. Only then will they acquire a suitably mature and well-rounded conception of what is intellectually important.[39]

Ilyenkov is famous for his reflections on *activity*, and his educational writings reflect this emphasis. As we have seen, children are represented as developing abilities as they learn through problem-solving, resolving contradictions that confront them as they engage with the subject at hand. This might suggest a somewhat individualistic picture, on which the child learns in an individual confrontation with recalcitrant reality. However, the contradictions the student confronts lie not just in situations she confronts alone. She encounters those problems in dialogue with others. Sometimes the contradictions manifest themselves precisely in a conflict between individuals – one person says one thing; another denies it. In this case, the dialectical problem is how to find common ground with one's interlocutor that will enable the disputants to get beyond the conflict. Sometimes, of course, conflict is resolved by one side withdrawing its claims, but most disagreements find resolution in the space that opens between the opposed positions, transforming them into a new unity. This involves the exercise of the intellectual virtues discussed above, including interpretative imagination and generosity, as well as the ability to listen attentively yet critically. To this end, Ilyenkov emphasises the importance of understanding the perspective of others, as well as the ability to take the position of a 'generalised other', an ability, he claims, that is central to human self-consciousness.[40]

Ilyenkov did not write much about teachers' rapport with their students, or about mentorship and inspiration, though he does emphasise that teaching must respond to the child's individuality.[41] However, treatments of Ilyenkov's own practice as a mentor repeatedly return to such themes, for Ilyenkov was

---

39   For parallels between Ilyenkov's views and the educational philosophy of Michael Oake-
      shott, see Bakhurst 2019b, pp. 236–8.

40   Ilyenkov 2002b, p. 92; 2007c, p. 82.

41   In a striking passage, he writes: 'It is impossible to teach a child – or, indeed, an adult –
      anything, including the ability (skill) to think independently, without adopting an attitude
      of the closest attention to his individuality. The old philosophy and pedagogy used to call
      such an attitude "love"' (Ilyenkov 2002b, p. 14; 2007c, p. 16).

an inspiring figure who exemplified the spirit of creative inquiry, by his passion for ideas and his opposition to dogmatism and mindless orthodoxy. It was, he thought, the duty of any teacher to bring ideas to life in this way and inspire and transform her students, while being open in turn to being inspired and transformed by them.

8   Conclusion

Ilyenkov's educational philosophy has a distinctively moral dimension. No child can flourish without education, because education makes us what we are. Access to education is therefore a matter of *justice*. All children deserve the opportunity to enter the domain of human knowledge and acquire the powers of critical deliberation and judgement necessary to be at home there. No-one should be left behind because educationalists or politicians have decided they are not 'naturally' able. The working assumption should be that all children, who are not suffering from the severest impairment or illness, are able to develop their talents and flourish. Any appeal to limits set by 'natural inability' is just an excuse for not working harder to create conditions that will permit children to succeed. Of course, different children will have different interests, motivations and aptitudes, and will thrive in a variety of contrasting ways. That is as it should be – diversity and plurality are goods. But education must never give up on children's potential.

This fundamental commitment was central to Ilyenkov's vision of communism – the harnessing of social powers for the all-round flourishing of humanity – and he saw, more clearly than many, that education was of paramount importance to the communist project. Much of his work, therefore, argues that the Soviet Union must take greater responsibility in enabling the well-being of its citizens by cultivating creative, critical thinkers, able to question and challenge received wisdom, and not quiescent sheep that willingly submit themselves to authority – themes visible in the contributions of Ilyenkov's cohort to the roundtable with which we began. His writings are therefore interesting as polemics, but they are more than that: they uphold a vision of the scope and purpose of education that is relevant far beyond the confines of the former USSR. Ilyenkov's role as a public intellectual was not dissimilar to that played by John Dewey, and his ideas, as much as Dewey's, maintain their significance. Indeed, we see arguments that parallel Ilyenkov's being made today by American thinkers emphasising the importance of critical thinking to sustaining a vibrant political culture, in which citizens are empowered to resist indoctrination and oppression and contribute to informed discussion in a healthy democracy.[42] The Soviet Union may seem a long way from contemporary America, but Ilyenkov's educational vision is no less relevant to the latter than the former. Or so I believe.

∴

Next we turn to another neglected part of Ilyenkov's legacy: his work on aesthetics. In 1964, on a rare trip to the West, Ilyenkov visited an exhibition of pop art in Vienna. He was disgusted by what he saw and wrote a scathing critique entitled 'Chto tam, v Zazerkal'e?' ('What's There, Through the Looking Glass?'). Does Ilyenkov's antipathy to pop – and, indeed, to so-called modern art in general – show him to be enamored of a narrow, reactionary form of socialist realism? If so, how can this be squared with his reputation as a creative, critical voice within Soviet Marxism? To answer these questions, I examine Ilyenkov's other writings on aesthetics in search of a nuanced interpretation of his reaction to pop. I consider his idea that art should serve to cultivate higher forms of perception and his attendant concepts of aesthetic sensibility and imagination, and explore how these notions contribute to his view of the unity of the cognitive virtues, his hostility to the division of labour, and his ideal of genuine human activity, guided by reason. Such themes are vital constituents of Ilyenkov's humanism, which celebrates free, creative activity as a life principle that must assert itself against the mortifying forces of mechanisation and standardisation. Although these ideas may not entirely redeem Ilyenkov's hostility to modern art, they reveal his stance to be far more sophisticated than appears at first sight.

---

42   See, for example, Nussbaum 2010.

Ilyenkov on Aesthetics: Realism, Imagination, and the End of Art

Of all Ilyenkov's writings, the most neglected are his works on art. This is unfortunate, for his views on aesthetics help us to place Ilyenkov and his ideas in a broader context and to appreciate how the dominant themes of his philosophy are woven together into a single humanistic vision.

Art is a species of the ideal, a significant aspect of cultural reality, and one which gives expression to, and trains and transforms, the imagination, a vital cognitive capacity. It is thus no surprise that the aesthetic should have a prominent place in Ilyenkov's thought. Yet although the relevance of aesthetics to Ilyenkov's philosophy is not difficult to discern, his writings on art are by no means straightforward. Indeed, they present significant interpretative problems.

1   Beauty, Goodness, Truth

Between 1960 and 1972, Ilyenkov wrote a series of papers on art in which he discussed such questions as the nature of beauty, the concepts of aesthetic sensibility and imagination, and the relation of artistic and scientific understanding.[1] The papers focus mainly on the visual arts, though reference is made to literature and music. I begin by concentrating on one: '*Chto tam, v Zazerkal'e?*' ('What's there, through the looking glass?'), published in 1969. This is a curious article, which displays some of the best and the worst of Ilyenkov's philosophical style. It shows his talent for combining abstract philosophical speculation with anecdotal material of a popular and accessible kind. It is typically passionate, witty, and forceful. However, the position Ilyenkov advances is so problematic that it seems to cast his entire philosophy in an unfavorable light.

'*Chto tam, v Zazerkal'e?*' begins by posing the question of the relation of beauty, goodness, and truth. Ilyenkov immediately endorses what he describes as the ancient solution that the three somehow represent a unity in diversity.

---

1   Ilyenkov 1984a; 1984b; 1984d; 1984e; 1984f.

On this account, the good, the beautiful, and the true all spring from the same source; they represent three different expressions of one and the same thing.

Ilyenkov admits that this solution sounds counterintuitive to contemporary ears. We feel today that there are no internal relations between these concepts. Insofar as science is governed by the regulative ideal of truth, it is a morally neutral endeavour. The facts science discovers can as easily be put in the service of evil as of good, as Hiroshima stands witness. Likewise, we do not feel there need be anything morally edifying about the beautiful or aesthetically pleasing about the good. The beautiful is morally relevant only insofar as it is one among the things we care about. A painting is not more beautiful for its being morally uplifting, nor is it morally edifying merely in virtue of its beauty, and, of course, the pursuit of beauty need not coincide with the pursuit of truth. In fact, the simple yet high ideal of the classical solution seems wholly at odds with the modern temperament, habituated as it is to the ideas that evil is unavoidable, that violence and cruelty can be objects of aesthetic appreciation, that the progress of science may lead us to the abyss. In such a climate, we may expect to see a loss of confidence in art – with the art world oscillating between the reduction of art to amusement and varieties of anti-art – but not an affirmation of the coincidence of the beautiful with the true and the good.[2]

Ilyenkov does not so much argue for the classical position as expound a form of humanism that locates the coincidence of truth, beauty, and goodness in the ideal of properly human relations among human beings and between human beings and nature. He counsels us not to portray the relation of beauty, truth, and goodness as if it were one between Platonic forms. Rather, we should see their relation as disclosed by the relation between art, science and morality, the practices that have beauty, truth, and goodness as their respective objects. Ilyenkov argues that these practices form three different expressions of human self-consciousness and as such they represent three distinct mirrors in which we see ourselves. Pursuing this metaphor, he argues that when the images reflected by these three disciplines are somehow incommensurate with one another, we are tempted to conclude that each reflects a distinct realm. There is, however, an alternative conclusion: that the human relations they reflect are somehow out of kilter or 'abnormal'.[3] Where our relations to each other and to

---

2 Nietzsche (1913) held that the affirmation of the coincidence of the beautiful with the true and the good amounted to an act of bad faith: 'It is absolutely unworthy of a philosopher to say that "the good and the beautiful are one"; if he should add "and also the true", he deserves to be thrashed. Truth is ugly. Art is with us in order that we may not perish through truth' (p. 265, § 822).

3 Ilyenkov 1984a, p. 312.

nature are harmonious, Ilyenkov maintains, the images cast by science, art, and morality coincide, and truth, beauty, and goodness are seen to be one. 'Hence', he writes, 'the harmonious unity of truth, goodness, and beauty is a criterion of the maturity of genuine human relations'.[4]

In light of this, Ilyenkov argues, it is urgent that we define a criterion to determine what is real or proper (*podlinnoe*) art. We must not avoid this issue, in the style of Pontius Pilate, by feigning a commitment to relativism, aesthetic or epistemological. No such views carry conviction. They are just an excuse to remain silent on the hard questions, and silence, Ilyenkov tells us, 'is a nightmarish thing'.[5] Despite these bold words, Ilyenkov fails to make explicit what he takes the true criterion to be. He answers the question largely in the negative. Real art, he asserts, cannot be in the service of evil:

> Genuine art cannot be immoral by its very nature and, by the same token, immoral art is always false art – not art but a talentless surrogate, formally adroit perhaps, but an essentially contentless falsification of aesthetic values.[6]

Nor can real art further the aims of pseudo-science. Genuine art cannot perpetuate images of beauty that in some or other way reinforce the bogus conceptions of 'pseudo' or 'half-scientific' theories 'empty of humanistic values'.[7]

Ilyenkov's view seems to be that genuine art is distinguished by the contribution it makes to human flourishing, to the furtherance of free and fulfilled humanity. There is a suggestion that he thought that the same criterion can be applied to genuine science or morality. The measure of these forms of self-consciousness is their contribution to the self-realisation of humanity.

2   Vienna, 1964: Through the Looking Glass

In case this humanism appear too abstract, Ilyenkov illustrates his position with a story. He describes visiting an exhibition of pop art in Vienna in 1964, when he was part of a Soviet delegation to a philosophy congress. Ilyenkov tells how, because he was already acquainted with pop art though reproductions, he entered the exhibition in suitably ironic mood. However, 'after ten minutes

---

4   Ilyenkov 1984a, p. 311.
5   Ilyenkov 1984a, p. 309.
6   Ilyenkov 1984a, p. 311.
7   Ilyenkov 1984a, p. 313.

my ironic-sarcastic apperception – being "a priori", though certainly not "transcendental" – had been completely swept away and destroyed by the avalanche of direct perceptions pounding my senses'.[8] In its place, Ilyenkov found himself overcome with a mixture of disgust, dismay and abhorrence.

Ilyenkov discusses some works that provoked this reaction and, though he cannot bring himself to mention the artists by name, it is clear that the exhibition contained works by Warhol, Rauschenberg, and possibly a number of earlier pieces deemed precursors of pop art, such as Duchamp's *Fountain*. Ilyenkov discusses his soul-searching efforts to explain to himself his antipathy. He considers the view that pop art expresses not frivolity but agony; that it embodies the death, or perhaps the suicide, of art. (He puts this view into the mouth of the director of the museum trying to placate the bemused Soviet delegation.) Ilyenkov rejects the idea that his reaction is really one of grief and counters the death-of-art thesis with an alternative interpretation: Pop art is a mirror which shows us an image of people in an alienated world. It displays

> what human beings are turned into by this mindless, upside-down and inside-out world. A world of things, mechanisms, instruments, a standardised, formulaic world of dead schemata, a world made by human beings but flying beyond the control of their conscious wills. An incomprehensible and uncontrollable world of things made by man in his own image. A world where dead labour has become a despot ruling over the labour of the living.[9]

Thus Ilyenkov explains his gut reaction to pop art: It is depressing because it is a true reflection of a distorted world and, because it cannot see itself for what it is, it simply serves to affirm and perpetuate that mindless world.

3   Ilyenkov in the Mirror of Pop Art

Ilyenkov's dismissal of pop art is undeniably rather crude. Indeed, such is his exasperation that one wonders whether he simply lacked the cultural resources to form a nuanced understanding of the art he derides. For example, there is a moment of pathos in the article when Ilyenkov describes his horror at confronting a canvas consisting of numerous reproductions of the Mona Lisa.[10] Ilyenkov

---

8   Ilyenkov 1984a, p. 314.
9   Ilyenkov 1984a, p. 320.
10   Probably Warhol's *Thirty are Better than One* (1964).

expresses outrage at this act of defamation and laments that if he were now ever to see the real Mona Lisa, his experience would be ruined by the memory of this parody in which all the enigmatic individuality of the original is lost through the repetition of the image.

How sad, one feels, that during Ilyenkov's precious trip to the West, Vienna should have been staging an exhibition of Warhol rather than da Vinci. But the real pathos is that had Ilyenkov's conference taken him to Paris rather than to Vienna, his sighting of the Mona Lisa in the Louvre would no doubt have been as disappointing as Warhol's pastiche. For, of course, the relatively small canvas hangs under glass and must be viewed at some distance, as one must fight with the hordes of visitors, mainly tourists 'doing' the Louvre. The canvas cannot be studied; it must rather be glimpsed, and one's glimpses serve merely to remind one of the hackneyed image known so well from reproductions. This is what the mystique of the Mona Lisa has become, and this is surely part of Warhol's target, but the point was lost on Ilyenkov.

It may nevertheless be argued that Ilyenkov's unease with pop art is ultimately defensible. After all, pop art existed in an air of permanent paradox. Although at its beginning the movement was undoubtedly subversive – exposing the vacuity of mass imagery and fleeting images of television and advertising, and parodying consumerism and celebrity – it so reveled in what it exposed that it only served to affirm the culture it pastiched. Nor can pop be redeemed by casting it as intellectual, rather than sociopolitical art, designed to pose the great question, 'What is art?' Although it certainly posed this question, it has absolutely nothing meaningful to say in response to it.[11] The result

---

11   Those familiar with Arthur Danto's writings, particularly his exceptional book, *The Trans-figuration of the Commonplace* (1981), may complain that my treatment of this issue is too cursory. For Danto, the significance of pop art – especially pieces like Warhol's *Brillo Boxes* – is precisely that it brings to consciousness the vexed philosophical question, 'What makes some object a work of art?' At the opening of *Transfiguration*, Danto envisages an exhibition of several works that are physically indistinguishable: They are all identical red rectangles, though they have been produced by different artists for different reasons, given different titles, and so on. The status of these objects as works of art is not determined by their physical constitution, a point literally embodied by Warhol's brillo boxes and soup cans. The general philosophical question Danto takes pop to pose so vividly is a version of Ilyenkov's problem of the ideal; that is, in virtue of what can a material object (or configuration of such objects) be a vehicle for ideal (in this case, aesthetic) properties? Thus, if Danto's reading is right, it seems that Ilyenkov showed a striking lack of imagination when he failed to see the point of pop art. However, it may not be that Ilyenkov failed to perceive the philosophical dimensions of pop so much as that he thought them trite. All works of art, not just mundane objects posing as art, stand before us as instances of the ideal. Moreover, the problem of the ideal is quite general in kind, having no special locus

of this supremely knowing but ultimately inarticulate reflexivity was that art
was reduced to consumption. An object is art insofar as it is something collect-
ors will buy, a position that Warhol happily embraced. With this, the apparently
democratic elements of pop became eclipsed, for not anyone can turn junk into
art: Only celebrated artists have the Midas touch. Hence pop's cult of celebrity
and Warhol's corresponding vision of equality: 15 minutes of fame for everyone.

It would thus not be difficult to gloss over the infelicities of Ilyenkov's argument and grant him at least that the phenomenon of pop art reflects something
about the confusions of Western culture in the 1960s.[12] I think, however, that
there are two reasons why such a reading would be unduly sympathetic to Ilyenkov.

First, Ilyenkov's scorn was not directed at pop art alone; rather, he saw pop
as the inevitable culmination of the whole modernist tradition, which 'from
beginning to end, from cubism to pop' represents 'a form of aesthetic adaptation of human beings to the conditions of an "alienated world".[13] Although it is
at least possible to present pop art as a reflection of the bankruptcy of capitalist culture, it is hardly plausible to portray, say, cubism in such a light. Ilyenkov
comes across as an unimaginative socialist realist. Moreover, Ilyenkov's realism
seems to be more than a moral injunction that progressive art should further
the revolution. It appears to rest on the idea that the function of all art is ultimately to reflect or represent reality: to show what is, what may be, what should
be. Thus he tolerated modernist art only where it is plausible to see the artist as
striving to represent reality. Ilyenkov seemed to approve, therefore, of Picasso's
Guernica, which he could portray as a depiction of the horror of the bombing of
the Basque town, but a cubist still-life made no sense to him.[14] Cubist art could
only be a mirror of a twisted reality. It seemed not to have occurred to him that
representation may not be the only legitimate purpose of art. As he saw it, if art
does not reflect reality then its purpose can only be to amuse or entertain, and
the latter role is far too frivolous to be the essence of art.

Second, although the idea that the measure of art is its contribution to
human flourishing is a defensible, if contentious, position, it invites abuse in

---

in the aesthetic. We must remember that although Warhol's work, conceived as a philosophical gesture, had a point in Danto's milieu, where problems of the ideal were much
neglected, such issues have always been absolutely central the Hegelian tradition of which
Ilyenkov is part. Ilyenkov did not need Warhol to remind him of them.

12   Cf. Marcuse 1978.

13   Ilyenkov 1984a, p. 323. Ilyenkov expressed his hostility to modernism in other writings; see
for example, Ilyenkov 1984e, where surrealism is the target, and Ilyenkov 1984b, pp. 329–
30.

14   See Ilyenkov 1984e, pp. 272–3.

familiar ways. Combined with a dogmatic conception of where our flourishing lies and a teleological conception of history, such a position, for all its humanistic ideals, can be invoked to license the criticism of art on political grounds, a distinction between progressive and reactionary art, and so on – in short, well-known techniques of Soviet criticism. Ilyenkov made no attempt to acknowledge how arbitrary such criticism can be and how much damage it can do to an intellectual culture. One wonders what he made of those Russian avant-garde artists who saw their work as an expression of the ethos of revolution and a contribution to the new order, before they were swept aside in the Stalinist cultural revolution.

Finally, Ilyenkov's position seems equally to license the critique of scientific theories on political grounds. To maintain that science without humanistic ends is pseudo-science is to suggest that it is legitimate to dismiss a scientific theory because it fails to serve humanity. In 'Chto tam, v Zazerkal'e', Ilyenkov seems to criticise his bête noire, cybernetics, on just these grounds. However, this is to deny that science should be governed by the regulative ideal of truth, unless of course Ilyenkov was prepared to identify true conceptions of the world with those that promote human well-being. This appears to put him perilously close to endorsing a conception of proletarian science.

Ilyenkov's humanism appears to contain a sinister element that affirms the very Stalinist orthodoxy that he is so often represented as opposing.

4   A Second Look

The examination of Ilyenkov's views on art has led toward some uncomfortable conclusions, yet the idea that Ilyenkov was a one-dimensional socialist realist does not ring true. Ilyenkov's writings on art contain none of the Russian chauvinism that marks so much Soviet socialist realist criticism. And his devotion to the integrity of philosophical inquiry, evident in much of his other writing, is hard to combine with the idea of the criticism of scientific theories on class grounds. I will thus consider some of Ilyenkov's other writings on aesthetics in search of a richer understanding of his position.

In 1960, at the height of his creative powers, Ilyenkov wrote a short paper, 'O "spetsifike" iskusstva' ('On the "Specifics" of Art'), and he followed this in 1964 with the lengthy 'Ob esteticheskoi prirode fantazii' ('On the Aesthetic Nature of the Imagination'). These writings cast Ilyenkov's philosophy of art in a rather different light. They too advance a radical humanism, but insofar as they accord art a 'purpose', it is simply to 'develop the productive forces of humanity', where the latter are understood 'in the broadest possible sense' as the 'capacity creatively to transform nature'.[15] Moreover, the contribution of art is not principally to provide appropriate representations of reality but to cultivate in us a form of aesthetic sensibility that enables certain higher forms of perception. In harmony with the cultural-historical psychology of Vygotsky and his followers, Ilyenkov argues that whereas the fundamental forms of human perception emerge spontaneously as the child assimilates the basic patterns of life-activity of the community, the higher forms must be actively developed. The history of art, Ilyenkov maintains, is a key resource in this process. Art teaches us to see things differently.

Ilyenkov argues that aesthetic sensibility, as he understands it, essentially involves the exercise of creative imagination. By imagination, he means not just the capacity to envisage what is not, but the ability to see particular facts in a way that simultaneously captures their uniqueness and reveals how certain general schema are applicable to them. As Ilyenkov puts it, imagination enables us to see the 'universal individuality' of the facts. This is illustrated by the kind of creative recasting of an object in certain acts of discovery. Suddenly, a way of solving a hitherto intractable problem emerges by, as it were, reorganising the facts. The facts acquire a new 'shape' – a new profile – in which what was formally salient has receded, throwing new features into relief. In like manner, imagination is also at work when we grasp how various features, hitherto perceived as distinct and isolated, in fact constitute parts of an organised whole. Imagination enables us to see significance in things, significance we grasp in an act of perceptual apprehension rather than through ratiocination. The history of art, Ilyenkov asserts, is a treasure trove of examples of the creative exercise of imagination so conceived, and it presents for us a gallery of problems we may solve only through the acquisition of imagination.

It is important that, for Ilyenkov, aesthetic sensibility is a capacity that has application in all dimensions of cognition, and not just in the appreciation of art: 'Art develops a universal sensibility, by means of which human beings enter into active contact (*deistvennyi kontakt*) not only with each other but also with nature'.[16]

Ilyenkov repeatedly stresses that the exercise of imagination is as crucial for scientific and philosophical cognition as it is for art. In this, he explicitly departs from Hegel's vision of art (which he admired), according to which art, though it represents an essential stage in the path of spirit to self-understanding, is superseded by philosophy. In contrast, Ilyenkov argues that art and science (which,

---

15   Ilyenkov 1984d, p. 217.
16   Ilyenkov 1984d, p. 215.

for Ilyenkov, includes philosophy) are necessary partners. Science cannot live without art, as it demands the cultivation of imagination; art cannot despise science insofar as its object is the very world that science discloses to us.[17]

Ilyenkov insists on the universality of aesthetic sensibility in part to defend art against positivistic attacks inspired by the scientific-technological revolution of the 1960s, attacks that celebrated the objectivity of natural science and relegated art to a vehicle for the expression of emotion and attitude. There is, however, a further, deeper reason for Ilyenkov's insistence, one that we anticipated in the last chapter. At the root of his Marxism lay a disdain for the division of labour, where human beings are able to reproduce their existence only by the partial or one-sided development of their capacities. Ilyenkov was not just concerned about the specific effects of the division of labour under industrial capitalism. Rather, he attacked any form of specialisation that forces us to cultivate some capacities at the expense of others and urged the creation of conditions that facilitate the individual's 'all-round' development.[18]

It is important to understand Ilyenkov's talk of all-round development properly. It is not, for example, intended to evoke a utopia in which everyone is somehow capable of anything. The hallmark of distinctively human activity is that it is informed by reason, and the hallmark of reason is universality. Ilyenkov sometimes explains this by saying that human beings have the power to adapt their activity in light of novel and peculiar circumstances, and he loves to invoke Spinoza's example of how the human hand is not antecedently determined by its structure to manipulate objects of any particular shape but is able to

---

17   Ilyenkov 1984b.

18   As I stressed in the previous chapter, it is important to appreciate the significance of the individual in Ilyenkov's philosophy. The collectivist elements in his thought – this emphasis on society, culture, tradition, history, and so on – figure in an exploration of the preconditions of the development, and flourishing, of individual human beings. This is a significant aspect of his reaction to Stalinist collectivism. I think Ilyenkov would have endorsed (most of) the following passage from Marcuse, an essay that bears interesting comparison with Ilyenkov's aesthetic writing, and also his educational philosophy and its recognition of the value of autonomy. Marcuse (1978, pp. 38–9) wrote: 'To be sure, the concept of the individual as developing freely in solidarity with others can become a reality only in a socialist society. But the fascist period and monopoly capitalism have decisively changed the political value of these concepts. The "flight into inwardness" and the insistence on a private sphere may well serve as bulwarks against a society which administers all dimensions of human existence. Inwardness and subjectivity may well become the inner and outer space for the subversion of experience, for the emergence of another universe. Today, the rejection of the individual as a "bourgeois" concept recalls and presages fascist undertakings. Solidarity and community do not mean the absorption of the individual. They rather originate in autonomous individual decision; they unite freely associated individuals, not masses'.

adapt its form to accommodate the object before it.[19] The activity of a rational animal is not simply called forth by the interplay of its internal structure and causal forces impinging upon it. Rather, rational animals conform their activity to the objective requirements of the circumstances in which they find themselves. Their activity is guided by reasons rather than produced by causes. The key thought is that our activity is rational – and thus evinces our humanity – to the degree that it is not (or not merely) causally determined but an expression of the recognition of objective reasons. Rationality demands that our psychological powers are supremely plastic, able to accommodate the form of any circumstance reality presents us with.

Ilyenkov sees the division of labour as a hindrance to this plasticity, and for this reason he resists views that drive a wedge between scientific cognition and aesthetic appreciation and privilege science over art. It is not that he aspires somehow to incorporate the scientific and the aesthetic into a single mode of cognition. Rather, he endorses what we may call the unity of the cognitive virtues: No particular cognitive capacity can be properly attuned to reality unless it is part of a whole in which all the other psychological capacities are equally so attuned.

Ilyenkov's vision of rational action is intimately connected with his conception of freedom. Freedom is manifest in human actions that are guided by reasons – that issue from an appreciation of what ought to be – and a being is free to the degree to which it possesses the capacity to act in appropriate recognition of reasons as they present themselves. Thus, Ilyenkov endorses the famous adage of German classical philosophy that freedom involves the recognition of necessity. This does not mean, of course, that we are free to the extent that we knowingly acquiesce before causal forces but that free acts are those that are dictated by rational necessity, by an appreciation of objective reasons. Individuals manifest freedom insofar as they chart an appropriate course through the world of reasons, a course for the most part dictated by the geography of that world. On this view, free acts are contrasted with behaviour that is the outcome of causal forces beyond our control, but they are also contrasted with acts that are merely arbitrary (*proizvol'no*) expressions of the will and hence cannot be explained as issuing from an appreciation of objective reasons. The existentialist idea that a truly free choice is one unencumbered by constraint rests on a mistake: Free acts must chart a course between the Scylla of causal determination and the Charybdis of arbitrary volition.[20]

---

19   Ilyenkov 1974a, pp. 33–5 (2009b, pp. 25–6).

20   For further discussion of the idea of freedom, see Chapters 10 and 18 below. The idea that

I have made a brief tour of certain important ideas that figure in Ilyenkov's writings on the philosophy of art in the early 1960s (and which, it goes without saying, have their origins in the German tradition): his notion that art serves to cultivate certain higher forms of perception and the attendant concepts of aesthetic sensibility and the creative imagination; the idea of the unity of the cognitive virtues; his hostility to the division of labour; and his ideal of essentially human activity, rational and free. Ilyenkov saw the activity of the artist, engaged in the production of real art as a paradigm of free, creative activity. With these ideas in place, Ilyenkov's hostility to modern art is more understandable.

Modernism represents a rupture, a self-conscious breaking of tradition, a search for a new conception of the role of art, which was often cast in terms of an explicit opposition to everything that had gone before. The negativity of modernism, provoked of course by the emergence of technologies that threatened to make representational art obsolete, affronted Ilyenkov's vision of the history of art as a coherent, ever-expanding and developing repository of resources for the education of the senses. Much modern art (though not all) scorns such a conception and embodies that scorn in its works.

Ilyenkov looks to art above all to cultivate the development of creative imagination. In much modern art, however, Ilyenkov only sees imagination in league with arbitrariness. Where art celebrates the unconstrained and the nonsensical, or where it is simply an expression of the arbitrary will of the artist, we see the free play of the imagination, but not imagination in the service of freedom, which is always constrained by reason. These works cannot be represented as expressions of the genuine exercise of creative imagination but merely as objectifications of arbitrary will. They do not, therefore, cultivate the imagination as a cognitive resource. Moreover, Ilyenkov takes the irrationalism of modernism to affirm the division of labour by dramatically opposing art to genuine cognitive inquiry. Thus he sees modernism as a natural partner of early twentieth-century positivism, with its strict opposition between the

---

human beings are rational animals is now often disparaged for neglecting the emotional, appetitive side of our natures and encouraging the myth of the disengaged and dispassionate cognising subject. It would be a mistake, however, to object to my reconstruction of Ilyenkov's position on such grounds. To say that someone is rational in the sense I use it here is simply to say that he or she is responsive to genuine reasons for belief and action. No stark contrast is intended between reason and feeling, emotion, passion, and so on. On the contrary, some reasons may only be perceptible to agents with appropriate emotions, feelings, and concerns (this is, I believe, an aspect of the idea of the unity of the cognitive virtues I attribute to Ilyenkov). By the same token, rationality is not to be understood simply in terms of a fidelity to certain logical or formal modes of reasoning.

factual and the normative, belief and desire, description and expression. To embrace these dichotomies is to relegate aesthetic sensibility and thereby to advance an impoverished conception of cognition.

My purpose is not to defend Ilyenkov's position. He was, I believe, wrong to suppose that modern art (if we can talk as if modern art were a single phenomenon) does not cultivate the exercise of creative imagination, as he understood it. Good modern art certainly encourages new ways of seeing; indeed, it shows how much more there is to see than can be captured by traditional representation. Nevertheless, once cast in its proper context, Ilyenkov's position is certainly defensible and far from a crude, unreflective reduction of the aesthetic to the political. This conclusion does not, however, excuse the way Ilyenkov made his case in '*Chto tam, v Zazerkal'e?*' which, though often amusing, obscures the philosophical content of Ilyenkov's aesthetics and invites a plethora of misunderstandings.

5   Art and the Affirmation of Life

This discussion has helped draw out some themes that lie deep within Ilyenkov's humanism. I conclude by exploring them further.

Ilyenkov's notion of free, creative activity lies at the heart of his concept of genuinely human relations among human beings and between humans and nature. Our relation to nature is not merely to a local environment that impinges upon us and causes us to act in various ways; rather, we see ourselves as inhabitants of a world, which our concepts disclose to us and in which we find significance.[21] We see this world at once as infinite in its ever-receding horizons and as the setting, the home, of our life-activity. To relate to another person in a genuinely human way is to recognise that person as a source of rational subjectivity like oneself, to see him or her as the subject of a life charted though the world. In relating to another, an individual's activity expresses rationality in responding to the expression of rationality manifest in the activity of the other. Intersubjectivity is premised upon such reciprocal attunement to the meaning in each other's movement.

I suggest that, for Ilyenkov, free creative activity is a kind of life principle. Such activity represents life in its fullest expression. His famous response to the problem of the ideal can be seen as an attempt to explain the origin of this prin-

---

21   My way of putting this is inspired by Gadamer (1999), as developed in McDowell 1994, Lecture VI.

ciple, one that explores how free, creative activity develops through a kind of bootstrapping. As a result of collective human action, significance is objectified in the natural world making possible a normative relation to nature in which agents respond to their surroundings in light of their meaning, molding their activity to ideal rather than merely physical forms. A world of reasons is created that calls forth rational activity that issues in the objectification of further modes of significance, facilitating further activity, and so on. Crucially, Ilyenkov saw this process as the enlivening of the brute physical environment, the breathing of life into dead nature. Human beings express their rational powers insofar as they assimilate the capacity to inhabit the world so animated by the life-activity of humanity.

This humanistic vision informs all of Ilyenkov's thought, including his thinking about art. It is present explicitly in 'Ob esteticheskoi prirode fantasii', where he advances the anthropocentric (indeed, anthropomorphic) view that in cognition we are always in touch primarily with nature humanised by activity and then invokes this idea to argue that judgments of beauty, even natural beauty, are always derived from our conceptions of the fittingness of artefacts to human purposes and ends.[22] However, the key idea is the notion that free creative activity is the highest expression of life, and such activity is possible only in a world laden with significance through the objectification of human agency, the process that, as it were, gives life to reason. Throughout Ilyenkov's writings, this concept of life is contrasted with mechanism, with the workings of dead physicality, with the production of behaviour through the causal efficacy of structures blindly interacting in accord with physical law. For Ilyenkov, the mechanical, the standardised, the formulaic represents death in contrast to the life-affirming character of free, creative activity. He rails against the social circumstances that make human beings behave like machines and against those theories that portray human behaviour in mechanistic terms. Hence his horror of cybernetics, with its celebration of the machine, and of all forms of reductive, deterministic materialism.[23]

The metaphors of the living and the dead are found throughout Ilyenkov's writings, and his humanistic affirmation of life against forces of mortification may be deemed the overarching theme of his philosophy. This certainly helps clarify Ilyenkov's celebration of what he called genuine art, an expression of our rational power to animate nature through free, creative activity, as well as his antipathy to pop, with its celebration of mass production and mechanical

22   See Ilyenkov 1984e, pp. 257–75.
23   See Maidansky 2023.

reproduction. 'I want to be a machine', Warhol declared.[24] This, for Ilyenkov, could only mean the suicide of the artist. To attack the whole of modernism on these grounds must be misguided, though we can see now why Ilyenkov, with his historicist conception of art, was appalled at the idea that the history of art might culminate in this. For Ilyenkov, pop represented not so much the death of art as the art of death.

6   Conclusion

In this chapter, I have tried to take a fresh look at prominent themes in Ily-enkov's philosophy by approaching them from the perspective of his writings on aesthetics. My argument has, I hope, cast new light on the humanism that informs his whole work. I conclude by reflecting briefly on what is living and what is dead in Ilyenkov's humanistic vision.

The concept of activity, as it figures in Ilyenkov's writing on the ideal, is usually taken to be the most significant part of his legacy. Its importance lies in particular insights that it forces upon psychology and the philosophy of mind, namely to take account of the extent to which our capacity to transform our environment influences dramatically the scope and limits of human minds. In the grand philosophical scheme – as a kind of derivation of the very possibility of the relation of subject and object – the position confronts epistemological problems of the kind that dogged Kant about our knowledge of things in themselves and of the kind that haunted Hegel about bootstrapping explanations. Moreover, Ilyenkov's secular historicism, within which philosophical anthropology tells the story of the self-creation of humanity, is arguably too anthropocentric; it accords human beings too great a place in the order of things, a sentiment that invites ethical as well as metaphysical objections.

For all that, however, I believe that Ilyenkov's essentially Kantian conception of free creative activity as responsiveness to rational necessity is very powerful. The claim that our humanity is expressed in the manner in which we navigate the world of reasons and in the way in which we respond to others as bearers of rational subjectivity is an insight of deep significance. It is an idea that has regained some currency in Western thought, notably in McDowell's work, and I believe there is potential for Ilyenkovian ideas to prosper in a fruitful dialogue.

Ilyenkov's affirmation of reason, freedom, and life gives his philosophy an optimistic and inspiring character, yet it is also haunted by darker themes, one

---

24   Cited in Hughes 1980, p. 348.

of which is the morbid image of humanity overtaken by mechanistic forces. Sometimes I wonder whether Ilyenkov, as he grew older, feared that his own imagination was becoming ever less creative, that his writing was becoming formulaic, and that the intellectual life force so evident in his very early writings was weakening. I wonder whether his way of responding was to become more aggressive and dogmatic while trying to mask his failure of imagination with a kind of desperate wit. Perhaps writings like '*Chto tam, v Zazerkal'e?*' were the result. Ilyenkov must have known that his strategy could only fail, and perhaps it was the recognition of that failure that was among the causes of his suicide in 1979. Now, more than 40 years after his death, we must work towards a balanced appreciation of his legacy, one that is cognisant of his failings as well as his strengths, and that does not shy from the humanity, and tragedy, of Ilyenkov's life and work.

∙∙
∙

The next chapter examines Hegel's place in Ilyenkov's philosophy and reflects further on the circumstances in which he found himself towards the end of his life. Hegel's ideas had a huge impact on Ilyenkov's conception of the nature of philosophy and of the philosopher's mission, and they formed the core of his distinctive account of thought and its place in nature. At the same time, Ilyenkov was victimised for his 'Hegelianism' throughout his career, from the time he was sacked from MGU in 1955 to the ideological criticisms that preceded his death in 1979. After considering Hegel's influence on the history of Russian thought, the chapter focuses on Hegelian themes in Ilyenkov's 1974 book, *Dialectical Logic* and evaluates their philosophical significance. Finally, parallels are explored between Ilyenkov's situation at the end of his life and the plight of Nikolai Bukharin, incarcerated in the Lubyanka prison in 1936 and at work on *Philosophical Arabesques*. Both thinkers confronted the contradiction between their confidence in the rationality of history and the tragic absurdity of Soviet reality, and both responded by affirming their fidelity to Lenin and his vision of Marxism. In this way, they sought to make sense of their respective situations in the face of extreme adversity. That they so much as thought it worth trying owed much to Hegel's influence.

Ilyenkov's Hegel

1. This chapter examines Hegel's place in Ilyenkov's thought. As I have affirmed in previous chapters, Ilyenkov was a significant figure in the rejuvenation of Soviet philosophical culture after Stalin. In the 1950s, he was one of a number of young scholars who produced compelling research focused on Marx's method. Ilyenkov defended his Candidate's dissertation, *Nekotorye voprosy materialisticheskoi dialektiki v rabote K. Marksa 'K kritike politicheskoi ekonomii'* at Moscow State University (MGU) in September 1953. Alexander Zinoviev, also at MGU, defended on a similar topic the following year. Ilyenkov and Zinoviev had a dramatic influence on the intellectual climate of Soviet philosophy in the mid-1950s. Both taught seminars at Moscow State University, and what they taught and how they taught it, stood in stark opposition to the ossified dogma that Marxist philosophy had become under Stalin. In the words of Vladislav Lektorsky, himself at that time a final year undergraduate in Ilyenkov's seminar, 'it was as if a new world had been discovered'.[1]

The inhabitants of the old world, however, were none too impressed, and before long Ilyenkov was in trouble. As we saw in Chapter 5, in 1954, he and another junior faculty member at MGU, Valentin Ivanovich Korovikov, were asked to stage a discussion in their unit (*Kafedra istorii zarubezhnoi filosofii*) on the nature of philosophy. To this end, they wrote the infamous theses on philosophy, arguing principally that the subject matter of philosophy is *thought*. The Ilyenkov-Korovikov theses immediately sparked controversy. They were taken to be at odds with the then-orthodox view that philosophy's province was the universal laws of being (encompassing nature, society, and thought), to privilege epistemology over ontology, thereby undermining Lenin's 'theory of reflection', and to dismiss historical materialism as a non-subject. Ilyenkov and Korovikov were subjected to severe criticism, and in the Spring of 1955, they were sacked from MGU for (among other things) 'Hegelianism'.[2] Korovikov left the profession and became a journalist. Fortunately, Ilyenkov managed to retain his principal position, which was at Moscow's Institute of Philosophy, a post held for the rest of his life.

Even in the more liberal climate of the post-Stalin thaw and with the support of such senior philosophers as B.M. Kedrov and M.M. Rozental', Ilyenkov con-

---

1 Lektorsky 2012, p. 328.
2 Novokhat'ko 1997, p. 5.

tinued to have difficulties. The next storm came in 1958 when it became known that, the previous year, he had given the manuscript of his first book, then in preparation for publication in Russia, to an agent for an Italian publisher in the hope that it might also appear in Italian translation. Unbeknownst to Ilyenkov, the publishing house, *Feltrinelli Editore*, was about to publish Pasternak's *Doctor Zhivago*. Ilyenkov was subjected to severe criticism and narrowly escaped expulsion from the Party. The publication of his book was delayed until 1960.[3] More controversy (though less dramatic) erupted over his 1962 article *Ideal'noe*, which appeared in the second volume of the landmark five-volume *Filosofskaya entsiklopediya*. Ilyenkov's defence of the objectivity of ideal phenomena – and his corresponding denial that the realm of thought can be reduced to brain functioning – was met with astonishment. As with his work on Marx's method, its effect was to infuriate the orthodox while inspiring the younger generation, and the more it did the latter, the more it did the former.[4]

There is no doubting Ilyenkov's influence. Many of the more inventive figures in late Soviet philosophy were either his students or they formed their views in dialogue with, or opposition to, his. As V.S. Bibler put it, 'We all came out from under Ilyenkov's overcoat'.[5] Ilyenkov's career continued much as it had begun. Though his achievements were recognised by his supporters and admirers – he received the Chernyshevsky prize in 1965, saw his books translated by Progress and his articles published in *Voprosy filosofii* and *Kommunist* – he continued to be a target of ideological accusations. As Korovikov attests, Ilyenkov's work could be decorated by the Academy one moment and denounced as a distortion of Marxism the next. The accusations reached a peak in the mid-1970s, by which time Ilyenkov was thoroughly worn down.[6] Ten years after his untimely death in 1979, Korovikov wrote: 'Pogroms big and small cost Evald Vasilievich a lot of strength, time, creative energy, driving him to distraction. He would have done significantly more for our spiritual life and philosoph-

---

3   Arguably it was only published then to avoid the embarrassment of it appearing in an Italian edition alone (the Italian text was indeed published in 1961). The 1960 Russian text was abbreviated and restructured to make it more acceptable to officialdom. An English translation was published by Progress in 1982. A more complete version of the manuscript did not appear until 1997 (Ilyenkov 1960, 1961, 1982a, 1997). Materials on 'the Ilyenkov affair' can be found in Ilyenkov 2017. Lektorsky (2012) and Novokhat'ko (1991) describe the circumstances of the 1960 publication.

4   Lektorsky 2012, pp. 284–5.

5   Lektorsky (2012) cites this remark but does not attribute it. In a personal communication, he revealed it was Bibler who said it.

6   See Oizerman 2009, pp. 36–8.

ical thought, were it not for constant oppression from the vigilant defenders of ideology'.[7]

Korovikov is not alone in this assessment. A similar picture is painted by Mikhailov, Mareev, Novokhat'ko, and myself.[8] But not everyone sees things the same way. Boris Kagarlitsky, for example, reports that 'in the sixties, and even more in the seventies, some quickening of dialectical philosophical thought was observable in our country', and he recognises Ilyenkov's centrality in this. However, he continues: 'Later, in the view of many philosophers, E. Ilyenkov failed to follow up his own conclusions but tried instead to reconcile his dialectics with the official schemas, mitigating its critical sense of the negation of reality'.[9] To put it starkly, Kagarlitsky, or at least his sources, counter the interpretation of Ilyenkov as a creative force downtrodden and martyred by relentless ideological oppression, with the image of him as someone who did not stand up to officialdom for long, and who fundamentally compromised his independence of mind.[10] Which is it?

I want to suggest that to understand Ilyenkov's contribution, and to arrive at a balanced evaluation of his legacy, it helps to reflect on his relation to Hegel. Many of the most interesting thoughts in Ilyenkov's writings are Hegelian in inspiration, and it is precisely those ideas that provoked his critics to attack him and that helped cost him and Korovikov their jobs at MGU. Moreover, Hegel informs not only Ilyenkov's conception of philosophy, but his understanding of the role and mission of a philosopher, and this sheds light on the way Ilyenkov saw himself and his situation at the end of his life.

2. It might seem strange that a person's integrity might be measured, by others or by himself, by his reading of Hegel. But ever since the Russian intelligentsia took an interest in Hegel in the 1830s and '40s, the interpretation of Hegel's ideas was charged with a kind of moral significance, as if it were a mirror in which a person's true colours showed themselves. Herzen famously describes the mood:

> [T]here was not a paragraph in all three parts of the 'Logic', in the two of the 'Aesthetic', in the 'Encyclopedia', etc., which would not have been the subject of desperate disputes for several nights in a row. People who

---

7   Korovikov 1998, p. 478.
8   Mikhailov 1998, Mareev 1994, Novokhat'ko 1991, Bakhurst 1991; 1995a.
9   Kagarlitsky 1989, p. 273.
10   Mikhailov confirms that such criticisms were made of Ilyenkov's character by his contemporaries (see p. 128n60 above).

loved each other parted ways for whole weeks at a time because they disagreed about the definition of 'all-embracing spirit' or had taken as an insult an opinion on the 'absolute personality and its existence in itself'. Every insignificant pamphlet ... in which there was a mere mention of Hegel was ordered and read until it was tattered, smudged, and fell apart in a few days.[11]

Hegel was important, of course, because his Eurocentric philosophy of history graphically posed the problem of whether Russia's destiny lay in its 'Westernisation' or in its fidelity to its own unique character. At first, Hegel's confidence that the rational is actual provided the Westernisers with an argument that enabled reconciliation with the oppressive reality of Russian life under the Tsars: however contrary to reason Russian actuality might seem, in all its Gogolian weirdness, it was part of a process in which rationality and freedom would eventually flourish in the form of the European nation state. Before long, of course, talk of reconciliation gave way to a discourse of revolt, as the Hegelian dialectic was read as an affirmation of the creative power of negation. For the Slavophiles, in contrast, Hegel's preoccupation with freedom and reason stood for a form of rational individualism that ran counter to everything valuable in the Russian soul. Russia, they urged, must reject Hegel's conception of world history and remain a world apart.

Later in the nineteenth century, when Russian radicals turned to Marxism, the interpretation of Hegel once again became a matter of passionate controversy, as the revolutionary intelligentsia agonised over the extent to which Hegelian ideas were integral components of an authentically Marxist stance. The issue exercised Lenin in the years preceding the Revolution, as is evidenced by his *Philosophical Notebooks* of 1914, which contain conspectuses of some of Hegel's works, particularly the *Science of Logic*.[12]

And after the Revolution, in the mid-1920s, Hegel's significance was again contested in the passionate dispute between two schools of Soviet Marxists: the 'dialecticians', led by A.M. Deborin, who argued that a materialist philosophy, invoking dialectical principles derived ultimately from Hegel, was an essential component of a scientific world-view, and the 'mechanists', positivist philosophers who maintained that natural science could look after itself. Not

---

11   Herzen 1956, p. 18, quoted in Silyak 2001, p. 338.

12   Lenin 1960–78, vol. 38. It is a matter of controversy whether, and to what extent, Lenin's studies of Hegel represent a departure from the positions he took in his earlier *Materialism and Empiriocriticism* (1960–78, vol. 14) with its scathing attack on Bogdanov and other Russian followers of Mach and Avenarius.

that the mechanists were hostile to Hegel as such. What they complained about was the codification of dialectics into abstract schema. Liubov Akselrod wrote: 'Dialectical method must be a tool for the cognition of reality, but the dialectic must not intrude upon reality, it must not prescribe to objective reality from its formal laws. Hegel himself, despite his absolute idealism, was incomparably more empirical than the "orthodox" and "militant" materialist Deborin'.[13] 'Thanks to the universality of the laws of dialectics', Akselrod complains, the Deborinites find it 'possible to talk about everything while knowing nothing, to talk in abstract terms, imparting a scholarly appearance to pure contentlessness'.[14]

In 1929, the Mechanists were defeated by the Debornites, who were themselves soon after routed by a group of young party activists, reputedly sponsored by Stalin himself. This new generation called for the 'bolshevisation' of philosophy, and once in power, they oversaw the codification of dialectical materialism into something far more rigid than anything proposed by Deborin. Their conception was expressed with terrifying simplicity in the infamous fourth chapter of the *Short Course* published in 1938.[15]

It might be supposed that there is nothing else to say about the reception of Hegel in this period, and hence that the next chapter begins with Ilyenkov and others trying to renew materialist dialectics in the 1950s and '60s. But we must not overlook Nikolai Bukharin, who in 1937 was incarcerated in the Lubyanka Prison facing certain death, and at work on (among other things) *Philosophical Arabesques*, a treatise on Marxist philosophy, thoughtfully composed and elegantly written. One of Bukharin's primary aims in this book is to come to terms with 'the great treasure trove of thought' that is Hegel's dialectics.[16] There is something wonderful about Bukharin's prison writings, but there is also something bizarre, for how could someone think that his desperate

---

13   Akselrod 1927, p. 148. There is a helpful website devoted to Akselrod's life and work, which includes a number of Russian texts and some in English translation: http://sovlit.org/lia/index.html (last accessed, 18 February 2023).

14   Akselrod 1927, p. 159. Some 30 years later, Marcuse (1958, p. 137) concurred with Akselrod's assessment: 'Soviet Marxism is nowhere more "orthodox" than in its painful elaboration of the dialectical method ... [Dialectic] has been transformed from a mode of critical thought into a universal "world outlook" and universal method with rigidly fixed rules and regulations, and this transformation destroys the dialectic more thoroughly than any revision ... [T]he very essence of dialectics rebels against such codification'. As we have seen, Ilyenkov made similar criticisms of the Soviet philosophical establishment in the 1950s (though not of Deborin) (see Chapter 5 above and Ilyenkov 2017, pp. 25–37).

15   See Bakhurst 1991, pp. 95–9.

16   Bukharin 2005, p. 160.

situation, and the desperate situation of his country, called for this, a vindication of materialist dialectics? After all, writing this book was not something Bukharin did just to pass long hours in confinement. He saw the survival of this treatise as more important than his own, pleading with Stalin, 'Don't let it be lost! ... Have pity! Not on me, on the work!'[17] In his powerful article, 'With Hegel to Salvation: Bukharin's Other Trial', Jochen Hellbeck suggests that we should understand Bukharin as putting himself through a *second* trial: 'an extended process of self-interrogation and an attempt to transform himself as a thinker and revolutionary actor'.[18] Hellbeck argues that Hegel has a lot to do with why Bukharin felt he had to undergo this. First, in his 1922 'Testament', Lenin famously qualified his estimation of Bukharin as 'a most valuable and major theorist of the Party' by describing him as an undialectical thinker.[19] This was not a gratuitous criticism: throughout the 1920s Bukharin was allied with the Mechanists. Fifteen years after Lenin's assessment, Bukharin was trying to show that he now understood the significance of dialectics, thereby affirming his fidelity to Lenin's vision. Second, in undertaking this process, Bukharin's judgement was informed by a vision of history, and of historical agency, that had its source in Hegel. Bukharin could not fail to think in terms of a single world-historical narrative. He could not cease caring about Russia's place, and his own, within that narrative. And he could not stop *trying to make sense*, unifying, ordering, synthesising, rationalising. What he failed to see was that Marx and Engels's famous characterisation of the bourgeois epoch as one where 'all that is solid melts into air and everything sacred is profaned' now applied with appalling irony to the circumstances in which he found himself.[20] Bukharin's confidence in the rationality of history, and of his place in it, derived ultimately from Hegel.

3. Now let us turn to Ilyenkov. As we have seen, the vision advanced in the Ilyenkov-Korovikov theses is that philosophy is the theory of thought (*nauka o myshlenii*). On this view, the primary subject matter of philosophy is logic, not in the narrow sense of symbolic logic, but logic as the study of the nature and possibility of our fundamental forms of thought, of categories and concepts, and of the movement of thought and the norms that govern it. Since this is a

---

17   Quoted in Hellbeck 2009, p. 76 (Hellbeck is himself quoting Stephen Cohen).

18   Hellbeck 2009, p. 78.

19   'Bukharin is not only a most valuable and major theorist of the Party; he is also rightly considered the favourite of the whole Party, but his theoretical views can be classified as fully Marxist only with great reserve, for there is something scholastic about him (he has never made a study of the dialectics, and, I think, never fully understood it)' (Lenin 1960–78, vol. 36, pp. 593–611). The material was first published in *Kommunist* in 1956, No. 9.

20   Marx and Engels 1968, p. 38.

logic of content, not merely form, its account of the evolution of thought forms, and of the nature of reasoning and argument, encompasses questions about the nature of knowledge and scientific method, together with questions about (what philosophers would now call) the sources of normativity. This is the rationale for understanding philosophy as the identity of logic, dialectics, and the theory of knowledge. This identity was famously asserted by Lenin in the *Philosophical Notebooks*,[21] but Ilyenkov's allegiance to it is not mere lip-service to Lenin. Rather, Ilyenkov sees this as a profound consequence of Hegel's legacy, which Lenin understood.

To examine what Ilyenkov makes of this idea, I propose to consider his 1974 book, *Dialekticheskaya logika*.[22] According to Kagarlitsky, or rather his unnamed sources, by the time Ilyenkov wrote *Dialekticheskaya logika*, the rot had already set in: here begins Ilyenkov's reconciliation with Soviet dogma.[23] I do not think this is a fair assessment. The book is an attempt to weave material from a number of Ilyenkov's earlier writings into a coherent story about the emergence of the conception of logic just outlined (it incorporates several previously published works, including the famous 1962 essay on the ideal, and material from Ilyenkov's doctoral dissertation (Ilyenkov 1968a)). In the course of this, we are treated to characteristically deferential statements about the founders of Marxism, but the resulting picture amounts to an affirmation of the conception of philosophy Ilyenkov had expressed with Korovikov twenty years earlier. It is therefore superficial to portray *Dialekticheska logika* as an attempt at reconciliation with the tenets of official Soviet philosophy.

The overarching question that motivates Ilyenkov's inquiries is the problem of thought's relation to its objects: How is it possible for thought to bear on the world? Ilyenkov's concern is to transcend philosophical conceptions that think of the relation between mind and reality as one between 'two worlds', the internal world of thoughts and experiences, on the one hand, and the external world of objects, on the other. Such conceptions are naturally preoccupied with philosophical bridge-building, trying to show how the two worlds are related, metaphysically and epistemically (What is the relation of mind and matter?

---

21   Lenin 1960–78, vol. 38, p. 319.
22   Ilyenkov 1974a (2009b). A second edition with supplementary materials appeared in 1984. An English translation was published by Progress in 1977 and is reprinted in its entirety in Ilyenkov 2009b. In what follows, page references are to the 1974 Russian edition with parenthetical references to the 2009 English text. The identity of logic, dialectics and the theory of knowledge is the subject matter of Chapter 9. An important collection of Ilyenkov's writing on Hegel has recently appeared in English translation (Ilyenkov 2018b).
23   Kagarlitsky writes (1989, p. 273), 'From this standpoint his book *Dialectical Logic* (1974) was already a step back'.

How is knowledge possible?). In my earlier writings, I tended to portray this as a matter of transcending Cartesian oppositions, and while this is not wrong, it fails to acknowledge the pivotal role played by Kant's philosophy in the German tradition that shapes the way Ilyenkov understands his project.

Kant famously argued that our experience of the world is essentially structured by a priori forms of intuition (space and time) and thought (the categories). The world as we experience it issues from the unity of sensibility and understanding, a unity that makes possible objective knowledge of an independently existing world. But Kant's achievement is qualified. It is a consequence of his view that we cannot represent the world as it is out of all relation to experience. Thus, his famous slogan, 'things in themselves are unknowable'. As a result, Kant too finds himself talking of two worlds, this time the 'phenomenal' and the 'noumenal', the world of experience and the world 'in itself', and his philosophy leaves human beings peculiarly bifurcated.[24] We are inhabitants of the phenomenal world, and as such we are natural beings subject to natural law, but freedom and rationality are aspects of the noumenal or 'intelligible' world. As Allen Wood puts it:

> So the same actions that we regard as naturally necessitated in the world of appearance can be regarded as transcendentally free in reference to their noumenal cause. When we think of ourselves as appearances, we are determined, but when we think of ourselves as moral agents, we transport ourselves into the intelligible world, where we are transcendentally free.[25]

In response to this Kantian picture, Ilyenkov draws from Hegel the following insights:

i. We must *historicise* the categories. The fundamental forms of thought are not given a priori, but are realised historically as social consciousness.

ii. The vehicle of social consciousness is not just language, but action: thought is embodied not just in utterances, but in the results of human activity:

> The thought of which Hegel spoke discloses itself in human *affairs* every bit as obviously as in words ... man's *actions*, and so too the results of his actions, the things created by them, not only could, but must, be

---

24 Of course, there are themes in Kant that suggest he is himself trying to overcome this two-worlds picture, as I maintain in the 'Kantian reading' I offer Ilyenkov in Chapter 5 above.

25 Wood 2008, p. 135.

considered *manifestations of his thought*, as acts of the objectifying of his ideas, thoughts, plans, and conscious intentions.[26]

Thought is therefore realised in culture and the humanised environment, in what Marx called the 'inorganic body of man'. This is an anti-psychologistic vision of thought, one where 'the whole immense objective body of civilisation' is portrayed as 'thought in its "otherness"'.[27]

iii.   We must think of the mindedness of individuals, not as given, but as emerging through the appropriation or internalisation of those modes of thought that are embodied in the practices of the community constitutive of social consciousness. Individuals acquire powers of reason – they become persons, rational agents, through *Bildung*.

iv.   We must recognise that all modes of mindedness are penetrated by conceptuality: thought is present in sensation (intuition), imagination, intelligent activity and embodied coping.[28] Moreover, the world is in no way alien to the conceptual: objective reality is thinkable. The world as we think it, as we sensuously perceive it, and as it is, is one and the same world; namely, the real world.[29] That is, as McDowell puts it, there is no gap between mind and world inherent in the very idea of thought.[30] Thought can be at one with the world. This is the sense in which Ilyenkov embraces the idea of the identity of thinking and being and follows Hegel in rejecting the Kantian idea of the thing-in-itself.

v.   We must acknowledge that contradiction is the notion central to understanding the movement of thought. There can be 'objective contradictions' in the sense that circumstances force thought into dilemmas and antinomies that can be resolved only by changing reality.

vi.   Empirical concepts function, or ought to function, not just as means of identifying phenomena of the same kind in virtue of shared characteristics, but as tools for expressing the essence of the phenomenon in question understood in its historical concreteness. A 'concrete universal' expresses the essence of an object understood as a self-developing totality, all the components of which are united by unity of genesis.[31]

---

26   Ilyenkov 1974a, p. 128 (2009b, p. 101).
27   Ilyenkov 1974a, p. 128 (2009b, p. 101).
28   Ilyenkov 1974a, pp. 131–2 (2009b, pp. 104–5).
29   Ilyenkov 1974a, p. 160 (2009b, p. 128).
30   McDowell 1994, p. 27.
31   Ilyenkov 1974a, p. 256 (2009b, p. 204). The final two chapters of *Dialekticheskaya logika* are devoted to contradiction and the universal respectively. There is much more on these

4. Ilyenkov embraces all of this. Moreover, he explicitly rejects as superficial the criticisms that Hegel's philosophy is mystagogical, that it 'logicises' reality or reifies logical forms. On the contrary, the dialectic captures the evolution of the thought forms we bring to bear on reality, by which reality is manifest to us and by which we come to attain self-consciousness as thinking beings aware of our power to embrace the world in thought. The primary problem with Hegel's philosophy, Ilyenkov tells us, is that it portrays thought as a self-determining creative principle and the material world as its expression. It therefore denies itself an account of the origin of thought itself.[32] To correct this aspect of Hegel's philosophy, we need to naturalise Hegel's conception of thinking, so that thought is reconceived as an aspect of the existence of embodied, material beings. Ilyenkov portrays this correction more as a minor adjustment than as a wholesale inversion. He is keen to stress how Hegel, as Lenin tells us in his conspectus of the *Lectures on the History of Philosophy*, comes 'very close to materialism'.[33]

To make the necessary adjustment, Ilyenkov offers his philosophy of the ideal, which is inspired by Marx – not just the Marx of the 1844 Manuscripts, whose influence is obvious, but the mature Marx of *Capital*, whose labour theory of value illustrates an instance of the origin of an ideal form (value) out of material activity (labour). The message of Ilyenkov's discussion of the ideal, by which he means the realm of thought (broadly construed as in (i) and (ii) above) is that the ideal exists objectively in forms of human life-activity. As he puts it, Hegel teaches us that:

> All the spontaneously emerging forms of the organisation of human social (collectively realised) life-activity, forms that exist *prior to, outside, and completely independently* of individual minds, are one way or another materially embodied in language, in ritually-prescribed customs and rights and, further, as 'the organization of the state', with all its material means and agencies for the protection of traditional forms of life. [These forms] stand over against the individual (the physical body of the individual with his brain, liver, heart, hands and other organs) as a whole, organised 'in itself and for itself', as something 'ideal', *within* which all particular things acquire a different significance and play a different role, than they do 'in themselves', that is, outside this whole. Therefore, the

themes in Ilyenkov's works on the dialectics of the abstract and the concrete, discussed in Bakhurst 1991, ch. 5.

32   Ilyenkov 1974a, p. 173 (2009b, p. 137).

33   Ilyenkov 1974a, p. 129 (2009b, p. 102), citing Lenin 1960–78, vol. 38, p. 278.

'ideal' definition of anything, or its definition as a 'disappearing' moment in the movement of the 'ideal world', coincides in Hegel with its role and significance in the body of social-human culture, in the context of socially-organised human life-activity, and not in the consciousness of an individual person, which is here regarded as something produced out of the 'universal spirit'.[34]

To turn this picture into a materialist one, we just need to recognise that the objectification of human activity is the source of the nature and possibility of thought, both at the level of the species and the individual. It is *doing* that is the ultimate source of normativity, and since our freedom resides in our ability to respond to norms, we have to understand that freedom as manifest in the life-activity of embodied material beings or 'thinking bodies' as Ilyenkov liked to say. The adjustment to Hegel's philosophy is anticipated by Goethe's Mephistopheles and his famous correction to scripture: In the beginning was, not the word, *logos*, but the deed – 'Im Anfang war die Tat'.[35] There remains a sense in which each mind is derived from universal spirit, in the sense that each individual becomes a minded being only though initiation into the practices that sustain the ideal realm, but the universal spirit has no reality independently of those practices.

If we make this adjustment correctly, then we can say that logical forms are not expressions of thought thinking itself, but 'universal forms of the development of reality outside thought':[36] 'all the dialectical schemas and categories revealed in thought by Hegel were universal forms and laws, reflected in the collective consciousness of man, of the development of the external real world existing outside of and independently of thought'.[37] This is to say that the realm of thought is the means by which human beings bring the world into view, the means by which the world is disclosed to them, or at least *can* be disclosed if circumstances permit its veridical apprehension. When things go right, thought embraces reality as it is.

---

34   Ilyenkov 2009a, p. 250, my translation; Ilyenkov 2014, p. 51. The passage also appears in Ilyenkov 2009b, pp. 263–4.

35   One interesting (and neglected) essay of Ilyenkov's on the relation of Hegel and Marx is 'Gegel i "otchuzhdenie"' (Hegel and "Alienation"'), published in Ilyenkov 1991b, pp. 141–52. Here Ilyenkov speaks of Marx liberating himself from the notion of the objectification of absolute spirit in favour of a view of the alienation of human practical activity in the form of its products (pp. 147–8).

36   Ilyenkov 1974a, p. 128 (2009b, p. 102).

37   Ilyenkov 1974a, p. 183 (2009b, p. 146).

Though there are places in *Dialekticheskaya logika* where Ilyenkov is more conventionally critical of Hegel, the respect he shows him in the pivotal chapters of that work leaves no doubt about the centrality of Hegel to Ilyenkov's vision.[38] Thus the idea that the work represents the beginnings of a compromise with orthodoxy seems to me to be a profound misreading.

It is worth observing that the recent interest in Hegel within the Anglo-American tradition only serves to bring out the continuing relevance of Ilyenkov's treatment of Hegel. Terry Pinkard, for example, represents the whole post-Kantian tradition in German philosophy as grappling with what he calls the 'Kantian paradox'.[39] This is a paradox about the nature of normativity. For Kant, I am free in so far as I conform my actions to norms that I give myself. Yet if my endorsement is to be rational, it must be grounded in reasons, but then it seems that my conformity is determined by something outside of myself – namely, the cogency of the reasons in question – and hence I am not *self*-determining but *un*free. According to Pinkard (and others), Hegel's solution to the paradox depends upon recognising the sociality of reason. We are free insofar as we conform our actions to norms *we* give *ourselves*: the sources of normativity reside in our mutual recognition of each other as sources of normative authority. This debate is in the same territory as Ilyenkov's discussion of the problem of the ideal, which as we have seen, invokes the notion of collective human activity in response to the question of how the realm of thought – that is, the realm of the normative – is possible. It is a matter of contention whether Ilyenkov would have had sympathy for Pinkard's rendition of the problem, let alone endorsed his account of a Hegelian solution, but there is no doubt that their respective approaches can be brought into dialogue, and that suggests that *Dialekticheskaya logika* not only preserves some of the more creative themes from Ilyenkov's early work, but does so in a way that is of enduring philosophical interest.[40]

5. I have been arguing that Hegel is at the very centre of Ilyenkov's argument in *Dialekticheskaya logika* and that Ilyenkov's reading of Hegel is an attractive one. Hegel's insights are brought to bear to reconcile mind and world, individual and community, reason and nature. The grand philosophy of history that

---

38   Ilyenkov's criticisms of Hegel are restrained. For example, he never goes as far as Bukharin, who, for all his sympathy with Hegel, writes (2005, p. 81) that Hegel replaced 'the world of reality, the material world, by a game of self-motivated ideas' and speaks of 'the panlogistic gibberish of objective idealism elevated to the status of a grandiose universal system'.

39   Pinkard 2002.

40   For further discussion of this theme see Chapters 16 and 18 below.

casts reason as 'substance' and 'infinite power', 'that by which all reality has its being' has no place,[41] but neither is there room for an Engelsian metaphysics of nature. Rather, the attentions of philosophy are turned towards the activity – the everyday life-activity – of embodied subjects at home in an environment that is leant value, meaning, and normative significance by their collective activity. Of course, the founders of Marxism are recognised for their development of this vision (which, at least in the case of Marx is appropriate), and lip service is paid here and there as needs must, but the substance of this work is '*sovershenno normal'naya filosofiya*', as my mentor Felix Mikhailov might have said.

But of course this is not the end of the story. The fact is that some of Ilyenkov's writings after *Dialekticheskaya logika* do come across as allied to official Soviet Marxism-Leninism, not just in their rhetoric but in their choice of subject matter. This is not true of the long article, 'Problema ideal'nogo', published posthumously in *Voprosy filosofii*, in which Ilyenkov returns to his views on the ideal and brings them into dialogue (or rather confrontation) with then current Soviet work in the philosophy of mind.[42] But it *is* true of his last book, *Leninskaya dialektika i metafizika pozitivisma*,[43] and a number of contemporaneous articles.[44] In these writings, Ilyenkov gives centre-stage to Lenin's contribution, defending his stance in *Materialism and Empiriocriticism*, with its critique of Russian empiriocriticism, and praising the insightfulness of Lenin's deliberations in the *Philosophical Notebooks*, especially his reading of Hegel. Significantly, Ilyenkov argues that Lenin's philosophical vision represents a coherent, unified whole. He discerns no tension between Lenin's 1909 critique of Bogdanov, his 1914 writings on Hegel, or his 1922 intervention 'On the Significance of Militant Materialism'.[45] The message is that Lenin was right all along.[46]

Let me quote from the conclusion of *Leninskaya dialektika*:

41   Hegel 1956, p. 9.
42   Ilyenkov 1979a; Ilyenkov 2009a; Ilyenkov 2014.
43   Ilyenkov 1980. The 1982 English translation (Ilyenkov 1982b) is included in Ilyenkov 2009b, pp. 285–391.
44   Some of these articles (e.g. 'Materializm voinstvuiushchii – znachit dialeticheskii' ['Militant Materialism Means Dialectical Materialism']) were included to supplement the text of the 1984 edition of *Dialekticheskaya logika* (pp. 286–304; translated in Ilyenkov 2018b: 229–47). If my reading of the 1974 edition is correct, they detract from the spirit of the original text.
45   Lenin 1960–78, vol. 33, pp. 227–36.
46   Lektorsky 2012, p. 337, observes that during the discussion of the Ilyenkov-Korovikov theses, A.S. Arsen'ev argued (bravely) that *Materialism and Empiriocriticism* should be read as an immature work in comparison to the *Notebooks*. It is revealing, therefore, that Ilyenkov takes the contrary view in his own late writings (as does Bukharin).

In place of the Machist conception of cognition which he demolishes, and in the course of this 'destruction', Lenin gives an explanation of dialectics as the genuine theory of knowledge and logic of Marx and Engels. This is the advantage of Lenin's criticism of Machism over Plekhanov's.

The *Philosophical Notebooks* continue the same line ...[47]

...*Materialism and Empirio-Criticism* now continues to be the most timely Marxist work in the field of philosophy where until now the front lines have run in the war of Marxism-Leninism for materialist dialectics, for the logic and theory of knowledge of modern-scientific, intelligent, dialectical materialism. This is the war for militant materialism, without which there is not and cannot be a Marxist-Leninist world outlook.

Revolution is revolution, regardless of whether it occurs in the socio-political 'organisms' of an enormous country or in the 'organism' of contemporary scientific development. The logic of revolutionary thinking and the logic of revolution are one and the same thing. And this logic is called materialist dialectics.

Materialism and Empirio-Criticism teaches this above all else if it is read in the light of the entire subsequent history of the political and intellectual development in Russia and the entire international revolutionary movement of the working class. History has clearly shown where the path of Lenin has led and is leading. It has also shown the crooked pathways of revising the principles of the logic of revolution from the point of view of positivism.[48]

One might conclude that, since such passages clearly seem to speak for Kagarlitsky's interpretation of the trajectory of Ilyenkov's career, the dispute between us can only be over *when*, rather than *if*, Ilyenkov compromised his philosophical principles.

But I think we need a more nuanced understanding of Ilyenkov's situation. In my earlier discussions of this material, I argued that although Ilyenkov is unquestionably to be faulted for his uncritical reconstruction of Lenin as philosopher, these late writings have redeeming features. True, Ilyenkov ignores the fact that, whatever might be said for views Lenin endorses, Lenin's *manner* of doing philosophy, in which arguments are embroidered with name-calling and abuse, helped create the very philosophical 'culture' that Ilyenkov set himself against and that ultimately swallowed him up. For all that, however, *Leninskaya*

---

47   Ilyenkov 2009b, p. 389–90.
48   Ilyenkov 2009b, p. 391.

dialektika is not without philosophical interest – it includes, for example, a lengthy discussion of Bogdanov's views – and it contains a progressive subtext; namely, that positivism has triumphed in contemporary Soviet intellectual life, just as scientism and technocracy has in Soviet political culture. Small wonder that message had to be concealed under a layer of orthodoxy.[49] Moreover, I think that this sympathetic reading can draw support from my reflections on *Dialekticheskaya logika*, as it is clear from the first of the quotations above, that what Ilyenkov seeks to defend by appeal to Lenin's authority is precisely his favoured conception of logic as the unity of the philosophy of thought, dialectics, and the theory of knowledge, that same thesis he and Korovikov defended.

I do not want, however, to engage in apologetics on Ilyenkov's behalf. The task is to understand Ilyenkov's situation towards the end of his life. To this end, I think it is helpful to reflect on the parallels between Ilyenkov and the incarcerated Bukharin at work on *Philosophical Arabesques*.[50] In the mid-1970s, Ilyenkov faced a crisis, one more mundane than Bukharin's nightmare, but nonetheless one that had a devastating effect on him. The Sector at the Institute of Philosophy at which he worked (*Sektor dialekticheskogo materializma*), now led by Lektorsky (who had become Head in 1969), became the target of vicious ideological criticism.[51] Ilyenkov's latest work on the ideal, which was to appear in a book of papers by members of the Sector, was denied publication by the Institute's Scientific Council in a painful and long-drawn out controversy.[52] Ilyenkov took this hard. His reaction, I think, was to put himself through the same internal 'trial' that Bukharin did. Like Bukharin, Ilyenkov's response was to try to reassert his identity as a revolutionary thinker, an exponent of a living Marxist tradition of thought. And again like Bukharin, he sought above all to affirm his allegiance to Lenin, to make peace with, to prove himself to, the father figure of the Russian Marxism.[53]

---

49   Mikhailov encouraged me to see this as the book's message; see Mikhailov 1998, p. 448.

50   In what follows, I focus on parallels between the ways in which their respective predicaments caused them to address the issues they did, rather than parallels between their philosophical views themselves. The latter topic, however, is worthy of exploration. There is a remarkable congruence between positions at which Bukharin arrives in *Philosophical Arabesques* and some of Ilyenkov's key ideas.

51   See Lektorsky, 2012, p. 286. Lektorsky mentions (pp. 360–61) that one of the most vocal critics of his section was former KGB operative E.D. Modrzhinskaya (see also Motroshilova 2009, p. 73). It transpires that this is the Elena Modrzhinskaya who was the KGB's leading expert on the UK in the 1940s and wrote a well-known report of the activities of the Cambridge Spies. See West and Tsarev 2009, pp. 313 ff.

52   See Ilyenkov 2018a.

53   In Bakhurst 1991, ch. 4, I discuss different ways in which Lenin's philosophy can be inter-

It is also significant that, although Hegel's philosophy of history has no real place in Ilyenkov's philosophy, Ilyenkov, once again like Bukharin, saw his situation in world-historical terms. Ilyenkov was a more modest figure than Bukharin, in several respects, and I do not think that he was particularly concerned about his legacy, his place in history. But I do think that Ilyenkov must have asked himself some difficult questions about what had been achieved since the heady days in which he and Korovikov set out to refashion Soviet philosophy and, as Korovikov attests, to help their students to think for themselves. And the answers to those questions must have been difficult to live with. Bukharin could see himself as swept up by tremendously powerful historical forces, which though they might dash him on the rocks, would flow onward and fashion something beautiful and joyful.[54] Ilyenkov, in contrast, could hardly summon that kind of optimism. At the height of his powers, he had seen his mission as the development of a critical, humanistic form of Marxism, and much of what he found in Hegel he deployed to that end. But after the Soviet invasion of Czechoslovakia in August 1968, the project of establishing 'socialism with a human face' was in dire jeopardy. Ilyenkov was not only bitterly disappointed by events; his situation within the academic world had worsened. After the Prague Spring, intellectuals were especially targeted as potential threats and Ilyenkov was identified as the primary exponent of the Soviet version of Marxist humanism. For a while, he was protected by the leadership of the Institute of Philosophy, first by V.P. Kopnin, who was Director 1968–70, and Kedrov, who led the Institute 1973–74. But when B.S. Ukraintsev took over in 1974, the climate worsened significantly. As Korovikov remarks, Ilyenkov left this world at a time when the momentum of history had gone from the Soviet project and Russian society was utterly stagnant, to use the metaphor that came to characterise the period. What killed Ilyenkov, according to his friend, was the unspiritual ('antidukhovnaya') atmosphere, from which all the oxygen had been sucked by careerists, cynics, and petty bureaucrats.[55] In such a world, it was no longer possible to define one's intellectual identity as a moment in the unfolding of a grand historical project. What history was teaching was the irrelevancy of the idea of history as Marxist-Hegelians typically understood it. Ilyenkov's reaction was first to resist this lesson, and to keep try-

---

preted (distinguishing between a 'conservative' and a 'radical' reading), and explore the nature of its influence on Ilyenkov.

54   Bukharin ends *Philosophical Arabesques* with the words, 'New questions of world significance are ripening, questions of the worldwide victory of socialism and its youthful culture, full of the joy of life' (2005, p. 376).

55   Korovikov 1998, p. 473.

ing to make sense, but this was not a stance that proved possible to maintain for long. On 21 March 1979, Ilyenkov took his own life.

∙ ∙
∙

In the next section, we return to the legacy of one of Bukharin's contemporaries, Lev Vygotsky, whose ideas influenced many of the more creative Soviet philosophers of Ilyenkov's generation. Vygotsky's thought has also had a significant influence in the West, particularly among developmental and educational psychologists, thanks in part to the advocacy of such thinkers as Jerome Bruner and Michael Cole, who looked to Vygotsky's insights to inspire and refresh psychological inquiry. Of course, not all Western psychologists see things that way. I remember mentioning my interest in Vygotsky to a colleague in the Psychology Department at Queen's. 'Oh, Vygotsky's alright', he said, 'but it's all theories'. This struck me as odd. What else could it be but theories? I suppose my colleague meant that Vygotsky's ideas are speculative, and not, by today's standards, confirmed by experiment. But to make that complaint about Vygotsky is really to miss everything that is interesting about his contribution, because Vygotsky is a font of exciting and thought-provoking insights that invite us to see the entire discipline of psychology in a new light. In this regard, Vygotsky is as much a philosopher as he is a psychologist. The next section begins by exploring the philosophical content of his legacy, before turning to explore two of the most fertile, and most contested, concepts in his work *oposredstvovanie* and *perezhivanie*.

PART 3

Vygotsky

..

CHAPTER 10

Vygotsky's Demons

This chapter examines the philosophical dimensions of Vygotsky's legacy. Vygotsky was a profoundly original thinker, but he was not one whose independence of thought caused him to neglect the ideas of others. On the contrary, Vygotsky was exceptionally well-read. He had an impressive command of the European psychological literature and considerable knowledge of adjacent fields, such as anthropology and educational theory. His appreciation of literature and literary theory is well-known and justly celebrated. Less often remarked upon, however, is his debt to philosophy. In this field, too, he was well-versed, having majored in philosophy and history at the Shanyavsky People's University. Vygotsky was much influenced by the philosophical vision of Marx and Engels: Almost all of the many references to their writings in Vygotsky's *Collected Works* are to philosophical themes.[1] He was also inspired by a number of philosophers who had influenced Marx and Engels, notably Hegel (whom Vygotsky had read in high school), Spinoza and Feuerbach. Marxism and its antecedents, however, by no means exhaust Vygotsky's philosophical interests. He cites numerous other philosophers, including Aristotle, Bergson, Brentano, Descartes, Dewey, Dilthey, Fichte, Hobbes, Husserl, James, Kant, Lichtenberg, Malebranche, Nietzsche, Neurath, Plato, and Scheler.[2]

---

1 There is no credibility in the once-popular idea that Vygotsky's references to Marx and Engels are simply the obligatory lip service demanded of Soviet scholars. It is true that Vygotsky was critical of the idea of 'Marxist psychology', but this was not out of contempt for Marxism. On the contrary, he felt that Marxism should inform all psychological inquiry, just as Darwinism informs all biology (Vygotsky 1997d, pp. 338–41 [*ss* 1, pp. 431–5]). Vygotsky's most extended discussion of Marxism is his 'The Socialist Alteration of Man' (Vygotsky 1994b). Please note that where I refer to Vygotsky's writings that appear in the six-volume *Collected Works of L.S. Vygotsky*, I cite the English translation and give the reference to the appropriate volume of the original Russian edition in square brackets (e.g. [*ss* 3, p. 32] = *Sobranie sochinenii*, vol. 3, p. 32). Note that the numbering of the volumes in the English version differs from the Russian original.

2 The only Russian philosopher regularly cited by Vygotsky is Semyen Frank, whose *Filosofiya i zhizn'* (1910) and *Dusha cheloveka* (1964) clearly impressed him. Vygotsky also alludes to Lev Shestov (Vygotsky 1997d, p. 266 [*ss* 1, p. 336]; Vygotsky and Luria 1994c, p. 14). As for the Russian Marxists, Vygotsky discusses Plekhanov (e.g. Vygotsky 1997d, pp. 313–15 [*ss* 1, pp. 397–400]; 1997h, pp. 178–80 [*ss* 1, pp. 214–17]) and Lenin, especially the latter's notes on Hegel (Vygotsky 1998b, pp. 79n, 119–20, 147 [*ss* 4, pp. 107, 158–60, 196–7]; 1987d, p. 88 [*ss* 2, p. 75]), and in *Thinking and Speech* he takes a swipe at Bogdanov's view of truth as socially organised experience (1987d, pp. 85, 87 [*ss* 2, pp. 71, 75]). It seems that Vygotsky,

It would be wrong, however, to treat the study of the philosophical elements of Vygotsky's thought merely as an archaeological exercise designed to uncover some of the sources of his ideas. This is because Vygotsky warrants consideration as a philosopher in his own right. What endures most in his legacy are not the results of his empirical inquiries, but the portrait he paints of the mind and its development, together with his reflections on the nature of psychological explanation. The contemporary significance of Vygotsky's work resides, to a significant extent, in its philosophical content.

In what follows, I begin by setting out Vygotsky's vision of the mind and his attendant conception of the obligations of psychology. I proceed to argue that his vision is steeped in the tradition of philosophical rationalism. I then consider the argument that the fecundity of Vygotsky's insights depends on liberating them from this rationalist perspective, which, it is claimed, has a deleterious, indeed reactionary, influence on his thought. In response, I argue that Vygotsky's ideas draw much of their power from their rationalist heritage. Their contemporary import cannot be properly appreciated without due recognition of this fact.

1   Vygotsky's Vision

As we observed in Chapter 3, Vygotsky saw himself as responding to a crisis in the psychology of his times. He argued that psychology was typical of a young science: it comprised a variety of schools each with its own distinctive concepts and methods (e.g. Behaviourism, Reflexology, Stern's Personalism, Gestalt Psychology, Psychoanalysis). Each school illuminated certain phenomena, but their respective insights were incommensurable. Moreover, they each had colonial ambitions, stretching their central concepts to the point of vacuity in an effort to encompass the whole of the discipline. Psychology was thus far from discharging its obligation to provide a comprehensive scientific account of the human mind. The discipline's shortcomings were particularly evident in the study of consciousness. Although subjectivist psychology saw consciousness as accessible only by introspection, thereby placing it outside the realm of scientific inquiry, the dominant scientific schools, premised on such concepts as 'reflex' or 'stimulus-response', lacked the resources to capture consciousness altogether. Indeed, some proposed to make a virtue of their ineptitude

---

no doubt wisely, paid little attention to the Soviet philosophical scholarship in the 1920s and 1930s, but he does cite V.F. Asmus's book on early modern philosophy (Asmus 1929) in his treatise on the emotions (Vygotsky 1999, pp. 124, 199 [ss 6, pp. 166, 269]).

by explicitly advancing a 'psychology without consciousness'. Vygotsky, in contrast, held that consciousness was 'an indisputable fact, a primary reality'.[3] No plausible science of the mind could fail to address its nature.

That Vygotsky was scornful of the prevailing approaches to consciousness is plain. His own view, however, is much less clear. He certainly does not think of consciousness as a kind of 'mysterious flame' or 'inner light' illuminating the theatre of the mind. Rather, he takes a broadly functionalist approach that identifies consciousness with a certain set of capacities. In his early works, he invokes the notion of 'doubled' (*udvoennyi*) experience. When I perceive an object before me, I am aware of the object, but I am also aware, or can become so, of my perceiving the object. Human beings are able to have 'experience of experience': we have reflexive awareness of our own mental states and act in that light.[4] Vygotsky identifies consciousness not just with such multilayered awareness, but with the function of selection and control that it enables. For him, the problem of consciousness is one of 'the structure of behaviour', not of phenomenology or subjectivity, and despite his wariness about the explanatory pretensions of the reflex concept, he suggests in his early papers, that 'consciousness is merely the reflex of reflexes'.[5]

In his later writings, Vygotsky takes a broader view, using the term 'consciousness' as a synonym for 'mind'.[6] He maintains that there is a profound distinction between the infant and the mature human mind. Normal children are endowed by nature with certain 'elementary mental functions' (e.g. prelinguistic thought, preintellectual speech, associative memory, basic forms of attention, perception, volition). These are modular in character and fundamentally explicable within the causal framework of stimulus and response. The mature descendants of these functions, in contrast, represent a holistic system of interfunctionally related capacities. Each 'higher mental function' (e.g. linguistic thought, intellectual speech, 'logical' memory, voluntary attention, conceptual perception, 'rational' will) is what it is in virtue of the relations it bears to the others. Memory, as we have seen, does not simply serve up material for thought, it is permeated and organised by thought, for remembering the past involves reconstruction and narrative; we 'think through' past events to make sense of them. By the same token, memory provides the constant background for thought and reasoning: each act of thinking takes place in the context of

---

3   Vygotsky 1997g, p. 47 [*ss* 1, p. 59].
4   Vygotsky 1997b, p. 68 [*ss* 1, p. 85]. One might say that, for a human being, consciousness and self-consciousness are one.
5   Vygotsky 1997b, p. 79 [*ss* 1, p. 98]; see also 1997g, p. 46 [*ss* 1, pp. 57–8].
6   In keeping with the Russian word 'soznanie', literally 'with knowledge'.

our awareness of the past. Similarly, perception and attention are structured by concepts and categories from language and thought, the will is directed to objects represented as desirable, and so on.

The cornerstone of Vygotsky's 'dialectical method' is the idea that everything in time must be understood in its development.[7] Accordingly, he argues that to understand the mature human mind, we must comprehend the processes from which it emerges. The higher mental functions, he argues, are irreducible to their primitive antecedents; they do not simply grow from the elementary functions as if the latter contained them in embryo. To appreciate the qualitative transformations that engender the mature mind, we must look outside the head, for the higher mental functions are distinguished by their mediation by external means.[8] Vygotsky's first and most straightforward example of such mediation is the tying of knots to assist memory. Although elementary memory is simply a causal process in which stimuli evoke an idea of some past happening, higher forms of memory deploy artificial devices intentionally to call forth the past. Such 'mediational means' are described as 'psychological tools' that enable human beings to master and control their own mental functions.[9]

It is important that such mediational means are fundamentally social in nature. The development of the child's higher mental functions thus rests upon her appropriation of culture. Following Janet, Vygotsky formulates the 'general genetic law of cultural development':

> [E]very function in the cultural development of the child appears on the stage twice, in two planes, first, the social, then the psychological, first between people as an intermental category, then within the child as an intramental category. This pertains equally to voluntary attention, to logical memory, to the formation of concepts, and to the development of will.[10]

Here, the leading idea is that the child first grasps external mediational means – e.g. the practice of tying a knot in a handkerchief as a reminder – and then she 'internalises' such techniques, coming to deploy mnemonic devices in thought.

---

7   Vygotsky writes, 'To encompass in research the process of development of some thing in all its phases and changes – from the moment of its appearance to its death – means to reveal its nature, to know its essence, for only in movement does a body exhibit what it is' (1997e, p. 43 [ss 3, pp. 62–3]).

8   Vygotsky writes, '[T]he central fact in our psychology is the fact of mediation' (1997j, p. 138 [ss 1, p. 166]).

9   Vygotsky 1997e, pp. 61–2 [ss 3, pp. 86–90].

10   Vygotsky 1997e, p. 106 [ss 3, p. 145].

Internalisation, Vygotsky explains, is not a matter of merely transplanting a social activity onto an inner plane, for the internalised practice is transfigured in the act of internalisation. Nevertheless, the developmental roots of the higher mental functions lie in the mastery of social practices: 'Genetically, social relations, real relations of people, stand behind all the higher functions and their relations ... [T]he mental nature of man represents the totality of social relations internalised'.[11]

Two points of clarification. First, each higher function has its own specific developmental story. Although concept acquisition and volition are the fruit of internalisation, their genetic roots are very different. The former emerges from practices of grouping, categorising, and from the development of early language; the latter from the internalisation of the social expression and mediation of preferences, and the acquisition of techniques that enable the child to cope with the frustration of her preferences and to reflect critically upon her wants. Second, Vygotsky does not see the child's appropriation of culture simply in terms of facility with discrete mediational means. From his earliest works, Vygotsky invokes the phenomenon of cumulative cultural evolution: human beings transmit vast amounts of knowledge across generations not biologically, but culturally.[12] The child inherits whole traditions of thought and experience. In addition, the cognitive powers of individuals are greatly expanded by their relations to culture and community. Much of an individual's knowledge rests on the testimony of authorities, and much inquiry is collaborative.

As his position developed, Vygotsky increasingly gave pride of place to the concept of meaning.[13] While he initially portrayed mediational means as artificial stimuli triangulating the basic stimulus-response model,[14] he later recognised that mediation undermines the whole reflexological framework. Medi-

---

11   Vygotsky 1997e, p. 106 [ss 3, pp. 145–6]. Cf. the discussion of internalisation in Chapter 2 above (pp. 43–4, 58).

12   Vygotsky 1997b, p. 68 [ss 1, p. 84]. The term 'cumulative cultural evolution' is Michael Tomasello's (see Tomasello 1999).

13   There is an intriguing passage in Vygotsky's 'The Problem of Consciousness' (which is in note form), where Vygotsky seems to set his position, premised on the concept of meaning, in contrast to an approach based on activity: '"In the beginning was the deed" (but not: the *deed* was in the beginning), at the end came the word, and *that is most important of all* (L.S.). What is the significance of what has been said? "For me, I'm content with this knowledge", i.e. it's enough that the problem has been posed' (Vygotsky 1997j, p. 138 [ss 1, p. 166]). I have modified the translation, which suffers from a serious error ('deed' is mistranslated as 'thing'). The passage contains allusions to Goethe's *Faust* and Pushkin's *Covetous Knight*.

14   E.g. Vygotsky 1997f [ss 1, pp. 105–8].

ational means are not simply intervening causes. They influence us in virtue of their significance, and their significance depends on how they are understood or interpreted by human subjects.[15] By the time Vygotsky wrote his masterpiece, *Thinking and Speech* (1934 [*ss* 2]), *word meaning* [*znachenie slova*] had become his fundamental 'unit of analysis', the key to the relation of thought and speech and, thereby, the essence of the whole system of higher mental functions. In this work, Vygotsky argues that thought and speech have different developmental roots; thought is grounded in basic problem-solving activities, speech in primitive communicative utterances. The critical point is when the two lines of development merge and the child relates to her own utterances as meaningful and employs them to communicate in virtue of their meaning. At this point, thought becomes linguistic and speech rational. This is a developmental moment of enormous significance for, with meaning as their common currency, thought can permeate all the higher mental functions.[16] Even perception becomes an essentially meaningful process: the child experiences a world of objects that have meaning for her.[17] Such a world influences her, not just causally, but normatively in virtue of its significance. The child thus enters a distinctively human mode of engagement with reality.

We can now see Vygotsky's rationale for identifying consciousness with mind, understood as the system of higher mental functions. Vygotsky's view of the relation of mind and meaning leads him to a sophisticated successor to the notion of 'doubled experience'. Mental phenomena take as their objects meaningful states of affairs in the world, or representations thereof, and any mental state can itself become the object of another: my thought can become the object of attention, reasoning, memory, volition, and so forth. Any being capable of such reflexive mental acts is conscious. With this, consciousness is fundamentally related to meaning and Vygotsky concludes that 'consciousness as a whole has a semantic (*smyslovoe*) structure'.[18] We might say that a conscious being occupies the space of meanings.[19]

---

15   See Vygotsky 1997j, p. 137 [*ss* 1, p. 166], and Chapter 3 above.

16   Vygotsky 1987b, p. 324 [*ss* 2, p. 415]. I discuss Vygotsky's view of the relation of thought and speech at length in Bakhurst 1991, pp. 68–81.

17   Vygotsky 1987b, p. 295 [*ss* 2, p. 372]; Vygotsky 1997j, pp. 136–17 [*ss* 1, pp. 164–5].

18   Vygotsky 1997j, p. 137 [*ss* 1, p. 165].

19   What, then, is the relation between the idea of a conscious being as an inhabitant of the realm of meanings and the idea of consciousness as the possession of 'an inner life'? After all, as Vygotsky admits, one can navigate the realm of meanings with greater or lesser awareness. I do not think Vygotsky would have held that his 'semiotic' view of consciousness displaces the need for an account of phenomenal awareness, of what it is like to be conscious. The latter account, however, will be subservient to the former. See Chapter 11 below.

Vygotsky's is a vision of the social constitution of mind: 'through others we become ourselves'.[20] We owe our very mindedness, our personhood, to our appropriation of culture, and our mental lives are lived in communication and activity with others, either directly or through the mediation of culture. Education in the broadest sense makes us what we are. Vygotsky's pedagogical and 'defectological' writings are premised on this vision. He argues, for example, that the significance of a disability such as blindness is that it inhibits the child's acquisition of culture. The task therefore is not to compensate for a specific physical defect (Vygotsky urges us to shun the very notion of defectiveness[21]), but to create conditions in which culture becomes accessible to the child. To this end, Vygotsky puts special emphasis on the disabled child's development of language.[22] He insists, however, that the '*principles and the psychological mechanism of education are the same here as for a normal child*'.[23] And for Vygotsky, the ultimate aim of all educational practice is the same: to promote the full and active life of an intellectually and morally accomplished social being.

Vygotsky's vision thus has a profoundly normative dimension. His cultural-historical theory of mind is perfectionist – in that it strives to understand and promote the conditions in which minds can flourish – and egalitarian, in that he sought that flourishing for all.[24] He hoped that the new psychology would prosper in Soviet Union, where its insights would contribute to the creation of a new and more just society that would facilitate the well-being of all.

---

20   Vygotsky 1997e, p. 105 [*ss* 3, p. 144].

21   He writes: 'Education must, in fact, make a blind child become a normal, socially accepted adult and must eliminate the label and the notion *defectiveness* which has been affixed to the blind' (Vygotsky 1993a, p. 108 [*ss* 5, p. 100]).

22   Vygotsky therefore urges that deaf children learn to lip-read and, if possible, speak the natural languages of the hearing culture(s) in which they live. Thus, his view is at odds with the contemporary received opinion that sign languages of the Deaf are not primitive protolanguages but possess all the syntactic complexity necessary for full semantic efficacy and that sign languages can and do sustain Deaf culture, initiation into which is sufficient for the development of higher mental functions and full and flourishing personality (see Padden and Humphries 1988, 2005; Sacks 1989). Were he alive today, I do not think it would be hard to persuade Vygotsky of the power of sign languages and the reality of Deaf culture (see Vygotsky 1993d, p. 168 [*ss* 5, p. 171], where he writes: 'Speech is not necessarily tied to the sound apparatus; it may be embodied in another sign system, just as the written language may be transferred from the path of vision to the path of touch'). He would never have granted, however, that the Deaf should confine themselves to their own culture, on the grounds that the members of any minority culture should have the wherewithal to engage with a wider cultural milieu.

23   Vygotsky 1993e, p. 112 [*ss* 5, p. 104], Vygotsky's emphasis.

24   I am inspired to describe Vygotsky as an egalitarian perfectionist by Christine Sypnowich's writings in political philosophy (see Sypnowich 2000a; 2000b; 2017).

2   Rationalism

In presenting Vygotsky's vision as 'philosophical', I do not mean to suggest it is a purely a priori conception. On the contrary, it is informed by extensive empirical inquiry and stands or falls to the extent to which it can inspire psychological theories that are empirically corroborated and vindicated in practice. It remains the case, however, that Vygotsky's brilliant portrait of the mind's place in nature far outruns the empirical data that prompted it. It is the fruit of much speculation, in the best sense of the term. Vygotsky's writings are less presentations of 'results' as injunctions to *think of the issue in these terms, to see things this way.* The 'general genetic law of cultural development', for instance, is not so much a law as a piece of advice about how to represent the relation between the 'inner' and the 'outer'; between the psychological capacities the exercise of which is constitutive of our inner lives and the social practices that constantly mediate our engagement with the world. It could remain good advice even if Vygotsky had the empirical details of internalisation wrong. In this sense, his legacy endures as a kind of prolegomenon to empirical psychology rather than an instance of it. Not that Vygotsky merely offers us some helpful ways of thinking. The significance of his contributions resides in his relentless interrogation of the theoretical framework of psychological inquiry. He appreciated very well that 'science is philosophical down to its ultimate elements, to its words' and that the methods and theoretical vocabularies of any science must be constantly subjected to critical reflection.[25]

How, then, should we characterise Vygotsky's philosophical cast of mind? When I conducted research in Moscow in the early 1980s, I was fortunate to be able to discuss Vygotsky's work with a number of Russian philosophers and psychologists, among them V.S. Bibler. Bibler maintained that Vygotsky's work should be seen against a philosophical tradition he called 'High Rationalism' (*vysokii rationalism*), a tradition that originates with the Ancient Greeks and that numbers Descartes, Leibniz, Spinoza, Kant, Hegel, and Marx as its most prominent modern representatives.[26] At the time, Bibler's view struck me as eccentric. I was anxious to portray Vygotsky as a post-Cartesian, post-

---

25   Vygotsky 1997d, p. 291 [*ss* 1 p. 369].

26   See Bibler 1975, pp. 137–61, where he describes the 'high rationalist' tradition and explores the affinity between Vygotsky and Hegel. See also Bibler's contribution to the seminar transcribed in Chapter 2 of this volume.

Enlightenment thinker, so it seemed puzzling to associate him with rationalism. Over the years, however, I have come to see the wisdom of Bibler's suggestion.[27]

I am not the only Western philosopher to endorse such a view of Vygotsky's legacy. Jan Derry has argued forcibly for a similar position.[28] But ours is a minority opinion. It is not difficult, however, to find the roots of prominent Vygotskian ideas in the thinkers of this tradition. For example, Vygotsky's conception of development through qualitative transformation is profoundly Hegelian,[29] as is his vision of the emergence of the individual intellect through the appropriation of culture as the repository of collective wisdom. Vygotsky, of course, endorses Marx's attempt to provide a naturalistic reading of such Hegelian insights. Indeed, his cultural-historical theory can be seen as an attempt to give content to Marx's Feuerbachian assertion that the essence of man is 'the ensemble of social relations'.[30] The key notion of mediation is also Hegelian.[31] Spinoza's idea that free, creative activity presupposes (in Vygotsky's words) the 'intellectualization of all mental functions' is a crucial influence on the latter's view of the mastery of the intellect through the creation of psychological tools.[32] Vygotsky's conception of freedom is also indebted to Kant, albeit Kant refracted through Hegel. In addition, Vygotsky's method of 'unit analysis' owes much to *Das Kapital*, where Marx deploys the commodity form as the key concept in explicating the development of capitalism. Indeed, Vygotsky's constant preoccupation with questions of method was inspired by Marx's methodological sophistication. Finally, Vygotsky appreciated Descartes's significance in defining the questions that psychology still struggled to address, especially the mind-body problem. 'The tragedy of all modern psychology', Vygotsky writes, 'consists in the fact that it cannot find a way to understand the real sensible tie between our thoughts and feelings on

---

27   My initial resistance was no doubt born of an uncritical acceptance of the kind of sharp
      cultural transitions that people attempt to mark with the prefix 'post'.

28   See Derry 2013, which I discuss in Bakhurst 2015b.

29   In their peerless book on Vygotsky's thought, van der Veer and Valsiner find the roots of
      Vygotsky's conception of development in Hegelian dialectics. They are rather too quick,
      however, to characterise dialectical transformation in terms of a simple 'thesis-antithesis-
      synthesis' model, which is, I believe, far too formulaic to capture the nuances of Vygotsky's
      conception of qualitative transformation (see van der Veer and Valsiner 1991, p. 26).

30   Marx 1968.

31   Vygotsky 1997e, p. 61–2 [*SS* 3, p. 89].

32   Vygotsky 1987b, p. 324 [*SS* 2, p. 415]. I have modified the translation better to reflect the
      original.

the one hand, and the activity of the body on the other hand'.[33] He was also well aware of the shadow Descartes's dualism cast over the history of psychology. Many attempts to develop a monistic picture had failed, Vygotsky argued, because they had allowed Descartes to define the terms of debate and tried to reduce mind to matter conceived mechanistically.[34] This was a further reason Vygotsky believed that psychology could learn from Spinoza, whose response to Descartes, he felt, represented a far superior variety of monism.

I contend that we must recognise the extent of Vygotsky's debt to these thinkers. They profoundly influenced his conception of the problems of psychology and the style of thinking with which he addressed these problems. Moreover, Vygotsky repaid the debt by making a genuine contribution to the rationalist tradition. No attempt to understand his psychology, or to develop his ideas, can fail to appreciate this.

3   Summoning the Exorcist

Many of Vygotsky's contemporary followers will be sceptical. They will grant that an appreciation of Vygotsky's favorite philosophers is sometimes relevant to understanding his ideas, just as it is also important to know something about the many psychologists he discusses. But it would be a mistake, they will argue, to emphasise the rationalist tenor of Vygotsky's thought.

The antirationalist will argue, first, that it is misleading to portray Vygotsky as a philosophical rationalist, and second, that in so far as there are rationalistic elements in his thinking, these are better purged rather than celebrated. As a cursory perusal of the relevant entry in any reputable philosophy encyclopedia will show, 'rationalism' is a rather vague appellation. Rationalists, it appears, are committed to what we might call the priority of reason. They are thus united in their hostility to the traditional empiricist idea of the individual subject constructing a conception of the world out of materials provided exclusively by sense experience. There is little unanimity among rationalists, however,

---

33   Vygotsky 1999, pp. 196–7 [SS 6, p. 265]. I have followed the translation in van der Veer and Valsiner 1991, p. 335.

34   See Vygotsky 1997b, p. 65 [SS 1, p. 81], where Vygotsky argues that Reflexology's 'basic assumption that it is possible to fully explain all of man's behaviour without resorting to subjective phenomena (to build a psychology without mind) is the dualism of subjective psychology turned inside out' (also cf. 1997g, p. 46 [SS 1, p. 57]), and the extensive discussion of the Cartesian elements of the James-Lange theory of emotion throughout Vygotsky 1999 [SS 6, pp. 91–328].

about the nature of reason's 'priority'. Rather, there are a variety of overlapping themes that are given contrasting expression by different philosophers. Yet, our antirationalist will insist, none of the themes most commonly associated with rationalism is found in Vygotsky. For example, he is not a devotee of a priori knowledge. He does not think that philosophical speculation can establish substantive truths about the nature of reality prior to or independently of scientific inquiry. Nor does he believe in innate ideas: what innate structure the infant mind possesses is radically transformed by enculturation. Nor does Vygotsky subscribe to the Hegelian thesis that the real is rational and the rational is real. Nor does he think the course of history is dictated by laws that might be discerned by reason. Nor is he a friend of teleological explanation. Spinoza and Hegel impressed Vygotsky, as they did Marx, but both Vygotsky and Marx are thorough-going naturalists. Human beings are part of the natural world, the character of which is to be disclosed by scientific inquiry. If there are laws of development – historical, cultural, or psychological – they must be established by attention to the facts, not discerned by speculation. It thus serves no purpose, the antirationalist concludes, to portray Vygotsky, or Marx for that matter, as a contributing member of the rationalist tradition.

Of course, the antirationalist will concede, there are themes in Vygotsky's work that are 'rationalistic' in the conventional sense of that term: he was, as it were, a 'small-r rationalist'. As Nadezhda Mandel'shtam observed, 'Vygotsky was fettered to some extent by the rationalism common to all scientists of that period'.[35] What the antirationalist will insist, however, is that such rationalistic elements must be eliminated from Vygotsky's thought if cultural-historical psychology is to flourish on the contemporary scene. These elements are demons that distort the real content of his insights. As such, they should be exorcised, not extolled. Harping upon Vygotsky's links to philosophical rationalism only threatens to make them stronger.[36]

The antirationalist invites us to consider the following six demons:

3.1   *Realism*

Vygotsky, the antirationalist begins, suffered from a naïve acceptance of the concepts *truth* and *reality*. He never doubted he was engaged in the search for

---

35   Mandel'shtam 1970, p. 241, quoted in van der Veer and Valsiner 1991, p. 11.

36   A number of Vygotsky's Western followers have made such a case, focusing on one or more of the six elements discussed here. In this chapter, I prefer to work with a stylised antirationalist opponent than to complicate matters by associating points with particular commentators. Derry 2013 contains a helpful discussion of some of the relevant Western literature.

truth. 'What can shake a person looking for truth!', he wrote, 'How much inner light, warmth, support there is in this quest itself'.[37] Psychology, he imagined, aspires to disclose the true nature of mind. But surely, the antirationalist continues, a genuinely cultural-historical psychology should recognise that what we take truth and reality to be – and, indeed, the very concepts of truth and reality themselves – are a cultural inheritance. What presents itself to us as 'reality' is the outcome of our culturally forged modes of conceptualisation as they organise and structure the deliverances of experience. A thinker like Vygotsky, who appreciated the extent to which our methods and vocabularies determine the objects we study, should have perceived that cultural-historical psychology is better served by admitting that reality is a social construct and that 'truth' is simply a compliment we pay to views currently accepted within the community.

3.2   Scientism

The antirationalist proceeds to argue that Vygotsky, in harmony with his realism, uncritically privileged scientific knowledge. This emerges in his preoccupation with psychology's status as a science. But it is also evident in his conception of psychological development, which he portrays as an ascent from spontaneous, fragmented, and particular forms of awareness to integrated and general modes of theoretical knowledge. Thus, for Vygotsky, a major pedagogical ideal is the transformation of the child's intellect through the assimilation of scientific concepts. However, a truly cultural-historical psychology ought to recognise that cultures contain a plethora of contrasting tools for engaging with reality of which science is only one, useful for certain types of explanatory and technical projects pertaining to the manipulation and control of nature, but inept in other respects.

3.3   Universalism

In keeping with his privileging of science, Vygotsky commends abstract and universal modes of cognition. For him, it is a virtue of cognitive abilities that they can be disengaged from particular contexts and transferred to others. He takes the sophistication of our concepts and other psychological tools to be directly proportional to the degree of their 'decontextualisation'. Yet, the antirationalist argues, a theory that emphasises the relation of cognitive development and enculturation should acknowledge that there are powerful ways of

---

37   The passage is from a letter to Levina in which Vygotsky describes how his work lends meaning to his life. It is quoted from van der Veer and Valsiner 1991, p. 16.

knowing that are culturally situated and context-bound. Failure to appreciate this has a number of unfortunate consequences. It results, for instance, in the privileging, in educational contexts, of abstract modes of reasoning that are remote from everyday practice and it obscures the significance of effective local solutions to culturally specific cognitive tasks.

3.4 Eurocentrism and Progress

Vygotsky's universalism is part of an elitist, Eurocentric conception of historical progress. In his view, cultural evolution proceeds on a linear scale from primitive to scientific, and individual psychological development undergoes a similar progression. Just as the spontaneous, untheoretical modes of conceptualisation characteristic of 'primitive' peoples give way to the sophisticated cognitive and technological powers of scientific cultures, so a child's psychological development moves from elementary forms of mental functioning to the full-blown rationality of a self-conscious subject of scientific knowledge. Once again, the antirationalist concludes, this is at odds with what a cultural-historical approach ought to say. For once we admit the intimate relation of culture and mind, proper recognition of cultural difference suggests that there is no single path of psychological development from ineptitude to rationality. It is therefore absurd to classify individuals or cultures as 'primitive' or 'advanced'. Psychology and educational theory need to recognise the diversity of intelligences and eschew altogether the idea of psychological 'progress'.

3.5 Didacticism

Consistent with his elitism, Vygotsky advances a profoundly 'top-down' conception of child development. His view that the emergence of mind depends upon the child's assimilation of the collective wisdom of her elders suggests an extremely instruction-based, teacher-orientated conception of learning. This might seem surprising because Vygotsky's emphasis on collaborative cognition is often celebrated. Yet consider the famous 'the zone of proximal development', which is defined by the difference between what a child can accomplish unaided and what she can achieve in collaboration with others. Its outer limits are determined by adult instructors who lead the child through the zone. The child is pictured as absorbing antecedently existing information, rather than building concepts and constructing knowledge. Surely, the antirationalist insists, a properly cultural-historical approach would acknowledge our agency in the creation of culture and portray the child as an equal partner in meaning making with others.

3.6   *Individualism*

Despite his emphasis on the socio-cultural foundations of psychological development, Vygotsky's thought remains centred on the individual subject conceived as a discrete, autonomous person. A cultural-historical approach, however, ought rightly to stress the dialogical character of the self. We do not just become persons through our interaction with others; we *are* ourselves only in relation to others. Selves are sustained through communicative practices, and our identities are forged through the negotiation of meaning. The growing appreciation of the significance of the semiotic that marks Vygotsky's later work should have led him to dialogism, for if consciousness is a semiotic phenomenon, and if meaning is a cultural product, then the very content of consciousness is fixed in social space (just as the meaning of an author's words is not determined by her say-so). A psychology that grasps this insight will attend more to the negotiation of meaning in public contexts and focus less on events in individual minds. Vygotsky, the antirationalist laments, could never shake free of the idea that the individual is the primary unit of psychological analysis.

These are the demons that the antirationalist would have us exorcise so that the real potential of cultural-historical psychology may be unleashed. From this perspective, situating Vygotsky's legacy squarely in the rationalist tradition is a profoundly reactionary move.

4   The Demons Confronted

Let us consider the antirationalist's first claim: that Vygotsky is not, in any meaningful sense, a member of the tradition of philosophical rationalism.

In my view, the critical factor is that, for Vygotsky, the distinctive characteristic of human minds is their responsiveness to reasons. Our engagement with our environment expresses our mindedness insofar as our thoughts and actions issue from an appreciation of reasons. Human beings are not mere playthings of causal forces. We do not simply react to stimuli, however complex and multilayered those stimuli may be. Rather, we think and act in light of what there is reason to think and do. Perception is not just a matter of the world impinging causally upon the subject.[38] The world beyond the mind is a meaningful ter-

---

38   In the 'Lectures on Psychology', Vygotsky writes of 'the meaningful nature of perception':
'It has been shown experimentally that we cannot create conditions that will functionally separate our perception from meaningful interpretation of the perceived object. I now hold a notebook in front of myself. I do not perceive something white with four corners and then associate this perception with my knowledge of the object and its designation,

rain, a 'space of reasons', that is disclosed to us in experience. Our relation to the meaningful is a normative, rational relation, rather than a merely causal one.

The idiom in which I have expressed this point is not particularly Vygotskian.[39] So let me develop the point with reference to an issue Vygotsky often discusses: freedom.[40] Vygotsky subscribes to a thesis endorsed by many within the rationalist tradition: freedom is identical with the recognition of necessity.[41] This thesis seems paradoxical. After all, it is common to *contrast* freedom and necessity; surely a person is free only if her actions are not necessitated but issue from her will. Thus, those familiar with the thesis only in its Marxist version often see it as a piece of Orwellian 'double speak', urging us to acquiesce before the inevitable triumph of communism. But although the thesis did take on this sinister dimension under Stalin, Vygotsky (who was no fan of dogmatic Marxism[42]) was faithful to its original point, which can be stated like this: Freedom pertains to actions (including mental actions, such as the making of judgments). Something is only an action if it can be represented as done for a reason: the difference between something an agent does and something that simply happens to her is that her actions can be portrayed as issuing from her awareness of reasons. Reasons stand in a normative relation to actions; that is, they determine what we *ought* to think or do. It follows that acting for reasons involves attunement to a certain sort of necessity: the recognition of what one must, or must not, think or do. For the rationalists, rational necessitation is not just compatible with freedom; it is constitutive of it.[43] The contrast

---

that is, with my understanding that this is a notebook. The understanding of the thing, the name of the object, is given together with its perception' (Vygotsky 1987b, p. 295 [ss 2, p. 372]).

39   The notion of 'responsiveness to reasons' is drawn from the work of John McDowell (1994), who also deploys the metaphor of 'the space of reasons' (which comes from Wilfrid Sellars). I discuss McDowell's philosophy at length in Bakhurst 2011. The affinity between McDowell's work and Ilyenkov's is addressed in several chapters of this book. Derry deploys McDowell's work to illuminate Vygotskian themes in Derry 2013.

40   See Vygotsky 1987b, pp. 351–8 [ss 2, pp. 454–65]; Vygotsky 1999, pp. 168–72 [ss 6, pp. 226–37]. This picks up a discussion begun in Chapter 8 above and continued in Chapter 12 below.

41   Vygotsky 1997e, pp. 209–10, 218–19 [ss 3, pp. 277–8, 290–1]; 1999, p. 172 [ss 6, p. 232].

42   See Vygotsky 1997d, pp. 228–332 [ss 1, pp. 417–23], where he writes: 'I do not want to learn what constitutes the mind for free, by picking out a couple of citations, I want to learn from Marx's whole method how to build a science, how to approach the investigation of the mind' (p. 331 [p. 421]).

43   There is an important subtlety here that complicates matters. Not all reasons necessitate some particular belief or action. Some reasons permit us to act in such-and-such a way, or

is between the autonomous, self-determining agent, who acts out of recognition for what she has most reason to think or do, and the heteronomous agent, whose actions are not motivated by reason, but by error, weakness, passion or emotion. Autonomy does not reside in acts of will that transcend necessitation; it is a matter of how our actions are necessitated. This position left its mark on Vygotsky.

The notion of the maximally rational person – the person who thinks what she should think for the reasons she should think it and does what she should do for the reasons she should do it – is an ideal. Real human beings are less than wholly rational and subject to all kinds of contingent influences and distractions. But fidelity to this ideal lends Vygotsky's psychology a certain teleological dimension. For him, human beings are not born responsive to reasons, but become so only through enculturation. The example of the free, rational agent becomes a norm to guide our educational practices. We must endeavour to create the conditions in which our children can, as they mature, reach as close as possible to this ideal.

Vygotsky's conception of freedom and rationality is linked to an idea that is a cornerstone of his thinking: the idea that reason must conquer nature. As Vygotsky puts it, 'Man overcomes nature outside himself, but also in himself, this is – isn't it – the crux of our psychology and ethics'.[44] We are free insofar as we are authors of our lives and not the playthings of external forces and this demands the mastery of nature. Although some see the conflict between reason and nature as a matter of the individual intellect subordinating the bodily promptings of emotion and desire, Vygotsky works with a more refined notion of 'the mastery of nature in our own person'. For him, the very development of the higher mental functions rests upon the mastery of nature through the creation of psychological tools to control our own psychological processes. Because this involves the creation of external technology – in the form of symbolic systems established in the environment – the task of mastering ourselves is one with the project of the control of nature outside us. We can find this

---

to think so-and-so, without requiring that we do; some reasons require us to bring about an act of a certain kind, but allow a variety of ways of doing so, and so on. Because permissibility is not necessity, the proper way to state the rationalist thesis is this: the notion of free action can be elucidated only with reference to the way in which reasons necessitate, determine, constrain or license action, and that the degree of our freedom is not inversely proportional to the extent to which reasons limit what we ought to think or do. On the contrary, we are free beings precisely because we are influenced by reasons, even if those reasons leave no rational option about what to think or do.

44   Vygotsky writes this in a letter to Morozova, quoted by van der Veer and Valsiner (1991, p. 15); see also Vygotsky 1997c, pp. 51–2, 350–51.

theme in Marx's philosophical anthropology, but it is taken to a higher level by Vygotsky's sophisticated vision of psychological development.

The idea of human mindedness as constituted by responsiveness to reasons, the identification of freedom and rational necessitation, the ideal of the maximally rational agent, and the vision of reason's mastery of nature are classic themes of the rationalist tradition, even if they are given very different expression by different thinkers. It is on this basis that I believe Vygotsky should be seen as heir to the rationalist tradition. But, in addition, a number of other rationalist ideas appear in his work, albeit ingeniously transformed. Consider, for example, innate ideas and a priori knowledge. Vygotsky does deny that children are born with innate ideas. The elementary mental functions with which we are endowed by nature enable only a prerational engagement with the world; the child's mind develops insofar as she appropriates 'forms of thought' (psychological tools, conceptual structures, and common knowledge) that are borne by the child's culture. In a sense, however, these forms of thought represent a kind of 'cultural a priori'. What Kant saw as forms of thought innate in each individual mind, Vygotsky saw as a cultural legacy.[45] In both cases, the forms of thought are antecedent to experience. For Vygotsky, as for Kant, the child is not a subject of experience in the full sense of the term until she possesses them.

Let us now confront our demons.

4.1 *Truth and Reality*

Vygotsky was certainly a realist, in the philosophical sense of the term. His inquiries assume that we are inhabitants of a world that is, for the most part, not of our making. He took it that thought is accountable to reality in that we are beholden to bring our conception of the world into line with how things

---

45   As we have seen, this view is explicitly endorsed by Ilyenkov 2009a, p. 33; 2014, p. 51. It should be noted that although Kant is often read as supposing that our fundamental concepts (categories) are innate, he is in fact only committed to the view that these concepts must be possessed by any being that can experience the world. This leaves open the possibility that these concepts are acquired.

The whole question of innateness is a vexed one. As David Wiggins has pointed out to me, it is superficial to think that Vygotsky would have entirely embraced Locke's famous critique of innate ideas (Locke 1975). Although Vygotsky would have had no time for the view that the mind is endowed with ideas by the deity (one of Locke's main targets), Vygotsky would have found much to admire in Leibniz's critique of Locke, especially where Leibniz enjoins us to see innate ideas not as representations, but as the fundamental predispositions of mind that influence how we think, reason, form conceptions, and so forth (Leibniz 1981).

actually are. Although Vygotsky appreciated that our research methods, language and other conceptual tools influence our conception of the objects of our inquiries, he never lost confidence in the idea that many of those objects are independent of our forms of understanding them. He does not argue for this conviction. He takes it as a presupposition of inquiry.[46]

In all of this, I believe that Vygotsky was absolutely correct. Suppose someone invites a seminar group to consider the proposition, 'There is a child in the courtyard'. Lengthy discussion might ensue about the boundaries of the concept 'child', the mutability of the child/adult distinction, the historical contingency of the idea of 'childhood', and so on. The seminar might conclude that there is no 'fact of the matter' about who is or is not a child: childhood is 'socially constructed'. Now imagine that a frantic parent interrupts the seminar to ask whether her missing child has been seen in the courtyard onto which the seminar room looks. Here, all the niceties of constructionism evaporate. Given that we define the concept *child* in a certain way, there is a fact-of-the-matter whether something answering to that concept has been in the courtyard. Our natural assumptions are entirely realist. Only someone in the spell of an extravagant philosophical theory could possibly take a different attitude.[47]

There is nothing demonic about Vygotsky's realism. To believe that there are facts of the matter is not a recipe for arrogance, intellectual conservatism or similar sins; it is perfectly consistent with a proper appreciation of the difficulties of inquiry and our proneness to error and fallibility. No exorcism necessary.

4.2   Science

It is beyond doubt that Vygotsky admired science. The key issue, however, is what he understood by science. His writings suggest that he took scientific explanation to have three distinguishing marks.[48] Scientific explanations are (1) *naturalistic* in that they invoke only phenomena that are constituents of the natural world; (2) *causal* in that they explain events by showing how they are necessitated by prior conditions; and (3) *systematic* in that their intelligibility depends on a background system of theoretical knowledge. It is crucial to note, however, that Vygotsky did not take a narrow view of nature, cause and system.

---

46   I do not mean that he merely assumes realism on pragmatic grounds. Rather, the reality of objects is treated as a precondition of the possibility of our cognitive relation to the world. (Of course, the objects of psychology are not necessarily independent of our modes of understanding them; many psychological phenomena are essentially self-conscious.)

47   For further discussion, see Bakhurst 2011, ch. 2.

48   See Vygotsky 1997d, ch. 15, § 2 [ss 1, pp. 309–23].

His conception of causation is not mechanistic, and he was consistently hostile to reductive modes of explanation, as is evident from his dialectical conception of development through qualitative transformation. He understood well that any naturalistic monism must admit diverse forms of causal interaction and adopt relaxed, open-minded strategies to integrate the various elements in our conception of the world to reflect the unity of nature.

It is also important that Vygotsky did not disparage 'nonscientific' modes of understanding. He was not the kind of rationalist who preferred to see human beings as cold, abstract reasoners. On the contrary, he insisted on the importance of the emotions in guiding and informing cognition. In his early book, *Educational Psychology*, he wrote:

> The ancient Greeks said that philosophy begins with wonder. Psychologically, this is true with regard to all knowledge, in the sense that every bit of new knowledge must be preceded by a certain sense of craving. A certain degree of emotional sensitivity, a degree of involvement must, of necessity, serve as the starting point of all educational efforts.[49]

And in *Thinking and Speech*, he goes so far as to argue that consciousness involves '*a unity of affective and intellectual processes*. Every idea contains some remnant of the individual's affective relationship to that aspect of reality which it represents'.[50] There is no inconsistency between this view and the idea that reason must master the emotions. The latter entails only that unreflective affective responses should not dictate our thoughts and actions. Emotion may nonetheless be essential to our responsiveness to reasons, in part because it facilitates the intellect, and in part because some reasons can be discerned only by beings with the appropriate emotional sensitivity. Consider, for example, our understanding of music or poetry, and our appreciation of the subjectivity of other people.

Vygotsky's admiration for scientific inquiry, and his general conception of rationality, were far from myopic or one-dimensional. Once again there is nothing demonic to exorcise.

4.3   *Context, Concept, and Cognition*

Those critical of Vygotsky's affection for science, also tend to disparage his apparent admiration for abstract and general forms of cognition. Vygotsky did

---

49   Vygotsky 1997c, p. 107.
50   Vygotsky 1987d, p. 50 [ss 2, p. 22], Vygotsky's emphasis; see also 1993g, pp. 238–40 [ss 5, pp. 254–6].

believe that psychological tools are more potent the less they are tied to specific contexts. The power of ordinary linguistic concepts, for example, derives from their generality. The concept 'dog' can refer to all and any dogs; 'water' to any instance of water, and so on. One of the miracles of language acquisition is that the child effortlessly learns to 'decontextualise' such concepts from the specific settings in which she encounters them. Though the child may at first, to the amusement of listeners, use the word 'dog' as if it were a proper name of a particular dog, or as if it referred only to dogs of a certain sort, she soon catches on to its universal character. Mathematical concepts and techniques exhibit similar generality. We use number systems capable of counting any discrete objects; we design systems of measurement that apply as universally as possible. And in science, we construct theories that aim to subsume as much as possible under the minimum possible number of scientific laws with maximum generality. Generality is linked to transferability: the more general a concept or technique, the greater its sphere of application.

In themselves, these observations are innocuous. It would be a mistake to conclude that someone who acknowledges their truth must embrace a view of the subject as a disembodied reasoner and disparage forms of situated knowledge. A talented footballer, for example, has sophisticated knowledge of how to read and play the game that is both uncodifiable and extremely context-sensitive (though, of course, it had better be transferable from game to game and from situation to situation within a game). An experienced salesperson at a street market might have impressive abilities to estimate quantities and calculate prices in ways that are unlike techniques taught in school mathematics. There are many examples of such situated knowledge. But they are hardly inconsistent with an appreciation of the significance of the abstract and the universal. It is not 'either-or'.

It is important to understand that Vygotsky does not applaud abstraction and generality for its own sake. On the contrary, his conception of abstraction is informed, I believe, by Hegelian–Marxist accounts of cognition as an 'ascent from the abstract to the concrete'.[51] By way of illustration, consider his view of

---

51   See Vygotsky 1997d, pp. 310–32 [ss 1, pp. 386–423]; 1993c, pp. 204–5 [ss 5, p. 214]. The
      present discussion merely touches on what is a most complex issue. Its point is simply to
      argue that abstraction and generalisation are movements of thought that serve our under-
      standing of the concrete and particular. The best Russian discussion of the dialectic of the
      abstract and the concrete, considered as a model of both scientific knowledge and indi-
      vidual cognition, is Ilyenkov 1960 [1982a]; see Bakhurst 1991, ch. 5. As noted in Chapter 7

concepts. Vygotsky offers a sophisticated typology of concepts,[52] but one basic distinction he draws is that between 'everyday' and 'scientific' concepts. The child's initial 'spontaneous' concepts are formed in relation to concrete experience; they sort entities into kinds according to criteria formed by abstraction from the entities' surface characteristics. In contrast, scientific concepts unite the kind in question by establishing a principle of its unity, a principle that explains why members of the kind are what they are. So although the everyday concept *tiger* individuates tigers by their characteristic appearance and behaviour, the scientific concept individuates them as members of a certain taxonomic category, the criteria for membership of which are established by biological theory (which might, for example, hold that something is a tiger only if it has a certain genetic make-up). Because such scientific concepts are verbally articulated, theoretically embedded, and tightly related to many other concepts, they seem abstract, general and remote from concrete experience. But appreciation of such concepts, properly integrated into a system of knowledge, actually facilitates the understanding of objects in their particularity (e.g. to understand exactly why *this* tiger has developed in just *this* way). Therefore, abstraction allows us to ascend to a detailed understanding of the concrete and particular.

It is thus misleading to deploy a sharp distinction between abstract, general, universal forms of cognition, and concrete, specific, situated ways of knowing. Vygotsky, who had a deep feeling for poetry, understood brilliantly how language, in virtue of its generality, enables us both to commune with infinity and to glimpse the fleeting and particular. Words allow us to express thoughts that span the whole of logical space and to say just how things are in the unrepeatable here and now. The trick is not to disparage the abstract and general, but to acknowledge the subtle relation of the universal and the particular in the life of the mind.

4.4   *Progress*

Vygotsky was a child of his time. He believed in progress. For him, humanity was on a path of intellectual, scientific and social evolution issuing in ever more powerful knowledge and technology and in the emergence of ever more just forms of social organisation. Unlike doctrinaire Marxists, he did not think that progress was guaranteed by the laws of history; but he believed in pro-

---

above, Ilyenkov had an enormous influence on one of Vygotsky's later followers, V.V. Davydov (see Davydov 1972).

52   See van der Veer and Valsiner 1991, pp. 264–6.

gress nevertheless. Because he saw enculturation as the source of mind, he naturally held that an individual's potential is constrained by the level of sophistication of the mediational means offered by their culture. This prompted him to draw parallels between the child's elementary mental functioning and the forms of representation and reasoning typical of so-called primitive societies.

Such a linear notion of historical development no longer carries conviction. The key question, however, is how to reject it without embracing a vapid cultural relativism. We must appreciate the rich varieties of local knowledge in cultures remote from our own without conceding that it is senseless to speak to their respective strengths and weaknesses. Of course, we should not be so arrogant as to suppose, for example, that cultures whose members have no grasp on theoretical science have nothing to teach us about the natural world or human life. However, we should also not conclude that the radical differences between such cultures and our own make our respective conceptions incommensurable, so that they cannot be explained and appraised in a common discourse. One can excise the linear view of cultural evolution from Vygotsky's psychology while leaving a position recognisably his own; no Vygotskian, however, can hold that the recognition of cultural difference requires us to forsake our confidence in the unity of nature and the possibility of genuine intercultural understanding.

The pernicious influence of Eurocentrism in Vygotsky's works must certainly be countered. We should not, however, exorcise the idea of progress as such. After all, progress in the search for truth, well-being and moral excellence was a guiding idea of Vygotsky's scholarship and a central constituent of his understanding of the ideals of education. It may be essentially contestable where truth and flourishing lie, but we cannot forsake the ideal of movement toward them.

4.5 Enculturation and Pedagogy

It is natural that a theory of psychological development giving pride of place to enculturation should embrace 'top-down' conceptions of upbringing and education. It is not fair, however, to accuse Vygotsky of representing the child as a merely passive recipient of culture. One problem is that Vygotsky's Western critics often look for agency in the wrong place. They want to portray the child's acquisition of knowledge as a matter of negotiation rather than assimilation. Much of Vygotsky's account, however, focuses on the child's acquisition of basic linguistic and conceptual structures and fundamental psychological tools and techniques. It makes little sense to think of these as negotiable, for until the child acquires a repertoire of concepts and forms of thought and reasoning, she lacks the wherewithal to negotiate anything. At the same time, not much of this repertoire is explicitly taught to the child; she 'picks it up' through her engagement in various practices that are, of course, initiated or scaffolded by caregivers. It is important, however, that such a picture must nonetheless acknowledge the child's agency, for our criterion of the child's acquisition of some concept or technique is her ability actively to deploy it. For Vygotsky, the child who has 'internalised' a psychological tool has 'made it her own'. The child may inherit rather than construct her basic concepts, but she possesses them only when they become a vehicle of her activity.

When we turn from infancy and the kindergarten to consider, say, the education of an 11-year-old child, the situation looks rather different. Now we have a child equipped to engage actively in her own education, and it seems appropriate to ask whether Vygotsky's vision of the zone of proximal development represents an unduly teacher-centred view of learning. After all, he argues that 'instruction must lead development'; that is, to encourage intellectual growth, instructors should teach at a level somewhat ahead of the child's actual ability.[53] The dictum that *'the teacher must orient his work not on yesterday's development in the child but on tomorrow's'*[54] is wonderfully forward-looking, but does it not hand too much initiative to the teacher to direct the educational process?

It is important, however, to set Vygotsky's view of instruction against his broader vision of education. For Vygotsky, educators must encourage in their students a critical, independently minded appreciation of whatever subject matter is before them, for the aim of education is not the assimilation of received wisdom, but its critical interrogation by each new generation. In his earliest writing on education, he asserts:

> The student educates himself ... For present-day education, it is not so important to teach a certain quantity of knowledge as it is to inculcate the ability to acquire such knowledge and to make use of it ... Where he [the teacher] acts like a simple pump, filling up students with knowledge, there he can be replaced with no trouble at all by a textbook, by a dictionary, by a map, by a nature walk .... Where he is simply setting forth ready-prepared bits and pieces of knowledge, there he has ceased to be a teacher.[55]

---

53 Vygotsky 1987d, pp. 208–14 [ss 2, pp. 246–55].
54 Vygotsky 1987d, p. 211 [ss 2, p. 251]; Vygotsky's emphasis.
55 Vygotsky 1997c, p. 339.

Vygotsky never abandoned this position, and his subsequent reflections on teaching and learning must be read in this light. The assimilation of culture is thus not the absorption of some fixed, stable collection of facts, but the internalisation of traditions of thought and inquiry that are essentially open to reflection, contestation, and development. Although the child initially confronts the knowledge embodied in her culture as something external, the appropriation of that knowledge is, or ought to be, a voyage of discovery on which she makes that knowledge her own and emerges as a creative voice in its expansion and development.

4.6   The Autonomous Individual

As should be clear from these reflections, Vygotsky does indeed treat the individual as the ultimate focus of psychological inquiry. What he seeks to explain is the development of the individual human mind, conceived, in its mature form, as conscious, self-aware, rational, creative and autonomous. Vygotsky appreciates, perhaps better than any other thinker, the social preconditions of this development. We owe our very being to others, and we are what we are, only in relation to others. In this sense, our essence *is* dialogical: 'The individual becomes for himself what he is in himself through what he manifests for others'.[56]

There are constraints, however, on how far these ideas can be taken. They cannot be allowed to undermine the very idea of the autonomous self; that is, of a self that is the subject of an integral mental life and the author of its own utterances. My conception of the world may be the product of my initiation into traditions of thinking; my very way of expressing myself may be structured by speech genres embodied in my culture. Yet, even if the words I speak are the product of numerous influences, the voice in which I speak is nonetheless *mine*. I speak these words; they do not speak me. This is even true of a work such as this chapter, which is easily detached from any specific context of utterance. But it is especially clear of the paradigm of utterance: where one speaker addresses another. In an encounter between persons, mediated by language, the assumption is that the encounter is one between autonomous, integral selves. Where language makes possible a meeting of minds, such selves are brought into contact with one another, but they do not thereby meld, fuse or dissolve. You and I are, and remain, ourselves.

In cultures dominated by political individualism, it can appear that people have become atoms divided from and closed to one another. Those who lament

---

56   Vygotsky 1997e, p. 105 [ss 3, p. 144].

this sometimes yearn nostalgically for lost community, and that yearning prompts interest in thinkers who, like Vygotsky, celebrate the socio-cultural foundations of the self. It can then seem puzzling that Vygotsky never loses confidence in a robust sense of the individual. But the divisiveness of individualist politics is not best countered by denying autonomy in favor of romantic images of 'relational' selves. The idea that we are autonomous individuals is a deeply entrenched aspect of our understanding of ourselves. This is evident if we consider, for example, our conception of the ideals of education. What we seek for our children is that they should become independent, critical and responsible, and that they should be the authors of their own identities. Vygotsky's brilliance is that he sees both the significance of autonomy and how we owe our status as autonomous selves to history, culture and society. The creation of the conditions in which we may attain genuine autonomy is therefore a social project that requires the political commitment of community. It is precisely this idea that political individualism – for all its interest in autonomy understood as freedom of choice – fails to discern.

5   In Lieu of a Conclusion

I have sought to defend the view that Vygotsky's legacy should be set against the tradition of philosophical rationalism. I have also argued against those who would seek to purge his thought of various rationalistic tendencies. Apart from Vygotsky's Eurocentrism and his linear vision of historical progress, none of these elements is threatening. They are not demons that must be vanquished if the true potential of Vygotsky's legacy is to come forth. On the contrary, if Vygotskian psychology is to flourish, we must let loose these ideas. If there is anything demonic about them, it is the havoc they threaten to wreak simultaneously on much mainstream psychology and on the ideas of many who attack it from the margins.

It is certainly the case that a heightened appreciation of the philosophical content of Vygotsky's legacy will enable a fruitful dialogue between his ideas and contemporary philosophical developments. Let me conclude by briefly mentioning two possible avenues of inquiry. One problem that haunts Vygotsky's work is the exact form nonreductive monism is to take. In recent Western philosophy, it is common to develop such a position by appeal to different modes of explanation. Although all events are events within the natural world, mental events are rendered intelligible by explanatory principles different in kind from natural laws. An event described using psychological terms is to be 'rationalised' by appeal to normative principles that express what it is appropriate for the subject to believe, desire, infer, or do in the circumstances in light of their existing mental states. Events described in physical terms, in contrast, are explained by appeal to causal laws. These two modes of explanation are fundamentally different in kind.[57]

Is such a position available to a Vygotskian? Its advocates sometimes invoke Dilthey's famous distinction between the natural and the human sciences. Yet Vygotsky is consistently critical of Dilthey and strongly resisted the idea that psychology should be divided into, on the one hand, a descriptive or hermeneutical discipline dealing with the higher mental functions and, on the other, a causal-scientific discipline treating the underlying physical mechanisms of behaviour. It is important, however, that Vygotsky treats descriptive psychology as a throwback to the Cartesian idea of mind as a special subjective realm. This is very different from those contemporary invocations of Dilthey that view psychological explanation as one among several irreducible modes of understanding the activity of an embodied being. Yaroshevsky[58] has suggested that Vygotsky worked with three levels of causal explanation: physical, biological and socio-historical.[59] It seems possible that such a reading, if suitably developed, might bring Vygotsky's position into fruitful dialogue with contemporary nonreductive materialism.

Attention to developments in contemporary philosophy thus promises to strengthen Vygotsky's position. There is also the possibility of a reciprocal influence. For example, the view that initiation into social or cultural practices is a precondition of the development of mind is a position that has been voiced by some prominent philosophers.[60] But all too often the philosophers write as if the acquisition of conceptual capacities occurs at a discrete point in the child's development, usually identified with the acquisition of language, as if we all undergo a kind of cognitive baptism. Prior to this moment the child is not a minded being in the full sense; after it she is a full-fledged inhabitant of the space of reasons. There is something absurd about such a view, which seems to treat a complex developmental process as if it were a single all-or-nothing transition. Vygotsky saw the *Bildungsprozess* as drawn out in time, extending across the life of the subject, and, as such, his vision offers an antidote to these

---

57   Examples of such a view are Davidson's famous 'anomalous monism' (see Davidson 1984a) and McDowell's contrast between explaining events by placing them in 'the logical space of reasons' or 'the realm of law' (McDowell 1994). The distinction between hermeneutical and scientific-causal explanation is also prominent in Jerome Bruner's cultural psychology (Bruner 1990).

58   Yaroshevsky 1999.

59   See van der Veer and Valsiner 1991, pp. 356–9.

60   E.g. McDowell 1994, Lecture VI.

austere philosophical renditions of enculturation. His interest in development made him ever alive to the not-quite-present, to shades of grey, to twilight and dusk. Philosophical accounts of the relation of culture and mind would do well to reflect on his sophisticated appreciation of the circumstances of mind's becoming.

•   •
•

Among the most enduring features of Vygotsky's legacy are the philosophical conceptions that informed his psychological theories. Perhaps the most important among these is the concept of mediation. Vygotsky is well known for arguing that human psychological functions owe their distinctive character to the fact that 'psychological tools' mediate the relation between thinking subjects and the objects of their thoughts. Yet although the significance of this idea is widely acknowledged, there is little consensus on how it is to be understood and developed. In the next chapter, I critically explore the philosophical significance of mediation and propose a thoroughly pluralistic account: mediation is not one kind of process, but many, and in some of its forms it brings us closer to the world, disclosing it to us, rather than distancing us from reality as it is in itself.

On the Concept of Mediation

1. Any account of the philosophical significance of Vygotsky's legacy should linger on the concept of mediation. Vygotsky himself described mediation as 'the central fact of our psychology':[1] it stands at the heart of his view of the higher mental functions, of the distinctive character of human activity, and of the social nature of mind. Moreover, the notion has a long philosophical pedigree in Hegel's thought and in its appropriation by Marx, Engels, and their many successors. In Vygotsky's vision of mediation, a whole philosophical tradition is condensed. The concept by no means exhausts the philosophical content of Vygotsky's thought – as I hope the previous chapter has shown – but it plays so pivotal a role that no account of his import for philosophy can fail to reckon with it.

2. The importance of mediation has not been lost on commentators. James Wertsch, for example, describes the concept as Vygotsky's 'most important and unique contribution', and makes much of the notion in his own research, as do many of Vygotsky's followers.[2] I am not sure, however, how well the notion is understood. The philosophical potential of the concept of mediation lies in its power to illuminate the nature and possibility of thought, broadly conceived. But this is a profoundly multifaceted topic, and the role of mediation is by no means straightforward.[3] If we set out to complete the schema (S) 'M mediates [between] x and y if and only if ...' do we know exactly what can substitute for the variables and what should come after 'if and only if'? And what are the constraints on the adjectival use of the term in expressions such as 'mediated activity', 'mediated memory', 'mediated attention', and so on, that Vygotskians use regularly?

It might be thought that I am being obtuse. Surely, the heart of mediation is simply the denial of immediacy. Mind is something essentially relational; that is, a creature with a mind is equipped to enter into certain kinds of relation to the world: we take in the world in perception; we judge of the world that things are thus-and-so; we strive to change the world through intentional action. We also enter into communicative relations with other minded beings. The psy-

---

1 Vygotsky 1997j, p. 138 [ss 1, p. 166].
2 Wertsch 1985, p. 15. See also Wertsch 2007.
3 See Daniels 2015.

chological relations we bear to reality, and to others, are never immediate: we do not simply drink in the world in perception, mirror it in thought, or change it by pure acts of will. We have no telepathic access to other minds. In perception, thought, action and communication the mind deploys psychological tools, of which language and other forms of representation are crucial. So, in schema (S), *M* is a psychological tool, S is a person (or subject), and O is the object of the person's perception, judgement, or activity. Many discussions of mediation begin from a schema like this:

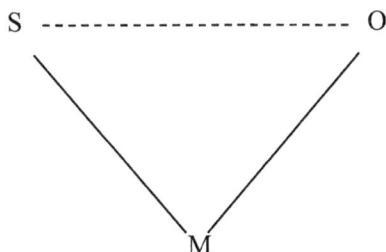

$$S \;\text{-----------------------}\; O$$
$$\diagdown \qquad\qquad \diagup$$
$$M$$

(Of course, it starts to get complicated if the object is another subject, but let us set that aside for now.) And we can also account for the adjectival use of 'mediated': mediated attention is attention facilitated by psychological tools, and so on.

3. This is a plausible start, but before proceeding I want to sound two notes of caution.

First, in this, as in all things, it is important to avoid vacuity. In *The Historical Meaning of the Crisis in Psychology*, Vygotsky comments perceptively that psychological schools often burst on the scene with a powerful organising concept that captures the imagination. People then become so excited by this concept that they begin to see it at work everywhere (e.g. everything is a 'reflex' or a manifestation of the 'unconscious'). The concept begins to take on an explanatory burden it cannot possibly bear and it eventually collapses into emptiness.[4] There must be a danger of the concept of mediation meeting such a fate. Someone might say that the idea of mediation makes good sense in contexts where we can identify well-defined 'psychological tools' at work. But what kind of mediation is involved when, say, you see your daughter walking towards you across a soccer field?

---

4 Vygotsky 1997d, pp. 245–6 [*ss* 1, p. 308].

To this, the Vygotskian might reply that perception, considered as a higher mental function, is informed by concepts. You see the figure before you *as* a person of a certain age and build, engaged in a certain activity, a person whom you recognise as your daughter (the word 'recognise' can mislead here, making the process seem too inferential: what you see is *your daughter coming towards you* – it's not that you see something less than that in which you *recognise* your daughter). But in all this, concepts are at work. Indeed, one could go further, for it is not just a matter of our perception of the present involving the application of sortal concepts and other categories. Our perception of the here-and-now is informed by our conception of the past: the present carries the past within it, as it were.

This response is attractive. But it threatens to stretch the notion of mediation too thin. For if the exercise of any higher mental function is mediated by concepts, if awareness of the present is mediated by recollection of the past, then mediation is universal and ubiquitous. It is true that any mental act will have its background conditions, that thought needs a mode of expression, that anything we do intentionally is done in some way or other, and so on. But if we call all this 'mediation', the notion will surely lose its explanatory force. Or so a sceptic might argue.

One way to respond to the risk is to return to schema (S) and stipulate clear boundaries to the concept. This is not, however, a strategy I recommend. We should not try to regiment the concept of mediation. Its significance lies precisely in its universality – the fact that it leaves its mark on every facet of the life of the mind. The important thing is to realise that its universality encapsulates a variety of contrasting forms, so that there can be significant differences between the character of mediation in different contexts. The universality of the concept is not an invitation to reduce all species of mediation to one. On the contrary, pluralism about the nature of mediation is the only approach that will preserve the concept's explanatory potential.

4. My second note of caution is that our account of mediation must not put us at remove from reality itself. We should not portray whatever does the mediating as coming between us and reality, so that we lose our grip on the idea that thought can embrace an independent world. When I see my daughter coming towards me, what I see is nothing less than an independently existing being: it is *she* who is the object of my awareness and thought and not some representation or construction of mind.

In recent Anglo-American philosophy, it is common to hear the argument that epistemology must dispense with mental intermediaries. We must abandon the idea that experience is mediated by ideas (as the classical empiricists called them), sense-data (as the positivists called them) or other representations, in favour of a view that, as Davidson puts it, re-establishes 'unmediated touch with the familiar objects whose antics make our sentences and opinions true or false'.[5] The difficulty with mental intermediaries is that they lead us into a number of familiar, and seemingly intractable, problems. The first is scepticism, of the kind dramatically illustrated by Descartes's evil genius hypothesis: if the mind is acquainted directly only with ideas, how can we know that these ideas are actually faithful to a world beyond the mind? The second problem, familiar from Berkeley, is yet more radical. If all experience is essentially mediated by ideas, then our awareness of these ideas supplies all the materials we have for empirical thinking. But if this is so, how is it even possible for us to form a conception of the world as it is out of relation to our ways of conceiving of it? The third problem is 'the myth of the given'.[6] The deliverances of experience are supposed to play a justificatory role, forming the empirical foundation on which all knowledge claims ultimately rest. Yet mental intermediaries are typically conceived as non-conceptual in character, as brute, pre-conceptualised appearances. How could appearances, so conceived, ever stand in normative relations of justification to something like beliefs?

It is thus commonly argued that if we invoke mental intermediaries, we will make it impossible to explain how the mind can reach out to the world and how the world can rationally impose itself on the mind. One solution, of course, is to acquiesce in the mind's encirclement by appearances and renounce altogether the idea of a mind-independent world, portraying reality as a construction of the mind. But this, in my view (and Vygotsky's), is the path to philosophical disaster. Rather we need to reconcile the universality of mediation with the mind's presence in, and access to, a world that is not of the mind's own making.

The first thing to observe is that Vygotsky's mediators are nothing like the kind of mental representations beloved of the empiricists and positivists. Some of his 'psychological tools' are not mental phenomena at all: they are in the world and of the world. This is exactly why the tool metaphor is especially apt. For if we consider a simple tool like a hammer, it is clear that it does not intervene between the user and the object on which it is used so that the user no longer acts on the object itself. This remains the case even if we acknowledge that new technologies can open up a new space of possibilities, creating possible objects of activity that formerly did not exist.

---

5   Davidson 1984b, p. 198.
6   See Sellars 1956; McDowell 1994, Lecture I.

I think that, happily, Vygotsky and Davidson are at cross-purposes. Vygotsky does not admire the kind of position Davidson attacks. But Davidson is certainly at odds with the tendency to 'lose the world' in a good deal of discursive or constructionist psychology that is supposedly Vygotskian in inspiration. What we need, I believe, is to develop a sense of how mediation – in Vygotsky's sense – enables us to bring the world into view, to make contact with reality. For example, in the context of communication, mediation is the means by which our minds can meet and genuinely engage with one another, rather than the murky lens through which our essentially solitary selves peer at each other.

5. So with these cautionary words in mind, let us proceed by recalling how Vygotsky's view of mediation evolved in his own thought. The notion entered his work as part of his attempt to transcend stimulus-response behaviourism. Let us reflect once again on one of Vygotsky's favourite examples: memory. Memories are sometimes simply caused – a certain stimulus evokes a particular image of the past. Human beings, however, create artificial stimuli to help them remember. The paradigm is the knot in the handkerchief. By tying the knot, we attempt to master the conditions of remembering. This psychological tool immediately reveals the limits of the stimulus-response model. First, the subject is an *agent*, manipulating the world to control its influence upon her mind, not a merely passive recipient of stimuli. Second, the knot's influence is *normative*, and not merely causal; that is, we tie the knot to remind us of something in particular and its results are subject to normative standards of correctness. This last point is important. The knot seems to function as an artificial cause, but it really does its job through something like meaning. That is why it is often more successful to replace the knot with a psychological tool that overtly uses iconic or linguistic meaning: a picture, diagram, note or list. Having grasped this insight, Vygotsky became increasingly preoccupied with the *semiotic* character of mediation. But where mediation proceeds through meaning, the relation of mind and object is transformed. Mind must be seen, not as a set of dispositions to react, but as the vehicle of a person's active conception of the world, and the world in turn presents itself to the person as pregnant with meaning, as yielding reasons for belief and action. In the mature Vygotsky's theories, meaning also mediates the relations between psychological capacities (what Vygotsky calls 'interfunctional relations'). Linguistic meaning becomes the common currency of the mental, facilitating propositional thought, articulate desire, narrative memory and the other higher mental functions, or in other words, the realm of the intentional.

With this, we can define the first philosophical question to which the notion of mediation is clearly relevant: the question of the nature of distinctively human psychological capacities. For Vygotsky, it is human beings alone who actively deploy psychological tools, whose psychological activity is subject to normative standards of assessment, and for whom meaning permeates the life of the mind.

6. It might be protested that we have already begun to lose focus, having moved swiftly from the accessible (if not very impressive) example of the knot in the handkerchief into rather vague talk about meaning. So let us consider for a moment a mundane example. A man keeps a diary. Every day he records events in his life, making entries like:

> **May 15th** Slept badly but pepped up by leftover kedgeree for b-fast. Home in morning; wkd on mediation paper. Met CAS at airport. Kids music next week. Spurs win 2–0 – match live. Watched half of *Unmarried Woman*.

This commonplace example illustrates mediation at work in a number of respects. First, the diary is, of course, a psychological tool, what Wertsch calls a 'mediational means'. Like the knot, it is an aid to memory, but while the knot is forward-looking, the entry looks backwards. It leaves a trace. The practice of making entries like this is one way the man gives shape to his life. Second, it is also the case that, in the man's words we see his beliefs, desires, intentions, etc., standing in their characteristic interrelations and expressed in verbal form. Third, each entry, both in its form and content is mediated by what has been written before. And fourth, the case brings out a prominent aspect of mediation that we have so far not considered: the influence of culture. Diary writing is a speech genre, and what is written about is culturally mediated in various ways (even this tiny entry mentions diet, hobbies, work, relationships, duties, cultural media (film, sport)). It is important not to think of culture as *determining* what the man writes, or what he has to write about. Rather we inherit psychological tools from culture, and culture provides the context in which our activity makes the sense it does. Understanding the culture is a precondition of understanding the man, a truth that the man himself must reckon with when he goes in search of self-understanding. Thus, this slender example brings out numerous issues, each of which requires separate, careful treatment.

Some may be anxious to draw more robust conclusions. After all, it is characteristic of human beings to do things like keeping a diary, and this is the sort of fact that a contextually rich psychology must keep in view. Can we say what role the practice plays in the man's life? Well, someone may keep a diary and refer to it regularly, and the diary may thereby profoundly influence how the man understands himself and his life. But someone might keep such a diary and read it only occasionally, or never read it at all. In the latter case, the making of entries gives shape to the present and immediate past, and the practice of making them might serve somehow to fortify the man's life. But that's it. Tools, even psychological tools, may be used for various purposes. It's difficult to generalise, so here we must be particularists in psychology.

But, some may protest, surely the example displays something deep about the narrative construction of identity. Diary writing is a species of autobiography, and this is one of the practices that have come to be known as 'self-making'. And here we see another crucial dimension to the mediating role of culture. For the diary is text and its meaning is not within the author's control, just as the significance of our lives is not down to us. The diary entry, it might be argued, is one small piece of the very complex puzzle of the cultural constitution of the self.

It is important not to exaggerate the significance of narrative in the constitution of identity. There is indeed a sense in which a person's life story is an account of 'who she is', but what it is a story of – the life of a person – is not itself a story. A person is a living human being, not a text. Sometimes, accounts of the narrative construction of identity lose sight of this. Nevertheless, the diary entry does shed light on questions of identity because it reminds us of the centrality of mediation to the most intimate relation of all: our relation to ourselves. Self-consciousness is impossible without mediation. The self has no natural mirror: it needs to see itself at work in something that is other to it. Since self-consciousness is present in all human awareness and thought, if only implicitly, mediation is a precondition of mind. This is the second philosophical problem that the concept promises to illuminate.

7. The diary entry also reminds us of the relevance of mediation to questions of creativity. The entry is reminiscent of the form of inner speech, sharing something of the latter's compressed and abbreviated character. Vygotsky thought that inner speech gave us a window into thought's becoming, into the creative process in which reason finds expression in words. How, though, are we to understand the possibility of creativity, when any explanation of the creative act threatens to rob it of its novelty and thereby extinguish the very problem it was designed to address? Here mediation helps us move towards an answer. Every thought emerges in answer to a question or as a move in a conversation, though often with a merely hypothetical interlocutor. Thought is therefore mediated by desire – the desire to solve a problem, respond to a question, etc. and by otherness – by the interlocutor who raises the issue that prompts the desire to respond. The logic of creative thought is therefore dialogical in char-

acter, as the philosopher V.S. Bibler was fond of arguing, taking his cue from Vygotsky's reflections at the end of *Thought and Language*.[7]

8. This dialogical moment brings to mind yet another philosophical theme to which mediation is critical, a theme that some would portray as the most significant in Vygotsky's legacy, though it tends to be obscured in discussions of 'psychological tools' and 'mediational means'. This is the idea that the emergence and growth of the child's subjectivity is mediated by her engagement with the subjectivity of others. At the core of the self's dialogical essence lies the fact that the self emerges as self-for-another. It is not just that self-consciousness requires that the self recognise itself in its externalised activity. Rather, the self needs to find itself in the present subjectivity of others; reflected, as it were, in the gaze of primary caregivers to whom it is turned towards from the moment of its birth. Such thoughts are present in Vygotsky's wonderful passages on the emergence of the child's ability to point, and they have inspired some of the work on parent-child relations conducted by his followers. But they are often lost in Western treatments of dialogism that are preoccupied with acknowledging multiple voices, with democratising the society of mind. Vygotsky's concern, however, is predominantly with what the philosopher Felix Mikhailov calls *obrashchenie*, which translates (poorly) as the *addressivity* of subjectivity.[8] This notion, Mikhailov thinks, is key to mind's becoming, but its relevance is not restricted to questions of development, for addressivity is critical to the mind's on-going existence. Mind is essentially 'turned outward' to the world and to the minds of others.

9. The final philosophical problem to which mediation is often argued to be relevant is the problem of the mind's place in nature. Hegelian Marxists commonly argue that the mediating power of activity (labour) is the key to how 'man overcomes the estrangement between the objective world and the subjective world'. The quotation is from Marcuse,[9] but a similar theme is found of course in the writings of Ilyenkov, whose solution to the 'problem of the ideal' involves an account of activity humanising the natural world.[10]

It is important, however, not to invoke mediation to answer a question that has been wrongly posed in the first place. I fear we are prone to take a leaf

---

7   Vygotsky 1987d [ss 2, pp. 5–361].

8   See Mikhailov 2003. Consider also Mikhailov's remarks reported towards the end of Chapter 2 above.

9   Quoted in Kozulin 1990, p. 120.

10   Ilyenkov 2009a; 2014. See Chapters 6–9 above.

out of Descartes's book and cast mind and nature as so utterly different that it becomes impossible to see how a physical world could contain minded beings. We are then tempted to tell a story about how the supposed estrangement between mind and world is to be overcome, and here we look to the mediating role of activity to bridge the gap by endowing nature with qualities that are not alien to mind. But this looks like a just-so story of monumental proportions. Once mind and world are torn asunder in our metaphysics, nothing, not even activity, will put them back together. Better not to pose the problem in a way that opens up and metaphysical gap between mind and world that needs to be bridged. In any case, although metaphysical problems about the place of mind in nature are clearly Ilyenkov's concern, it is less clear to me that these are problems that really exercised Vygotsky himself.

10. To conclude, our tour of the philosophical significance of the Vygotskian concept of mediation has brought out the relevance of the concept to five dimensions of the question of the possibility of thought. These are:
(i)   the character of distinctively human psychological capacities;
(ii)   the possibility of self-consciousness;
(iii)   the nature of creativity;
(iv)   the preconditions of the development of subjectivity;
(iv)   the unity of mind and nature.
Though these phenomena are intimately related, the role mediation plays varies in each case. Here I have merely scratched the surface, but I hope I have done enough to show that a great deal of interest lies beneath.

∴

The next chapter takes up another fascinating notion of Vygotsky's, though one that has only recently been the subject of sustained discussion by commentators – the concept of *perezhivanie*. In 2018, I was invited to visit the Faculty of Education at Monash University. I elected to present a paper on *perezhivanie*, on which a number of faculty members there – including Marilyn Fleer and Nikolai Veresov – had published important work. I set out to liberate the concept of *perezhivanie* from the mystery in which it is sometimes shrouded and show its relevance to certain central debates in philosophy of education. That presentation formed the basis of the chapter that follows. Although the present 'Revisionist Revolution in Vygotsky Studies' may have fanned flames of controversy about the true nature of Vygotsky's legacy, one thing remains incontestable: Vygotsky's writings are a rich source of insights that invite development in ways that continually cast fresh light on contemporary issues. That is, I think, a true mark of Vygotsky's genius.

CHAPTER 12

Vygotsky's Concept of *Perezhivanie*:
Its Philosophical and Educational Significance

1. It often happens that words or phrases from one language are taken up into another. Sometimes they are 'naturalised', becoming part of the language that imports them. But some foreign expressions, though widely used, retain their foreign character. These are often phrases or compound words that resist grammatical integration. Familiar examples in English are *nouveau riche, status quo, modus operandi, persona non grata*, and so on *ad nauseam*. Such phrases are adopted because they strike hearers as particularly apt at capturing some phenomenon and there is no obvious English equivalent or natural translation. So speakers just insert the foreign words into English sentences.

Sometimes we find this phenomenon in theoretical discourse. A term figuring prominently in a theory expressed in language A starts to capture the imagination because it picks out a distinctive phenomenon unrecognised in the theoretical discourse of language B. Usually it is not just that the word or phrase refers to something B-speakers have missed; it is because it has conceptual connections and connotations not made perspicuous in language B. The term is integrated into discourse in language A in a fruitful way that has no parallel in B. This makes it difficult to translate, so B-speakers just adopt it as is. Even where there is a translation, the foreign term is often preferred. For example, someone might insist on speaking of *mauvaise foi* rather than 'bad faith' to invoke the distinctive web of conceptual connections and allusions evoked in the original French discursive context.

2. One term presently much discussed is the Russian *perezhivanie*. A number of thinkers inspired by the psychologist Lev Vygotsky have recently made claims about the significance of this notion and its theoretical promise, especially for educational theory.[1] The claims are diverse, but everyone is agreed that the term does not translate easily into English, and so it is increasingly common simply to drop the Russian word into English sentences. But since Russian is not a language that has lent many words to English, most non-Russian speakers

---

1 See Fleer, Rey, and Veresov 2017, and the special issues of *Mind, Culture, and Activity* (2016, vol. 23, no. 4) and *International Research in Childhood Education* (2016, vol. 7, no. 1).

will struggle to guess what the term means, so those who use it have to explain it. However, notwithstanding the burgeoning literature,[2] the concept remains shrouded in mystery.[3] For example, although Veresov and Fleer proclaim that *'perezhivanie* is one of the key concepts of cultural-historical [i.e. Vygotskian] theory', on the very same page they concur with Smagorinsky that it remains 'more a tantalizing notion than a concept with clear meaning'.[4]

This is cause for concern. Elusive concepts that seemingly get at something deep can engender a kind of cultish fascination. As time goes on, they may gain a life of their own, people tire of explaining them, and it becomes accepted that they denote something of critical importance when in fact their meaning remains obscure. So my aim here is to clarify the concept's significance and how best to capture this in English. In my view, we should avoid appropriating the Russian term and find ways that are natural in English to express what the Russian concept is so apt at revealing.

3. The term *perezhivanie* derives from the word *'zhit''* which means 'to live', conjoined with the prefix *'pere-'*, which means variously 'across', 'under', 'over', 'through', or 're-' or 'again' (so *perekhod* is the name for an 'underpass', 'crossing' or 'overpass'; *perekhodit'* is the verb 'to cross', *peredelat'* means 'to re-do', *peredumat'* means 'to re-think', and so on). So the verb *perezhivat'* conveys 'living through' or 'going through' something. For example, suppose a mother is meeting her 13-year-old daughter. The daughter is late and the mother is worried. When she finally arrives the mother says, '*Ya kak perezhivala!*' – meaning 'I was so worried', or 'I was really going through it'. Thus here the verb is used to convey a sort of experience, usually involving anxiety, suffering and distress. The emphasis is not only on the phenomenology. It is important that a specific something is the focus of worry, in this case, the child's absence. So the noun form, *perezhivanie*, conveys an experience, or an experiencing, in the sense of a living-though or going-through something.

It is tempting to think that the term delineates a particular *type* of experience (an *enduring* of something, characterised by emotional turmoil). That is, Vygotsky means to pick out a distinctive phenomenon distinguished from other modes of experiencing. However, I don't think that's the best interpretation. When Vygotsky discusses *perezhivanie* in the 'Problem of the Environment',[5] he describes the situation of three children with an alcoholic single-mother.

2   E.g. Blunden 2016; Mok 2017.
3   Kozulin 2016, p. 357.
4   Veresov and Fleer 2016, p. 351, citing Smagorinsky 2011, p. 339.
5   Vygotsky 1994a.

He argues that in order to understand how the environment influences the children's development, we have to appreciate how they experience their situation. The influence is not merely causal in the way that the children's development might be influenced by a toxin in the air. The environment affects them in virtue of their respective ways of making sense of their circumstances. In the case of the oldest, this is a complex dynamic, which plays out over time as he struggles to understand and orientate himself within his situation, and to influence it. Vygotsky deploys the concept *perezhivanie* to argue for a suitably rich, or 'thick', conception of experience that encapsulates the dynamic development of the child's self-conscious understanding of himself as being-in-the-situation.

4. Let us try to characterise this thick conception of experience, which I shall dub 'experience*'.

4.1. In Kantian terms, we can say that *experience* * *is a unity of spontaneity and receptivity*. It is a taking in of the situation by the subject. As such it has content – it is an experience *of* something. In experience*, this object is 'given to' the subject, but it is not *merely* given: it is present to the subject only through the mediation of concepts. Moreover, the way it is apprehended and understood is influenced by the subject's existing beliefs and attitudes, fashioned in light of past experience, her dispositions of character, and so on.

In many cases where we apprehend something familiar and unproblematic, we do not confront an issue about how we are to understand the situation before us. So as I sit and write this paper in an office at ANU, my awareness of my immediate environment does not present me with significant interpretative problems. I am equipped with a repertoire of concepts adequate to make sense of my surroundings. This is not entirely so, since, having just arrived from afar as a visiting academic, my surroundings are unfamiliar. The office contains a few objects mysterious to me (*that* must be some kind of computer dongle left behind by a previous visitor; *this* must be the thermostat, etc.). Of course, if we look beyond the perceptual apprehension of my immediate environment to encompass other dimensions of my experience* as a visiting scholar, then I quickly encounter rather more problematic issues, such as whether I am meeting expectations and making a good impression, whether I feel 'at home' here, whether everything is 'going well'. These questions pervade the way I experience* my surroundings. However, I generally have the conceptual resources to address all this, it is just not clear to me what to think. Of course, my experience* is mediated not just by concepts but by everything I bring to the situation, which includes the influence of past experience, aspects of my personality, temperament, powers of imagination, and so on.

In the case Vygotsky considers, the oldest boy initially lacks resources to cope with his situation. He cannot draw on relevant past experience*, he lacks the powers of imagination and qualities of character necessary to decide how to act, and his grasp on the concepts he needs to make sense of his circumstances is inadequate. In Vygotsky's story, the boy gradually comes to assume responsibility for his mother and siblings, by taking over the role of his absent father. In the course of his experience*, his conceptual resources are enriched in a way that enables him to act. His understanding matures. He now sees what the concept of responsibility asks of him. And this understanding is of a piece with his finding within himself the strength of character and the powers of imagination that enable him to perform the role he sees he must play.

So when we say that experience* involves the unity of spontaneity and receptivity, we need to recognise the dialectical interplay at work as experience* engenders the development of the subject's conceptual resources, which in turn transforms the subject's experience*, thereby engendering further conceptual development. And all that plays out in relation to the child's developing personality and powers of mind.

4.2. *Experience* has essentially evaluative and emotional dimensions.* Its content is permeated by value and emotion. These evaluative and emotional components are not merely projected by the subject onto an evaluatively-neutral object. Rather, experience* is apprehended as something that contains value for the subject to discover and that warrants certain emotional responses. So the subject experiences* the object as beautiful or ugly, uplifting or disgusting, noble or contemptuous, etc., and the subject's delight, indignation, joy, anger, jealousy, fear, depression, etc. are understood as responses merited by the character of the object experienced*.

It is crucial that these emotional and evaluative dimensions are intrinsically part of the experience* itself. It is not that the real object of experience is, strictly speaking, an object of intellectual apprehension, and the evaluative components are subjective responses that lend value to objective reality. Rather, subjects always-already find themselves in situations which call from them evaluative and emotional responses the appropriateness of which they must discern and assess. Recognising this helps illuminate the intimate relation between experience*, action and activity. If the world as I experience* it calls forth evaluative and emotional responses from me, then experience is not motivationally inert. On the contrary, the world as I experience* it will demand (or permit, suggest, etc.) that I act in certain ways; my experience* will require that I do such and such, allow me to do so and so, render this way of acting appropriate and that one inappropriate, and so on. Once again, we see a dialectical interplay: by acting I change the world, and hence change my experience* and what it calls upon me to do. And, of course, our two dialectical processes are really one: experience* wrings from me both understanding and action, which in turn changes the situation and my understanding thereof, prompting further transformation on both sides of the subject-object relation.

4.3. *Experience* is essentially self-conscious* in at least two respects. First, the subject is necessarily aware of her experience*. She may misinterpret what she is experiencing, but she is necessarily aware *that* she is experiencing. One might say, experience* is an object of subjective awareness (though 'subjective' is ultimately redundant).

This is not to say that aspects of experience* may not influence subjects in ways of which they are unaware. My traumatic experience* may cause in me dispositions of character that I do not know I have, and if I later become aware of them I may remain ignorant of their cause. However, though elements of my experience* may not reach awareness, or may exercise unconscious influence, they must be understood as elements of an experience of which I was aware.

Second, experience* is an object of self-conscious reflection. Indeed, if the object of experience* is troubling, as in Vygotsky's example, then experience* will be essentially such as to invite reflection. Subjects will not just be aware of what they are experiencing*, but of *how* they are experiencing it, of the evaluative and emotional dimensions of the experience*, and they will self-consciously attempt to make sense of the experience*. At first, this might be an inchoate struggle, which only later begins to offer illumination as the subject finds the resources to render her experience* intelligible and to understand how it is appropriate to think, feel and act in its light. (Of course, subjects might resist engaging in self-conscious reflection. But experience* is *such as to* prompt such reflection, even if it does not do so in some particular case. What needs explanation is why the subject does not reflect, not why she does.)

5. What, then, is experience*? As I mentioned above, a natural response is to say that experience* is a particular *kind* of experience; namely, the conceptually-mediated, personality-inflected, emotionally-evaluatively-agentially self-conscious and reflection-inducing kind. Experiences of this type are to be found in certain particular contexts (e.g. of trauma, turmoil, struggle, suffering, etc.) and lend themselves to certain forms of analysis, therapeutic or phenomenological.

I want to suggest a different interpretation. In my view, experience* is just experience. We can drop the asterix. All experience contains the dimensions illuminated in the discussion of experience*, it's just that the emotional, evaluative and agential dimensions of experience are often familiar, undramatic and unproblematic, and don't pose questions for us that prompt reflection, or at least reflection that is enduring, agonising and transformative. Sometimes my experience may leave me nonplussed about how to react, but this may not matter. Although the situation as I perceive it is laden with evaluative, emotional and agential significance, there may be nothing much at stake, so its elusiveness doesn't provoke a struggle for meaning. Moreover, even where I recognise that I don't know what to think or feel, I may hold that the best course is to relax and be patient: in time things may come to make sense and the issues resolve themselves. Perhaps too much reflection on my experience will only inhibit understanding and impede resolution.

Moreover, to hold that experience is essentially value-laden, emotion-inducing and action-orientated is not to deny that some experiences may just leave us cold. My drive home from work warrants no particular emotional reaction, I see it as neither good nor bad. Similarly, reading a book or seeing a film might be a profound emotional experience that changes my life in some way, but some books and movies may just leave me indifferent. We should not conclude there are two kinds of experience, the emotionally laden sort and the indifferent sort. Rather, we should say that experience has emotional, evaluative, agential dimensions, but sometimes they are dialed down, even to zero (though something may occur to dial them up, causing me, e.g. to see the book that once left me cold in a different light).

So my recommendation is that we translate *perezhivanie* as 'experience', so long as we work with a thick conception that acknowledges the phenomena Vygotsky wanted to highlight. That way, we can wean ourselves off the temptation to insert the Russian term into English sentences, and decisively counter the cultish implication that *only* the Russian will do.

The plausibility of this recommendation can be difficult to see precisely because philosophers and psychologists have often used the term 'experience' in a thin and denuded sense to denote perceptual experience understood as the in-the-moment apprehension of the immediate environment. And they posit as the vehicles of experience, sensory representations, which go by many names ('ideas', 'impressions', 'sensations', 'appearances', 'sense-data', and so on) but which, given the prominence of vision in epistemological discussions, are treated on the model of pictorial representations (something akin to retinal images, only in the mind rather than the eye). Notwithstanding the notorious difficulties individuating and identifying such phenomena, philosophers have been wont to construe perceptual experience as comprised of the apprehension of such perceptual entities (or the apprehension of the world via the mediation of such entities). If we allow ourselves to think of experience as something complex and enduring (a person's experience of a sunset in the Rockies, for instance), then it is understood as a complex composed of many more fundamental perceptual experiences, conceived as elements of the whole.

A Vygotskian ought to resist such a compositional view of experience and argue that the supposed entities we pick out as the component parts of an enduring experience are not free-standing atoms, but merely abstractions from the whole, upon which they ultimately owe their nature and identity. At present, as I take in the room in which I am sitting, I cannot characterise the parts of my experience out of relation to my experience as a whole. Of course, I can focus in on *that* green cabinet, and make its 'greenness' the object of perceptual attention. But it is folly to think I am thereby getting at one of the perceptual simples out of which my experience is composed. Our experience forms a unity and we articulate its parts only by abstraction therefrom. We shouldn't kid ourselves that the parts have an independent existence.

Once we overcome the tendency to think of experience as so much philosophy and psychology has,[6] we can make better sense of *perezhivanie*, understood not as something we invoke to supplement the traditional conception of experience, but as a plausible alternative to it.

6. In my view, this rich conception of experience is in harmony with Vygotsky's thinking when he deploys the concept *perezhivanie*. Commentators make much of the supposed differences between Vygotsky's use of the term in his early *Psychology of Art*,[7] and the later writings 'The Problem of the Environment'[8] and 'The Crisis at Age Seven'.[9] It is not uncommon to read that, in his later works, Vygotsky's treatment in *perezhivanie* marks a transition in his thinking: it is part of his developing interest in semiotic mediation, in a psychology of sense and subjectivity, which Vygotsky never lived to develop, and that is why the concept remains pregnant and mysterious. *Perezhivanie* is thus presented as a potentially fruitful, but ultimately incomplete and underdeveloped notion that Vygotsky perceptively invoked on his journey towards the cultural-historical theory he never managed to articulate. So now it falls to us to continue that journey ...

6　Though by no means all, of course. Dewey is a notable exception (e.g. 1934; 1938); see also Ryle 1949, McDowell 1994, Noë 2004.
7　Vygotsky 1971 (1987c).
8　Vygotsky 1994a.
9　Vygotsky 1998a, ch. 11 [*ss* 4, pp. 376–85].

However, once we interpret Vygotsky's remarks about *perezhivanie* in light of the rich conception of experience articulated above, it becomes clear that there is continuity between Vygotsky's early and late thinking, at least on this score. A thick conception of experience is precisely what one needs if one is trying to understand the aesthetic experience of, say, an actor working her way into a role, or an audience being transported into the world of the play. In turn, such insights in the psychology of art might be expected to illuminate the nature of pretend play and its role in the psychological development of the child (a classic Vygotskian topic), and as we saw, they bear on how we are to understand the influence of the environment on the developing child. I think Vygotsky appreciated throughout his career that such a concept must figure centrally in any theory of individual development, for it allows us to portray the child's consciousness of herself and her situation as a function of her developing intellectual, conceptual, emotional, attitudinal, imaginative and evaluative capacities, as well as personality, memory and so on. This is a conception of experience that invites us to see the mind as an organic unity of psychological powers, powers of an embodied agent engaged with the world, so that we might do psychology cognisant of what Vygotsky calls 'the full vitality of life'.[10]

7. Let us now consider how this notion of experience might be deployed. In the present context, I propose consider the application of the notion to an issue in education.

Before I begin, however, I want to make a general remark about the application of theoretical concepts in cultural-historical inquiries. Very often, Vygotskian concepts are used to interpret 'data', often taking the form of observations of activity (e.g. classroom activities), or perhaps accounts of activity provided by participants (e.g. a teacher describing her situation, or a transcription of students' commentaries on what they are doing, or of conversations between teachers and students). All too often, the purported analysis simply amounts to a re-description of the material using the concepts in question. So, if we can, say, describe a conversation between teacher and student using the concepts in question, it is assumed that this illuminates the situation under study. Now, sometimes this *is* illuminating – finding the right terms to describe events can be explanatory. But often it achieves little or nothing. We cannot assume that just because we can put something into 'Vygotsky-speak', we are closer to understanding it. Sometimes, in fact, we understand the phenomena under investigation perfectly well *before* the theoretical analysis and it is only in virtue

---

10   Vygotsky 1987d, p. 50 [*ss* 2, p. 21].

of that prior understanding that we grasp the sense of the purported analysis. This is particularly true of certain applications of the term *perezhivanie*.

When I speak of 'applying' the concept of experience I have something different in mind. Rather than thinking about how we might use it as a tool of qualitative data-analysis, I propose to use it to reinterpret some familiar educational terms of art. At my university, for example, there is a lot of talk about 'the student experience', both in discussions of the university's strengths (e.g. we offer a 'unique student experience') and in discussions of the pros and cons of possible innovations (e.g. such-and-such is desirable because it will enhance 'the student experience'). Now although everyone thinks they know what 'the student experience' means, few would be able to unpack this idea in any detail. They can point to some special things about the student experience at Queen's that differentiate it from other institutions, and they can point to metrics that supposedly indicate quality of student experience (e.g. high retention and graduation rates). But that's about it. Part of the problem is that it won't do simply to enumerate the kinds of facilities and opportunities open to Queen's students because what is at stake is something about the *ethos* and history of the institution, about *what it is like* to be a member of the student body and how all that influences one's 'whole experience' of life at Queen's. To get a handle on the idea of 'one's whole experience' we need precisely the thick notion of experience I have characterised with Vygotsky's help.

Talk of 'the student experience' is a manifestation of a still broader notion that is in common use, and which is no easier to define. This is the idea of *educational experience*, a term that can be applied to anything from a moment of insight in a lesson to a person's entire educational career (a person might speak, for example, of her 'educational experience in the UK', which ranges from her entering primary school to her completing her doctorate). For present purposes, let us focus on the concept of educational experience as it might be applied to a course, a module, a lesson, or some mid-sized unit of educational activity. I want to suggest that our thick conception of experience is exactly what is needed to give content to the idea: that is, to understand and evaluate educational experience, we must have in play a conception of the student's evolving awareness and understanding of the object of learning, and of themselves as engaging with the object, which incorporates precisely emotional, evaluative and agential dimensions, in their evolving interplay, and which thinks of educational activity as world-disclosing and situated in 'the full vitality of life'.

The task of characterising educational experience can be approached in various ways. Our idea might be to articulate a developmental-explanatory account of learning and instruction, an account that attempts to explain the causal preconditions of learning. Or one might have a normative agenda: one's interest might be in the *quality* of educational experience, and one's concern might be to distinguish 'positive' educational experiences from 'negative' ones. If one works with a sharp distinction between description and evaluation, facts and norms, it might look like these are different matters, though of course, it is hard to pursue an interest in the facts of learning without normative considerations entering at every turn. Education is a good, so normative considerations are always in view.

Here I shall focus directly on the normative and ask by what criteria we should evaluate educational experience. First, I want boldly to suggest that the axes of evaluation should comprise the following interrelated dimensions. We should ask whether the experience is: (i) fulfilling, (ii) enriching, (iii) inspiring, (iv) affirming, (v) personal, and (vi) authentic. An outstanding educational experience will exhibit some or all of these qualities to an appropriate degree and in appropriate balance. An unsatisfying educational experience will be wanting in some or all of these qualities. Second, I want to claim that to understand these criteria, and to grasp their mutual relations, we should operate with the thick conception of experience we have inherited from Vygotsky's discussions of *perezhivanie*.

7.1 To say that an educational experience is *fulfilling* is not merely to say that the learner derives satisfaction from it. Fulfilment is not a merely subjective measure. It presupposes that the outcome of the educational activity is the acquisition of knowledge, which might include the cultivation of valuable skills. Whatever the learner feels about the process, it cannot be fulfilling unless its object and outcome are worthwhile, useful, meaningful, illuminating, and so on. The emotional and evaluative dimensions of the educational experience have to be understood in light of the learner's relation to the world and her agency within it.

7.2 The same goes for *enrichment*, where intellectual, emotional and evaluative dimensions are again all in play. And once again, whether some educational activity enriches us is not a merely subjective matter. It depends upon the value of what is learnt and how it complements our existing knowledge and competencies. At its best, enrichment involves not merely adding to, enhancing and illuminating students' present conceptions and capabilities, but expanding their horizons, so that new and hitherto-unexpected opportunities for learning come into view. Students are enriched by learning x, because it now enables them to learn y. Here I have in mind, not merely an instrumental relation (as when learning to add enables one later to learn to multiply), but of cases where, until one has learnt x, one cannot even see the point or value of y. (So, say, taking a certain course in music might open up to one a world of musical appreciation that was simply not available to one before.)

7.3 An educational experience is *inspiring* if it excites the learner to see beyond the internal logic of the educational moment itself, moving her, for instance, to study or inquire further, to embrace certain values, take up certain activities, and so on.

7.4 To say that an educational experience is *affirming* is to say that the learner understands herself to have been fulfilled and enriched by the activity in a way that enhances her flourishing, sustains her commitments, stimulates her growth, and contributes to her living a meaningful life. In an education, what we learn becomes a part of ourselves; the learner has to be able to 'make it her own'. This does not entail that all learning must serve to endorse the learner's prior conception of herself. Some learning is genuinely transformative – but in that transformation we reject our former views or values in order to embrace others that better conform to our evolving conception of ourselves and the world.

7.5 Educational experiences are thus *personal* in the sense that they speak to the learner, who recognises (or endeavours to recognise) their value and significance, not merely impersonally, but in relation to herself and her life. Of course, this does not imply that these experiences may not happen in consort with other people. Indeed, certain educational experiences will be possible *only* in consort with others. Some things can only be learnt in dialogue with peers, and sometimes students' relation to their teachers is essential to the educational experience.

7.6 Finally, to say that the educational experience is *authentic* is to acknowledge that it enhances and illuminates in a way that respects the integrity of the object of learning and of norms of reasoning and inquiry. It is important that, in our educational endeavours, we recognise that we are accountable, not just to ourselves and to others, but to the discipline, and ultimately, to reality. This is an important part of what it is to understand oneself as seeking knowledge, theoretical and practical (knowledge of what to think, of what to do, and how to do it ...).

It should be clear that my six criteria are not independent components of an educational experience. We can think of them as 'virtues' that together comprise a unity of mutually-enhancing qualities. Whether the list is complete is contestable, as is my characterisation of the virtues listed. Moreover, we can expect the question of whether and to what degree some educational experience exhibits these virtues also to be contentious. This is not a checklist of easily identifiable qualities that can form a litmus test for educational excellence. Educational administrators, who like to measure quality, may be disappointed by the complexity of the picture I have offered. I do not preclude the articulation of metrics that might capture something of this picture: but before one can devise means of measurement one has to know what one is trying to measure.

Much could be said by way of explanation and qualification, but for now I will restrict myself to one qualification. Nothing in this picture is supposed to deny that learning can be difficult, distressing, disorientating, disturbing, and so on, and that sometimes the quality of an educational experience is enhanced by the fact that one achieves one's goals in spite of (or because of) adversity. And this is not just a feature of the emotional-motivational aspects of learning: it may be that a person's understanding of the subject matter is enhanced by her struggles with it (you don't fully appreciate the character of a philosophical theory unless you appreciate how difficult it is to understand it, and you don't appreciate that unless you have been through the turmoil of trying to make sense of it). So fulfilment, enrichment, affirmation, and so on, do not preclude struggle, from within the midst of which they may seem a long way off. This is, in fact, just another dimension to the authenticity of learning.

8. Having parlayed the Vygotskian notion of *perezhivanie* into a recognisable notion of experience, and having used that notion to illuminate the concept *educational experience*, I now propose to reflect on how the insights so far accumulated might be applied to a particular issue: the evaluation of new learning technologies.

In recent years, there is much discussion about the power and potential of emerging educational technologies, a discussion which has suddenly become unavoidable, as the COVID-19 pandemic has forced schools and universities into a vast experiment in distance education. The issues around new learning technologies have long provoked strong feelings, and at the extremes of the spectrum we see, at one end, utopian visions of escaping the constraints of the traditional classroom for the garden of digital delights and, at the other, dystopian speculations about the displacement of teachers by computers and a brave new world of technologically-enhanced learners.

These extreme positions pose deep and dark philosophical questions (e.g. ethics for cyborgs in conditions of posthumanism ...), but if we concern ourselves with the evaluation of technologies designed to enhance learning in educational contexts familiar to us – such as remote learning under conditions of pandemic – what tools do we have? Of course, there are no plausible general philosophical arguments against the use of learning technologies. After all, books and blackboards are technologies, and we would now view arguments against their use as absurd. Everything depends on what the technology enables teachers and learners to do, and whether its use enhances or detracts from something we regard as of genuine educational value. So technologies must be carefully evaluated for their particular merits and failings. And this is no easy matter because we often have to confront difficult questions about what is educationally important, and these questions are not easy to treat in the abstract.

I suggest we approach the evaluation of educational technologies by exploring their effects on the educational experience understood in the way I sketched above. Of course, this does not offer a simple test of some proposed technology that will quickly settle the controversy. But it does enable us to ask meaningful questions about the role and value of the innovation in question, and it equips us with resources in which to frame answers and debate the strengths and weaknesses. We must ask: How does this proposed technology contribute to a learning experience that is fulfilling, enriching, inspiring, affirming, personal and authentic? Debating that will bring into view what is really at stake. Indeed, such questions need to be asked, not just about new technologies, but about existing, familiar ones. The ubiquitous use of PowerPoint or of 'pop quizzes' in university instruction, for example, might be fruitfully evaluated by these criteria.

9. To conclude. We began by considering the present interest in the notion of *perezhivanie*, as it finds expression in the work of Vygotsky. Because it is difficult to find a single English word to translate *perezhivanie*, the Russian term is now finding its way untranslated into English papers. I argued that this is unfortunate. Better to try to understand the gap that this term is being used to fill. I argued that what it offers is a way of capturing a thick conception of experience – experience as world-directed, but as permeated with emotional, evaluative and agential dimensions, and open to reflective, self-conscious awareness and critical evaluation. I further argued that we should not see this as a distinctive, and perhaps rare, kind of experience. Rather, *all* experience has these dimensions. So we just need to work with a suitably rich concept of experience, abandoning the narrow and denuded notions that have dominated so much philosophical and psychological thinking. I then sought to draw on this thick notion to illuminate the (much used but usually unanalysed) concept of educational experience. I offered an account of the criteria by which to evaluate the quality of educational experience in the form of six interrelated virtues. Having done that, I showed how the resulting conception might be applied to the evaluation of new learning technologies.

Vygotsky's legacy has been rightly influential in educational theory and psychology. However, notwithstanding Vygotsky's intensely philosophical cast of

mind, his work has not had a major impact in philosophy of education.[11] Bringing the discussion of *perezhivanie* into view promises, I believe, to connect
Vygotskian ideas to debates at the centre of philosophy of education (advocates of Deweyian or phenomenological approaches may find much of interest).
In any case, I hope to have shown that the Vygotskian concept of *perezhivanie* is
rightly inspiring, and it can be freed of the mystery in which it is often shrouded.
Such mystery as remains is due to the depths of the phenomenon it denotes:
human experience in all its richness and complexity.

∴

This chapter explored a Vygotskian concept – *perezhivanie* – in which a number of scholars today find contemporary relevance. One of the most striking
features of the ideas of both Vygotsky and Ilyenkov is that they continue to be
seen as fertile sources to refresh and invigorate debates in philosophy, psychology and educational theory. Indeed, my own interest in these thinkers has from
the outset been focused on the fecundity of their theories. I have never wished
merely to chronicle their thought, but to treat their ideas as living contributions to enduring controversies of profound importance. The next and final
section addresses head-on the contemporary relevance of our subject matter
and brings it into dialogue with like-minded thinkers from other traditions.

In 'Minds, Brains and Education', I draw on Ilyenkov's famous controversy
with Dubrovsky to imagine what he would have made of debates about the
relevance of brain science to educational theory and practice. Three papers
then follow that examine the rise of activity theory in Russia and the West
and consider how the concept of activity can be deployed to illuminate our
understanding of action, self-consciousness and the human life form. The final
chapter surveys the themes of my 2011 book, *The Formation of Reason*, which
brings ideas gleaned from Vygotsky, Mikhailov and Ilyenkov into conversation
with one of the most inspiring philosophers of the (post-)analytic tradition,
John McDowell. The section begins, however, by returning to the topic of collective remembering and examing how that phenomenon might be treated in
the cultural psychology of Jerome Bruner, a figure instrumental in introducing
Vygotsky's psychology to the West in the early 1960s. Although I admire the creativity and erudition of Bruner's vision, which enables us to place the marvels
of human memory against a far richer background than that typically counten-
anced by empirical psychology, I venture a critique, inspired by Ilyenkov and

---

11   Though see, e.g., Derry's important book (2013); Su and Bellman 2018; Luntley 2018.

McDowell, of the constructivist dimensions of his approach, which, I feel, open the door to a debilitating relativism. As I have suggested in earlier chapters, such a framework impedes, rather than stimulates, the fruitful interpretation of the Vygotskian ideas to which Bruner is indebted.

PART 4

Contemporary Applications

CHAPTER 13

Memory, Identity and the Future of Cultural Psychology

I begin with two examples. The first is a case of experiential memory.[1] Whenever I hear the opening of the Beatles' 'All My Loving' I experience an uncanny sensation of the past. I am transported to my early childhood in the 1960s, when the song was new. Unlike paradigmatic cases of experiential

---

1 An experiential memory is one which essentially involves memory experience or imagery. When A experientially remembers O, A has a memory experience of O, and O's having been the case is appropriately related to A's present experience of O (e.g. that O was the case is part of the explanation of why A now has memory experiences of O). Experiential memory is to be contrasted with 'propositional' or 'factual' memory: memory that p. I remember that my parents moved to such and such an address before I was born, or that Napoleon was born in Corsica, without bringing to mind experiences of the events or persons remembered, or indeed any experiences at all.

Experiential memory involves (in some sense) 'reliving' the past. Thus, David Wiggins writes that remembering once climbing the stairs of the Eiffel Tower involves rehearsing to oneself 'something and enough of that climbing of those stairs ... rehearsing it from the point of view of the climber' (Wiggins 1992, p. 339). This is obviously close to the truth, but some qualifications are necessary. First, we are prone to think that experiential memory is like a mental video recording of events, but the imagery that comprises experiential memories is often fragmented and disjointed, and sometimes pertains to the mood of the events or states of affairs remembered. Second, Wiggins may be wrong to imply that experiential memories must represent the past events from the point of view from which the events were originally experienced by the rememberer. Sometimes, our experiential memories (like our dreams) represent us as we were from a *third-person* perspective, although such images are often juxtaposed with others that are first-personal (e.g. I see myself as a little boy riding a tricycle in the garden from the perspective of a spectator, while at the same time remembering how the peddles felt, how the handlebars looked as I rode, etc.). It is too quick to rule out these third-personal representations of self as not genuine memory experiences on the grounds that they are obviously constructions (perhaps based on stories we have heard about the events in question). After all, many first-personal memory images also involve significant elements of construction; moreover, the constructions in question may themselves have been formed at the time of the original events (perhaps we often form a (usually unconscious) representation of our body as if from a third-person perspective), and hence our present awareness of these images is related to representations of events causally grounded in past experience in a way that is, arguably, sufficient to count as experiential remembering of how things were.

It would be a mistake to sharply counterpose experiential and factual remembering, for many cases of remembering involve both propositional and experiential dimensions. Memories that p are often engendered by, or engender, experiential memories.

remembering, this memory does not involve determinate imagery or the reliving of specific events. The sensation is a seemingly unmediated presentment of the past; one so bare that my present self cannot impose itself upon it and domesticate it. I am somehow able to recapture the mood of how things were, to be fleetingly 'back then'. This brings me nostalgic pleasure, tinged with sadness, as one might feel coming across a scrap of handwriting of a long dead relative.

This case brings out the close relation between memory and identity. Just as the sensation reminds me intimately of who I am, so the example reminds us that our identity depends on an enduring stream of self-conscious experience that rests, in turn, on memory's power to place present experience in a temporal continuum.[2] Our personal histories are histories of lived experience. This fact is central to our understanding of ourselves.

Now an example of collective remembering. Consider the following passage:

> In March 1979 the strangeness began. I called on him one day and was immediately struck that he appeared peaceful, reconciled. His usual state was one of inner turmoil, as if he felt all the sorrows of the world as a sharp pain in his soul. Now suddenly he was lighter. I was even more surprised to find, sitting at his trusty typewriter, his three year old nephew, Van'ka, banging at the keys with all his might. I voiced concern for the machine. He replied, 'Ah, it doesn't matter'.
>
> His melancholy worsened. He began to ignore meetings at the Institute of Philosophy. One day, as I left the Institute, I phoned him. He answered my questions in monosyllables. When I suggested that he get some rest (as if anyone were forcing him to work) he answered, 'Yes, yes, for good'. And when I said goodbye, he replied abstractedly, 'Farewell'.
>
> Why farewell? After all, he wasn't going anywhere ... It seems, however, that he had long known where he was going. He just wasn't clear about the method. But soon that was decided too. The pathologist examining his body asked suddenly, 'Did this man know anatomy?'[3]

---

2 This is not to say that I hold a 'psychological continuity theory' of personal identity, according to which a person, A, is the same person at time, t2, as at an earlier time, t1, only if there is the right kind of continuity, underwritten by A's memory, in A's mental states (beliefs, desires, memories, dispositions of character, etc.) between these times. I hold only that psychological continuity is an important dimension of our conception of (normal) personhood, not that it is a strict condition of personal identity (see Bakhurst 2011, ch. 3).

3 Mareev 1994, pp. 17–18.

So Sergei Mareev describes the last days of Russian philosopher Evald Ilyenkov.[4] Although the text presents an individual's recollections, it is nevertheless an instance of collective remembering, a contribution to a joint endeavour: remembering Ilyenkov. Such biographical writing, however personal in mood, is a social utterance in a social medium (language mediated by specific narrational devices), addressed to others and subject to their scrutiny. It contributes a part to a picture that is collectively sustained, and its significance depends on that wider picture.

Biography is, of course, just one of innumerable ways we sustain an image of our past. Through the written word, photograph, film, audio and video recording, ritual and memorial, and so on, the past is constantly made present. This is no small fact, but a defining feature of the human condition as it now is.

Collective remembering, no less than experiential memory, pertains to matters of identity. The question, 'Who was Ilyenkov?', may only be explored by engaging in practices of collective remembering that aspire to tell the story of his life and work. In a sense, Ilyenkov *just is* the focus of that narrative. Of course, after Ilyenkov's death, all that remains is the story of his life. But that story was hardly less crucial when he was alive, for Ilyenkov was *for himself* the subject of the emerging story of his life. So we all see ourselves, as we aspire to live meaningful lives. As Alasdair MacIntyre has stressed, the integrity of an individual's life depends on its being seen as a narrative which runs from birth to death.[5]

MacIntyre, we might note, has sympathies with the Greek view that the character of a person's death – the point of closure – is a crucial factor giving shape to her life as a whole. Thus we might surmise that Ilyenkov felt the narrative coherence of his life demanded his suicide, or perhaps it was a belief that his life had ceased to constitute a meaningful narrative that provoked his death. The issue is contestable, and might remain so even if we had access to Ilyenkov's testimony. The special relation of an individual to the events of his life provides no guarantee that his version of events is authoritative, as those who mourn Ilyenkov have reason to lament.

---

4   Mareev's book is a collection of personal reminiscences about Ilyenkov. It was published in an edition of 250 copies, a poor reproduction of a rough typescript, barely superior in quality to a *samizdat*, and evidence of the fragility of collective memory.

5   MacIntyre 1981, ch. 15.

1   The Social and the Individual: Priority Disputes

We might say that our examples illuminate distinct species of memory, related
to different aspects of identity. On the one hand, there is the 'inner-worldly',
first-personal acquaintance with the past that sustains our identities as enduring subjects of experience; on the other, there are the public, 'third-personal'
practices of collective remembering, vital to our identities as subjects of lives
lived in social space. It is tempting to keep the two phenomena apart, arguing
that they represent contrasting modes of awareness of self in time.

Yet this manoeuvre obscures the fact that the individual and social dimensions of memory are so evidently interrelated. Collective remembering depends, obviously, on episodes of first-personal awareness. Mareev's account, for
instance, is composed of reports of experiential memories, supplemented by
factual memories (he may not actually have heard the pathologist's remark). It
is part of a narrative presentation of Ilyenkov's life, but of course its focal point
is a subject of experience. And Mareev's account stands or falls on the evidence
of experiential memory, which plays a key role in the epistemic evaluation of
narrative.

At the same time, experiential memory, as we possess it, depends on our
ability to place memory images into context. Without a framework in which to
locate the deliverances of memory, only fractured presentments, disconnected
images, and stark propositions would remain. Voluntary acts of remembering
would be impossible. Thus the socially entrenched skills that structure collective remembering are implicated in the possibility of experiential memory. We
might speculate that a being unable to see itself as the focus of a life-story could
not have experiential memories as we understand them. Thus our identities
as self-conscious subjects of experience depend on our identities as 'narrative
selves'.

It is nevertheless inviting to try to subordinate the social dimension of
memory to the individual, or vice versa. Traditionally, psychology has treated
personal memory as the primary notion. It is awfully tempting to try to turn the
tables and argue that all memory, even in its most intimate personal aspects,
is imbued with the social. Such a position might be developed from Vygotsky's
writings, as discussed in Chapter 3 above, or discerned in views inspired by him,
such as social constructionist and discursive psychology, and my focus here –
Jerome Bruner's cultural psychology.

One argument for the primacy of the social takes up the idea that experiential memories are nothing without interpretation. We talk as if self-interpreting
images pop up on the mind's stage. But this, it is argued, is Cartesian claptrap.
There are no self-interpreting images and no theatre of the mind for them to

populate. The self is not a passive spectator of the mind's show, but an active interpreter. And interpretation involves skills of classification and narrative that are socially forged and sustained. The mind's objects are thus, in a significant sense, fashioned by cultural 'tools' and all memory is thereby imbued with sociality.

This position is insightful, but flawed. Consider again the 'All My Loving' example. This involuntary remembering yields a sensation with an obscure content that I must respect. Because it is obscure, I have to deploy powers of thought and interpretation that are, no doubt, culturally mediated. But my memory experience is not itself a social or cultural construct, for it is not a construct at all. It is a presentment of the past that *warrants* one or other interpretation. The same is true of many less curious memory experiences. The past intrudes upon us in personal memory (I almost mean that literally), and our beliefs and interpretations must conform to its deliverances.

This might suggest that I am reinventing the idea of 'the given' in the domain of memory. Such a strategy, it will be argued, is hopeless, for there are no 'raw' memory images, no 'bare presences' like the sense-data of old. Anything contentful before the mind is already conceptualised, construed, interpreted. This is as true of memory (truer?) as of perception.

I am no advocate of the myth of the given. I do think, however, that we need to revise the pictures of the relation of mind and world that influence much debate about social memory, in particular the assumption of the ubiquity of interpretation that informs much cultural and constructionist psychology.[6] We must abandon the idea that what the mind confronts is the product of interpretation, together with the key metaphor that motivates it: the idea of the mind as organising experience. To see why, consider how these problematic ideas figure in Bruner's work.[7]

---

6   See, e.g., Bruner 1991, pp. 8–9.

7   The metaphor of the mind 'organising' experience – central to many empiricist views, and to neo-Kantian versions of the dualism of 'conceptual scheme' and 'sensory content' – takes various guises in Bruner's work. In *In Search of Mind*, for example, Bruner describes 'the world we perceive directly' as 'a filtering, a sorting out, and finally a construction' and writes that '[t]he nature of the filter and of the construction processes that work with it – these constitute the *real* philosopher's stone. It does not turn base metal into gold, but turns physical "stimuli" into knowledge, a much more valuable transformation' (1983, p. 66). For a lengthier treatment of Bruner's position (which also includes a discussion of the relevance of Ilyenkov's philosophy to Bruner's views), see Bakhurst 1995b (revised as Bakhurst 2005a).

2   Cultural Psychology on the Road to Irrealism

Bruner presents cultural psychology as an alternative to two psychological orthodoxies. The first is Piaget's universalistic view of psychological development, which, Bruner argues, fails to appreciate that psychological development involves the acquisition of a variety of domain specific capacities designed for tasks that are, to a large degree, culturally defined.[8] We must recognise that culture is a repository of psychological skills (a 'tool kit'), a support-system for the acquisition of mental powers, and a site of distributed knowledge. Piaget's approach is also scientistic, portraying all knowledge as scientific theory-building and casting children as little mathematicians, logicians, scientists. This is a poor basis to explain their developing knowledge of social reality and of other minds, which involves normative modes of explanation, narrative structures of interpretation, empathy and hermeneutical sensibilities.

The second rejected orthodoxy is the legacy of the cognitive revolution, which ousted behaviourism only to substitute a no less impoverished view of human beings as information-processors.[9] This, Bruner argues, renders psychology unable to understand *meaning*, a concept crucial to any plausible theory of mind. Meaning is no by-product of formal systems, but something *made* by human agents as they navigate cultural reality. We will never understand children's 'entry into meaning', their knowledge of the minds of other 'meaning makers', unless we look beyond the head and explore how meaning is culturally created, sustained and negotiated.

In all this, Bruner preserves the metaphor of the mind as organising experience. He simply argues that many resources for the organisation of experience reside in the culture and must be appropriated therefrom. Bruner sometimes seems to accept a relatively traditional dualism between the 'inner world' of the mind and the 'external world' beyond its frontiers. In *In Search of Mind*, for example, he writes that the 'metaphor of an "outer reality" that could never be directly known and an inner one that one "constructs" to represent it has always been a root one for me – the drama of Plato's prisoners in the cave'.[10] For Bruner in this mood, cultural psychology's principal insight is that the conceptual scheme that defines the structure of mind, and which shapes the 'construction' of our conception of the world, cannot be understood without essential reference to culture.

---

8   See Bruner 1991, pp. 2–3.
9   See Bruner 1990, ch. 1.
10   Bruner 1983, p. 134.

Increasingly often, however, Bruner appears to advance a more radical position, one that plays up the sceptical theme implicit in the quotation above. Bruner argues that our 'folk psychology' is an ineliminable aspect of our self-understanding.[11] He takes a richer view of folk psychological explanation than many writers, arguing that it includes not just explanation in terms of the propositional attitudes, but an appreciation of the cultural context of behaviour and a facility with narrative. Nevertheless, he endorses the mainstream belief that folk psychology is primarily a tool for the explanation of behaviour, a device for organising our experience of the behaviour. This inclines Bruner to a constructivist view of mental states and the 'self' that possesses them. Mental states are seen as creatures of attribution, and the self is portrayed as an explanatory construct. Earlier, we saw how we are led to view the self as an active interpreter. Now we find ourselves saying that its essence is to exist for-itself as an object of its own interpretation: the narrative self is all. The self is a virtual object, an artefact of strategies of self-interpretation. It exists, in Dennett's words, as 'a centre of narrative gravity', akin to a fictional character, as much made by meaning as making it.[12]

There is something ironic in this progression of ideas. A primary objective of Bruner's position is the *repersonalisation* of psychology. He aims to make possible a new psychology of the individual that ousts the dominant, dehumanising models of mind and to put personal meaning at the foundation of our mind. Yet Bruner's willingness to fictionalise the self undermines this objective. The self is restored to psychology only to be declared a mere artefact, less than wholly real.

Some would say that Bruner's position is yet more radical, representing a full-bloodied constructivism where everything 'real' is, in a sense, an artefact of our modes of interpretation and categorisation. Bruner insists that there is no 'aboriginal reality': the world as we encounter it is a product of the organising power of mind, of the 'narrative construction of reality'. So we do not diminish the self by admitting it is artefactual. For even science, on this radical reading, is just one more set of discursive practices which 'structure reality', one more 'way of worldmaking', as Nelson Goodman put it.

With this, the idea that the mind organises experience has led us down the well trodden path to global irrealism. The resulting position is fashionable, particularly when endowed with postmodern flourishes, and convenient, since it

---

11   Bruner 1990, ch. 2.
12   See Bruner 1995, pp. 26–7.

allows the cultural psychologist to write-off criticisms from mainstream psychology, which can be dismissed as labouring the delusion that there is a 'real' mind to study.[13]

3   McDowell: Navigating the Space of Reasons

I think this irrealism is profoundly misguided. I believe we should aspire to a vision of mind and world that countenances the reality of personal being in, and in cognitive contact with, an enduring world which, for the most part, is not of our making. The task is to embrace this realistic vision while giving full weight to the socio-cultural dimensions of mind.

What alternative is there to the idea that, since experience is organised by the mind, the reality we encounter in experience is a product of interpretation? This is where I draw inspiration from John McDowell's *Mind and World*. As we saw in Chapter 6 above, McDowell argues that epistemology has typically been caught between two unsatisfying views of experience. First, there is the position pejoratively called 'the myth of the given', where sensations are portrayed as providing the basis for belief. The problem for this position is to provide a satisfying account of how my receiving impressions of such and such a kind is supposed to *ground* my belief that things are thus and so. For if impressions are conceived as they typically are – as raw sensory 'feels', non-conceptual in nature – then it is hard to see how their occurrence could constitute *reasons* for belief. That I receive certain impressions might *cause* me to form certain beliefs, but it could not justify them, for only something conceptual in structure could do that. So conceived, experience is part of the causal order but lies outside (what McDowell, following Sellars, calls) 'the space of reasons'.

It is tempting to recoil from this picture into a form of coherentism that admits that nothing can provide a rational warrant for belief but another belief. Thus if we continue to represent experience as a causal impingement on the mind, we are forced to argue that something must be 'done' to the deliverances of experience before they present themselves to the mind. We are brought to the view that experience must be conceptualised, interpreted, and organised to enter the economy of thought.[14] This is Bruner's position. But now we have

---

13   Not that Bruner himself seeks to insulate cultural psychology from serious engagement with the mainstream. Some of his many followers, however, are wont to do so.

14   I am aware that here I run together the *conceptualisation* and the *interpretation* of experience. This conflation is one I suppose (perhaps unjustly) my opponents to make (sliding, for example, from the idea that the theory-ladenness of scientific observation means that

to admit that the results of this process of interpretation are at several stages removed from 'reality' itself. Indeed, this coherentism makes it hard to see how thought can be rationally constrained by reality at all. Bruner's response to this problem, as we have seen, is not to care.

The novelty of McDowell's stance is that he denies that these two positions exhaust our alternatives, for we can think of experience, not as the result of the organising of raw sensation, but as an *openness* to reality. What experience yields are *appearances of how things are*. Such appearances have no special epistemic privileges; nothing guarantees they are correct. They must be scrutinised in light of our existing system of concepts and beliefs. But when experience correctly presents how things are, thought reaches right out to reality. There is no gap between mind and world; the world is present to us in thought.

McDowell's position depends on the idea that the deliverances of experience are already conceptual in nature. Experience is not an apprehension of raw data, but an awareness *that things are thus and so*. In other words, the deliverances of experience are already within the space of reasons. (In Kantian terms, the receptivity of experience and the spontaneity of reason form an indissoluble unity.) What experience yields is already fit for our concepts and hence nothing need be done to experience before it can represent reality to the mind. Thus the world we experience is not, on McDowell's view, at a distance from the world as it is.

Many will argue that we cannot think of experience as simply offering the world to the mind. Meaning is the currency of the mental, but the world beyond the mind is empty of meaning, or 'disenchanted', in Weber's famous phrase. The 'external world' is the domain of objects interacting according to natural, causal laws, and nothing in that domain need be explained by appeal to meaning. It follows that nothing can be conveyed from the 'realm of natural law' into the 'space of reasons' without first being endowed with meaning. That is why we must see conceptualisation or interpretation as the world's passport into the mental realm.

McDowell urges us to drop the view that reality is disenchanted as one more scientistic presumption. We must not confine the conceptual, the meaningful and the rational to a bounded domain called 'mind' and set this against the meaningless 'external' realm of the causal, the natural, the nomological, as if nature stops where the space of reasons begins. We must rather see how the

---

there is no uninterpreted data to the idea that sensory experience is never encountered in an uninterpreted (rather than unconceptualised) form). A fuller treatment of the issue will need to substantiate that supposition, and to distinguish clearly the respective contributions of these two activities of mind.

conceptual permeates the natural, and vice versa. In this, I see a striking parallel between McDowell's position and Ilyenkov's work on 'the problem of the ideal'. Both seek to 're-enchant' reality to avoid the dilemma that philosophy must either bridge the gulf between mind and world, or declare the world is a construct of mind.[15]

McDowell's account of experience is focused largely upon perception. But just as he would have us see perception as an openness to reality, so we can portray memory as affording an openness to the past, to how things were. Of course, in memory the mind does not (directly) receive something from beyond its frontiers. But memory is nevertheless analogous to sense experience – indeed it is a genuine form of 'receptivity'. As the 'All My Loving' example illustrates, memories are often brought to mind by causal processes no more under rational control than sense experience. Indeed, memory underscores how the contrast between mind and world does not coincide with that between the rational and the natural, for the contrast between phenomena within the 'realm of law' and those in 'the space of reasons' also arises *within* the mind.[16] McDowell's position allows us to see memory experiences as examples of how things meaningful can impinge upon us in experience, presenting us with glimpses of how things are or were which warrant the formation of certain beliefs.

But what of the socio-cultural dimension of experience in general and memory in particular? Significantly, McDowell's position continues to afford a central role to the notion of culture. Both he and Ilyenkov see an individual's ability to inhabit the space of reasons as requiring the possession of sophisticated conceptual skills acquired through the child's assimilation of culture. These skills are aspects of our 'second nature' and their acquisition brings the child into contact with the *world*, with its ever-receding horizons, rather than a merely local environment. Such is the character of *human*, rather than merely animal existence.

---

15   Those familiar with Ilyenkov's work might be puzzled by the harmony I detect between Ilyenkov and McDowell. McDowell wants to hold that experience yields some kind of direct access to reality. But Ilyenkov, in his work on ideality, seems to argue that the world becomes a possible object of thought only in virtue of its endowment with meaning, or 'idealisation' by human activity. Does it not follow from Ilyenkov's view that the mind has access only to the world in so far as it is mediated (constructed?) by activity and hence that we lack access to reality as it is in itself? But as I have argued in previous chapters, I believe Ilyenkov thinks the mediating power of activity can bring us into contact with the world as it is, rather than engendering an object of thought which somehow comes between us and things as they are (see also the discussion of mediation in Chapters 10 and 11 above).

16   See Bakhurst 2011, ch. 6.

In my view, it is in the exploration of these thoughts, rather than in a global cultural constructivism, that the future of cultural psychology resides.

4   Enabling versus Constitutive Views of Culture

Both McDowell and Ilyenkov represent culture as *enabling* the emergence and exercise of mind. For them, the child's inauguration into culture represents the acquisition, or actualisation, of conceptual powers that make possible experience of the world. A being that has these powers is a full-fledged inhabitant of the space of reasons; that is, it is able to organise its activity in response to rational requirements on belief and action. Such a being guides its thought by good reasons for belief, and acts in light of good reasons for action, and only such a being can be said to have a conception of the world and to be the subject of a life conceived as a story played out within that world.

McDowell argues that the crucial component of the process in which the child assimilates culture, or *Bildung* as he calls it, is the acquisition of language, conceived 'as a repository of tradition, a store of historically accumulated wisdom about what is a reason for what'.[17] Initiation into language is initiation into a medium that already embodies conceptual relations and which enables the exploration of the geography of the space of reasons. Ilyenkov takes a broader view, urging us to see that assimilation into culture involves the appropriation of many forms of socially significant activity that are non-linguistic in kind and which form the basis for the subsequent development of language. For Ilyenkov, what is at issue is the infant's emerging capacity to guide her activity by norms, so that her behaviour is not simply called forth by biological imperatives. This process begins with the manipulation of artefacts, of objects that elicit behaviour because they are seen as significant, and occurs far earlier than language acquisition.

The differences between McDowell and Ilyenkov on this point are important, for the central task of any cultural psychology must be to provide a rich and satisfying account of *Bildung*. Both agree, however, that initiation into culture is a precondition of the possibility of the emergence of mind. Hence, to say that, on this position, culture *enables* mind is not to say that initiation into culture merely assists the exercise of capacities that could be exercised inde-

---

17   McDowell 1994, p. 126.

pendently of the influence of culture. Rather, entry into culture makes possible the very 'responsiveness to meaning' that is the quintessence of human mentality.[18]

Another crucial point of agreement is that what we acquire though our initiation into culture is the ability to respond to rational requirements on belief and action, to guide our activity by rational norms. These rational requirements are thought of as objectively binding, as 'there anyway' whether we recognise them or not. Culture's gift is to make available to us the contours of the space of reasons, to enable us to see reasons that have force regardless of whether that force is perceived.

Contrast this idea with what I shall call a *constitutive* view of culture's influence.[19] On the constitutive view, what is a good reason for belief or action is held to be so because it conforms to accepted practices in the culture, because it conforms to what the community *counts* as a good reason. Here, the practices of the community simply constitute the norms of rationality – what the community does defines the space of reasons – and the individual is required to conform to those practices to count as rational.

The constitutive view naturally entails that the assimilation of culture, in the sense of conformity to the community's practices, is a precondition of mindedness, and hence it appeals to some who seek a philosophical rationale for cultural psychology. In addition, it has a certain philosophical pedigree. It appears, for example, in influential readings of Wittgenstein and of Richard Rorty's critique of traditional philosophy.[20]

---

18   McDowell 1994, p. 123.

19   McDowell himself invokes a similar distinction between 'enabling' and 'constitutive' questions and explanations in McDowell 1998a, in a discussion of the explanation of mental content. Note, however, that in that context McDowell identifies an enabling explanation with a causal one. In my version of the distinction, an enabling explanation need not be causal in any straightforward sense of the term.

20   For such readings of Wittgenstein see, e.g., Wright 1980, ch. 11 and Kripke 1982. Compare McDowell 1994, pp. 92–4 and McDowell 1998c. (The interpretation of Wittgenstein I develop in Bakhurst 1995c embraces the constitutive view as a transcendental thesis, which, I there argue, is nonetheless compatible with empirical or 'internal' realism. I am now less confident in this strategy.) Rorty's position is complex. Although he writes that 'there is nothing to be said about either truth or rationality apart from descriptions of the familiar procedures of justification which a given society – *ours* – uses in one or another area of inquiry' (1991, p. 23), he would deny that he embraces the constitutive view. The latter, he would argue, is a misguided attempt to provide a philosophical theory of the nature of rationality and truth. Better to give up the hope of any such theory and let justification rest with an appeal to 'the ordinary, retail, detailed, concrete reasons which have brought one to one's present view' (Rorty 1982, p. 165). One may nevertheless suspect that

The constitutive view is, in my view, a disastrous basis for cultural psychology. It does violence to our conception of ourselves and our relation to the world to think that what constitutes a compelling reason for a belief or action is ultimately a matter of communal agreement. This represents the community as policing the requirements of rationality and ultimately truth (or even worse – as constituting the requirements they police). It thus fails to do justice to the idea, which is a precondition of all our reasoning and inquiry, that thought is answerable to a world which is not of our making.

The attractions of the constitutive view have so eclipsed alternatives that the McDowellian option is only just being entertained. Why is the constitutive view so attractive? I think there are three principal reasons.

The first derives from the power over us of a certain kind of scientific naturalism, one which embraces the disenchanted conception of reality.[21] In the grip of that conception, we search in desperation for an account of the place of reasons, values, meaning in the world. How, deploying only resources available from the disenchanted perspective, can we give an account of responsiveness to reasons? The only option, it seems, is to construct the rational out of patterns of behaviour, patterns that conform to the majority practice. But this is to suggest that mere behaviour could be turned into something rational simply through coincidence with the mere behaviour of others. And, to turn to parallel concerns about meaning, that the mere noises that issue from a person's mouth are made meaningful in virtue of their congruence with the mere noises made by others. The whole doomed project is misconceived, for it is driven by an unduly austere conception of what is real.

Second, I believe the constitutive picture appeals to those who are over-impressed by sceptical arguments. In the midst of our practices, we typically have a strong sense of what constitutes a good reason for some belief or action, and we understand the character of disputes about whether some purported reason is in fact a good one. For example, my reason for believing that I am presently typing at my computer is that I see the keyboard and feel the keys, my action upon the keys produces exactly the effects I expect, and so on. In short, everything in my present experience speaks in favour of this belief, and nothing against it. I understand how one might dispute whether, say, unusual fluctuations in the weather are a reason to believe in the deleterious effects of global warming, but not whether things as I presently take them to be consti-

---

Rorty's constant reference to society and solidarity are a vestige of the constitutive view, or something like it, according to which our everyday reasons need a social warrant to be the reasons they are.

21   See McDowell 1994, Lecture V.

tute grounds to believe I am working on my computer. Traditional epistemology, however, counsels us not to rest content with reasons of the latter variety, because they can be attacked by sceptical arguments of the Cartesian kind. We are thus urged to look for further reasons that are immune from sceptical attack and serve to justify those we typically adduce.

It is now widely agreed, of course, that those who seek a foundational rebuttal to scepticism will be disappointed: there simply are no reasons that are immune from sceptical attack and sufficiently substantive to provide the foundation for everything else we believe. The fact that sceptical concerns cannot be answered leads many to dismiss the sceptic's arguments as in some way misconceived and, indeed, to ridicule the pretensions of the foundationalist (Rorty's critique is an obvious example). They find it difficult, however, to rid themselves of the idea, implanted by the sceptic, that there is something lacking in the reasons we normally give. Unable to supplement these reasons by philosophical argument, they find the necessary addition in the endorsement of the community. On this view, what makes such-and-such considerations a reason for a particular belief is that these kinds of considerations are counted as a reason for belief among members of our epistemic community. Agreement thus becomes the ultimate epistemic warrant. But the idea that there is a place to be filled here by communal agreement is a mistake, and one that is a legacy of scepticism. The trick is to recognise that our normal modes of justification stand in no need of supplementation, either by foundational epistemology or 'post-foundational' conventionalism.

Third, and finally, there is a streak of self-aggrandising anthropocentricity in the constitutive view. It makes human beings arbiters, indeed creators, of the true, the rational, and (no doubt) the good. Such a view seems empowering, but it really bespeaks immaturity: an inability to come to terms with a properly secular worldview. For the constitutive conception cannot free itself of the idea that truth, rationality, and value are ultimately expressions of *personality*. I believe this is an illusion, and a dangerous one.

It might be replied that the real attraction of the constitutive view is that it enables us to appreciate the extent to which communally accepted practices deeply influence what we are and what we may become. Only it can fully capture the extent of the social construction of identity. But this too is a mistake, for the opposite is true. We can only appreciate the extent to which the community influences us, for good or ill, if we preserve a robust sense of how things are. For among the things that participation in the practices of our community empowers us to do is to navigate an independent course through life, responding in our distinctive way to reasons that have a force independent of communal assent. And among the ways our participation can diminish us is because the community distorts or obscures truths which are not of its making. We cannot hope, for example, to illuminate the phenomenon of collective memory unless we keep a firm grip on the idea that our practices do not 'construct' the past, but illuminate and disclose or distort and conceal it. Those practices issue in reasons for belief and our guiding light in assessing those reasons is the idea of accountability to the way things were.

5   Conclusion

This last thought returns us to the theme of memory, the topic with which this paper began. Memory is a topic that vividly displays both the promise of cultural psychology and the complexities it faces. Although mainstream psychology has typically treated memory in extremely individualistic fashion, the socio-cultural dimensions of memory are not hard to see. And once perceived, they appear to be of enormous import for psychology. Memory, after all, is crucial to identity. The problem, however, is to find a way properly to accommodate both the individual and the social dimensions of memory in a plausible account of the integrity and persistence of the self. It is, I believe, a criterion of adequacy for any cultural psychology that it give credence to the socio-cultural character of mind while preserving due sense of the inner, intimate and private dimensions of our mental lives. But this is a difficult criterion to meet, for cultural psychology cannot proceed by simply grafting a number of hitherto overlooked socio-cultural factors onto an individualistic picture of the mind inherited from some existing branch of the cognitive sciences. Cultural psychology requires us to rethink our very conception of mind and its place in the world, to reconceive the relations we bear to nature and to each other. It demands a conceptual – a *philosophical* – transformation.

Bruner understands this as well as anyone, for he has always been aware of philosophy's importance. This is not because he looks to philosophy to provide a foundation for psychology, but because he has always recognised the power of speculative inquiry to illuminate and enthuse, to counsel and inform, and because he holds psychology to especially high ideals. For Bruner, psychology's object is self-understanding, the attainment of a satisfying picture of our place in nature, and, moreover, one which will inspire us to live better. It might be said that, for Bruner, psychology is a kind of empirical philosophy, a contemporary descendant of the 'moral sciences' that should never lose sight of its speculative roots.

I have tried to show that, although Bruner appreciates the importance of philosophical inquiry, his own philosophical sensibilities incline him into positions that represent an untenable premise for cultural psychology. Bruner's commitment to the dualism of scheme and content leads him to embrace, or at least to flirt with, forms of radical cultural constructivism and philosophical irrealism that fail what I take to be a second criterion of adequacy for any cultural psychology: that it acknowledge the social dimensions of the mind without forsaking a sensible realism in which minded beings inhabit a world which is, to a large extent, not of their making. I suggested that the seeds of a more satisfactory vision of the relation of mind and world can be found in the work of John McDowell, which has interesting parallels with the ideas of Ilyenkov. Both reject the dualism for the view that, in favourable circumstances, perception represents an awareness of how things are and thought is to make contact with an independent reality.

As we saw, both McDowell and Ilyenkov attribute a vital role to culture in the development of mind, for they argue that initiation into culture enables the individual to acquire the cognitive powers to navigate the space of reasons. Moreover, we might add that their positions are entirely compatible with the view that 'cultural tools' mediate our awareness of reality. As I have counselled in earlier chapters, we must insist that 'mediational means' do not necessarily come between us and reality itself. Rather, their use can serve to bring reality within our reach. In this, it is important to take the tool metaphor seriously. Just as the use of a hammer does not somehow remove us from the object on which we are working, so our concepts, models, theories, and so on need not create a barrier beyond which we cannot see. We use them to disclose the world to us, not to obscure it. Such a view, I have argued, is precisely what Vygotsky had in mind when he invoked the concept of mediation, though this is often lost on his followers. I conclude, therefore, that though much remains to develop in McDowell's position, it is a promising ally of cultural psychology.

While I am sure that Bruner would have found much to argue with in the case I have made, I am equally certain that he would have welcomed my effort to reexamine critically the guiding metaphors of cultural psychology and the pictures of mind and world that inform its research. For he appreciated more than anyone that such speculative reflections are not just a preliminary to the 'real' research, but an integral part of mature psychological inquiry. And there was no greater advocate of such inquiry than Jerome Bruner himself.[22]

---

22   Bruner replied to this essay in Bruner 2001.

∴

It is now often argued that neuroscience can be expected to provide insights of significance for education. Advocates of this view are sometimes committed to 'brainism', the view (a) that an individual's mental life is constituted by states, events, and processes in her brain, and (b) that psychological attributes may legitimately be ascribed to the brain. Inspired by Ilyenkov's famous dispute with David Dubrovsky, the next chapter considers the case for rejecting brainism in favour of 'personalism', the view that psychological attributes are appropriately ascribed only to persons and that mental phenomena do not occur 'inside' the person but are aspects of her mode of engagement with the world. Supplementing Ilyenkov's argument with insights from John McDowell and Peter Hacker, I argue that, since plausible forms of personalism do not deny that brain functioning is a causal precondition of our mental lives, personalism is consistent with the claim that neuroscience is relevant to education, and not just to the explanation of learning disorders. Nevertheless, as Ilyenkov counselled, we must be careful that fascination with scientific innovation and technological possibility does not distort our conception of what education is or ought to be, leading us to portray education, not as communicative endeavour, but an exercise in engineering.

CHAPTER 14

Minds, Brains and Education

1. From the mid-1960s to the mid-1970s, Ilyenkov published a series of writings about the mind-body problem. In these texts, he argued passionately against what I shall call 'brainism', the view (a) that an individual's mental life is constituted by states, events, and processes in her brain, and (b) that psychological attributes may legitimately be ascribed to the brain.[1] 'The brain does not think', Ilyenkov maintained, 'a human being thinks with the help of her brain (*s pomoshch'iu mozga*)'.[2] The psychological subject is the person, not the brain,

---

1   I owe the term 'brainism' to my late colleague E.J. Bond. As I define it in the text, the term serves well to characterise Ilyenkov's target. Ilyenkov himself sometimes describes himself as attacking 'naturalism' about the mind, but even though this is in keeping with how the term subsequently came to be used in Western philosophy of mind, it is not ideal, since there is a clear sense in which Ilyenkov himself embraces a form of naturalism, albeit one more expansive than his opponents. 'Reductionism' about the mental is too narrow to describe Ilyenkov's target, since he would reject some forms of non-reductive physicalism, as well as eliminative materialism (which, despairing of reducing the mental to the physical, proposes to displace our 'folk psychological' idioms altogether). 'Physicalism' is too broad a term, since there are a huge variety of physicalist views of mind. For example, Ilyenkov would have rejected both traditional identity theory, which holds that for each type of mental state there is a type of physical state with which it is identical, and functionalist theories, according to which mental states are identified with their functional roles, the latter being portrayed as realised by causal processes in the brain. But Ilyenkov might have tolerated *some* versions of non-reductive physicalism. Ilyenkov did not occupy himself with the fine detail of nuanced positions in the philosophy of mind. He was rather concerned with our most basic conceptions of the nature of mind and his target was any view that casts the brain as the location of thought. Hence 'brainism' is as good a term as any to describe his *bête noire*.

2   Arsen'ev, Ilyenkov, and Davydov 1966, p. 265; see also Ilyenkov 1974a, p. 183 (Ilyenkov 2009b, p. 146). The translation of the quoted remark is not entirely straightforward. First, the Russian '*chelovek*' serves for both 'human beings' and 'person' (the term has rich etymological associations, suggesting a being whose 'face is turned towards the infinite'). However, the potential ambiguity is of no consequence in this context, since Ilyenkov would hold that the paradigm of a person is a living human being. More problematic is the expression '*s pomoshch'iu*'. The literal translation, 'with the help of', is awkward, but so are the alternatives 'by means of', 'with', or 'using', none of which seem wholly appropriate to characterise a person's relation to their brain. This is perhaps only to be expected. If we deny that we can construe the mental in terms of brain functioning, we should not suppose that we will be able to represent the relation of person and brain on the model of some familiar relation, such as a person's relation to a tool. It should not surprise us that the relation is a singular one, in some respects like other relations, and in other ways unique and elusive.

and moreover, the person in unity with nature and society. Human beings are creatures of the natural world, but our mindedness does not consist in the occurrence of a special class of events inside us; rather, it lies in our mode of engagement with the world, a mode of engagement possible only because we are social beings.

Ilyenkov was by no means the only Soviet philosopher to take such a position. In many ways, his views are representative of the generation of Hegelian Marxists who sought to reanimate Soviet philosophical culture in the post-Stalin era. These thinkers typically adopted a strongly socio-historical view of mind that they deemed inconsistent with brainism.[3] But Ilyenkov's contribution was distinctive. He more than anyone sought to link philosophical controversies about mind and brain to social and political issues. He was adamant that Soviet fascination with artificial intelligence and cybernetics was a symptom of a growing cult of technology that looked to the development of science to solve socio-economic problems, thereby distracting attention from their true source.[4] He also sought to bring the issues to a wide audience by writing in a lively, accessible style and publishing not just in philosophical journals, but in popular books and newspapers.[5]

Ilyenkov was especially concerned about the influence of brainism in the domain of education. He thought it would be disastrous for teachers to see education as a matter of training brains. He feared such a view would not only misrepresent the educational process, it would encourage nativist ideas about students' potential to learn. Since the brain's capacities are determined by its physical organisation, and since that organisation is in part determined by genetic considerations, a brain's capacity to learn must be constrained by innate factors. This seems to compel the conclusion that whether someone is intelligent, whether she is talented or 'gifted', how much she can benefit from some or other programme, and so on, is a function of the kind of brain she has.

---

3 Witness Felix Mikhailov's *The Riddle of the Self*, first published in 1964, and discussed in Chapter 1 above, and the work of psychologists influenced by Vygotsky, such as A.N. Leontiev and V.V. Davydov.

4 Of course, in the Soviet political context, Ilyenkov had to be extremely cautious in making such points, often casting them as criticisms of *Western* society, but the sub-text would have been clear to many Soviet readers.

5 Ilyenkov's more scholarly treatments of the issue are Ilyenkov 1974a, ch. 8 (Ilyenkov 2009b, pp. 146–67); Ilyenkov 2009a (Ilyenkov 2014). Ilyenkov 1968c (1969) is a good example of his more polemical writing. See Chapter 7 above for discussion of Ilyenkov's writings on education. Ilyenkov 1968b is a lively book-length treatment that integrates themes from the philosophies of mind and education.

Ilyenkov felt that such reasoning only leads educators to blame children's failure to learn on their supposedly innate abilities, or lack of them, when the real culprit lies in the education system.[6] It also encourages the idea that a future brain science might enable us to stream students for specialised programmes in light of their innate abilities, a strategy which, as Ilyenkov was quick to point out, is at odds with Marxism's commitment to abolish the division of labour for the cultivation of 'all-round individuals'.[7] In contrast, Ilyenkov urged that we liberate ourselves from the idea that a normal child's developmental trajectory is significantly predetermined by genetic factors. He embraced a thoroughgoing 'nurturism', maintaining that a child's capacity to learn has unlimited horizons and that we should educate for people's all-round development. If something goes awry in the learning process, we should look for social, rather than biological, causes.

Especially in his more popular writings, Ilyenkov adopted a strident polemical style and made abundantly clear that he deemed his opponents' views pernicious and reactionary. His opponents, of course, thought that the shoe was on the other foot.[8] They deemed it inappropriate of Ilyenkov to suggest that brainism was inconsistent with Marxism. After all, Marxists are materialists, and the obvious materialist approach to mind is to recognise that mental processes are brain processes. In any case, it is manifestly unscientific for philosophers to declare that neuroscience and cognate disciplines have nothing to tell us about our mental lives. It is an empirical matter whether, say, the capacity to learn is significantly influenced by genetic factors, so philosophers are in no position to pronounce on the matter. To disregard empirical research and embrace extreme nurturism on a priori grounds is not just unscientific; it is utopian, idealistic, and patently absurd.

Ilyenkov was undeterred, insisting that:

> The *substance* of mind is always the life-activity [of a person] ... and the brain with its innate structure is only its biological *substrate*. Therefore, studying the brain has as little to do with studying the mind as investigating the nature of money by analysing the physical composition of the material (gold, silver, paper) in which the monetary form of value is realised.[9]

---

6   Ilyenkov 2002b, pp. 76–7 (Ilyenkov 2007c, pp. 67–8).
7   Ilyenkov 1968c, pp. 147–51.
8   See Dubrovsky 1968; 1990, pp. 6–9.
9   Ilyenkov 2002b, p. 98 (Ilyenkov 2007c, p. 88).

2. Half a century has passed since this controversy played out in the Soviet Union. The USSR is no more, and Marxist philosophy is distinctly out of fashion. Ilyenkov is long dead. Philosophy of mind, cognitive science, neuroscience and evolutionary biology have been busy – very busy – in the intervening years. So why dwell on a thinker like Ilyenkov, who is so remote from the contemporary scene?

It is striking, however, that for all that has changed, much remains the same. The problems that exercised Ilyenkov remain with us, and in many respects we are no closer to resolving them. Consider, for example, the jointly-authored book *Neuroscience and Philosophy*, published in 2007. In this text, neuroscientist Maxwell Bennett and philosopher Peter Hacker maintain, as Ilyenkov did, that psychological attributes cannot be ascribed to the brain. They argue that it makes no sense to say that a brain thinks or reasons, decides or remembers. Such things are done by people, not brains. In response, the philosophers Daniel Dennett and John Searle argue, in their respective ways, that Bennett and Hacker are wrong. Searle holds that consciousness is a biological phenomenon caused by the brain, and that mental states exist in the brain. Dennett argues that attributing psychological predicates to sub-personal brain systems has produced genuinely explanatory cognitive-scientific theories, and if, as Dennett puts it, such a strategy 'lets us see how on earth to get whole wonderful persons out of brute mechanical parts', who is the philosopher to say that such attributions make no sense?[10] In response, Bennett and Hacker deny that cognitive science lets us see anything of the kind, and disdain Searle's idea that the brain causes consciousness. This discussion would be very familiar to Ilyenkov, as would the acrimonious tone that sometimes creeps into it. Bennett and Hacker write of neuroscientists 'fostering a form of mystification and cultivating a neuro-mythology that are altogether deplorable'; Dennett describes their philosophical methods as 'deeply reactionary'.[11]

Ilyenkov would also find sadly familiar the burgeoning literature on the relevance of neuroscience to teaching and learning. The most comprehensive summary of how contemporary brain science can inform education is Sarah-

---

10   Bennett et al. 2007, p. 89. *Neuroscience and Philosophy* issued from an 'Author and Critics' session at an American Philosophical Association conference in 2005 that discussed Bennett and Hacker's *Philosophical Foundations of Neuroscience* (2003), a book that gives a comprehensive statement of their position and includes substantial appendices criticising Dennett and Searle.

11   Bennett et al. 2007, pp. 47, 92.

Jayne Blackmore and Uta Frith's *The Learning Brain: Lessons for Education*. Although the authors are enthusiasts for their discipline, speculating that in 'the future there will be all sorts of new and radically different ways to increase the brain's potential to learn',[12] it must be said that the concrete educational recommendations issuing from the research they review are remarkably modest. Some examples:

> One clear implication for education from this research [on grammatical processing in the brain] is that there *may be* a finite time for the most efficient type of grammar learning. After the age of 13, we are still able to learn grammar, but we will *probably* be less efficient and use different brain strategies than if we had learned grammar earlier.[13]
>
> [Research on the adolescent brain suggests that] If 0–3 years is seen as a major opportunity for teaching, so should 10–15 years. During both periods, particularly dramatic brain reorganization is taking place. This *may well be* a signal that learning in certain domains is becoming ultra-fast during these periods.[14]
>
> [Research on brain mechanisms underlying imitation (specifically mirror neurons) suggests that] Learning from observation is *usually* easier than learning from verbal descriptions, however precise and detailed the descriptions may be. This *might be* because, by observing an action, your brain has already prepared to copy it... [Thus] In education, imitating attitudes, mentalities, and emotions *may be* more important than imitating simple movements.[15]
>
> [Research on brain activity during sleep suggests that] it *may be* a good idea to take a nap after learning[16] [and that] learning sessions could also be scheduled in the evening, permitting the beneficial aspects of sleep to improve the performance of the learned tasks.[17]

However, notwithstanding the underwhelming character of these conclusions, Blakemore and Frith's book paints an engaging picture of a young science uncovering numerous thought-provoking findings, some of which certainly

---

12   Blakemore and Frith 2005, p. 167.
13   Blakemore and Frith 2005, p. 47, my emphasis.
14   Blakemore and Frith 2005, p. 121, my emphasis.
15   Blakemore and Frith 2005, p. 161–3, my emphasis.
16   Blakemore and Frith 2005, p. 175, my emphasis.
17   Blakemore and Frith 2005, p. 176.

appear to have application to educational matters. This is especially true of research into the neurophysiological basis of conditions that impede learning, such as dyslexia and autism.[18]

As is evident from the claims quoted above, Blakemore and Frith are under no illusions about the need for caution in making educational recommendations on the basis of the present state of research. Such caution, however, is not shown by many proponents of 'brain-based education', who are quick to invoke contemporary neuroscience to recommend 'brain-based curricula' and 'brain-compatible learning programmes'.[19] Although Blakemore and Frith ignore this literature, suggesting they give it no credence, others have been unable to suffer in silence. John Bruer, for example, has criticised brain-based education since its inception.[20] Bruer rightly complains that 'the brain-based education literature is produced not by neuroscientists but by educators and educational consultants'. Though they purport to ground their conclusions and recommendations on science, 'the primary "scientific" sources cited in this literature are popular books written by neuroscientists and journalists'.[21] From these sources, they make cavalier inferences from premises about brain structure to conclusions about brain-functioning. The result is 'at best ... no more than a folk-theory about the brain and learning' dressed up as science.[22]

Ilyenkov would have applauded Bruer's stand. The worry about brain-based education is that pop-scientific speculation, grounded more in prejudice than science, might significantly influence educational policy, and this is exactly what concerned Ilyenkov, albeit in a very different political context. Of course, Ilyenkov would go further than Bruer. For one thing, Bruer does not question the potential relevance of brain science to education. He just thinks that, as things stand, serious scientific 'research on applications of brain science to general education is non-existent'.[23] Moreover, Ilyenkov would fault, not just brain-based education, but the more scholarly work of Frith and Blakemore. He would complain that, when they write that 'the brain has evolved to edu-

---

18   In these cases, what is contentious is not the potential relevance of brain science but the characterisation of the conditions themselves. For example, although we are now used to thinking in terms of an 'autistic spectrum', it is by no means clear that there is a single spectrum rather than, say, clusters of related conditions or behaviours. Such questions of typology are profound and neuroscientific data is unquestionably relevant to resolving them. I discuss autism further in Bakhurst 2015a and 2016a.

19   See, e.g., Jensen 2008.

20   See, e.g., Bruer 1997, 2002.

21   Bruer 2002, p. 1031.

22   Bruer 2002, p. 1032.

23   Bruer 2002, p. 1032.

cate and to be educated'; that it 'acquires and lays down information and skills'; that it 'learns new information and deals with it throughout life'; that it is 'our natural mechanism [that] places limits on learning', determining 'what can be learned, how much, and how fast', Blakemore and Frith foster the view that the real focus of education is brains, not people.[24] It is significant that from the very outset, their language is one of *limits* to learning, and that they portray education in terms of an engineering metaphor: education as landscaping.[25] Finally, for all their caution, Blakemore and Frith are not immune from utopian speculation, remarking that '[p]erhaps one day it will be possible to pop a pill to learn!'[26] All this would have provoked Ilyenkov.

No doubt Blakemore and Frith would protest that their view of education does not focus on brains at the expense of learners. On the contrary, the metaphor of landscaping is supposed to evoke the image of gardening, of cultivating the brain's powers so that *learners* should flourish. Their talk of limits is balanced by the desire to exploit neuroscience to maximise everyone's potential to learn. At best Ilyenkov's complaints are superficial, pertaining to infelicities of language rather than to matters of substance. I suspect, however, that Ilyenkov would have deemed their language indicative of a certain scientistic style of thinking that inevitably influences, perhaps tacitly, the setting of research priorities, the identification of research topics, and the categorisation of objects of inquiry. The best way to guard against this influence is to abandon the pretence that studying the brain is studying the mind at all.

As we have seen, Ilyenkov rejects brainism in favour of what we might call 'personalism' about the mental, the view that psychological attributes are properties of persons, not brains. This is a view I introduced in chapter one above, while discussing the views of Ilyenkov's friend Felix Mikhailov. The view is also endorsed by a number of prominent Western thinkers, including Peter Hacker, mentioned above, and John McDowell. In what follows, I consider the case for personalism and consider how its truth might bear on the relevance of brain science to education. It is not difficult to understand what a philosopher takes herself to be claiming when she claims that mental states are brain states or that consciousness is caused by the brain. These claims might turn out to be ultimately incomprehensible, but it is not difficult to grasp what their advocates are trying to say. It is also not hard to understand why brain-functioning might be thought relevant to questions of education. The science described in Blakemore and Frith's book is intellectually demanding, but the book's claims

---

24   Blakemore and Frith 2005, p. 1.
25   See Blakemore and Frith 2005, p. 10.
26   Blakemore and Frith 2005, p. 167.

are not conceptually challenging. The kind of view Ilyenkov favours, however, is not as intuitively plausible as his opponents' positions appear to be and it is easily misunderstood and misrepresented.[27] So my aim in this chapter is to do the best for it I can.

3. It is important to underline that personalism is not a form of dualism of the Cartesian variety. When the personalist denies that the brain thinks, or that mental states are in the brain, she is not claiming that thoughts reside in some immaterial substance or non-material organ of thought. The point is that mental states and processes are states of whole persons and persons are material things – human beings – who are inhabitants of the natural world. It is 'I', David Bakhurst, who sees, hears, imagines, infers, speculates, hopes, intends, wants, reasons, and so on, not my brain or any other part of me. It is also critical that the personalist does not deny that the proper functioning of a person's brain is a precondition for her having a mental life, and that neuroscience may be able to establish significant correlations, perhaps to a high degree of detail, between particular events in the brain and the occurrence of certain mental phenomena, and between activity in certain areas of the brain, and the possession or exercise of certain abilities and skills. But to establish a correlation is one thing, to affirm some kind of identity another. Brain functioning enables mindedness, but is not constitutive of it.[28] Or so the personalist maintains.

What, then, is the *argument* that psychological ascriptions can be made of persons but not brains? According to Bennett and Hacker, whether psychological states can be ascribed to the brain is not a question of fact, but a conceptual issue that precedes empirical inquiry.[29] They maintain that it is incoherent to use psychological predicates of anything other than persons. Following Wittgenstein, Bennett and Hacker argue that the meaning of an expression is determined by the conditions of its use. But the rules for the use of psychological expressions make no reference whatsoever to what is going on in the brain. You do not have to know anything about what is happening in someone's brain to be able to say of them that they believe it is Tuesday, or that they are deciding what to have for dinner, or that they are day-dreaming about Grenada. Indeed, a person can have an excellent mastery of psycho-

---

27   In Ilyenkov's case, his strident polemical tone, and the incautious way he attacks his
      opponents, positively invite an uncharitable reading. It is important to step back from
      the heat of the controversy and take a sober look at the best of the arguments.
28   The enabling/constituting distinction is discussed in the previous chapter (though in
      application to the social, rather than physical, constitution of mind).
29   See Bennett et al. 2007, pp. 15–33, 127–56.

logical discourse while knowing little about the brain and its relation to our mental lives (this was, after all, true of Aristotle). Psychological predicates are applied to creatures in light of their behaviour as they actively engage with their environment and with each other. Bennett and Hacker write: '[T]he *concept* of consciousness is bound up with the behavioural grounds for ascribing consciousness' to an animal. 'An animal does not have to exhibit such behaviour in order for it *to be* conscious. But only an animal to which such behaviour *can intelligibly be ascribed* can also be said, *either truly or falsely*, to be conscious',[30] and the same goes for other psychological states and processes. Since the brain does not engage in behaviour in the relevant sense, and its processes are unobservable to most speakers, it is simply not a candidate for the possession of psychological attributes. If we apply such terms to the brain, we do so derivatively and in a way parasitic upon ordinary psychological discourse. Of course, nothing prevents scientists from using psychological expressions metaphorically, or from coining novel usages, but as Bennett and Hacker think they can show, neuroscientists and cognitive scientists typically presuppose that they are using psychological expressions literally.

How good is this argument? Bennett and Hacker's critics see it as a futile throwback to ordinary language philosophy. Searle argues that they confuse the criteria for the use of psychological expressions with what these expressions pick out. Although we attribute a psychological state to someone on the basis of behavioural evidence, *what it is* that we are attributing to her is, we now know, a brain state.[31] Dennett, who is more sympathetic to the view that meaning is tied to criteria for use, argues that if ascribing psychological expressions to the brain yields explanatory theories, then the philosopher is in no position to declare the practice illegitimate. Cognitive science has indeed produced fertile theories by assuming that brains or their parts behave in ways that can usefully be described as 'thinking', 'remembering', etc. If there is a doubt about the coherence of these theories it must be established by close examination of the theories themselves, rather than general considerations about the rules for the use of words. In any case, Dennett comments, what are these rules? As Wittgenstein himself well understood, we are unable to state the rules for the use of most expressions, so philosophers only embarrass themselves by pretending to be the self-appointed guardians of the legitimate use of words.[32]

I think Ilyenkov, who was no fan of linguistic philosophy, would have agreed that personalism cannot be established by appeal to considerations about the

---

30   Bennett et al. 2007, p. 135.

31   Bennett et al. 2007, pp. 101–6.

32   Bennett et al. 2007, pp. 74–95.

meaning of psychological terms. A different style of argument favoured by the Russians starts from the claim that if you open up a person's cranium and look in their brain, you do not find mental images, sensations, beliefs, intentions, and so on. At best, all we can observe in the brain are *correlates* of mental processes.[33] What is the basis for this claim? Why deny that brain-imaging techniques allow us to observe mental processes themselves? It might be thought that the personalist is making an argument reminiscent of Thomas Nagel's famous paper 'What is it Like to be a Bat?'[34] This is the idea that occurrent mental states have a qualitative dimension. They have a subjective, phenomenological quality. Although we might be able to observe what is going on in a person's brain when she sees a red flag, we cannot observe *what it is like* for her to see it. The subjective dimension, which some claim to be an essential characteristic of conscious mental states, goes missing in any third-personal, physical description of brain states. Hence, we might conclude, all that is observable are the neural correlates of mental activity, not mental activity itself.

The personalist agrees with this conclusion, but I think she takes a different route to it, one that does not depend on considerations of phenomenology. She is more likely to begin from the premise that the human mind is a psychological unity.[35] A person's mental states are not just a rag-bag collection of representations. Any mental state has a place in a network of mental states. They form a unified system. Any new experience, any potential belief, any new intention or desire, must be evaluated in light of its fit with the subject's existing mental states. I can only adopt a new belief if it is consistent with what I already believe, and if it is plausible in light of my existing conceptions. I should only form the intention to do A, if doing A is consistent with my commitments and projects, or if I am willing to revise those commitments and projects to accommodate the action. The possibility of a network of mental states depends on two unifying factors. First, my mental states are unified, first, because they are all states of a particular person, me. Second, they are unified in that they express my orientation to the world, which comprises both a conception of how the world is and commitments to change the world in various ways

---

33   See, e.g., Ilyenkov 1974a, p. 54 (2009b, p. 42); Mikhailov 1980, pp. 115–42. Bennett and Hacker make a similar point: 'After all, the only thing neuroscientists *could* discover is that certain neural states are inductively well correlated with, and causal conditions of, an *animal's* being conscious. But *that* discovery cannot show that it is *the brain* that is conscious' (Bennett et al. 2007, p. 136).

34   Nagel 1979.

35   It is not that significant psychological disunity is impossible, just that it must be understood as a departure from the norm.

through action. It follows that if we are to understand the unity of a mental life we have to think of the person, rather than any of her parts, as the legitimate subject of psychological ascription, for it is the person that has an orientation to the world manifest in action, not her brain.[36]

One way to put this argument about psychological unity is to say that brainism struggles to make sense of the first-person perspective. A person does not typically stand to her own mental states as to objects of observation. If I ask myself what I believe about something, I do not determine the answer by observing the contents of my mind and coming across the relevant belief, as if surveying exhibits in a museum. I determine it by making up my mind what to think in light of the evidence as I understand it. The attitude we take to our own mental lives is one of agency: we are the authors of our orientation to the world, responsible for what we think and do and our attitude to our own beliefs is never one of passive observation.[37] Indeed, even in cases where our minds are passive recipients, as they are in perception, we are nevertheless under a standing obligation to evaluate the veracity of what we take ourselves to see, hear, and so on. Although we can observe the world, our observing of it is always charged with agency. But although a person does not relate to the contents of her mind as to objects of observation, her relation to her own brain states, as revealed, say, by MRI imaging, *is* one of observation. Thus, what she observes when she observes events in her own brain can only be brain events correlated with, an enabling of, her mental life, not her mental life itself.[38]

---

36   It was Kant who brought to prominence the question of the preconditions of psychological unity with his treatment of the transcendental unity of apperception. Kant held that the self that secured such unity was purely formal in nature. This, he believed, was the only alternative to Cartesianism. But Kant failed to see the possibility of taking persons – real living human beings – as genuine psychological subjects. See the excellent discussion in McDowell 1994, pp. 99–104.

37   See Moran 2001.

38   It is worth noting an important contrast with Nagel's argument in 'What is it Like to be a Bat?' That argument trades on the idea that there is a crucial aspect of the mental – namely its subjective phenomenology – that cannot be observed from a third-person perspective. Since physicalist accounts are cast from a third-person perspective, they will always fail to capture a crucial aspect of the mental. The personalist, in contrast, does not depend on the limitations of the third-personal perspective. Indeed, she can hold that much of our mental life is observable from a third-person perspective because it is manifest in the life-activity of the subject. The personalist's point is that the first-person perspective on the mental is not one of observation but agency, and this precludes a person adopting an attitude to their own mental states as if from the third-person (except perhaps in certain unusual circumstances). Our brain states, in contrast, are possible objects of observation.

4. The personalist's objective, as John McDowell puts it, is

> to restore us to a conception of thinking as an exercise of powers pos-
> sessed, not mysteriously by some part of a thinking being, a part whose
> internal arrangements are characterizable independently of how the
> thinking being is placed in its environment, but unmysteriously by a
> thinking being itself, an animal that lives its life in cognitive and practical
> relations to the world.[39]

Both McDowell and Ilyenkov supplement their personalism with a distinctive
view of human development. On this conception, the human child first lives
a purely animal mode of existence; that is, her bodily functions, including her
psychological functions, answer exclusively to biological imperatives – for food,
warmth, comfort, etc. At this stage, we might say that the child's psychological
functions are unified by the satisfaction of biological need, rather than by the
maintenance of an orientation, cognitive and practical, to the world. As the
child matures, however, she undergoes a qualitative transformation. She enters
a distinctively human, essentially social form of life and acquires distinctively
human psychological capacities that enable her to transcend existence in the
narrow confines of a biological environment and to hold the world in view.
With this, natural-scientific modes of explanation are no longer adequate to
explain the character of the child's mindedness.

Exactly what is it about the mature human mind that resists explanation
in scientific terms? When Ilyenkov characterises the distinctive character of
human thought, his emphasis is always on creativity, universality, and unpre-
dictability. Ilyenkov's point is that the human mind is universal in that it is
in principle open to *any* subject matter.[40] It is able to grapple with and solve
hitherto unencountered problems. The human mind constantly transcends
its own limits; it does not simply apply old techniques to new problems. On
the contrary, we set ourselves problems precisely to develop the methods to
address them, a process which in turn uncovers new questions, creating new
problem-spaces demanding further innovation, and so on. To understand this
dialectical process, we cannot represent the mind as determined by antecedent
conditions. If it is determined by anything, it is by the logic of the subject matter
it confronts.[41] But if it is to conform itself to an evolving, ever-novel object, the
mind must be able to transcend rules and principles that formerly governed its

---

39   McDowell 1998e, p. 289.
40   Ilyenkov 1974a, pp. 38–9 (2009b, pp. 29–30).
41   Ilyenkov 2002b, pp. 105–6; Ilyenkov 2007c, pp. 93–4.

operation. The human mind is not rule-bound. It follows that since the brain is a physical thing operating according to physical laws, its operations cannot be all there is to the life of the mind. A machine, even an astonishingly complex biological machine, can only do what it has been programmed to do by evolution or design. No machine can be truly universal in the way that human minds are universal.

As we observed in Chapter 1, in relation to Mikhailov's work, such an argument is harder to sustain today than it was in Ilyenkov's time. We are now familiar with computers capable of learning and of forming creative solutions to problems. So the idea that computers are rule-bound in a way that human beings are not lacks the intuitive plausibility it enjoyed in the early days of artificial intelligence and cybernetics. So Ilyenkov's opponents will likely dismiss his argument as no more than a misplaced affirmation of humanism.

But as I suggested above, the argument can be redeemed, however, if we bring into play something Ilyenkov does not usually discuss head-on: rationality. McDowell, like Ilyenkov, argues that human beings 'are born mere animals, and they are transformed into thinkers and intentional agents in the course of coming to maturity'.[42] But McDowell makes very clear human beings' distinctive psychological powers reside in their *responsiveness to reasons*. Human beings think and act in light of the reasons for so doing and their behaviour can be explained only with this perspective in view. Critical to McDowell's view is a distinction, ultimately derived from Kant, between two species of explanation or 'modes of intelligibility'. On the one hand, there is explanation by appeal to scientific law; on the other, there is explanation by appeal to reasons. The explanation of why Harry tripped over the carpet appeals to the physical conditions that were causally sufficient for the accident to occur. In contrast, we explain why Harry opened the door by appeal his reasons for so doing: we attempt to show the favourable light in which he saw the action. In like manner, we explain what Harry believes by appeal to what it is most reasonable for him to think in light of the evidence, his situation, and his existing beliefs, on the assumption that he is rational. These two species of explanation, rational and causal, are fundamentally different in kind.[43] The relations in which rational

---

42   McDowell 1994, p. 125.

43   McDowell prefers to cast the distinction as one between rational and scientific explanation because he does not want to make the scientific-naturalist a gift of the concept of causation. He wants to leave open the possibility that rational explanation can be genuinely causal. Conversely, not all scientific explanation is strictly causal in character. However, the rational-causal distinction will do for present purposes, so long we bear these subtleties in mind.

explanation deals are normative in character. When I decide that Jack must believe that q because he believes (a) that p and (b) that p entails q, I am not making a causal claim. I am assuming that Jack believes what he ought to believe if he is rational.

Earlier, I described the mind as a psychological unity. The relations that unite mental phenomena into a system are precisely normative, rational relations of entailment, probability, plausibility, and so on. These are not the sort of relations that are characterised by natural-scientific theories. The language in which we describe and explain mental events and processes, and the constraints that govern those explanations, are fundamentally different in character from the language of natural science. What goes on in the brain is exhaustively open to scientific explanation. The brain is within the realm of scientific law. But mental states and processes occupy a different logical space – the space of reasons. Since there is no possibility of reducing the items that occupy the space of reasons to those that populate the realm of law, it follows that psychological talk represents a fundamentally different discourse from talk of the brain, and these discourses have fundamentally different subjects.[44]

With this view of rationality in place, we can say that the qualitative transformation in the child occurs when she becomes an inhabitant of the space of reasons, a being whose life-activity must be understood by appeal to rational, rather than merely causal-scientific, considerations.[45] For McDowell, what is crucial is the acquisition of the conceptual capacities. These enable the child to have perceptual experiences of a kind that have a rational bearing on judge-

---

44   Those who know the work of Donald Davidson may want to resist the final step in this argument. Davidson holds that psychological and physical explanations are fundamentally different in kind, but contends that mental events are physical events (see, e.g., Davidson 1984a). Since an event can be picked out by different modes of description, we can say that any event described psychologically (e.g. my thinking of Vienna) is identical with some event that can be described physically (e.g. such-and-such neurons firing). Davidson argues that even though this particular (or 'token') mental event is the same as that particular physical event, the fundamental difference between psychological and physical modes of explanation entails that we cannot establish identities between types of mental and physical events or establish psycho-physical laws. He thus arrives at a form of nonreductive physicalism known as 'anomalous monism'. McDowell and others (e.g. Hornsby 1997) reject anomalous monism on the grounds that we cannot assume that psychological and physical discourses individuate the same events.

45   It is interesting to speculate why Ilyenkov says little about rationality as such. I think he would have taken the rational/causal distinction for granted as a staple of post-Kantian philosophy, but avoided overt talk of reason and rationality for fear of provoking accusations of idealism, Hegelianism, or rationalism – all of which were considered heresies in Soviet philosophy.

ment, and to entertain mental states of a kind that can stand in articulate rational relations with one another. Such a creature is a rational agent, a person. This conception of development consolidates the view that the person is the centrepiece of rational explanation, not her brain. It is persons whose beliefs are consistent or inconsistent, who act reasonably or unreasonably, who argue perceptively or stupidly, who judge carefully or precipitously.

It may seem that these considerations about reason and rationality are at some remove from the Ilyenkovian thoughts about creativity and universality that they were meant to redeem, but they are not. To take up a theme introduced back in Chapter 1, it is a presumption of rational explanation that agents are free and hence responsible for their thoughts and actions. Creatures capable of conceptual thought governed by norms of rationality are able to commune with the universal, first, in the sense that concepts can have universal content and, second, in the sense that there is no limit to what we can entertain in thought (of course there can be empirical limits to what we can entertain in thought, but there is no restriction of subject matter built into the very nature of thought itself). Finally, rational explanation is tolerant of novelty and creativity: it enables us to see how someone derived a novel solution to a problem without representing its derivation as a merely a piecing together of that which was already to hand. Even where judgement is compelled by rational necessity – where a person realises that there is nothing else to think but p – creativity may be required to perceive the significance of the considerations that compel judgement. This kind of creative insight can be understood and appreciated; it cannot itself be represented as necessitated by circumstance, or anticipated by substantive rules or procedures. Rational explanation is at ease with this.[46]

It is worth reiterating that although Ilyenkov and McDowell paint a similar picture of human development, there are marked differences in their views. McDowell links the acquisition of conceptual capacities to the learning of a first language. Ilyenkov, in contrast, argues that language learning is possible only once the child has already entered the human world by learning to interact with artefacts. Ilyenkov holds that the physical form of an artefact embodies the purposes for which it is used. Acquiring facility with artefacts is therefore a matter of coming to respond to a meaningful object, adapting to the 'ideal' form expressed by its physical form. The child inhabits a social world, not just because she constantly interacts with other people (indeed, she is dependent

---

46   The concept Ilyenkov deploys to capture the creative movement of thought is *dialectics* (see, e.g., Ilyenkov 2002b, pp. 26–34; 2007c, pp. 20–31).

on others for her very survival), but because her world is full of objects created by human beings for human purposes. Learning to negotiate this world is the child's entrance into the space of reasons, for to interact with the artefactual is to engage in activities are that are not just elicited by circumstance but mediated by meaning. So the child enters the human world, the world of meaning. Language, for Ilyenkov, is just another artefact, albeit it a supremely complex and sophisticated one.[47]

5. We have now considered some of the central arguments for personalism.[48] In conclusion, I shall consider the bearing of these arguments on the relevance of neuroscience to educational issues.

It is sometimes argued that although there are significant constraints on the extent to which brain science can illuminate learning, it does have a role in the explanation of dysfunction, deficit, and disorder.[49] Reflecting on the distinc-

---

47   There is an interesting discussion of the significance of artefacts in his writing on the education of the blind-deaf. Reflecting on the importance of the blind-deaf child's learning to eat with a spoon, Ilyenkov writes: 'The first and most fundamental form of human mind is revealed here as the *movement of the hands according to a schema* – according to a trajectory, not defined by biological need, but by a form and situation of objects created by human labour, created by human beings for human beings' (Ilyenkov 2002b, pp. 99–100; 2007c, pp. 89–90; see also Chapter 4 above).

48   But not all. For example, some argue the case for personalism on the basis of 'externalism' about meaning. It is sometimes argued that meaning, and hence mental content, is constituted in part by relations between the speaker/thinker and the external world. So, when I have a thought about tigers, what my thought is a thought about depends on facts about what tigers are. When I have a 'singular thought' about a particular object perceptually present to me (e.g. 'That lampshade is ghastly'), the content of the thought depends upon the existence of the object demonstrated. Such considerations led Putnam to conclude: 'Cut the pie any way you like, "meanings" just ain't in the *head*!' (Putnam 1975, p. 227). McDowell takes these ideas further, arguing that 'the moral of Putnam's basic thought for the nature of the mental might be, to put it in his terms, that the mind – the locus of our manipulations of meanings – is not in the head either. Meanings are in the mind, but, as [Putnam's] argument establishes, they cannot be in the head; therefore, we ought to conclude, the mind is not in the head' (McDowell 1998e, p. 276). McDowell takes this as an argument for personalism: 'Mental life is an aspect of *our* lives, and the idea that it takes place in the mind can, and should, be detached from the idea that there is a part of us, whether material or (supposing this made sense) immaterial, in which it takes place. Where mental life takes place need not be pinpointed any more precisely than by saying that it takes place where our lives take place. And then its states and occurrences can be no less intrinsically related to our environment than our lives are' (p. 281). Andrew Davis explicitly discusses the bearing of externalism about meaning on the question of the relevance of brain science to education (Davis 2004).

49   See Davis 2004, p. 31; Changeux and Ricoeur 2002, p. 49.

tion between rational and causal explanation can explain why this position seems attractive. Where learning is proceeding smoothly, we view the child from the perspective of rationality: she is a rational agent gradually taking command of some subject matter by coming to understand and appreciate the reasons for which she should form certain beliefs, make certain inferences, engage in certain practices, and so on. If the child encounters obstacles to learning, we try at first to explain this rationally. So, for example, we might propose that the child cannot see that she should infer that q, because she is missing some vital piece of information. Once she understands that p, then she will quickly realise that q... But sometimes we decide that such rational considerations cannot explain the child's difficulty. Her problem is not just that she lacks information or understanding in a way that is consistent with our viewing her as a rational agent. Her problem is of a different order. We then look for a causal explanation. Appeal to learning disabilities provides explanations of this kind. Such causal explanations look for underlying mechanisms, and in many cases it makes perfect sense to think that these might be a matter of brain functioning. It is plausible to suppose, for instance, that the particular challenges faced by people on the autistic spectrum have their basis in the way their brains work.[50] Once we adopt the causal perspective on the child's problems, we cease to see her as a rational agent, at least in this respect, and absolve her from responsibility, and hence blame, for her failings.

Yet why should we conclude that brain science is only good for explaining obstacles to learning? Why cannot brain science illuminate why someone is especially good at some practice? Admittedly, the explanation of why someone made some inference, or gave some excellent explanation, or solved some problem a certain way, will be a rational one, reconstructing the 'logic' of the achievement. But the explanation of why the person in question is particularly adept at this sort of thing – of her speed of thought, or her talent for seeing unusual connections – need not invoke rational considerations. It will speak to the causal preconditions of her rational powers. Why should we suppose, as Ilyenkov asks us to, that the only relevant neurophysiological fact is that her brain

---

50   Though, in harmony with what I say in note 18 above, I am by no means confident that, say, the condition formally known as Asperger's Syndrome (and now, since DSM-5, blended into the 'autistic spectrum') is really a single phenomenon, nor am I impressed with the assumption that the deficit is all on the side of the person diagnosed with the syndrome. We are good at describing the respects in which those with the syndrome fail to read other people, but we fail to ask what it is about 'normal' people that makes it difficult for them to read those with Asperger's.

is functioning normally? Surely we can aspire to a fine-grained explanation of exactly what it about the way her brain functions that enables her to excel as she does.

Ilyenkov insists that only social factors are relevant to the explanation of ability and achievement. Why? Consider the role that the social plays in Ilyenkov's and McDowell's respective accounts of the child's entrance into the space of reasons. McDowell gives pride of place to the child's acquisition of language, but he treats language, not just as a symbolic system, but as a living embodiment of cultural wisdom, so that the child's acquiring a first language represents her initiation into styles of thinking and reasoning. He writes that

> the language into which a human being is first initiated stands over against her as a prior embodiment of mindedness, of the possibility of an orientation to the world ... [Language is] a repository of tradition, a store of historically accumulated wisdom about what is a reason for what.[51]

Acquiring a language, so conceived, is acquiring a form of social life. Ilyenkov, as we observed, stresses that our form of life is embodied, not just in linguistic thought and talk, but in the very form the world takes in virtue of human interaction with nature. Our world is one 'humanised' by our activity, populated by created objects that are embodiments of meaning and purpose. The first step to becoming human is to learn to manipulate such objects in light of the 'ideal form' they have been lent by human agency. And it is not just that initiation into social forms of life kick-starts our mindedness. The life of the mind is lived in social space, mediated by forms of thought and inquiry that are essentially sustained by social practices.

Yet, notwithstanding the prominence both thinkers accord to the social, nothing in their arguments suggests that we should embrace a nurturism as thoroughgoing as Ilyenkov's can seem to be. They provide no reason to assume a priori that causal factors relevant to explaining this person's musical ability, or that person's proneness to anxiety, are all social. In the absence of real empirical evidence, that assumption can be based only on wishful thinking, on the hope that social factors can be controlled and improved in the way biological factors cannot be. Of course, there is as much reason to avoid crass biological determinism as there is to eschew a priori nurturism. It is critical to recognise that even though the acquisition and exercise of an ability (say, to sing a major scale) is enabled by biological factors, some of which may be innate, the ability

---

51   McDowell 1994, pp. 125–6.

itself is possessed by the person, not her brain. Moreover, *what* it is an ability to do is intelligible only in light of socio-historical considerations, and its acquisition must be seen as the appropriation of a social practice. Proper appreciation of these points gives the lie to any simple picture of abilities as 'hard-wired'. There is no reason to claim, as Ilyenkov appears to, that we can 'divide through' by biological considerations when considering the developmental trajectory of 'normal' brains.

I conclude that, even if personalism is true and psychological attributes cannot be legitimately ascribed to the brain, neuroscience remains relevant to understanding the brain processes that enable and facilitate our mental lives. There are no a priori grounds to declare brain science irrelevant to educational issues, or relevant only in 'deficit' cases. What is critical, however, is that interest in the brain should not distract attention from the fact that education is a communicative endeavour, not an engineering problem. Education is not about getting information into students' heads or of implanting skills in them. Learning history, for example, is a matter of acquiring facility with a discipline aspiring to critical self-consciousness about our relation to the past. Though a command of facts and skills of analysis are preconditions of historical understanding, they are not what that understanding consists in. This is not true only of high-brow humanities disciplines. When we teach carpentry, we are, or ought to be, introducing students to a craft, to an historically-evolving tradition of fashioning wood to make artefacts for various purposes. Once again, information and skills are not all that is at issue. Machines may possess those, or close surrogates, but machines have no practices and crafts. We must never lose sight of the wider communicative endeavour that is the heart of education: the meeting of minds in an encounter with a discipline.

Perhaps these reflections sound old-fashioned and high-minded. But I am amazed at the naiveté of scholars who ponder the possibility of 'popping a pill to learn'. If we object to athletes using performance-enhancing drugs, why should we welcome pharmaceutical ways of enhancing learning? If we stop students taking into examinations on which they have downloaded texts, should we look more favourably on the prospect of their downloading material directly into their brains? Such questions, however fanciful, raise ethical issues that force us to confront the issue of what education is and ought to be. My point is a familiar one: we must not let excitement about scientific innovation and technological possibility distort our conception of education and of the values it ought to embody. Above all else, this was the message that Ilyenkov sought to convey in his writings on education. Though many years have passed since he put pen to paper, this message is as relevant today as it ever was. I suspect it will remain so long into the future.

. .
.

It is sometimes suggested that *activity theory* represents the most important legacy of Soviet philosophy and psychology. But what exactly is activity theory? The canonical account in the West was forged by Yrjö Engeström, who identified three stages in the theory's development: from Vygotsky's insights, through Leontiev's articulation of the fundamental structure of activity, to a third generation incorporating difference, discourse and dialogue into the framework. The next chapter argues that the resulting position is in fact in tension with the concerns of the Russian founders of the tradition, and uses Ilyenkov's understanding of activity to bring out how this is so. While the Russians saw the concept of activity as a fundamental category to address profound philosophical questions about the nature and possibility of mind, activity theory in the West has principally become an empirical method for modelling activity systems. My chapter explores the strengths and weaknesses of views on both sides of the contrast and examines its consequences for the future of the 'activity approach'.

Reflections on Activity Theory

1. The subject of this chapter is the concept of activity, as that concept finds expression in the school of thought known as 'activity theory'. Activity theory is increasingly viewed as a potentially fertile paradigm for research in education, and the time is ripe for sustained theoretical reflection on the scope and limits of this approach.

When I did philosophical research in Russia in the early 1980s, I encountered two related ideas that I found challenging and exciting. These ideas were prominent on the Russian philosophical scene, but they were unfamiliar to me, schooled as I was in Anglo-American philosophy of the broadly analytic variety. The first was the notion of *the social self*, the idea that human individuals – persons – are essentially social beings; that the very nature and possibility of our minds depends in some deep sense on our membership in a community, or on our participation in culture. The second was the concept of *activity*. The Russian thinkers I studied were preoccupied with the claim that *activity* was a fundamental explanatory category in philosophy and psychology. There was lots of discussion of the so-called 'activity approach' or (less often) the 'theory of activity'. Indeed, among the reasons my mentors introduced me to Ilyenkov's philosophy was that he was one of the principal theorists of activity.

The social self is not so unusual an idea. It has long had a life in sociology and anthropology. Even though it did not figure in the sort of philosophy I was taught as an undergraduate, the idea has gained some currency in Anglo-American philosophy in the past three decades.[1] It has become prominent in communitarian political philosophy; some quarters of feminism, certain readings of Wittgenstein, and the work of philosophers such as Charles Taylor. In fact, interest in the social self may have peaked. Having brought the idea to prominence, the *Zeitgeist*, fickle as it is, seems to have moved on, and popular conceptions of persons are now heavily centred on matters biological. For all that, however, the idea that we are essentially social beings is no longer an unfamiliar one in Anglo-American philosophy.

The concept of activity, in contrast, had, and continues to have, no place whatsoever on the Anglo-American philosophical scene. Over the last thirty

---

1   See Bakhurst and Sypnowich 1995.

years, a great many high-quality reference works have been published in philosophy, but you will not find an entry on 'activity' in any of them. (I have in mind such works as the *Oxford Companion to Philosophy*, the multi-volume *Routledge Encyclopedia of Philosophy*, and the *Stanford Encyclopedia of Philosophy*.)[2] There is a vast literature on action and agency, but activity is not a live concept. Why? A representative of the Anglo-American tradition might argue along the following lines. Human beings engage in a vast number of activities (eating, playing, thinking, exercising, imagining, blaming, reading, breathing, lecturing, conversing, fighting...). Some of these activities raise philosophically interesting questions; some do not. What do we gain by subsuming them all under a single category? The question is even more pressing if we focus on more concrete activities: treating patients with multiple sclerosis, teaching seven-year-olds the basic grammar of their first language, designing cockpits for jet planes, creating computer viruses, sentencing criminals guilty of white-collar crime... Philosophical inquiry may be helpful in addressing some aspects of some of these things. But how could there be a theory of *activity* per se, that was not so general as to be utterly useless? This is a question to which activity theorists must have an answer.

2. The reader may now be expecting me to explain what Anglo-American philosophers are missing by telling a neat, coherent story about the role played by the concept of activity in the Russian tradition and explaining what it can do for us. Some of my previous writings might suggest that I have such a story.[3] But in fact, it is by no means easy to give a clear account of the role of the concept of activity in Russian philosophy and psychology. I am uncertain that there is anything that warrants the name 'activity theory', or even that there is any stable view of what the 'activity approach' is or might be. I wonder if we really know what it means to say, of activity, that it is a fundamental 'unit of analysis', or that, as Leontiev writes, activity is 'the substance of consciousness'.[4]

I am by no means the only one who has worked within this tradition who feels this way. If you consult two of the most useful Russian symposia on activity, you will see that no settled view emerges about the nature and significance of the concept.[5] Indeed, you might conclude from these discussions that 'the

---

2 Honderich 1995; Craig 1998. *The Stanford Encyclopedia* is at: https://plato.stanford.edu/cite.html (last accessed 20 February 2023).

3 See, e.g., Bakhurst 1997a; 1997b.

4 Leontiev 1977, p. 202.

5 See Lektorsky 1990, and the papers collected in the Fall 2001 edition of *Russian Studies in Philosophy* under the title *The Potential of Activity Theory*.

activity approach' is in crisis. Of course, one might expect a certain disorienta-
tion among the Russian proponents of the theory of activity. Given Marxism's
fall from grace in Russia, any school of thought associated with Marxism – as
activity theory clearly was – is bound to confront a legitimation crisis. However,
the situation is considerably more complex. In its heyday in Soviet thought, the
concept of activity was a vehicle for the articulation of a critical and creative
species of Marxism that stood in a tense relation to the Marxist-Leninist orthodoxy of the Soviet establishment. As a result, the activity approach was a means
for the ventriloquation of all kinds of views. And now, when one steps back and
reflects on the tradition, many of those views appear rather difficult to render
coherent.

3. It might be objected that, even if the Russians have lost their bearings about
activity theory, the paradigm is alive and well outside Russia, where there exists
a far more stable view of what the tradition amounts to.

   Take, for example, the conception of activity theory advanced by Yrjö Engeström. In his 1987 book, *Learning by Expanding*, Engeström offers a very detailed account of the diverse sources, philosophical and psychological, that
inform activity theory. In subsequent years, however, a simplified picture has
emerged out of his work that has become part of the self-consciousness of
those in the West who work in the tradition. This is the idea that there are three
principal stages or generations of activity theory or 'cultural-historical activity
theory (CHAT)' as it is now often called.

   The first generation is said to have been inaugurated in the late 1920s by
Lev Vygotsky, who is credited with having established a 'triangular model' of
action.[6] This is because Vygotsky introduced the concept of mediation, principally in response to the defects of S-R behaviourism. As we saw in Chapter 11
above, the fundamental idea is that human behaviour is not simply called
forth by stimuli, but is mediated by artefacts and concepts that are created to
prompt or modulate action. One of Vygotsky's favourite examples is the knot in
a handkerchief, tied as a reminder. The knot acts as an artificial stimulus functioning to control mental behaviour. Vygotsky goes on to develop this insight
as crucial to the understanding of language. He schematises mediation in the
following way.[7] A and X are stimuli, B is a 'point' acted upon:

---

6 Engeström and Miettinen 1999, p. 4.
7 See Vygotsky 1997e, p. 79 [*ss* 3, p. 111]; cf. Vygotsky 1978, p. 40.

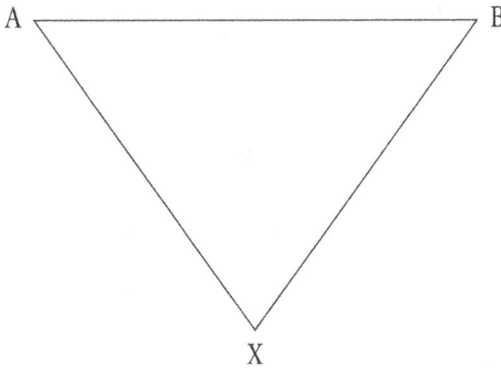

FIGURE 1
Vygotsky's model of mediation

Which activity theorists typically construe as the following:

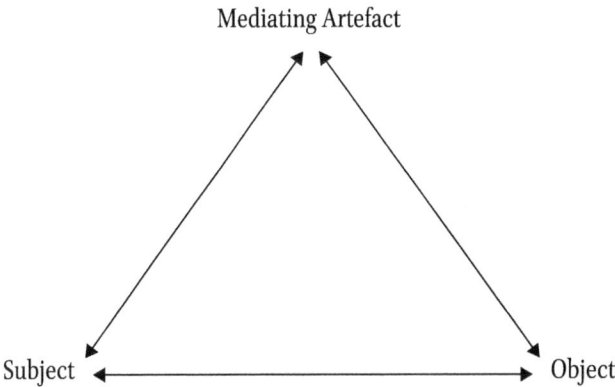

FIGURE 2
First-generation activity theory's (Vygotskian) model of action

A second generation is said to emerge on the basis of the work of Vygotsky's student, Alexei Leontiev. Leontiev distinguishes between 'action' and 'activity'. An action is conducted by an individual or group to fulfil some 'goal'. An activity, in contrast, is typically undertaken by a community (deploying a division of labour, and various means of production) and it has an 'object' and a 'motive'. Both action and activity are contrasted with 'operations', which are habituated behaviours provoked by certain conditions. Leontiev gives a much-celebrated illustration to develop these distinctions. He invites us to consider a member of a hunter-gatherer society who is a 'beater', startling animals so that others can catch them.[8] According to Leontiev, his action is beating a hedge to startle the game; his activity is hunting. The action is individual, the activity collective.

---

8 See Leontiev 1981, p. 210.

Leontiev is particularly interested in the contrast between the beater's behaviour and the behaviour of non-human animals. In the latter case, he argues, the object of an activity and its motive coincide. The animal's activity is always 'directed to objects of biological need and is stimulated by those objects' – e.g. the animal's activity is caused by its hunger and it sets out directly to satisfy that need.[9] In the human case, in contrast, object and motive can come apart. The beater's motive is the need for food or clothing, but his action does not address this directly. It is rather a contribution to a wider, social activity in which the participants each supply some part to the realisation of a common end. The point is not just that the beater is able to engage in means-end reasoning, recognising that his action contributes to an end he cannot realise alone. Rather, the very identity of his action depends on its relation to the broader social activity, which in turn draws its sense from the individual actions that constitute it.[10]

Engeström takes up Leontiev's position and schematises it in the following way:[11]

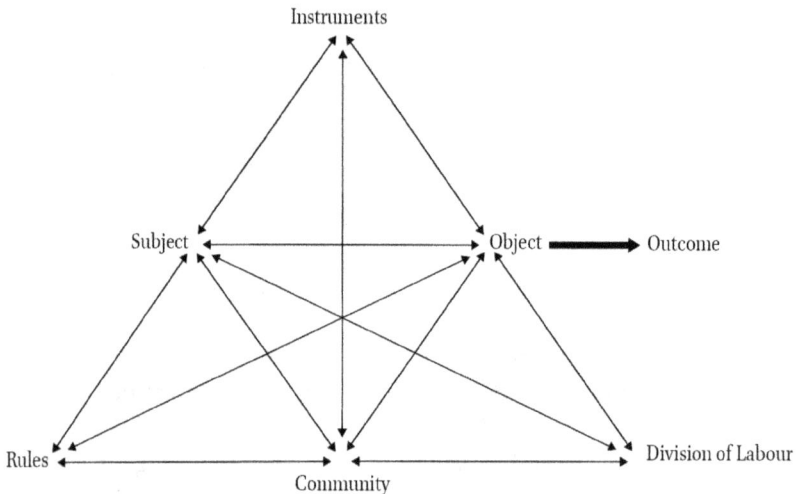

FIGURE 3   Second-generation activity theory's model of an activity system

Engeström refers to what the diagram models as an 'activity system', and he argues (invoking Ilyenkov) that the dynamics of the system – the forces of its development – result from 'contradictions' between its elements. The idea is

---

9   Leontiev 1981, p. 209.
10   See Leontiev 1981, pp. 212–13.
11   See, e.g., Engeström 1999, p. 31.

that the triangle can be applied to concrete subject matter; the terms 'subject', 'object' etc. are to be given specific interpretation depending on the particular case under scrutiny.

It is now common to speak of third generation of activity theory that examines the relations between activity systems and addresses issues of representation, voice, emotion, identity and difference, issues neglected by the 'troika' that founded the tradition – Vygotsky, Leontiev, and Luria – but which, it is now widely agreed, can and should be incorporated into the activity-theoretical approach.[12] Key here is the idea that we have to explore the conditions of the interaction of activity systems.[13] We arrive at:

So we are invited to think of activity theory as the result of the transition though the conceptions modelled in the diagrams above (Fig. 1–Fig. 4).[14]

4. The fact that this account of the nature of activity theory has become part of the self-consciousness of the tradition means that there is an important element of truth to it. A tradition is, after all, partly constituted by its understanding of itself. Nevertheless, there are aspects of this representation that I find unsatisfying.

One reason is that the account of the three generations of activity theory is something of a 'just so' story. The problem is not only the omission of numerous Russian thinkers who contributed to the Soviet school. Engeström would be happy to include reference to such thinkers as Luria, Rubinshtein, Zinchenko (father, Peter, and son, Vladimir), Elkonin, Davydov, Brushlinsky and Rubstov (as well as to various Western figures who have influenced activity-theory in the West, such as Dewey, Mead and Wittgenstein). The point is rather that, within Russian philosophy and psychology, the concept of activity was always seen as problematic and open to multiple interpretations. It is important that, as we have seen, Vygotsky's interest in mediation quickly led him to become preoccupied with *meaning*, as he recognised that mediating artefacts do not influence us simply as artificial stimuli, but in virtue of their significance, which cannot be understood merely causally. Once one had semiotic mediation in view, the whole behaviourist paradigm was blown apart. However, Vygotsky's fascination with meaning and culture laid him open to the politically-inspired objection

---

12   See, e.g., Roth 2007. The third generation was anticipated in Engeström and Miettinen 1999.

13   See, e.g., Hakkarainen 1999, p. 237.

14   Since I wrote this chapter a fourth generation has emerged which focuses on relations between activity systems within networks. See Spinuzzi's ingenious attempt to bring activity theory and actor-network theory into conversation (Spinuzzi 2008).

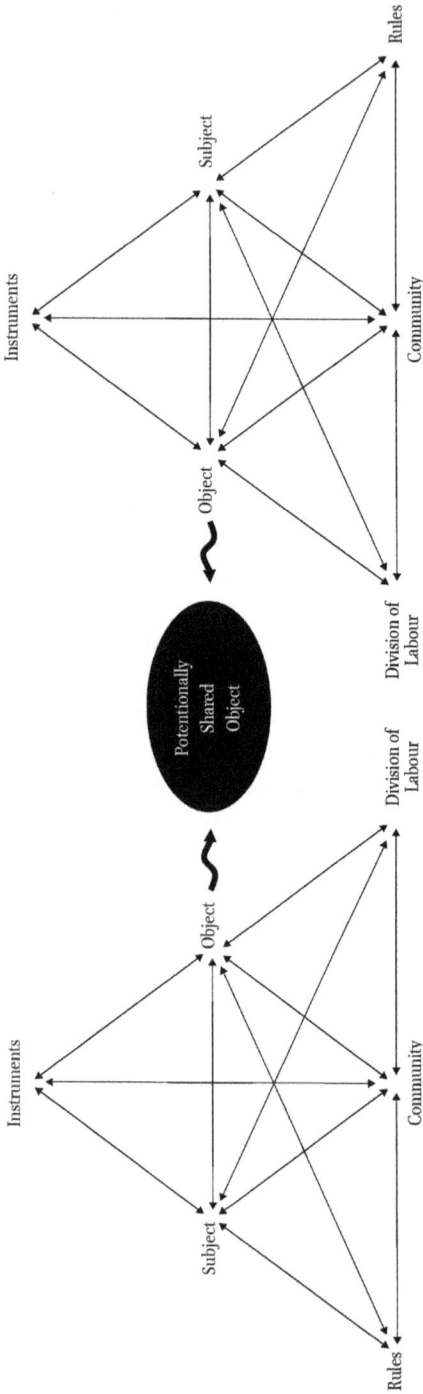

FIGURE 4   Third-generation activity theory's model of two interacting activity systems

that he was mired in an idealist worldview at odds with the true spirit of Soviet materialism. As I argued in Chapter 3, the concept of activity was brought to prominence by Vygotsky's students as part of an attempt to defend the general Vygotskian framework against this objection. To save the paradigm, and themselves, his followers rebuilt his psychology around the notion of *predmetnaya deyatel'nost'*, usually translated as 'object-orientated activity'. The adjective *'predmetnyi'* served the purpose well because it is suitably ambiguous, suggesting, on the one hand, material interaction with objects, and, on the other, the engagement of an enculturated subject with a conceptualised object situated in a socio-historical context (semiotic mediation was thus pushed out the front door and invited back in through the rear window). It is important, however, that these complicating factors were themselves very complicated. The coming to prominence of the concept of activity was the outcome of many forces that were not always transparent to the *dramatis personae* themselves, some of whom were genuinely committed to ridding Vygotsky of idealist tendencies, or at least had come to believe their own rationalisations for doing so.

One thing that is uncontroversial is that the emergence of the concept of activity pulled the Vygotskian approach towards the thought of the early Marx. Russian philosophers, however, were only able to address Marx's philosophical anthropology during the Khrushchev thaw in the early 1960s, when Ilyenkov and others sought to reanimate Soviet Marxism by returning to Marx's writings, including the early works that had only recently become available to Soviet scholars. This might help explain why there were some 40 years between Vygotsky's death and the publication of some of the better-known treatments of the activity approach, such as Leontiev's *Activity, Consciousness, Personality*.[15]

5. Another important consideration is that, on Engeström's account, what the activity-theoretical approach yields is a theory *of* activity, in the form of a model of activity systems. But the Russian founders of the tradition do not seem to be preoccupied with theorising activity as such, so much as deploying the concept of activity to explain something else – broadly speaking, our place in the world, the nature of consciousness, or personality. Their idea was that activity is the fundamental explanatory concept in philosophy and psychology because it is the central notion in any viable philosophical anthropology. On this approach, the claim that human beings are active creatures is not supposed to register as a merely empirical observation. No philosopher ever denied that human beings act. Rather, it is supposed to have deep philosophical signi-

---

15   Leontiev 1978.

ficance; that is, it is a claim about the very nature and possibility of thought and its bearing on the world. Ilyenkov is the Soviet philosopher who did most to develop this idea.

Ilyenkov argues against Cartesian and empiricist conceptions that activity is a precondition of the very possibility of mind. By actively engaging with reality we transform nature by lending it *meaning*. The world we confront in perception ceases to be a brutely external reality and becomes a space of significance and value. The results of our activity stare back at us with meaning and this creates new needs and desires, engendering further activity that further transforms the world, which then confronts us with new demands and opportunities. So activity is objectified in the world, and so the world invites or affords activity. It is not just that the things we create are charged with ideality; all objects we confront are meaningful for us in virtue of their relation to human activity. Our relation to the world is normative or rational from the outset; that is, the world is a space of reasons for belief and action and to be a thinking thing is just to have the capacity to navigate such a space. That capacity in turn is not innate, but is nurtured and sustained though *Bildung* or enculturation. We become beings that are responsive to reasons – persons in the full sense – as we appropriate the distinctively human forms of activity that manifest mindedness. Human beings are thus essentially social creatures because they owe their very status as minded beings, as persons, to their appropriation of culture.

It is important to understand just how ambitious Ilyenkov's position is. It aspires to explain both the nature of the world as a possible object of thought (of rational engagement) *and* the nature and origin of the powers that constitute our relation to the world as such an object. It thus appears to be nothing less than a derivation of the very distinction between subject and object, mind and world. And in this derivation, the concept of activity plays an absolutely crucial role. It is the key concept that explains both the emergence of the world as a possible object of thought through the objectification of significance *and* the emergence of our mental powers, which consist in a certain mode of active engagement with reality (responsiveness to reasons) and which develop in each individual through her appropriation of the specific modes of activity of her community, through initiation into a form of life. It is very typical of Russian philosophers of this tradition to look for such a root or core concept, the evolution of which encapsulates the logic of the system under scrutiny. Marx's treatment of the commodity form was the model for Ilyenkov, but you see the same strategy in Vygotsky, when he deploys the concept of word meaning as his so-called 'unit of analysis' in the evolution of the individual mind. So, for Ilyenkov, *activity* is the unit of analysis for the explanation of the very possibility of the relation of subject and object.

6. Any philosophical position as ambitious as this is bound to be fraught with difficulties and Ilyenkov's is no exception.

One problem is the status of the story Ilyenkov tells about activity. As I suggested above, it can be read as a kind of transcendental deduction of the mind-world relation. On this reading, Ilyenkov offers us a purely philosophical derivation: we start by acknowledging the reality of mind and world and work back to the preconditions of their relation, central among which is activity. Sometimes, in contrast, Ilyenkov writes as if he is telling a *historical* story; i.e. as if he is giving an empirical account of how minds evolved. We are offered a sort of speculative anthropology focused on, as Engels put it, 'the part played by labour in the transition from ape to man', where human history is portrayed as the history of the evolution of activity. Many of Leontiev's reflections on activity are of a similar kind.

So which is it, transcendental deduction or speculative anthropology? 'Im Anfang war die Tat' said Geothe's Mephistopheles. Is the 'Anfang' logical or historical? Either way, there are difficulties aplenty. First, the speculative anthropology is *very* speculative. What on earth is the evidence that supports the stories that, say, Leontiev tells? The answer, so far as I can tell, is very little.[16] That is, what looks like an empirical, historical account of anthropogenesis is actually an *a priori* derivation, or, if you like, it is just a good story.

So I prefer to read Ilyenkov's version as a purely philosophical argument that is not purporting to describe how minded beings actually evolved, but to explore the nature of mind and world in a way that delineates the limits of possibility. By so doing, Ilyenkov might succeed in establishing a framework that any account of anthropogenesis would have to respect (if we could tell it, which we cannot), but he is not really engaged in an historical account of the development of our species.

Yet, as I stressed in Chapter 6 above, if we read Ilyenkov's account as a transcendental deduction of the subject-object relation, it faces similar problems to those that beset Kant about our knowledge of 'things in themselves'. Ilyenkov seems to be saying that we lack access to reality prior to and independently of its idealisation by human activity. But if this is the case, it appears to follow that we are unable to attain a conception of reality as it is itself, out of all relation to human activity. Our conception of reality is fundamentally anthropocentric. Perhaps the reader is prepared to acquiesce in the idea that we have no immediate access to the world. But this is a view that Ilyenkov himself could not accept. For him, thought is accountable to reality: not just to reality-as-we-

---

16   Consider, e.g., Leontiev 1981, pp. 221–73, esp. pp. 232–44.

see-it, but to reality as it is. If we grant that all thought depends on mediation, then we have to see the mediational means as disclosing reality to us, not as coming between us and reality. I am confident that this issue can be insight-fully addressed, but devotees of activity theory should not assume that this is a philosophical issue that can be easily and definitively resolved.

This problem is not the only one Ilyenkov faces. Like Leontiev, Vygotsky and Marx himself, Ilyenkov operates with a very sharp distinction between human and animal minds. Human minds are responsive to reasons, free, creative, con-scious and self-conscious, and open to the world. Human experience is con-ceptual in character and we see reality as an integrated totality with (more or less) infinite spatial and temporal dimensions. We recognise the depth of the psychological reality of other persons, and their dignity and value. Non-human animals, in contrast, have a very different mode of psychological being. They are, of course, sentient and responsive to their environments, capable of cer-tain problem solving, and so on. But they do not inhabit the world as we do. They inhabit limited environments, which they perceive and respond to in light of biological imperatives. They do not think or act in light of concepts, they are neither free nor rational. As Marx put it: 'The animal is immediately one its life-activity. It does not distinguish itself from it. It is *its life activity*';[17] human beings, in contrast, are capable of critical reflection upon their own activity, of stepping aside and of seeing themselves through the eyes of another (or of a generalised other), and hence they are capable of heights of self-transformation that we do not see in the brutes.

Many contemporary readers will find this conception of our relation to other animals profoundly unattractive. It may appear to be no more than the age-old concern to set human beings apart from the rest of nature. In my view, the pos-ition can be finessed to extract a significant degree of truth from it, but it needs work to make it plausible.

The deep anthropocentrism of Ilyenkov's position is also evident in his gen-eral view of the relation of humanity to nature. As I also observed in Chapter 6, like many Marxists, Ilyenkov tends to view the physical world as the raw mater-ial on which human activity goes to work. Nature is the putty humanity fash-ions: the brute physicality of nature is endowed with meaning – given life, as it were, by agency. Nature as it is out of all relation to ourselves is pure other-ness; it only comes into focus when it is 'for us'. This is a highly problematic conception of our relation to our environment: it is ecologically disastrous to see reality simply as a resource for human activity. This needs to be radically

---

17   Marx 1977, p. 73. See Chapter 2 above, pp 44–8.

rethought. But it runs very deep within the broadly Russian Marxist tradition, and is a guiding theme in the activity approach, at least in its Russian version.[18] It is not clear to me that we can simply divide through by the prometheanism and leave a coherent theoretical position behind.

7. Although I raise these difficulties for Ilyenkov's philosophy, I firmly believe that there is a great deal of value in it. It contains many telling insights of enduring relevance. Ilyenkov's philosophy represents an affirmation of the autonomous, epistemically responsible agent – rational, perceptive, critical – combined with the recognition of the profound way in which rational autonomy depends on culture, society and history. He saw that rational beings are essentially embodied, finite creatures, in active engagement with the world of which they are part, and with each other. And he understood that human beings are beholden to one another for their very status as rational agents. Especially important in Ilyenkov's work is his attention to the significance of the character of the world in which human lives are led. He was acutely aware of the form the world takes on through our engagement with it in activity and of the endless dialectic of action and transformation this provokes. What philosophers of the Anglo-American tradition usually see as a contingent circumstance of marginal philosophical importance, Ilyenkov places at the very centre of the human condition: our active engagement with nature is the source of our humanity.

Thus, in criticising Ilyenkov, it is not my intention to diminish his ideas. By no means. My point is just that those who invoke his views, and views like them, should not take their philosophical cogency for granted.

8. In light of the discussion so far, it is natural to conclude that the activity-theoretical tradition contains two strands. First, there are those who see the concept of activity as a fundamental explanatory category that is the key to understanding the nature and possibility of mind. Ilyenkov perhaps best exemplifies this kind of thinking, but of course it is not a purely philosophical position. It is a philosophical stance designed to form the basis of a viable psychology, a psychology of the kind Leontiev sought to develop. Out of Leontiev's work then evolves the second strand, which is principally a method for representing activity systems with a view to facilitating not just understanding, but practice. Activity theory in the second sense is, among other things, a way of modelling organisational change.

---

18   See Davydov 1999.

I am not the only person to draw a distinction of this kind between two strands within activity theory. Victor Kaptelinin makes a similar move.[19] As I am a philosopher, when I draw such a distinction, people suspect that I believe that the first, philosophical strand represents the authentic theory of activity, and that the second strand is much less interesting. Since the first strand is preoccupied with rather abstract philosophical questions, I draw upon myself accusations of scholasticism (Engeström may have me in mind when he writes: 'when activity is taken *only* as a principle of [theoretical] explanation it seems that the outcome is often an endless conceptual exercise with meagre empirical grounding').[20] However, such an accusation would not really be fair. My main concern is that we do not lose sight of what the first strand of activity theory was all about. I do not want the first strand to be simply taken up into the second and to survive in people's imaginations only as its precursor. This is particularly important because, as I shall show, there is a very great difference in *style* of thinking between those who deploy activity theory to understand organisational change and thinkers like Ilyenkov (and not just because Ilyenkov would have been disappointed by the diminution of the Marxist framework that he held so dear).

9. I suspect that many who are drawn to activity theory find themselves in the following position. They want to look at a particular phenomenon (e.g. the way that treatment is delivered to stroke patients, or how a literacy programme is to be instituted in a certain community, or how a certain institution solves or fails to solve certain problems it confronts (say, how a bank institutes new technology which transforms the jobs of certain of its employees)). They recognise that the phenomenon is not easy to capture using the standard techniques of standard social science. This is in part because the phenomenon is part of a complex system and part because it involves a rich human texture. So what is needed is the right kind of qualitative research. But this has to be done properly, so what is required is an appropriate theoretical framework that will reveal the structure of the phenomenon and enable the researcher to generate and interpret data. This is what the second strand of activity theory – activity theory as a method for analysing activity systems – provides.

It is interesting to consider how Ilyenkov would have seen this. I think he would have raised a number of criticisms. First, it is not clear that what we have here is a theory at all. What we have is a model or a schema that has minimal predictive power. If activity theory is a theory, it warrants the name because it is a theoretical representation of the general structure of activity systems.

---

19   See Kaptelinin 2005.
20   Engeström 1999, p. 27.

But *does* the model capture the general structure of activity systems? It looks too true to be good. It is pretty much impossible to find something recognisable as an activity that does not fit the model. *What is wrong with that?!*, you might reply. *Isn't universality an advantage here?* Not obviously so. The fact is that the model seems to work particularly well for the sorts of activity systems that activity theorists typically study: health care, work settings, some educational contexts; that is, where you have a reasonably well-defined object, a pretty good sense of desirable outcomes, a self-identifying set of subjects, a good sense of what might count as an instrument or tool, etc. It is much less plausible for activities like, my writing and delivering this paper, or (rather more impressively) Beethoven's composing his 7th Symphony, Andy Warhol's producing his pastiche of the Mona Lisa, the dissemination of Bakhtin's ideas, or for modest activities such as having dinner with colleagues, walking the dog, visiting one's invalid relative. The point is not that you cannot make the model fit these activities – you can. It is just that it has no explanatory value for activities like this: they need to be understood using methods that are remote from the conceptual apparatus presupposed by the schema. This suggests that what we have here is a universal, but generally vacuous schema, that turns out to be a useful heuristic in reference to certain kinds of activity.

Moreover, the schema vastly underdetermines the description of the 'activity system' under scrutiny. Engeström speaks confidently of the triangular structure of activity. But what is the rationale for that (apart from the supposed authority of Vygotsky)? Why not just have a list of factors?

The model also says almost nothing about the relation that the various components bear to one another. The points of the triangles are joined by lines, but what do the lines represent? This is an important question because the items at the nodes are not just given: the relations they bear to each other will to some degree constitute them. In terms of understanding the dynamics of the activity system, a fair load is carried by the idea of a *contradiction*, but this notion is conspicuously vague.

It is also interesting that there seems to be no constraints whatsoever, apart from ideological ones, on employing any one of a number of other methods in conjunction with an activity-theoretical approach: discourse analysis, for example. The motivation for third-generation activity theory is precisely the need to incorporate into the framework considerations about, broadly speaking, the politics of representation. But there appears to be no obstacle to doing this in any one of a number of ways. This might seem like a strength of the approach; but it might also be a symptom of its emptiness.

Finally, I am sure that Ilyenkov would have been critical of the preoccupation with schematising activity that is so evident in the ubiquitous triangles that define the second approach. He would have said that they were tolerable as a heuristic, but it is crucial not to let these models acquire a kind of theoretical life of their own. By all means deploy something like this schema to get a handle on the interactions you are trying to understand. But from the outset you have to be alive to the limits of the model itself. You have to look for 'contradictions', not just within the subject matter the model discloses to you, but between the model and that very subject matter. The model is, after all, only another tool or instrument. This would be true of any model of activity that might be proposed within the activity-theoretical tradition. As Engeström recognises, to understand any complex interaction, you have to countenance at least two perspectives – the perspective of a theorist examining the interaction from outside, and the perspective of a participant (of course, there may be many different participant perspectives at issue).[21] You have to try and work your way into the system, to see how things look from the perspective of the various agents, and to sense the forces that influence their perceptions and their actions. To this end, you must bring to bear whatever tools seem appropriate to the task, but you have to be willing to step back from your own inquiries and submit them to critical scrutiny. This self-critical distance-taking is the very heart of human activity itself: the foundation of our rationality. And so it is especially important to see it at work when the subject under study is activity itself. The moral is that you must be very cautious about given, stable, structural representations where there is really dynamism, flux, reflexivity, and transformation.

10. If we grant that there are two main strands in the activity-theoretical tradition, it is natural to see their relation like this: the first strand forms the theoretical background to the section, so that conceptual problems in the second strand are to be addressed with resources supplied by the first. And hence the reader might think that I hold that the shortcomings of the second strand raised in the previous section should be addressed by a return to philosophical basics. But in fact I do not take this view. And this is not because of the contentious nature of the philosophical framework of the first strand. I'm just not sure that the kind of empirical work inspired by activity theory needs more theory. It might be better off with less.

Consider the recent debate about the nature of the object of activity.[22] The premise of this debate is that the object position in the triangle stands in need

---

21   See Engeström and Miettinen 1999, p. 10.
22   See Foot 2002, Kaptelinin 2005.

of theoretisation. This is because the triangle represents a dynamic system and we know the object of activity will evolve and transform over time. Does it help to answer this question if we return to the founders of activity theory? In my view, things only seem to get worse because of the familiar complexities of the *ob"ekt/predmet* distinction. Russian, like German, has two candidate words for object: *ob"ekt* – the term typically counterposed to subject, with connotations of brute objectivity and otherness, and *predmet*, with connotations of a conceptualised object – an object of inquiry, situated in a space of intention and purpose. What kind of thing should we be talking about when we're modelling activity systems?

I don't think we're going to make progress on this topic by going back to philosophical foundations. The fact is that term 'object of activity' in English is ambiguous. Under one interpretation, the most natural, it means the purpose or aim of the activity. So the object of what I am doing in writing this chapter is to get clearer about the present state and future prospects of activity theory. In this sense, citing the object of an activity is one way to answer the question, 'What are you doing?' The second interpretation is more obscure: in this sense, the object of activity is what the agent is acting *on*. This is clearest where some material is being fashioned: so the object of the carpenter's activity is *this piece of oak*. In this sense, the object of my activity now is *activity theory* or some such. Where this kind of object is an intellectual object, then we can speak of the 'subject' of our discussion. *Predmet* can also be used for subject in this sense, though we should observe that the two English senses I have enumerated do not correspond to the *ob"ekt/predmet* distinction.

My contention is that once we sort out the ambiguity in the English, we are home. We can seek to characterise the object of someone's activity in the sense of what it is she is trying to achieve. This is always a good question. And sometimes it might help to ask what the object of her activity is in the second sense: i.e. What is it that she is working on? But often there will be no answer to the latter question. This will be so, not because there is an object of her activity that is essentially elusive, as some theorists have concluded, but because for many activities the question is ill-formed. If someone asks, 'What was the object of the Russian Revolution?' we can only answer this as the question 'What was the revolution supposed to achieve?', 'What did the revolutionaries think they were doing?' But if we try to hear the question as asking for an object in the second sense, we'll get nowhere: the masses?, world-history?, the economy? The question makes no sense and to keep asking it is, in my view, the quintessence of pure scholasticism.

So I think recent discussions about the object of activity are a case where the second strand in the activity-theoretical tradition makes it seem as if there is a

deep theoretical problem to be solved, when in fact there is not, and that turning to the first strand to address this pseudo-problem only promises to make
matters worse.

11. The intention of my criticisms in this chapter is simply to increase the level
of self-consciousness within the tradition about its nature and origins. I admire
the philosophy that informed the activity-theoretical tradition. I admire Engeström and his colleagues, who have taken up the torch and are faithful to the
practical ethos of the Russian founders, in that they are concerned that theory should be deployed to transform the world for the better. My point is only
that activity theorists should not have a complacent attitude to the relation of
the different strands within the tradition, or blithe self-confidence that their
contemporary empirical inquiries are grounded in an unproblematic, coherent, theoretical paradigm. What is vital is that there is a rich and self-critical
dialogue between the different styles of thinking within the activity-theoretical
tradition. I hope this chapter will stimulate such discussion.

∴

The next chapter goes more deeply into the idea that the concept of activity
is a logical category fundamental to the explanation of the relation of mind
and world. After outlining Ilyenkov's position in ten theses, I take up a series
of objections articulated by Genrikh Batishchev. The later Batishchev sees
the activity approach as totalising and reductionist, construing reality as the
plaything of human activity conceived entirely in instrumental terms. This self-
aggrandising athropocentricity offers a distorted picture of human life, one that
finds no place for the transcendent and/or mysterious. In response, I gently
defend Ilyenkov from these criticisms, and offer a different, though perhaps
heretical view of the philosophical role of the concept of activity. Instead of
thinking of activity as the key concept from which we can derive the very possibility of the relation of mind and world – an interpretation of Ilyenkov's
philosophy I owe principally to Felix Mikhailov – we can say that the philosophical project of understanding mind and its relation to the world is to be
addressed by elucidating the distinctive character of our life-activity. A human
being lives in a way that is responsive to reasons, self-conscious and free; human
life is life that knows itself and that acts in light of what it knows. Philosophy's
task is to unpack these ideas in a way that reveals their interconnectedness,
their fundamental unity.

Activity and the Search for True Materialism

1. In the previous chapter, I argued that the concept of activity, as Ilyenkov and many other Russian thinkers deploy it, is not an empirical concept, but something more fundamental: a logical category. That is, the activity approach, properly understood, does not set out to describe or characterise human activity as an anthropologist or empirical psychologist might, or even to provide a philosophical typology of different kinds of activity (object-orientated, material, intellectual, instrumental, communicative, joint, interactive, or whatever). Rather, activity is supposed to be a basic explanatory category, charged with elucidating the relation between subject and object, thinking and being – with explaining the very possibility of a relation between mind and world. That is why it is central to the quest for true materialism. So when Ilyenkov says (echoing Marx) that 'both the *contemplating individual* and the *world contemplated* are products of history',[1] he means this not (or not only) as an empirical observation, but as a kind of transcendental claim: mind and world are possible only in and through activity.

In this chapter and the next, we shall continue exploring the philosophical potential of the concept of activity. Does this concept make a distinctive contribution to live philosophical questions? Or is its use by Ilyenkov and others now of merely historical significance?

2. In a 2005 article, I tried to characterise some key moments of an Ilyenkovian approach in the form of ten theses.[2] Here they are, slightly revised:

i.   To understand our distinctively human mental powers, we must comprehend our ability to commune with what Ilyenkov calls 'the ideal', that is, with all those putatively non-material phenomena (such as ideas, meanings, values) that comprise the domain of the conceptual.

ii.   Our relation to the ideal is essentially normative in character; that is, ideal phenomena influence our thoughts and actions rationally rather than merely causally. To possess a concept is to understand a set of rational (often inferential) relations; to grasp the meaning of an expression is to know how it *ought* to be deployed; to recognise the value of some object,

---

1   Ilyenkov 1974a, p. 207 (2009b, p. 165).

2   Bakhurst 2005a. I am grateful to Oxford University Press for permission to incorporate the material in this essay.

action or event is to appreciate something about what *ought* to be the case. The defining characteristic of human minded behaviour is that it is guided or determined by reasons, rather than merely dictated by causes.

iii.   To understand this, we must recognise that ideal requirements on thought and action have their authority independently of the consciousness and will of thinking subjects. In this sense, the ideal exists objectively. The realm of the ideal is not the projection of individual minds. On the contrary, the direction of explanation runs the other way: the objective existence of the ideal is a precondition of the possibility of individual minds, at least minds of the kind possessed by human beings.

iv.   This may look like a form of platonism, but objectively existing ideal phenomena do not constitute a supersensible reality or group-mind. We can think of them as elements of 'social consciousness', understood as a cultural formation, as something intelligible only in its relation to human activity.

v.   Cultural phenomena are embodied both in human practices and in the form the world takes on by virtue of human activity.

vi.   If we adopt a 'genetic' perspective – one concerned with the origin of the ideal – we can say that ideal phenomena are 'objectifications' of human activity. By virtue of our engagement with the world, nature is lent significance and value; it is 'humanised' or 'enculturated'. (We should, however, not reify the ideal: it exists only in the dynamic interplay of activity and world, 'in the unceasing transformation of a form of activity into the form of a thing and back – the form of a thing into the form of activity'.[3])

vii.   The point is not just that our ontology must admit 'social objects' – artefacts and institutions, for example – understood as embodiments of human activity. Of course, any form of Marxism will acknowledge the reality of such objects and distinguish them from natural phenomena. Ilyenkov's claim, however, is that 'in man, all objects are idealised'; that is, all objects brought within the compass of our 'spiritual culture' are made meaningful, and our relation to them engages our conceptual powers.[4] The world is given to us insofar as it is brought within the realm of the conceptual.

viii.   To be a thinking thing *just is* to have the capacity to commune with the ideal, to engage with the world normatively. We must orient epistemology away from what Elizabeth Anscombe called modern philosophy's 'incor-

---

3   Ilyenkov 1991a, p. 269 (2009a, p. 62; 2014, p. 78).
4   Ilyenkov 1974a, p. 202 (2009b, p. 160).

rigibly contemplative conception of knowledge',[5] with its preoccupation with the representation or picturing of reality, and towards a conception of mind as a specific mode of active engagement with the world. As Ilyenkov liked to put it when sympathetically expounding Spinoza, thought is the mode of activity of a thinking body.

ix.   Our distinctively human mental powers are not innate but are acquired through *Bildung* (education, enculturation). We become rational animals – persons in the full sense – as we appropriate the distinctively human forms of activity that manifest mindedness.

x.   This position aspires to explain both the nature of the world as a possible object of thought (that is, of rational engagement), and the nature and origin of the powers that constitute thinking, as emerging out of activity (or perhaps, in their essential relation to activity). It is thus a deduction (or dialectical derivation) of the distinction between subject and object, mind and world, in which the key concept – the 'cell', the '*arche*', the 'key', the 'unit' – is the concept of activity.

3. I believe that these ten theses capture important elements of Ilyenkov's philosophy. Of course, since I have mined them, removed them from their context, and cast them in a rather different idiom from Ilyenkov's own, it might be questioned whether my reading of Ilyenkov is faithful to the original. Some might complain that this is more like 'Ilyenkhurst' than Ilyenkov. But suppose these ten theses express a viable Ilyenkov-inspired variant of the activity approach. Is it a live philosophical option?

It will help to consider some objections to the activity approach made by thinkers who were broadly sympathetic to it. The most interesting such objection is Genrich Batishchev's claim that the activity approach is guilty of what he calls 'substantialism'. At first sight, this might appear to be the complaint that the activity approach treats object-orientated activity as a kind of material surrogate for Hegel's *Geist*. History, as the activity approach would have us see it, is not *Geist*'s voyage to self-consciousness and absolute knowledge, but material activity's journey to free, self-determined fulfilment under communism.

The problematic character of such a vision was certainly part of the accusation of substantialism, but there was also a good deal more to Batishchev's concerns, which contain many overlapping themes. For example, another of Batishchev's targets was monism, understood not so much as substance monism, but as what Paul Franks calls 'derivation monism' – the idea that all aspects

---

5 Anscombe 1957, p. 57.

of an adequate philosophical system are to be derived 'from a single, absolute first principle', which for the devotee of the activity approach is, naturally,
activity.[6] But this, Batishchev argues, entails the 'shameless elevation' of activity into a 'supercategory' from which we are somehow to deduce all aspects of
human life – mind, language, institutions, culture, art, religion, interpersonal
relations, and so on.[7] Such a derivation might be relatively trivial, in that it
is not hard to portray all these as aspects of human activity, but the activity
approach's preoccupation with object-orientated, goal-directed activity paints
far too instrumental a picture of our relation to the world, and to each other.[8]
So Batishchev writes, distancing himself from views he once held, 'activity is
not the only possible, universal, mode of being of man, culture, and sociality,
and ... not the only and all-embracing mode of man's relation to the world'.[9]
Any conception of activity needs to be complemented by other fundamental
concepts such as communication and community that are simply irreducible
to object-orientated activity.[10]

In addition, the activity approach does not simply distort our *relation* to
reality; it offers a distorted conception of reality itself, portraying the world
as merely the plaything of human activity. As Batishchev puts it, 'the whole
of objective reality outside human consciousness [is] reduced to a world of
objects – things that are axiomatically empty and a priori lower than man'.[11]
Such radical anthropocentrism not only slights the independence of objective reality; it also perpetuates the myth that, as V.S. Shvyrev boldly puts it,
'humans are basically capable of taking control of any "space" in the world,
any "sector" of existence'.[12] As such, the activity approach embraces a prometheanism that is as environmentally disastrous as it is philosophically base-
less. Moreover, even as a form of anthropocentrism the activity approach is
myopic in that its instrumentalism makes for a remarkably one-dimensional

---

6   Franks (2005, p. 17) casts derivation monism as a view about the derivation of the *a priori*
     conditions of experience. Such a view embraces Ilyenkov's philosophy, though Ilyenkov's
     explanatory ambitions are bolder. It is noteworthy that the entry on monism in volume 3
     of the *Filosofskaya entsiklopediya* essentially defines monism in terms of derivation mon-
     ism (see the references in Davydov 1990, p. 149).
7   Batishchev 1990b, p. 7.
8   See Batishchev 1990c, p. 171.
9   Batishchev 1990b, p. 9.
10   This was also a prominent theme in B.F. Lomov's reading of the activity approach in Soviet
     psychology.
11   Batishchev 1990b, p. 9.
12   Shvyrev 1990, p. 3.

view of human beings themselves.[13] Only consider the idea that the *Bildungs-process* can be understood as a matter of the 'internalisation' of social forms of activity; indeed, it is sometimes claimed that internalisation accounts for the very genesis of the individual mind. But such a vision has no way to acknowledge an authentic form of subjectivity or genuine modes of creativity.

What Batishchev called 'substantialism' is thus code for a whole host of sins, incorporating monism, reductionism, anthropocentrism and instrumentalism, which jointly preclude 'any undiscovered possibility, anything beyond the limit, any mystery'.[14]

4. There are certainly versions of the activity approach that warrant some or all of these criticisms. Indeed, there are those that invite the label 'substantialism' in its pure form. V.P. Zinchenko, for example, writes that

> Activity as a whole is an organic system whereby, as in a living organism, everything is reflected in something else and that something else reflects everything in itself. But this is not enough. In addition, activity with its highly complex structure is constantly developing. An indispensable feature of an organically developing system is its capacity to create during the course of its development organs that it lacks.[15]

To conceive of activity as *subject*, as Zinchenko does in this passage, is undoubtedly problematic, but it is hard to see Ilyenkov as guilty of this kind of totalising vision. Ilyenkov is a substance monist, but the substance is matter (understood as a dynamic system, not as human activity). Activity 'substantialises' itself in matter, but it is not itself substance, but form (or rather, that which creates form).

I also do not think that Ilyenkov gives the concept of activity all-encompassing explanatory pretensions. The concept plays a critical role in the solution to the problem of the ideal, which in turn explains the possibility of the relation between mind and world, but Ilyenkov is not committed to the view that the character of that relation has to be understood exclusively in terms of activity. To become a thinking thing, the child must acquire the capacity to commune with the ideal, and this involves initiation into the practices of the community and, thereby, the appropriation of forms of activity which, as it were, bear ideality within them. A being that has acquired that capacity is able

---

13   See Batishchev 1990c, p. 172.
14   Batishchev 1990a, p. 90.
15   Zinchenko, quoted by Batishchev 1990b, p. 11.

to engage in conceptual thought and communication, and to enter a meeting of minds with other such beings. Though this may be mediated by object-orientated activity, it does not *consist in* object-orientated activity, nor can it be reduced to object-orientated activity. Moreover, in the rare cases where Ilyenkov speaks of 'internalisation',[16] he is very clear that the appropriation of social forms of activity is to be understood as a precondition of the emergence of self-determining subjects, who are by no means 'products of society' in the pejorative sense. So there need be no tension between the notion of internalisation and the idea of autonomy or creativity.

Of course, there are elements in Batishchev's criticisms that hit their mark. The 'environmental' objection is spot on. The whole rhetoric of the activity approach portrays nature as an object of aim-orientated activity, as a resource, as the means of humanity's self-realisation. This is true of a great deal of Marxist thinking. But though this comes naturally to the activity approach, I do not think it *has* to see nature this way. If our active engagement with nature is the source of our very rationality, it does not follow that we must portray the world as subordinate to human ends. An ecologically saner perspective is perfectly possible, one which acknowledges that we are parts of nature, not masters of it.

Another serious issue is whether Ilyenkov's solution to the problem of the ideal commits him to a form of anthropocentrism that slights the independence of objective reality. This is an objection I have tried to address in a number of my writings, perhaps not entirely successfully.[17] Ilyenkov claims that the fundamental forms of thought that make possible our cognitive relation to the world are not innate in individual minds, but are inherent in the practices of the community – they are culturally, rather than psychologically *a priori*. Each child becomes a thinking thing by appropriating the practices constitutive of those forms of thought. By what right then does he think that our forms of thought disclose the world to us 'as it is', rather than as it is relative to the forms of activity of beings like us? Ilyenkov seems to hold that because our forms of thought are grounded in the modes of activity of beings engaged with an objective world, those forms of thought reflect the character of that world as much as they reflect our character as agents. However, it is hard to say whether this is an argument or an expression of faith. One might respond that the contrast between the world as it is in itself, and the world as it is by virtue of the influence of human activity, is a distinction that must be made *within* the conception of the world that issues from the application of our concepts. It is not as

---

16   For example, Ilyenkov 2002a; 2007b.
17   For example, in Bakhurst 1991, pp. 207–12, and Chapter 5 above.

if the distinction can be drawn from some vantage-point *outside* thought, from which we can compare the world as it is out of all relation to us with the world as we find it. And in our engagement with the world – in our life-activity itself – we constantly mark the distinction between things as seem and things as they are. Indeed, it is hard to see how we could even understand ourselves as acting in the world without recognising the objectivity of things, including of course our own bodies. The problem of reality is one posed for us within practice and is resolved practically, rather than philosophically, as the second of the 'Theses on Feuerbach' boldly affirms.[18]

Whatever one thinks of this resolution, there is no doubt that we are in the terrain of live philosophical issues: how to understand the preconditions of our cognitive contact with a mind-independent world. It might be complained, however, that we have arrived at this live issue via a route that is full of obscurity. What does it really mean to say that ideality is activity objectified, or that the ideal exists in the interplay between the form of practice and the form of reality? It will not do just to show that the activity approach has live questions in view; it has to have something intelligible to say about them. Is this really true of Ilyenkov's contribution?

5. A natural response to this objection would be to present Ilyenkov's famous work on the ideal as addressing a question familiar from post-Kantian philosophy: what is the source of normative authority? As we saw above, the influence that the ideal has on thought and action is *normative*. The problem of the ideal is thus the problem of how norms are possible, or how rational determination is possible, and we can see Ilyenkov as arguing that normative authority is objective, relative to the individual, but ultimately instituted by social human activity. This brings Ilyenkov into dialogue with the social-pragmatist tradition (the leading exponent of which is Robert Brandom).[19]

On such a constructivist view, normativity is standardly thought of as brought into being by something like self-legislation, understood not as the exercise of pure practical reason, but as a matter of social recognition. Ultimately, there is nothing to being a norm other than being taken to be one. As Jeffrey Stout puts it:

---

18   'The question whether objective truth can be attributed to human thinking is not a question of theory but is a practical question. Man must prove the truth – i.e. the reality and power, the this-sidedness of his thinking in practice. The dispute over the reality or non-reality of thinking that is isolated from practice is a purely *scholastic* question' (Marx 1968, p. 28).

19   See, for example, Brandom 1994.

Our norms are our doing. Each time we apply a concept we contribute something to the evolution of our norms ... As subjects, we are products of the norms as they currently stand, just as our norms are products of the social practice in which our predecessors carried out their cognitive projects by applying concepts to things they considered worth talking about. The inheritance now rests in our hands.[20]

So Stout characterises a view that finds various forms of expression in the writings of many different philosophers. Ilyenkov's version, with its emphasis on the material instantiation of what Hegel calls 'objective spirit' through the objectification of activity, is rather different in character from the work of many contemporary pragmatists, but it is similar in inspiration and objective. It portrays the source of normative authority as ultimately residing in us.

It is certainly possible to see Ilyenkov as contributing to this style of thought. And this is hardly surprising, since the social-pragmatist tradition has its roots in Hegel, Ilyenkov's favourite philosopher. I have reservations, however, about the idea that all normative authority issues from us. There is a good sense, for example, in which the rules of soccer are our norms, that we administer them, and so on. This is so because those norms are in the service of certain specifiable human interests and may be codified and modified to suit them. But things are not so straightforward when we consider norms of inquiry that are in the service of getting things right. Here the norms are as much a matter of discovery as the truths they enable us to disclose. In what sense, then, are they *ours*? They may be said to be so because we embrace them, thereby 'making them our own', but not because we put them into place. I believe we need to recognise a fundamental non-derivative kind of normative authority that is not constructed by us, but which we discover and to which we seek to conform our thoughts and actions. As John McDowell puts it, '[i]f self-legislation of rational norms is not to be a random leap in the dark, it must be seen as an acknowledgement of an authority that the norms have anyway'.[21]

We will take up this theme when we consider McDowell's position in more detail in Chapter 18. For present purposes it is enough to remark that if Ilyenkov's discussion of the problem of the ideal can be fruitfully read in relation to contemporary debates about the sources of normativity, then it is unmistakably a contribution to live philosophical issues, and moreover, one that

---

20   Stout 2007, p. 30.
21   McDowell 2009h, p. 105.

addresses them with greater imagination than is found in the writings of many thinkers who struggle with these matters.

6. I want to conclude by making a radical, even heretical, suggestion. Many of the problems of the activity approach, real or perceived, issue from the idea that activity is a category from which we can deduce the relation between subject and object, thinking and being. But suppose we forswear commitment to derivation monism and appease Batishchev by adopting a more modest project. Let us think of ourselves as trying to characterise our form of life, or the human life form, in a way analogous to the kind of natural-historical judgements by which we might characterise an animal species.[22] Any such account would have to describe our biological nature in terms anatomical, physiological, and so on. But it would also have to capture the distinctive character of human beings' modes of activity. Suppose we think of the philosophy of activity as trying to do just that. The task is not to give an empirical description of how human beings live or what they do, but to express the terms in which we must *think* human activity, the terms in which human activity must understand itself. Central to any such characterisation will be the idea that human beings are responsive to reasons, or that they commune with the ideal, as Ilyenkov might have said. It is not just that some of a human being's doings can, indeed must, be understood as guided or determined by reasons. It is that being subject to rational determination is an essential dimension of our mode of being. The ideas of object-orientated or goal-directed activity are in themselves less than adequate to capture this, for aim-orientated action as such is not distinctively human. What is critical is that a creature that is responsive to reasons is capable of deliberation, of making up its mind about what to think or do in light of an appreciation of what there is reason to think or do. Such a being is autonomous or self-determining. Its activity manifests freedom. Moreover, its freedom presupposes that it is self-conscious, for it can think and act for reasons only insofar as it knows what it thinks and does. Now any attempt to characterise human activity along these lines must reckon with the fact that in the course of their lives human beings undergo a certain transformation. We are not born responsive to reasons, but attain this status in the course of coming to maturity. A human life is marked by *Bildung*, by the formation of reason.[23]

---

22   This suggestion is inspired by Michael Thompson's work: see, for example, Thompson 2008.

23   See McDowell 1994, pp. 125–6; McDowell's philosophy is treated at length in Bakhurst 2011; see Chapter 18 below.

Suppose we give the philosophy of activity the task of continuing and deepening this characterisation, which picks up, of course, many of the themes in the ten Ilyenkovian theses I presented. Is this not really the project in which we have been engaged all along, once it is relieved of transcendental or Hegelian-Marxist baggage? It might be complained that Ilyenkov himself would not recognise the project. But I do not think that is true. For preserved in the approach is the idea, central to German idealism, that freedom, reason and self-consciousness are one, and hence the task of true materialism is to understand how a being that is self-conscious, free and responsive to reasons is, indeed can only be, a material substance. That is a question that Ilyenkov would definitely recognise as his own. Moreover, such an approach makes self-consciousness the primary object of philosophy: for the project of understanding how freedom, reason and self-consciousness are one is an exercise in self-knowledge, by thinking beings who understand their own nature as such. This issue, cast in this way, is very much alive in contemporary philosophy – witness Sebastian Rödl's impressive book *Self-Consciousness*.[24]

I think therefore that we can now conclude that the concept of activity is of more than merely historical significance. There is much in the activity approach, as exemplified by Ilyenkov, which engages with ideas prominent on the contemporary philosophical landscape. Indeed, I expect that as time goes on, and more and more lines of communication are opened between German idealism and Anglo-American styles of philosophy, the kind of theoretical insights that gripped Ilyenkov will come to seem increasingly relevant to our philosophical concerns, even as the political vision that inspired him becomes increasingly remote. Indeed, I suspect that the concept of activity, in one guise or another, may gradually edge its way towards the centre of philosophical attention and, with this, the reflections of Ilyenkov and like-minded Russian philosophers will come to seem strangely prescient. Whether I am right, only time will tell.

∴

In 2016, the editors of *Educational Review* asked me to write a short piece updating my 'Reflections on Activity Theory', which had appeared in that journal in 2009. The opportunity enabled me to bring the insights of the Russian originators of the activity approach into dialogue with recent developments in the philosophy of action. Building on the position proposed at the end of the

---

24   Rödl 2007.

last chapter, I argue that understanding how intentional human action is self-conscious action is essential to understanding the character of the human life form (or human life-activity) in its socio-historical reality. With both Marx and Ilyenkov in mind, the chapter examines and refines Leontiev's distinction between action and activity, arguing that some activities have ends that are infinite (that is, ends that are not exhausted by their realisation) and internal (that is, intelligible only to those immersed in the activity itself). Educating and philosophising, it is argued, are, in the ideal, such activities. This construal of the philosophical substance of the concept of activity gels nicely with Ilyenkov's vision of philosophy as logic, the science of thought, for human life is thinking life. In this regard, thinking is not one among the things human beings do; it is the manner in which they do things – as this is expressed in the activity of their 'thinking bodies', as Ilyenkov liked to say.

Activity, Action and Self-Consciousness

1 Further Reflections on Activity Theory

'Reflections on Activity Theory' (Chapter 15 above) explores the relation between activity theory, as it has been developed in the West, by Yrjö Engeström among others, and the tradition of Russian thought in which the theory originated, particularly as it found expression in the philosophy of Evald Ilyenkov. There is some tension in this relation. For Ilyenkov, the concept of activity forms part of an ambitious philosophical anthropology that sets the terms for empirical psychology. In contrast, activity theory in the West has evolved primarily into a framework for analysing, designing and transforming 'activity systems', exemplified by Engeström's writing on work. There is undoubtedly a difference of ethos between these two orientations. While Ilyenkov seems to invoke activity in a kind of transcendental deduction of the relation of subject and object, contemporary activity theory is essentially a collection of concepts, schematised into a framework to impose order on empirical data.

By drawing this contrast, my aim was to complicate the simplistic picture of the evolution of activity theory sometimes presented in the literature, and to suggest that much contemporary research in the tradition represents a rather different enterprise from the work of the tradition's founders. I also sought further to complicate the picture by noting that the concept of activity was highly contested in Soviet philosophy and psychology and that there was never a settled view of its significance.[1] I hoped thereby to raise the level of self-consciousness about the nature and origins of the 'activity approach' and to stimulate discussion about the different styles of thinking within it.

In addition, I wished to counter the idea that activity theory is best seen as a heuristic, a set of 'off the peg' tools to be adopted (perhaps along with resources furnished by other frameworks) on largely pragmatic grounds to conduct empirical research. Insofar as Vygotsky, Leontiev or Ilyenkov saw

---

[1] I am sure this is not lost on such thinkers as Engeström, Kaptelinin or Nardi whose work is informed by a real appreciation of the tradition's theoretical antecedents, and of the many variations on the theme of activity within it (see, e.g., Kaptelinin and Nardi 2006, ch. 8).

theories as tools, they were tools to disclose reality, to enable a uniquely satis-fying conception of the mind's place in nature. The criterion for their adoption was truth, not usefulness. And this imposed upon these thinkers the burden of ensuring their concepts were adequate to reality in all its rich complexity. The realistic spirit that infuses such work is at odds with the idea of activity theory as essentially a heuristic or technique, to be adopted so far as it is useful, and supplemented or revised so long as that proves expedient. For a thinker like Ilyenkov, such an approach fails to respect the depth of the concept *activity*. It would be a shame if contemporary activity theory lost touch with that senti-ment, and for that reason it is important that activity theorists appreciate their tradition's philosophical roots.

Since 'Reflections on Activity Theory' appeared in 2009 work in activity the-ory has continued apace. My paper traced the development of the paradigm from Vygotsky's initial insights about mediation, through the emergence of Leontiev's activity-theoretical psychology and its appropriation in the West, to the dawning of so-called 'third-generation' activity theory, with its recognition of issues of diversity and the interaction between multiple activity systems. Since then, AT 3.0 has matured and now there is talk of its succession by a fourth generation, incorporating greater recognition of the dynamics of 'the network society'. There has also been fascinating historical research on Vygotsky and his circle that challenges much received wisdom,[2] and important work on the tradition's philosophical foundations.[3]

Also important, I believe, is that the *Zeitgeist* within Western philosophy is shifting in a way hospitable, if not to Ilyenkov's boldest ambitions, then at least to finding significance in the concept of activity.[4] This has influenced how my own thinking has evolved, and this is reflected in my book, *The Formation of Reason*,[5] which has education as a central theme, and in subsequent writ-ings.[6] In this chapter, therefore, I propose to reflect further on some of the notions central to the activity approach – not least of all the concept of activity itself – and show how their philosophical elucidation illuminates the activity-theoretical framework.

---

2 Yasnitsky and van der Veer 2016b, though see Maidansky 2020.
3 Exemplified by Levant and Oittinen 2014 and Maidansky and Oittinen 2015.
4 I am thinking of the work of Sebastian Rödl (2007) and Michael Thompson (2008), among others.
5 Bakhurst 2011.
6 E.g. Bakhurst 2012 (Chapter 18 below); 2022.

2   Doing and Self-Consciousness

Let us begin with the Ilyenkovian idea that we always-already stand in relation to the world 'idealised'.[7] As I have often presented this, and as it is sometimes taken up in the activity-theoretical tradition, Ilyenkov holds that the world is meaningful for us because we apprehend and approach it in relation to, or under the aspect of, our activity. This is the source of what is sometimes called the 'as-structure' of the world of experience: objects are viewed in relation to doing – they are for us how they can be used, how they may figure in the ebb and flow of our activity. This is true not just of artefacts, but also of (seemingly) mind-independent objects, which we know only as they have a place in our activity.[8] This picture of the world, as a space of permanent possibilities for action, resonates with aspects of Heidegger's thought, with Gibsonian views of perception (his famous concept of *affordances*), and with certain pragmatist ideas, such as Dewey's philosophy with its pedagogically rich conception of inquiry.

In *The Formation of Reason*,[9] I embrace the view that our relation to the world is mediated, first and foremost, by *concepts*. This is the real source of the as-structure of experience. This might suggest the kind of contemplative epistemology that Marx disparages in the 'Theses on Feuerbach', and it is true that the inspiration for my view is John McDowell,[10] who starts from considerations about *perception*. But the conceptual need not be opposed to the agential. On the contrary, we can argue that the conceptual cannot be understood without essential reference to *doing*.

This is so in a number of ways. First, to possess a particular concept, say *cat*, is to be able to do certain sorts of things; namely, to individuate and identify cats, and form and entertain thoughts about them. This might provoke the response that this kind of activity is 'purely intellectual', rather than 'object-oriented'. But if we heed Ilyenkov, we will not construe thinking as a purely inner process, only contingently related to action. On the contrary, thinking is

---

7   See Ilyenkov 2014.
8   Ilyenkov writes, '... Nature "in itself" is given to us if and only if it is translated into an object, material, or means of production, of human life. Even the starry heavens, which human labour does not directly alter at all, becomes an object of human attention (and contemplation) when and only when it is transformed into a natural "clock", "calendar" or "compass", that is, into a means and an "instrument" of our orientation in space and time' (1964, p. 42; 1997b, p. 22).
9   Bakhurst 2011.
10   McDowell 1994.

part of the life-activity of an embodied being. We are 'thinking bodies', as Ilyenkov likes to say. To be minded is to engage with reality in a particular way.[11]
A being whose relation to the world is mediated by concepts can act in light of
reasons. This kind of engagement does not occur only in 'inner space', with the
silent apprehension of propositional thoughts. Thinking is essentially related
to forms of its expression, in linguistic utterances of course, but also in intelligent activity – in forms of embodied coping or spontaneous skilled activity,
where doing issues from situated responsiveness to context rather than deliberation in propositional form. Such forms of intelligence-in-action are no less
conceptual in character for being embodied and spontaneous, for acting 'in the
flow' is also informed by concepts (concepts of what to do, rather than of what
to think).[12]

This must be so, for intentional action is possible only where agents understand themselves as acting to realise some end. I cannot be intentionally taking
tea to Christine unless I know that I am. Of course, I can do something unintentionally (take tea to Marcia when I thought I was taking it to Christine),
just as my intentional actions can have unintentional side-effects and consequences, which I may or may not know are occurring. But what I achieve
intentionally requires me to know what I am doing: if I am intentionally φ-ing,
I must know that φ-ing is what I'm up to. Intentional action is self-conscious
action.

This is an important truth because it speaks to the nature of the human life-
form, to the character of our 'life-activity', as Ilyenkov might say. Human life
is rational life and rational life is self-conscious life. Intentional action presupposes that the agent knows what she is doing, and typically she will also know
why she is doing it, for she will be acting not just for, but *in the light of*, reasons. So rational life is marked by the constant relevance of the question, 'How
to act?' The inescapability of the Socratic question, 'How should we live?', is a
mark of the human condition.

This emphasis on self-consciousness might seem a retreat from the profoundly social perspective that informs the activity approach. Doesn't talk
about self-consciousness take us into the recesses of the individual mind?
No, for human self-consciousness is a social and historical reality. Our mental powers are actualised in us only though our initiation into social being –
into language, practices of knowing and inquiry, and traditions of thinking and

---

11   Of course, as Ilyenkov might have put it, the particular way in which a minded being
      engages with reality is a *universal* way.
12   McDowell 2009f, p. 325.

reasoning – as Ilyenkov never tires of arguing. We know ourselves only insofar as we are parties to this socio-cultural inheritance. So, self-consciousness, as we know it, finds expression only in beings whose lives are social through and through.

I have spoken of intentional *action*, but much of what I have said is true also of *activity*. Some activities are done intentionally, and perhaps cannot be done otherwise – playing soccer or listening to music, for example. In such cases, the activity is necessarily a self-conscious one. Of course, I can be listening to music and think I'm doing something else (e.g. listening to wind chimes in my neighbour's garden), just as I can be couriering messages for a spy ring while I think I'm merely delivering letters. But what I can't do is *engage* in such activities unintentionally, for the engagement presupposes awareness of what I am doing.

Of course, activity within biological or physical systems is non-intentional. We speak of activity in a hive, of an increase in activity in a test tube, and so on, without any presumption of self-consciousness or intentionality. This forces the question: When activity theorists speak of an 'activity system', is the activity in question intentional or non-intentional? Should our model be the hive or the string quartet? The answer must lie in the nature of the activity at issue. Sometimes people engage in collaborative activity with a broadly common aim: the activity system is intentionally set up to achieve some end. Of course, what the collaborators do may have unintended consequences or they may find themselves, knowingly or unknowingly, participating in activities that are antithetical to their ends. All this the activity theorist might seek to make explicit so that the collaborators can intentionally modify their ends or transform their activity. In other cases, however, the activity theorist may be better off thinking of the system as much more like a hive. This might be so if the ends of the system do not coincide with intentionally-adopted ends of the individuals acting within it; if the activity is dominated by forces that are causal rather than rational, shaping the ends of individual agents more than the agents shape them. In such a case, the system itself becomes the primary locus of agency – an impersonal agent, acting without intention or self-consciousness, and dictating to the agents who are compelled, willingly or unwillingly, to do its bidding. The activity theorist might model such a system, not just to understand it, but I order to wrest agency back and return it to the human agents acting within it. Many activity systems, of course, lie in the space between these two examples.

3   Activity and Action

Anglo-American philosophy has tended to focus exclusively on action. So what does the concept *activity* contribute that the concept *action* does not?

We tend to work with an intuitive distinction between activity and action. Actions are particular doings (raising one's arm; shifting from first gear to second; opening the can); activities are stretches of doing spread out in time (walking; listening to music; building a house). How, then, are action and activity related? On Leontiev's view, actions are the constituents of activity. To take an example: Sally is gardening. Now she plants *this* rose; now she plants *that* one; now she mows the lawn; now she trims the hedge. These separate actions comprise her activity: gardening. The activity renders the actions intelligible (because she is gardening she does *this*, then *that* ...).[13]

This picture looks plausible, but it is not without its puzzling aspects. First, the example asks us to treat planting a rosebush, mowing a lawn, or trimming a hedge as *actions*, but surely, they are, or are also, activities, engaging in which constitutes Sally's gardening. The problem is not just that, e.g. planting a rosebush is a doing that is extended in time and that inclines us to think of it as an activity, for actions can be extended in time. We might say that Jane's greatest action in the war was to crack the code, even though it took her three years to do it. The problem is that it is by no means clear how to decide what counts as action and what as activity. Moreover, some activities do not seem to be composed of actions: listening to music, for instance.

Perhaps we can distinguish action and activity, as Leontiev tries to, by appeal to their grounds: actions, he argues, seek to fulfil an end or aim (*tsel'*), while activities issue from motives. But the end/motive distinction is obscure. Everything Sally does intentionally has an end: she moves the wheelbarrow (action) to transport some soil; her end in gardening (activity) is to have a beautiful garden and to enjoy the great outdoors. Similarly, whatever Leontiev means by 'motive' (*motiv*) seems equally applicable to actions and activities. Whichever we are talking about, what motivates me is the prospect of realising my end.

To make progress, it is important to observe that 'action' is ambiguous. It can refer to (i) a particular doing or doings (*this* planting of a rose by Sally, a 'token' action, as philosophers say); or (ii) an action *type* (rose-planting). Some action-

---

13   On Leontiev's view, actions are themselves constituted by 'operations' which are non-conscious bodily movements, and just as activity helps render actions intelligible, so actions (e.g. planting the rose) render intelligible the operations that realise them (e.g. why her muscles are contracting as they are).

type concepts specify doings we intuitively call 'activities' (rose-planting is one such) and others not (opening the door, switching on the light). So, it is tempting to ask: what makes some action-types activities?

Now we must observe that the English term 'activity' is also ambiguous, though in a rather different way. It can be used akin to a mass noun (like 'gold' or 'sand'). In this sense, we may speak of an increase in activity or of some activity occurring (some walking, some gardening, etc.). The term can also be used as a count noun, as in 'My class did two activities this morning'. The Russian *deyatel'nost'* functions *only* like a mass noun – so we can speak of kinds of activity (object-orientated; end-mediated; creative; self-conscious; intellectual), of activity typical of human beings (talking, reading, dining). But the Russian term does not lend itself to speaking of *an* activity (as in a classroom or sporting activity, or the activities you have lined up for your guests). *Deyatel'nost'* does not let us speak of hunting as *an* activity, though we can of course speak of the hunter's activity.

Now consider the following example. Harry walked to Steve's house. That describes an action. What was Harry's end? To get to Steve's house. His action began when he started out for Steve's house and ended when he got there. Such an action has the logical conditions of its termination built into the specification of its end. Now, Harry's action involves activity. Of what kind? Walking. One might say that when we describe Harry's doing as an action, we focus on what he completes or fails to complete, but when we think of his doing as activity, we focus on the doing itself. Action and activity are of course a unity, but here it seems that the concept of action dominates. The idea of his action makes his activity into a particular doing: the measure of his activity is how well it gets the action done.

Sometimes, however, the reverse is true. This is so when the end of Harry's action is subordinate to the activity involved in completing it. The point of Harry's walking to Steve's house might be the walking, not the getting there. What matters is the character of the activity – e.g. that it should be entertaining, invigorating – not that it terminates in his arrival at a particular destination. Again, action and activity are a unity, but here the activity dominates. What matters is the doing, not what gets done; or rather, that what gets done is some walking, some activity.

Often, of course, both the action and the activity matter. Take a case of a classroom activity where children are learning a song. This has an end, that the song is learnt. But the realisation of the end is not the only point, the activity of singing is the end too.

So, I want to say, contra Leontiev, that actions are constituted by activity just as activity is (often, though not always) composed of action. How things look depends on whether we focus on particular completable doings (actions) or on the doing itself (activity).

As we observed (again seemingly contra Leontiev), some activities have ends. You might garden to earn money for a vacation. Having earned the money, your gardening is done. (Here, as in the case above, we might say that the activity is subordinate to an action: earning the money.) But some activity has no natural termination because its end cannot be realised in a way that completes it. If you garden in order to have a beautiful yard, there is no end to the gardening even if you realise your end. You can complete an episode of gardening, but you can't complete the gardening. Your gardening has an infinite end.[14] In some cases of activities with infinite ends, the ends are *internal* to the activity: you engage in the activity for its own sake. Gardening can be like this. You can garden for the delight of gardening, a value discernable only to those who appreciate the practice 'from within'.

Such activities are crucial to understanding the human condition. These are self-conscious activities, which the agent understands as activities of hers, perhaps as activities definitive of deeply held values, of who she is, of how to live. So understood, the activity can unify actions across swaths of time and place. Sally's planting *that* tree at her home in London in 1973, and planting *this* one in San Francisco in 2017, are both part of the same activity, her gardening.[15] Marx and Engels famously wrote in *The German Ideology* that, in communist society, it would be possible 'to do one thing today and another tomorrow, to hunt in the morning, fish in the afternoon, rear cattle in the evening, criticize after dinner, just as I have a mind, without ever becoming hunter, fisherman, herdsman or critic'.[16] Here, of course, Marx considers activities that one might do for their own sake, as well as for whatever other ends they might realise. Marx would not think it wrong as such to identify oneself with one's activity, and see oneself as a fisherman or a critic; his target is simply the conditions under which people are compelled to labour in order to live, and are thus made identical with their activity by circumstance rather than by their self-conscious identification with the activity's intrinsic value.

---

14   Rödl 2007, pp. 34–8.
15   Had *I* planted trees in those places at those times then those actions would not have been part of a single activity of mine, I not being in the relevant sense a gardener.
16   Marx and Engels in Tucker 1978, p. 160.

4   Conclusion: Activity and the Human Life Form

The activity approach emerged in the discipline of psychology, in an attempt to understand the nature of the human mind. One might surmise, therefore, that the activity it would be interested in, perhaps above all, is *thinking*. But it is wrong to portray thinking as one among human activities (as if one might hunt in the morning, fish in the afternoon, and think in the evening). Thinking characterises the form of human life-activity. Human agency is self-conscious agency, and so thought enters into everything we do. Such is the character of rational life.[17] Of course, we can pick out certain kinds of mental activity and call them 'thinking' – as in 'I wasn't daydreaming, I was thinking' – but such forms of ratiocination do not exhaust the concept of thought as it characterises the human life form. Marx, though he may have stood Hegel on his head, would not have denied this, hence his famous remark in *Capital* about the worst of architects and the best of bees.[18] And this is why Ilyenkov, seeking to understand Marx, places the concept of ideality at the centre of his philosophy and why he argues that philosophy is logic, the science of thinking, while all the while recognising that thinking is an activity of the person, a thinking body.

Consider now Leontiev's thought that action is to be explained by appeal to the activity of which it is a constituent. A person buys a fish. Why? Because she is shopping for food and she's doing that because she is preparing a meal. We need go no further to realise that, in the case of human beings, self-conscious activity is always a socio-historical reality. The question of what human beings eat and how they eat it, for example, cannot be answered in the kind of natural-historical terms to which we would resort in the case of non-human animals (e.g. 'The wolf is a carnivore that eats ungulates, as well as smaller mammals such as beavers, rabbits and mice. Wolves also scavenge ...'). To address the question of what human beings eat takes us immediately into a story about human culture, the history of agriculture, trade, colonialism, and so on, and of course, there is no giving a settled answer. The explanation is not just more complicated than one we give for a non-human animal, it is of a different kind, and one that can be given only for a being that acts in light of an understanding of what it seeks to bring about, an understanding it gains from education, in the broadest sense, since nothing is born understanding itself in such a way.[19] That understanding can be wrong, very wrong. But only a being

---

17   My remarks in this concluding section are much indebted to Sebastian Rödl.
18   Marx in Tucker 1978, p. 344.
19   See Rödl 2020.

capable of knowledge can err; only a rational agent can think and act irrationally; only a moral agent can do wrong; only the free can be enslaved. Such are the burdens of rational life, which Marx thought communism could alleviate by transforming the socio-economic conditions that breed error, irrationality and evil and thereby make activity a source of enslavement rather than fulfilment. Psychology, as Vygotsky and Leontiev understood it, does not study thinking as a discrete activity. It studies the thinking life, the life of thought, in its empirical manifestations, and as such it must always have the socio-historical in view.

Philosophy, for Ilyenkov, addresses the same subject matter, but not empirically. Philosophy articulates the forms in which rational life can and must understand itself and explores the preconditions of such understanding. Philosophy is an activity with ends that are internal and infinite. Some philosophers have believed that they could conclude philosophy, but this is a conceit. Philosophical insight and understanding are real, but they are always provisional, so there is no quieting the impulse to philosophical inquiry. Philosophy has no terminus – its object is one of infinite depth.

When a philosopher thinks of herself as doing philosophy, she understands herself in relation to the activity considered as an ideal: the pursuit of insight and understanding, for its own sake and with no prospect of closure. But philosophy can be done only in the real – by reading *this* book, developing *this* argument, writing *this* paper... – and often in an institutional setting, educating students, giving conference talks, publishing papers... All of these things are done for finite ends – to advance *this* philosophical conversation, to refute *that* argument, to cultivate critical thinkers, to get tenure, and so on. It is important not to allow these finite ends to obscure the infinite ends from which the activity gets its real point and value, and which are its true motivation. This is the case, of course, not just for philosophy, but many activities, including education, which, when viewed in the ideal, also has no terminus. One may teach something and a student may learn it, but there is no end to teaching and learning.

Activity theory strives to understand the reality of activity. But, as Ilyenkov might have said, we must countenance its ideality too if we are to understand the depth of the human condition and the practices that make us what we are.

••
•

The next and final chapter elaborates and defends the central thesis of my book, *The Formation of Reason*: that a human being gets to be free in the distinctive way that human beings are free through the acquisition of second nature. In my book, my treatment of this thesis is much influenced by the philosophy of John McDowell. McDowell himself, however, is notoriously reluctant to offer a theory of second nature. In my chapter, I explain his reasons for taking this stance and show how, for all that, his work contains much that illuminates the idea of second nature and its relation to freedom. Finally, I consider the objection that although McDowell recognises second nature as a property of individuals, he mistakenly rejects the Ilyenkovian idea of second nature in external form. I argue that his works do in fact contain resources to countenance second nature externalised, so long as we keep that idea insulated from the constructivist theories of normativity that McDowell rightly rejects. Understanding our thesis aright is, I maintain, a necessary condition of a compelling conception of the social dimensions of mind and of the end of education. In this chapter, as in *The Formation of Reason* itself, there is less overt discussion of Ilyenkov and Vygotsky. It should be clear from everything that has gone before, however, that the position I embrace is influenced through and through by their ideas.

Freedom and Second Nature in *The Formation of Reason*

This chapter explores some of the ideas presented in my 2011 book, *The Formation of Reason*, which appeared in the book series of *The Journal of the Philosophy of Education*. I did not set out to write on philosophy of education, but the book evolved in that direction thanks to the encouragement of colleagues in the field, especially Jan Derry and Paul Standish of UCL's Institute of Education. It was written over more than a decade and, though intended as a coherent whole, each of its six main chapters can be treated as freestanding. My overarching aim is to expound a socio-historical account of mind inspired principally by the philosopher John McDowell, whose work I have invoked many times in the writings collected in this book. Along the way, I discuss a variety of topics including identity and personhood, rationality, normativity, learning, freedom, and the limits of social constructionism. The outcome is a vision of education that understands its end as the cultivation of autonomy. In addition to McDowell, whose influence is ubiquitous, I consider many other thinkers, including Brandom, Davidson, Hacking, Korsgaard, Moran, Strawson, Wiggins and Wittgenstein.

In this chapter, I take up one prominent thesis and develop it in a way that makes connections with a number of the themes of *The Formation of Reason* as well as the current volume. This is the thesis *that a human being gets to be free, in the special way that human beings are free, only though the acquisition of second nature*. On this view, the development of a human being is marked by a transformation: we become beings whose lives manifest freedom as we acquire rational powers, powers whose exercise is second nature to us. There is thus an essentially social dimension to freedom, for the formation of reason involves not merely biological maturation, but cultural formation, or *Bildung*. Though my book focuses on this idea as it finds expression in McDowell's philosophy, there is an obvious congruence with the views of many of the Russian thinkers discussed in the present volume, whose intellectual roots are in Hegel and Marx. Though these thinkers do not figure prominently in *The Formation of Reason*, the book contains discussions of both Ilyenkov and Vygotsky, and their ideas indirectly inform many of its arguments.

The thesis looks like one of considerable importance that could form the core of a substantive theory of personhood expressing the unity of reason and nature. The aforementioned Russians certainly thought it momentous. For them, understanding it aright turned seemingly abstract questions about the relation of thinking and being into issues about the social conditions in which human freedom can find proper realisation. As such, they thought themselves immune from Marx's famous rebuke that philosophers 'have hitherto only interpreted the world in various ways; the point is to change it'.[1] For them, this *was* philosophy in the service of transforming the world. My aspirations for the thesis are rather more modest, but the recognition of its truth ought at least to do something for philosophy, bringing to centre-stage questions of human development that presently receive scant attention in Anglo-American thought, and providing a source of stimulating ideas for philosophy of education.

It might be thought surprising that I seek inspiration from McDowell, for many philosophers – some sympathetic to him, some hostile – have complained that though second nature has a claim to be 'the master idea' of his philosophy, he leaves the notion surprisingly underdeveloped.[2] Writing some 15 years after the publication of McDowell's *Mind and World*, Italo Testa laments that 'no fully fledged theory of second nature exists, and also the references to this concept to be found in McDowell and in the authors who have followed him are altogether fragmentary and limited for the most part to the authority of Aristotle or of Hegel'.[3] McDowell's response to such complaints has been entirely defensive: he simply denies that the notion stands in need of development. So my object in this paper is to explore the place of second nature in McDowell's philosophy and explain how, notwithstanding his reluctance to theorise it, his writings contain the resources to explicate the notion and illuminate its relation to freedom. In this way, McDowell's philosophy, as I understand it, helps consolidate a number of ideas that have emerged in the essays collected in this volume.

1   Freedom

Let's begin with freedom. When I say that the acquisition of second nature is a precondition of freedom, I have in mind freedom that pertains not just to action but to thought. A being is free in the distinctive way a human being is

---

1   Marx 1968.
2   Halbig 2008, p. 72.
3   Testa 2009, p. 347.

free if it can determine what to think or do in light of what there is reason to think or do. Freedom is responsiveness to reasons.

We are accustomed to understand freedom primarily in terms of choice. Casting freedom as responsiveness to reasons is at odds with this, for the balance of reasons may leave a person little or no choice about what to think or do. Indeed, McDowell follows Kant and declares that 'rational necessitation is not just compatible with freedom but constitutive of it', thereby suggesting not just that one is no less free in thinking or doing what one sees one must, but that freedom finds its fullest expression in acquiescence before rational necessity.[4] The air of paradox is dispelled by recognising that rational necessitation requires *self*-determination. In determining what to think or do I subordinate myself to requirements of reason that can move me only if I recognise and endorse them. By so doing, I make them my own, thereby realising the kind of 'being-at-home-in-another' that is Hegel's most general vision of freedom.[5]

It might be complained that the emphasis on deciding what to think or do yields a conception of freedom too narrowly intellectual. After all, someone can make up her mind what to think or do yet be prevented from expressing her thoughts or acting as she sees fit. One can be responsive to reasons, yet chained and bound. But it is not my intention to confine freedom to the realm of thought. The capacity to determine what to think or do is a power that properly finds expression in action. (In my book, I identify this with the power of autonomy;[6] I could less controversially have portrayed it as an ingredient or precondition of autonomy). Of course, the expression of that power can be frustrated, and in such a case we are free only in our judgement. But where we can and do act as we decide to, then the thought that is our deciding what to do does not stop short of our deeds, but enters the doing itself. We need to see the unsuccessful cases as partial realisations of a power that finds its proper expression in the bodily activity of its possessor. So there need be no tension here with the Hegelian view, as characterised by Frederick Neuhouser, that 'a will's self-determination is not complete until it successfully translates its ends into reality'.[7]

Though it is easiest to see such freedom manifest in cases where determining what to think or do involves *deliberation* – where the idea of 'making up

---

4 McDowell 1994, p. 5.
5 Neuhouser offers this translation rather than the more usual 'being-with-oneself-in-another' (2000, pp. 305–6 n34).
6 See, e.g., Bakhurst 2011, pp. 142, 158.
7 Neuhouser 2000, p. 84.

one's mind' has clear application – it is important to recognise cases where our responsiveness to reasons is more spontaneous. For example, a concert pianist giving an exhilarating performance is responsive to reasons and hence manifests freedom, though her playing as she does is not the outcome of deliberation in the sense of practical reasoning (she may deliberate prior to the performance but not during it). This is a very different case from one in which a person acts after having antecedently made up her mind what to do (such as when I decide that, all things considered, I should leave the party now and so say my farewells). An intermediate case is one of a scholar 'thinking on her feet' in a seminar. Here what she says is the outcome of deliberation in one sense, since her thinking on her feet *just is* a kind of deliberation; but in another sense, she is deciding what to say in the course of saying it and her utterances are not the outcome of prior, self-conscious reflection. The pianist and the scholar show us instances of *intelligence in activity*. What they do or say is subject to normative assessment and justification by reasons, and as such their respective performances exhibit freedom.

In *The Formation of Reason*, I try to do justice to the way freedom is expressed in these more spontaneous forms of responsiveness to reasons, as well as in what is sometimes called our 'embodied coping' with our environment.[8] It is important that for all the talk about reason and rationality, the McDowellian view I endorse does not think of responsiveness to reasons as something formal, abstract, rule-bound, unsituated, or otherwise 'rationalistic'. It is a matter of our attunement to the normative contours of our environment, or to the 'topography of the space of reasons', as McDowell might say. Sometimes this is mediated by judgment that issues from deliberation; sometimes it is more immediate. But the leading idea is that we become free in acquiring a second nature because we thereby attain the capacity to navigate the space of reasons.[9]

---

8   See, e.g., Bakhurst 2011, pp. 83, 124–6, 130. I am sure my efforts are not entirely successful. For one thing, under the influence of Richard Moran's impressive work (2001), I tend to overemphasise 'making up one's mind', thereby appearing to stress deliberation at the expense of responsiveness to reasons in its more spontaneous forms.

9   McDowell makes much use of the idea of the 'space of reasons', which he draws from Sellars 1956, and which I invoke in several of the essays in this volume. The notion is the focus of Chapters 5 and 6 of *The Formation of Reason*. The identification of freedom with responsiveness to reasons raises many other thorny issues (some of which I discuss in Chapter 4 of my book). For example, McDowell writes that the degree to which freedom is realised in action 'depends on the extent to which the supposed reasons in the light of which someone acts are genuinely reasons' (McDowell 2009g, p. 169). But this is ambiguous between the modest claim that an agent is free in so far as she moved by reasons as opposed to, say, external forces,

2   Second Nature

As McDowell has it, the responsiveness to reasons constitutive of human freedom is an aspect of second nature, a gift of *Bildung*. The concept of second
nature has a long history and the term is now deployed in a variety of ways.[10]
First, it can be used adjectivally to mark acquired dispositions so ingrained
that the resulting behaviour issues with the fluency of instinct and without
the mediation of thought (e.g. A music teacher enjoins her pupil to practice:
'Find it hard to shift from an E chord to a B7? Don't worry, keep practicing
and it'll become second nature'.) This is perhaps the most common, 'everyday'
use of the expression. Second, it can be used as a noun, as in the claim that
human beings 'acquire a second nature'. This use marks a supposed qualitative
transition in human development. To 'acquire a second nature' is to become a
fundamentally different kind of being – 'a being of a metaphysically new kind'.[11]
Third, 'second nature' is sometimes used to refer to features of the world that,
though they have objective existence (in the sense that they are there to be
discovered), are not aspects of 'first-nature'; that is, they would not figure in a
scientific description of the furniture of the world.[12] These features include, but
are not limited to, properties of human individuals.

McDowell uses the term in both the first and second senses,[13] but resists
the third. Let's review how the concept enters his work. McDowell holds that
human mindedness is *sui generis* in the sense that our rational capacities resist explanation by natural-scientific means. He contrasts two distinct modes
of explanation or intelligibility: (a) natural-scientific intelligibility, where phenomena are explained by appeal to scientific laws or principles, and (b) rational

---

and the bold claim that someone is free to the degree to which she thinks and acts in light
of what, objectively speaking, she has reason to think and do. I try to resolve the ambiguity
at Bakhurst 2011, pp. 90–91. McDowell comes at the issues by drawing on ideas from the
German tradition, but that is not the only route: see, e.g., Pettit and Smith 1996.

10   See Bakhurst 2011, p. 71n21.

11   McDowell 2009g, p. 172. Here one might protest that if human beings have a nature, surely
they have at most one. To speak of *two* natures is to invite the potentially misleading
question of whether second nature replaces or supplements our 'first' nature. Would it
not therefore be better to say that we are creatures whose nature it is to acquire rational
powers in the course of our development, rather than creatures who acquire a new nature?
I have some sympathy with this objection.

12   See, e.g., Halbig 2008.

13   See McDowell 2008, pp. 222–3. Though he does not distinguish the two uses and tends to
slide between them (as I have done so far in this chapter, as attentive readers will have
spotted).

or '"space-of-reasons" intelligibility', where states or happenings, such as an agent's holding a certain belief or doing a certain action, are explained by showing how the agent is (or at least takes herself to be) justified in believing what she believed or acting as she did. The latter mode of intelligibility essentially invokes normative notions. So when a vase falls to the floor what has occurred can be exhaustively explained by appeal to scientific law; but my action of taking a vase and dashing it to the ground requires a different kind of explanation, one that appeals to the *reasons* for what I did and reveals why I thought smashing the vase had something going for it.

The distinction between two modes of intelligibility is Kantian in inspiration, and McDowell adds to it another Kantian idea. To understand how our minds are in touch with the world in experience, we must recognise the unity of what Kant calls 'spontaneity' (thought, understanding) and 'receptivity' (sensory awareness). McDowell argues that our conceptual capacities, understood as 'aspects of our free responsiveness to reasons', are operative in perceptual experience.[14] It is not just that our minds put a conceptual construction upon non-conceptual content given to the senses. In human beings, experience is always-already mediated by concepts.

In combination these two Kantian theses present a problem, for taken together they seem to threaten the idea that perception is a natural capacity. For if (i) our conceptual capacities are at work in perceptual experience; and (ii) conceptual capacities elude scientific explanation; then, on the assumption (A) that everything natural is in principle open to scientific explanation, it follows that (iii) perception in human beings cannot be a wholly natural transaction between perceiver and world.

McDowell's response is to deny (A), arguing that although our conceptual capacities lie beyond the reach of scientific intelligibility, we can think of them as natural so long as we acknowledge they 'belong to our second nature' and develop in the course of the normal maturation and education of human beings.[15] Human beings are not 'born at home in the space of reasons'; they are 'born mere animals, and are transformed into thinkers and intentional agents in the course of coming to maturity'.[16] But this transformation does not somehow lift us out of nature. If we refuse to gift the concept of nature to natural science, we can say that there are 'two kinds of happenings in nature: those that are subsumable under natural law, and those that are not subsumable under

---

14   McDowell 2008, p. 219.
15   McDowell 2008, p. 220.
16   McDowell 1994, p. 125.

natural law, because freedom is operative in them',[17] and thus that 'exercises of spontaneity belong to our way of actualizing ourselves as animals'.[18]

3   Quietism

It is inviting to think McDowell owes us a substantial account of second nature to establish our entitlement to think that rationality is both *sui generis and* natural. McDowell, however, denies this. He claims he doesn't need a theory of nature, asserting that 'the only unity there needs to be in the idea of the natural ... is captured by a contrast with the idea of the supernatural – the spooky or the occult'.[19] As for second nature, the idea simply encompasses 'any propensities of animals ... imparted by education, habituation, or training'.[20] All we need recourse to, he argues, is the 'bare idea of *Bildung*'.[21] But if McDowell does not say more, won't the appeal to second nature seem no more than a verbal trick, a way of *calling* reason 'natural' but not explaining how it can be so?

To better understand McDowell's stance, we need to see how his reluctance to theorise second nature follows from what is sometimes called his 'Wittgensteinian quietism'. McDowell characterises this sensibility in the following way.[22] Sometimes we find ourselves confronted with philosophical problems of the form: How is x possible? We can respond to such questions in different ways. One is to accept the terms in which the question is posed and answer it with a philosophical theory. An alternative is to interrogate the question itself, challenging the idea that there is something problematic about x that calls for philosophical theory. The first strategy is *constructive*, answering the question by theory-building; the second, *therapeutic*, disclosing that the question itself is flawed.

McDowell illustrates the distinction with a familiar example. Wittgenstein invites us to consider a signpost pointing the way to a destination, let's say Kingston. It is easy to think there is something philosophically puzzling about how a signpost *can* direct us. In itself, it might be argued, the signpost is just a piece of wood or metal of a certain shape, perhaps with marks on it. It is natural to suppose that something like that could direct us only if it is inves-

17   McDowell 2006, p. 238.
18   McDowell 1994, p. 78.
19   McDowell 2000, p. 99.
20   McDowell 2008, p. 220.
21   McDowell 1994, p. 95.
22   McDowell 2009i.

ted with meaning by an act of interpretation. But this supposition cannot be correct, for the same query can be made of the putative interpretation. Suppose the interpretation takes the form of the statement: 'To get to Kingston from here, you need to go left'. Taking the alienated perspective from which the signpost appears as no more that a board with marks on it, the words offered in interpretation are no more than sounds in the air or marks on paper. If the signpost needs interpretation to be meaningful, so does whatever we offer by way of interpretation. We have a regress.[23] As McDowell reads Wittgenstein,[24] this shows there must be a way of understanding the signpost that is not an interpretation, a way exemplified in our everyday practices that nobody finds mysterious (except when doing philosophy). The moral is that once we adopt the alienated perspective, nothing will serve to answer the 'how is it possible?' question. The solution is to eschew that perspective and occupy the one familiar to us when we engage in the practice of using signposts. To this end, the philosopher's task is to 'assemble reminders', truisms (in this case about our use of signposts) to undermine the feeling that there is something standing in need of explanation.[25]

Wittgenstein's philosophy is therefore appropriately described as 'quietist', not because he identifies good philosophical questions that he declines to address, but because his aim is to quieten 'the felt need for substantive philosophy'.[26] McDowell invokes the idea of second nature with a similar purpose. (Indeed, the overall issue at stake is much the same as that Wittgenstein addresses in the remarks on rule following from which the signpost example is taken.) McDowell argues that much philosophical puzzlement about the mind's place in nature is a result of the deleterious influence of the disenchanted conception of nature we have inherited from early-modern science. Because the latter finds no place in nature for such things as meaning, reasons or value, it generates philosophical anxieties about how purely natural beings could have rational powers. But the idea of second nature can help us see that the disenchanted conception is not compulsory, and with this our anxieties are quietened and the supposed problem of the reconciliation of reason and nature evaporates. Here second nature figures as a Wittgensteinian 'reminder' – something that points to facts in plain view that we overlook when in a philo-

---

23   McDowell expounds this argument in McDowell 2009i, but a more detailed account can be found in his earlier writings on Wittgenstein, collected in McDowell 1998d (see, especially, 1998c, pp. 264–6).

24   Cf. Wittgenstein 1953, § 201.

25   Wittgenstein 1953, § 127.

26   McDowell 2009i, p. 370.

sophical cast of mind. It is not the first move in a constructive philosophical endeavour, but a discovery that 'gives philosophy peace'.[27]

4   Habituation: Aristotle

Is McDowell's quietism tenable? It is one thing to deny we need a theory of second nature, another to assert that invoking 'the bare idea' of *Bildung* will suffice. At his most defensive, McDowell seems to forget that in *Mind and World* he ingeniously argues that Kant is driven to a purely formal notion of the self in the unity of consciousness (the famous 'I think' that 'must be able to accompany all my representations') because he lacks 'a seriously exploitable notion of second nature'.[28] Armed with such a notion, McDowell maintains, we can understand the unity in a set of mental occurrences as residing in the fact that they are events in the life of a living thing, a human being, thereby enabling us to conceive the subject of experience as a bodily presence in the world. It is hard to see how a notion that can be 'seriously exploited' in so happy a way can be glossed as 'no more than the idea of a way of being ... that has been acquired by something on the lines of training'.[29] We surely need to say more than this.

So one of the tasks I assume in *The Formation of Reason* is to try to occupy a middle ground between McDowell's reticence and the ambitions of the constructive philosophy he eschews. I aim to bring into view the unity of the rational and the animal in our nature, to counter those tendencies that, as McDowell himself puts it, cause us to forget how 'to maintain a firm and integrated conception of ourselves as rational animals'.[30] Notwithstanding his defensiveness about constructive philosophy, McDowell's writings contain many resources to assist in this.

These resources include McDowell's treatment of Aristotle. In *Mind and World*, McDowell invites us to generalise Aristotle's theory of the formation of moral character into an account of the formation of reason itself.[31] There are a number of reasons why this strategy might appear problematic. McDow-

---

27   Wittgenstein 1953, § 133; McDowell 1994, p. 86.
28   McDowell 1994, p. 104. Here McDowell is possibly unfair to Kant, whose educational and anthropological writings do take *Bildung* seriously – '[t]he human being can only become human through education. He is nothing except what education makes out of him' (Kant 2007, p. 439). We must concede to McDowell, however, that Kant does not succeed in deploying such notions in a way that unifies the rational and the natural.
29   McDowell 2000, p. 98.
30   McDowell 1998f, p. 382.
31   McDowell 1994, pp. 78–84.

ell would have us move from a picture of moral development, in which the acquisition of second nature is a 'shaping' of the practical intelligence of a being already equipped with concepts, to an account of the coming-into-being of the understanding itself ('the faculty that enables us to recognise and create the kind of intelligibility that is a matter of placement in the space of reasons').[32] Thus it appears we are to shift from deploying 'second nature' in its familiar adjectival use, describing the formation of behavioural dispositions constitutive of moral character, to a vision of human beings 'acquiring a second nature' in the sense of a 'new essence'. But if the notion of habituation is at home in a discourse about character formation, it is less obviously germane to the elucidation of the formation of reason as such. For what is at issue in the generalised account is the acquisition of concepts; that is, of powers the exercise of which is essentially subject to normative standards.[33] But habits, understood as behavioural dispositions, are not so subject. Habits can be bad or good, but the standards by which we so judge them are external to the activity itself, which is simply ingrained, routine behaviour called forth by circumstances. Although, as Hegel observes, good habits enable our freedom in various ways, there is also a sense in which they can enslave us, for if habit is second nature, 'it is all the same still a *nature*, something *posited* which takes the shape of *immediacy*, an *ideality* of what is simply given, which is still burdened with the form of [mere] *being*, and consequently something not correspondent to free mind, something *merely* anthropological'.[34] Habit may be *'mediated* immediacy', but it is at some remove from reason, for the realm of freedom requires powers that equip us to decide what to think and do, but habits decide for us, as it were. Aristotle may have been at ease with the idea of virtue originating in habit because he took an uncritical approach to morality and saw moral education as a matter of conformity to the mores of his time. He operated with what Rüdiger Bubner calls 'a static anthropology' that knows not 'the productive unrest of the critical intellectual'.[35] But the latter is *sine qua non* for McDowell, for whom the formation of reason yields a subject who is responsive to reasons, knows that she is, and has a critical attitude to the reasons she finds herself with.[36] How could such a subject issue from habituation?

---

32 McDowell 1994, p. 79.

33 Sebastian Rödl defines a power as 'the cause of the existence of its acts in such a way as to be, at the same time, the cause of their conforming to a normative measure, which is thus internal to these acts' (2007, p. 141).

34 Hegel 1971, p. 410 ff.

35 Bubner 2002, p. 211.

36 See McDowell 2009g, p. 181.

To rebut this scepticism, we must look beyond McDowell's immediate discussions of second nature. In my book, I offer a number of ideas to elucidate the *Bildungsprozess*, reflecting upon the social influences on concept formation, suggesting parallels between McDowell and Vygotsky, and exploring the idea of 'learning by initiation' by drawing on Myles Burnyeat's rendition of Aristotle's ideas of moral development.[37] I want to return here to the latter discussion, for the treatment in my book neglects some of McDowell's own relevant writings on Aristotle.[38] These papers make clear that what McDowell finds in Aristotle is a model of the acquisition of genuinely conceptual capacities. The emphasis on habituation marks that the child does not acquire moral concepts by processes of reasoning and deliberation. She doesn't work out what is noble by hypothesis formation. But neither is she simply trained to conform unthinkingly to the moral conventions of the community. Rather, she is initiated into seeing certain acts as noble in the course of learning the language of moral evaluation. At first, as Aristotle tells us, she learns the *that* but not the *because*: she learns what acts count as noble and only later gets a sense of, and learns to articulate, the reasons why such acts merit that ascription.[39] Thus habituation does not yield a mere behavioural tendency that stands in need of an external rational warrant; it is rather initiation into a 'way of seeing' situations in which certain considerations stand out as morally salient in a manner that is unified under the moral concept in question.[40] Such 'ways of seeing' are conceptions of what matters that are inherently normative:[41] they are apt to be challenged and will stand in need of defence by the giving of reasons, so that the seeds of the *because* are implicit in facility with the *that*.[42]

---

37   See Bakhurst 2011, pp. 10–14, 150–7, 138–41; Burnyeat 1980.

38   Especially McDowell 2009c; 2009a; 1998g. In *The Formation of Reason*, I tend to resist talk of 'habituation' and 'training' on the grounds that those notions too readily imply the passive reception of routine 'unthinking' behaviours (hence my preference for 'learning by initiation'). I now feel my discussion (there and in 'Vygotsky's Demons' (Chapter 10 above)) takes too narrow view of habit. McDowell's various papers on Aristotle help to correct this and suggest richer possibilities for the notion of habituation. I have also benefitted from reflecting on Julia Annas's *Intelligent Virtue* (2011) and from discussions with Will Small and Jennifer Rothchild, who kindly invited me to a stimulating conference on habit held in Gainesville, Florida, in 2019.

39   McDowell 2009c, pp. 34–5; 2009a, pp. 55–7. For Aristotle, 'the noble' (*to kalon*) designates, not one virtue among others, but a quality of actions recommended by virtue. As McDowell puts it, 'the concept of the noble organizes the evaluative outlook of a possessor of excellence' (2009a, p. 46).

40   McDowell 2009a, pp. 50–52.

41   McDowell 2009a, pp. 44–6.

42   McDowell 2009c, pp. 36–7, 39; 2009a, pp. 56–7.

It is important that moral concepts cannot be treated atomistically, but are aspects of a moral point of view in which they are unified, so the acquisition of one moral concept requires the acquisition of many. Where there is moral uncertainty because situations exhibit characteristics that suggest different courses of action (where, say, justice seems to require one course of action and friendship another), the agent must discern the overall moral shape of the situation to decide what to do. A person with that ability has what Aristotle calls *phronesis* or practical wisdom.[43] This is a rational capacity or power: the power to decide what to do in light of what there is most reason to do. As McDowell sees it, practical wisdom is not an intellectual excellence that is external to the character traits formed by habituation; rather, it is the ability to integrate those traits with one another so as to determine what is a reason for what in concrete moral situations.

In *Mind and World* it is practical wisdom itself that McDowell describes as 'second nature'.[44] It is so in the (adjectival) sense that the practically wise person judges with the fluency and immediacy typical of a merely natural propensity or instinct. Of course, sometimes good moral judgement will not be immediate and spontaneous, but will require reflection and deliberation. There is no formal procedure to reach moral decisions and no rational warrant for them outside the moral point of view. Moral reflection is Neurathian,[45] in structure: it operates entirely within the domain of concepts, the intelligibility of which rests on 'the conceptual and motivational outlook that ... ethical upbringing imparts'.[46] There are no foundations for moral thinking that will support the moral point of view from without. Someone who is responsive to reasons in this way manifests a form of mindedness quite unlike merely animal mentality, and thus we can speak of the acquisition of a second nature. But that second nature must be seen as a modification of an animal form of life. Indeed, it brings that form of life into view as its object by posing the question: What makes a human life go well? No proper answer to that question can be indifferent to the contingencies of our animal being.[47]

---

43 McDowell 2009a, pp. 42–58.

44 McDowell 1994, p. 84; cf. 1998i, p. 192.

45 See McDowell 2009c, pp. 35–40; 1994, p. 81. For clarification about 'Neurath's boat', see note 36 in Chapter 5 above.

46 McDowell 2009a, p. 54.

47 It is important to stress that such a view of moral judgement can accommodate critical reflection leading to moral innovation. Of course, people can abdicate their responsibility to decide what to think by deferring to convention or custom, just as there are many ways of making bad judgements. And these failings can result from our upbringing. It is an achievement of modernity that our taking responsibility for what we think is recog-

5   Habituation: Wittgenstein

McDowell proposes we generalise Aristotle's account of moral development in the following way: Just as a child attains the capacity to make moral judgements by being initiated into concepts constitutive of the moral point of view, so she acquires reason as such by being initiated into her native language. If this move is not to seem too cursory, it needs to be placed in relation to other aspects of McDowell's philosophy, especially his reading of Wittgenstein on rule following.[48] McDowell holds that the moral is 'shapeless' with respect to the non-moral; that is, there is no way to characterise what unites items that fall under a moral concept, such as courageousness, in non-moral terms. What unites them can only be discerned from within the distinctive 'way of seeing' enjoyed by those who possess the concept in question. This is why the concept can only be taught by initiation. Now, one lesson of Wittgenstein's famous rule following considerations is that there is a shapelessness to *all* concepts if we try to characterise how they are to be applied in way that prescinds from the understandings of those competent to deploy them. A multiplicity of ways of extending a concept is formally consistent with the way the concept has been used in the past, and any attempt to formulate a rule for the application of the concept will itself stand in need of interpretation and we shall be in a vicious regress (the same regress we encountered when we considered the signpost example considered above). The 'principle' that unifies items under the concept must simply be grasped from within. As in the moral case, it is a matter of habituation (or 'training' as Wittgensteinians usually have it) into 'ways of seeing' what accords with the concept.

As in the moral case, these conceptual capacities cannot be viewed atomistically, but must be seen as integrated into a worldview or 'form of life'. Following Gadamer, McDowell asserts that to acquire language is to enter a tradition of thought, 'a store of accumulated wisdom about what is a reason for what'.[49] Entering language is not simply acquiring conceptual abilities that enable the expression of thought. It is a matter of learning what to say. Our entry into lan-

---

nised as constituting the freedom of self-determination, the exercise of which is partly constitutive of human flourishing. So McDowell's neo-Aristotelian picture of *phronesis* as second nature embodies an ideal of critical moral personhood. It is not simply a description of what happens in our upbringing.

48   McDowell's papers on Wittgenstein are collected in McDowell 1998d and 2009b. I discuss Wittgenstein on rule following and private languages in Bakhurst 1995c, and consider the relevance of such arguments to Vygotskian themes in Bakhurst 1986 (reprinted in Bakhurst 1991, ch. 3).

49   McDowell 1994, p. 126.

guage is a process in which, as Wittgenstein memorably puts it, 'light dawns gradually across the whole',[50] and we emerge thinking, speaking, and acting in ways that embody a conception of the world. What the child thinks or says is apt to be challenged by recalcitrant experience or contrary opinion, and she must learn to be ready to support her opinions by reasons. As McDowell insists, a standing readiness to engage in critical reflection is a hallmark of rational freedom, for by endorsing our thoughts in critical reflection we make them our own. Again, the process of reflection is Neurathian. There is no foundational standpoint beyond the trading of reasons by our best lights.

In this way McDowell generalises Aristotle's view of moral development into a vision of the formation of reason as such. In both, the movement is from habituation into the *that* to an appreciation of the *because*, from knowing what to say to understanding why one is justified in so saying. The conceptual capacities that enable the child's responsiveness to reasons are second natural in the sense that they are typically exercised fluently and spontaneously – with mediated immediacy – and in the sense that the orientation to the world they make possible is the possession of a rational agent that has overcome the 'merely animal' status it once had. But the Wittgensteinian framework keeps our animality firmly in view because it represents the fact that human beings can be initiated into language as simply a fact of human natural history. Freedom may coincide with rational necessitation, but, as McDowell puts it, that 'human beings can be initiated into the capacity to place themselves within a "normatively" structured space of possibilities – the realm of freedom, one might say' is a fact that is deeply and irredeemably contingent.[51]

To revert to the quotation from Hegel above, we can say that McDowell has a richer conception of habit than an 'ideality of what is simply given', combined with an insistence that something 'merely anthropological' *can* correspond to a free mind. Of course, this freedom is not total. Not everything we think issues from our power to make up our mind. As McDowell makes clear, there are irreducibly passive elements to perception. Perceptual knowledge draws into play conceptual capacities that have their home in active thinking, but it is not itself the outcome of deliberation or judgement (I can actively look, listen, or touch, but I am nonetheless the passive recipient of the outcome of this perceptual activity: I can decide what to think about some issue, but I cannot, in the same way, decide what to see, hear, or feel). Moreover, the worldview that informs all our active thinking is something given. As Wittgenstein puts it, 'I did not get

---

50   Wittgenstein 1969, § 141.
51   McDowell 1998b, p. 319.

my picture of the world by satisfying myself of its correctness; nor do I have it because I am satisfied of its correctness. No: it is the inherited background against which I distinguish between true and false'.[52] Of course, on McDowell's Neurathian scheme, any part of a worldview may warrant critical attention. But without proper cause for doubt, much of it simply remains in place. Indeed, when it comes to the propositions Wittgenstein identified as the 'hinges' on which many of our beliefs turn, it is usually the case that only flights of philosophical fancy can pretend to call them into question. This might appear to represent a limit to our intellectual freedom, but it is as much a precondition of our freedom as a limit to it. Our ability to determine what to think and do can be exercised only from within a worldview. What matters is that someone who has 'acquired a second nature' is able, *when called upon to do so*, to cancel the seeming naturalness of responses that have become second nature to her, step back, and subject them to scrutiny. That is what intellectual freedom is all about.[53]

6   Second Nature: Further Thoughts

At the opening of this chapter, I noted that McDowell has been criticised, by Testa and others, for his unwllingness to give a substantive account of second nature. I hope I have established that, notwithstanding McDowell's avowed reluctance to address the issue head-on, his work contains a rather rich picture of what it is to acquire a second nature. The account may not amount to a theory, but it is not fragmentary, nor does it rest on appeals to authority. Of course, the account might be still richer. Let me briefly mention two points. First, it is important not to allow the emphasis on concepts to yield an over-intellectualised view of habituation. When a child learns to speak, among the habits that must be formed are modes of vocalisation, so that it is second nature to her to make *these* sounds to say such-and-such. Habit formation is crucial to laying down the bodily capacity for the expression of thought, so that, as Hegel puts it, the child's body is transformed 'into the likeness of its ideality'.[54]

Second, in order to understand the preconditions of the child's initiation into language, we need a nuanced picture of the pre-linguistic child's relation to

---

52   Wittgenstein 1969, § 94.

53   For further discussion of philosophical complexities of the idea of acquiring a second nature, see Bakhurst 2015a and 2016b; Rödl 2016; Kern 2020.

54   Hegel 1971, § 412zu.

her caregivers in whom she first encounters reason-in-the-person-of-another. As we saw in Chapter 14, a significant theme in McDowell's philosophy is that mental states and occurrences should be seen as properties of the whole person, and not of any of a person's parts (such as the brain), and he portrays our mindedness as manifest in, present in, a person's life-activity.[55] On his view, to acquire a language is to acquire the ability to speak one's mind and to hear the meaning in someone's words.[56] The thoughts of others can be open to us to perceive in what they say and do, and their intentions present in their actions, so that action is movement that manifests thought. Our mindedness does not lurk somewhere out of sight, behind its bodily expression: our life-activity is itself infused with the conceptual. This invites a very different picture of what the pre-linguistic infant confronts when she interacts with her caregivers than is found in, say, the 'theory of mind' paradigm. On McDowell's picture, recognising another's personhood is not a matter of inference to the existence of unobservable causally-efficacious internal states, but of responding to the mindedness manifest in their activity as something of normative import. The seeds of this are present even in a simple game of peek-a-boo, where the infant comes to react, not just to the surprise appearance of the object, but to the other person as withholding it, so that there is mutual recognition around the expectation of its immanent appearance. We need to appreciate how a pre-linguistic responsiveness to reasons is cultivated in infants and refined in their engagement with the bodily mindedness of others. The child is summoned to mindedness by the proleptic recognition of mature individuals, who in finding the germ of reason in her in turn demand recognition of their personhood from her. In *The Formation of Reason*, I suggest that such reflections on the constitution of intersubjectivity promise to enrich our sense of the unity of the rational and the animal in our nature, for there is nowhere for caregivers to find the child's embryonic mindedness except in manifestations of her animal being.[57]

---

55   See Bakhurst 2011, pp. 16–18, 157–8. Although McDowell's view of the mental puts him at odds with most contemporary cognitive science, there are interesting parallels (and differences) with, e.g., Alva Noë's work (2004; 2009).

56   As McDowell puts it (1998h, p. 253), 'shared command of a language equips us to know one another's meaning without needing to arrive at that knowledge by interpretation, because it equips us to hear someone else's meaning in his words. ... a linguistic community is conceived [by Wittgenstein] as bound together ... by a capacity for a meeting of minds'. I try to express similar thoughts, e.g., at 2011, p. 39.

57   Bakhurst 2011, pp. 61–4.

7   Second Nature Externalised

Testa might accept all this and still complain of a major gap in McDowell's thinking; namely, that McDowell considers second nature only in its subjective (or internal) form as individual mind, but finds no place for second nature as objective spirit: that is, as 'external nature understood as an ensemble of the forms of objectified interactions together with the institutions of the social space in which individuals find themselves operating, presenting an immediacy analogous to that of the first-nature environment'.[58] Both sides of second nature figure in Hegel's philosophy, the first in the Anthropology section of the *Encyclopedia*, the second in the *Philosophy of Right*.[59] By thinking of second nature as the possession of individuals, and ignoring how our mindedness is externalised in our lifeworld, McDowell denies himself an account of the sociality of reason and a satisfying account of *Bildung*. In my book, I make what might appear to be a similar argument, drawing on Ilyenkov to urge a conception of second nature that encompasses not just the rational powers of human beings but aspects of the reality those powers enable them to respond to. In this way, I argue, we can better understand the space of reasons as a public domain, an aspect of the world as we find it.[60]

Testa proposes to give pride of place to Hegel's theory of 'recognition' (*Anerkennung*) in an account of the dialectical interplay of internal and external second nature, between the minds of individuals and mindedness as externalised in the environment. In this way, we can aspire to understand the formation of reason in the individual as a matter of the internalisation of external second nature. If the normative structures that constitute social space depend for their existence on the fact that we recognise those norms by recognising each other as subject to them, we can portray the child as acquiring rational powers – as entering the space of reasons – as she becomes capable of standing in the relevant relations of recognition. Then we can say, with Robert Brandom, that selves

> are synthesized by *mutual recognition*. That is, to be a self ... is to be taken or treated as one by those one takes or treats as one: to be recognized by those one recognizes. Merely *biological* beings, subjects and objects of

---

58   Testa 2009, p. 349.
59   Hegel 1952, §§ 146–51.
60   Bakhurst 2011, pp. 109–14.

desires, become *spiritual* beings, undertakers (and attributors) of commitments, by being at once the subjects and the objects of recognitive attitudes.[61]

Isn't this just what we need to make sense of *Bildung* as the process of 'acquiring a mind' and to express the affinity of freedom and second nature? For if the normative structures of social space are ultimately of our own making, then (if conditions are right) conforming to them is not a constraint on our freedom but an expression of it, one in which we are at one with an aspect of our own nature.

It is important that McDowell wants none of this. He rejects constructivist accounts of normativity that portray norms as *instituted* by us. To represent normative authority as originating in us only appears to render less paradoxical the identification of freedom and rational necessitation. For if the norms we institute are not to be arbitrary, our allegiance to them must be supported by reasons. It follows that the normative authority of those reasons cannot be instituted by us on pain of a regress.

Terry Pinkard and other prominent Hegel scholars see this paradox as the problem par excellence of post-Kantian philosophy and represent Hegel's theory of recognition, properly understood, as its solution.[62] McDowell, in more Wittgensteinian spirit, prefers not to let the paradox get going in the first place: he maintains that there is no avoiding a notion of underived normative authority. Responding to Robert Pippin, McDowell writes that 'we are subject to norms only in so far as we can freely acknowledge their authority, so that being subject to them is not being under the control of an alien force. But apart from special cases, their authority is not brought into being by acknowledgement'.[63] Of course, *some* norms are socially constructed (e.g. the rules of soccer), and others take shape behind the backs of individuals (e.g. economic norms), but we cannot treat all norms that way. The idea that thought is accountable to reality embodies a primitive conception of underived normativity.[64] It follows that

61   Brandom 2002, pp. 216–17.

62   See, e.g., Pinkard 2002. Pinkard (p. 60n) attributes the first articulation of the paradox to Robert Pippin. Pinkard, Pippin and Brandom all see Hegel as resolving the paradox through a social theory of normativity. Here we return to a theme discussed in Chapter 16 above.

63   McDowell 2009e, p. 201.

64   McDowell writes: 'If Hegel did think thought can be beholden to its subject matter only in the context of complete mutuality of recognition, the right response would surely be: "So much the worse for Hegel"' (2009e, p. 200) ... 'That objects are authoritative over thought – certainly over its expression – is a feature of a social practice that has evolved into being as

we cannot think of selves as 'synthesized by mutual recognition'. Someone is a 'self', or (better) a person, only if she warrants being described as such in virtue of, among other things, her powers of self-conscious thought. Recognition by others may enable the development of the conceptual capacities that are preconditions of thought, but recognition does not constitute the 'normative standings' their exercise makes possible.

I think McDowell's reluctance to entertain 'external' second nature issues in part from his hostility to constructivist accounts of normativity: he associates the interest in the former with optimism about the latter. I concur with him in his rejection of such accounts. But it is open to us to deny that the space of reasons is instituted by us while employing the idea of second nature to give sense to the Hegelian view that, as Bubner puts it, '[t]he world in which we live ... is universally shaped by spirit, in the meanings that surround us and in the cultural models we obey',[65] and that the child's rational powers develop as she is summoned into this world. We need to capture how the world into which the child is born is a normative space. Ilyenkov's insights, I argue in *The Formation of Reason*, can help us in this.

Such ideas are hardly foreign to McDowell's thinking.[66] Consider the ways in which a McDowellian can grant that reason is present in the environment encountered by the human child on the way to 'acquiring a mind'. McDowell clearly sometimes thinks of 'the space of reasons' as something external to the child (hence the frequent use of the metaphor of people as 'inhabitants of the space of reasons'). Moreover, the rational requirements that constitute its 'layout' or 'topography' are portrayed as aspects of the world that are there to be discovered. Why not think of these rational requirements as aspects of second nature? After all, they are not *first*-natural in kind. Although not *instituted* by us, they do not exactly float free of us either. 'The structure of the space of reasons', McDowell tells us, 'is not constituted in splendid isolation from anything

---

it is. The authority is genuine, because we freely acknowledge it. But the idea of bestowing it on objects does not apply to anything we do, or anything our predecessors did' (p. 203).

65   Bubner 2002, p. 216.

66   However, he is not always at ease with them. For example, in acknowledging the 'historicality of human spontaneity', McDowell (2002, p. 297) commends Bubner for stressing that 'the forms of life within which we come to be human beings at all ... are both products of drawn-out historical evolution and dependent for their continuation on continuing whole-hearted participation by mature individuals'. There are two awkwardnesses about this passage. First, better not to say that we *become* human beings; human beings become persons. Second, the idea that our form of life depends on our *whole-hearted* participation is odd, as if our form of life might be endangered by lack of commitment or conviction.

merely human'.[67] Hence, though he describes his position as a form of 'platonism', he calls it 'naturalised' or 'relaxed' platonism.[68] This suggests that we should see the space of reasons as second-natural in the third sense enumerated above.

Of course, the child first engages with reason in the person of another individual (this is an encounter with external second nature in an obvious sense). But *Bildung* also presupposes that the child also stands in relations to phenomena that have a life that transcends the individual. For example, McDowell writes, 'the language into which a human being is first initiated stands over against her as a prior embodiment of mindedness';[69] it is 'essentially the possession of a *we*'.[70] Thus contra Testa, one might say that McDowell *does* have a conception of objective or external second nature, expressed in the three cognate notions of language, tradition and worldview. What he doesn't elaborate is how they are expressed not just in what people say and have said, but in cultural practices and social institutions. Nor does he make anything of the fact that ours is a world in which intelligence is embodied in so many ways, not just in linguistic utterances and texts, but, as Ilyenkov teaches us, in non-linguistic representation, in artefacts as objectifications of human purposes and intentions, in machines and computers, in art and design, in schools and cities, in the very form the world takes on through human activity.[71] It would surely help McDowell's view that 'mindedness is operative even in our unreflective perceiving and acting' to admit that the world in which we live is pregnant with mindedness objectified. Moreover, the idea that our 'embodied coping is permeated by the conceptual' is critical to preserving 'an integrated conception of ourselves, as animals, and – what comes with that – beings whose life is pervasively bodily, but of a distinctively rational kind'.[72]

If the concept of second nature is to illuminate the unity of the rational and the animal in human life, we must elucidate not just how reason emerges in the course of the development of an individual human being, but how our form of animal life gives expression to reason. This latter inevitably leads us to mind externalised, if we are to capture how our form of life reproduces itself, how there can be traditions of thought for children to be initiated into, and how

67   McDowell 1994, p. 92.
68   McDowell 1994, pp. 91–2, 178.
69   McDowell 1994, p. 125.
70   McDowell 2009d, p. 149.
71   As John Haugeland (1995, p. 236) nicely puts it: 'Intelligence abides in the meaningful *world*: not just in books and records, but roads and ploughs, offices, laboratories, and communities'.
72   McDowell 2009f, p. 328.

there can be history which is the history of humankind. Until we have all this in view, the bare idea of *Bildung* will not be enough to eliminate the tendency to be puzzled by the idea of norms of reason. But once we get a sense of the myriad ways we live in a world imbued with meaning, then the appeal to second nature begins to look more plausible: we begin to see how it is an affront to the phenomenology of everyday life to raise the issue of how normativity can be possible, an affront motivated by a scientistic refusal to allow as real anything that doesn't figure in a scientific conception of the world.

Moreover, we need a suitably rich sense of what the child is initiated into when we speak of 'enculturation'. McDowell's work can appear to shrink *Bildung* to first-language acquisition. But it is not as if the process of cultural formation stops there. We need to appreciate how *Bildung* is spread out in time, enduring, potentially, across the whole of a human life.[73] The issue is not just how to characterise the formation of human beings; there are important normative questions at stake. McDowell describes human beings, equipped with rationality, as 'at home in the world', contrasting this with the condition of infants and non-human animals whose lives are confined to negotiating an environment under the influence of biological imperatives.[74] Recognising the diverse ways in which reason takes external form facilitates a corresponding appreciation of the variety of respects in which the child is called upon to 'cancel her otherness' (the child becomes at one with language by internalising it; but internalisation is obviously the wrong metaphor to express what is demanded in her encounter with the mindedness of others or with the intelligence embodied in artefacts). Being 'at home' in the world is not just a matter of being able to think how things are or might be; it is a matter of finding the world hospitable to the realisation of oneself as a rational agent, responsible and free.

Moreover, deploying the notion of second nature to understand institutions and practices is helpful in capturing the sense in which the social order can operate upon us with force akin to natural necessity. As Hegel famously writes: 'This ethical substance and its laws and powers are on the one hand an object over against the subject, and from his point of view they *are* – "are" in the highest sense of self-subsistent being. This is an absolute authority and power infinitely more firmly established than the being of nature'.[75] It also suggests the ideal that a person at home in social space conforms to the requirements

---

73   See Bakhurst 2011, pp. 8–10.
74   See Bakhurst 2011, pp. 158–62.
75   Hegel 1952, § 146.

it imposes upon her in virtue of her recognition that she has good reason to, where this recognition is genuine, both in the sense that the reasons she takes to be good reasons *are* good reasons (and good reasons of the right kind), and in the sense that this recognition is not confused, self-deceived, or the result of false consciousness. Here, one might say that the dictates of second nature in external form must be vindicated or refuted by second nature in the form of critical responsiveness to reasons.

8   Conclusion

I began by suggesting that the kind of position McDowell advances, and I try to defend in my book, can be a source of animating ideas for the philosophy of education. First, this is a view that puts education, in the broadest sense, up front and centre in our understanding of what a human being is. Human beings attain the rational powers that distinguish us from other species in a process of cultural formation. Our very mindedness is a gift of *Bildung*.

Second, on this view to possess rational powers is just to be responsive to reasons (this is not a view of rationality that is abstract, formal, instrument-alistic or rule-bound). A being that is responsive to reasons has the power to determine what to think or do in light of what there is reason to think or do. This is what it is to be autonomous or free. Now, nothing can count as a rational agent, a person in the full sense, unless it possesses that ability, but the ability can be exercised well or badly. It is something that can be cultivated, honed and refined. So McDowell's position brings with it an ideal of what a person is that can and should, I believe, inform educational thinking. It suggests that the cultivation of autonomy is a, or perhaps *the*, legitimate end of educational practice. This is not a view of autonomy focused primarily on the making of informed choices about how to live. It is in some respects narrower, because it thinks of autonomy as a matter of deciding what to think or do in light of what there is reason to think or do. But in some respects it is broader, suggest-ing that education must be focused on the cultivation of the child's power of self-determination in all aspects of her life: in thought and action.

In addition to these two leading ideas, there are fertile metaphors (the space of reasons, being at home in the world); there is the vision of learning by habitu-ation; there are telling reflections on how we are to think of a meeting of minds; there is recognition of the social preconditions of mind consistent with the idea that we are in touch with an independent reality, and much else besides.

In all this, there are significant connections between McDowell's philosophy and the thought of Vygotsky and Ilyenkov. Despite profound differences in the ways they conceive of philosophical reflection, and the enormous gulf between their intellectual environments, the common themes are rich and stimulating, and open up promising avenues of inquiry, and not just in the study of education, but in the philosophical apprehension of the human life form as such. Recognising this, I think, vindicates the excitement and optimism I felt when I first began my encounters with Soviet philosophy in Robert Daglish's apartment in Moscow, in conversation with Felix Mikhailov and Genia Lampert, all those years ago.

Permissions

Chapter 1: *'The Riddle of the Self* Revisited', *Studies in East European Thought*, 63, no. 1 (2011), pp. 63–73. Republished by kind permission of Springer.

Chapter 2: 'Social Being and the Human Essence: An Unresolved Issue in Soviet Philosophy', *Studies in East European Thought*, 47, no. 1–2 (1995), pp. 3–60. Republished by kind permission of Springer.

Chapter 3: 'Social Memory in Soviet Thought', in *Collective Remembering*, edited by David Middleton and Derek Edwards, London: Sage, 1990, pp. 203–26. Republished by kind permission of Sage Publications.

Chapter 4: 'The Meshcheryakov Experiment: Soviet Work on the Education of Blind-Deaf Children', *Learning and Instruction*, 1, no. 3 (1991), pp. 201–15. Co-authored with Carol Padden. Republished by kind permission of Professor Padden and Elsevier Publications.

Chapter 5: 'Punks versus Zombies: Evald Ilyenkov and the Battle for Soviet Philosophy', in *Philosophical Thought in Russia in the Second Half of the 20th Century: A Contemporary View from Russia and Abroad*, edited by Vladislav Lektorsky and Marina F. Bykova, London: Bloomsbury Academic, 2019, pp. 53–78. Republished by kind permission of Bloomsbury Academic.

Chapter 6: 'Meaning, Normativity and the Life of the Mind', *Language and Communication*, 17 no. 1 (1997), pp. 33–51. Republished by kind permission of Elsevier.

Chapter 7: 'Ilyenkov, Education and Philosophy', in *Ilyenkov: Cosmos and Practice*, edited by S. Freyberg and A. Rozhkov, Venice: Verum Factum, 2023. Open Access. Published here with thanks to the Verum Factum Collective.

Chapter 8: 'Ilyenkov on Aesthetics: Realism, Imagination, and the End of Art', *Mind, Culture, and Activity*, 8, no. 2 (2001), pp. 187–99. Republished by kind permission of Taylor & Francis.

Chapter 9: 'Il'enkov's Hegel', *Studies in East European Thought*, 65, no. 3–4 (2013), Special Issue, *Hegel in Russia*, edited by David Bakhurst and Ilya Kliger, pp. 271–85. Republished by kind permission of Springer.

Chapter 10: 'Vygotsky's Demons', in *The Cambridge Companion to Vygotsky*, edited by Michael Cole, Harry Daniels and James V. Wertsch, Cambridge: Cambridge University Press, 2007, pp. 50–76. Republished by kind permission of Cambridge University Press.

Chapter 11:   'O ponyatiye oposredstvovaniya', *Kul'turno-istoricheskaya psikhologiya*, no. 5 (2007), pp. 61–6. Previously unpublished in English. By kind permission from *Kul'turno-istoricheskaya psikhologiya.*

Chapter 12:   'Vygotsky's Concept of *Perezhivanie*: Its Philosophical and Educational Significance'. Previously unpublished.

Chapter 13:   'Memory, Identity and the Future of Cultural Psychology', in *Jerome Bruner: Language, Culture, Self*, edited by David Bakhurst and Stuart G. Shanker, London: Sage, 2001, pp. 184–98. Republished by kind permission of Sage Publications.

Chapter 14:   'Minds, Brains and Education', *Journal of Philosophy of Education*, 42, no. 3–4 (2008), pp. 415–32. Republished by kind permission of John Wiley & Sons.

Chapter 15:   'Reflections on Activity Theory', *Educational Review*, 61, no. 2 (2009), pp. 197–210. Republished by kind permission of Taylor & Francis. With thanks to Yrjö Engeström for permission to use the Figures.

Chapter 16:   'Activity and the Search for True Materialism', in *The Practical Essence of Man: The 'Activity Approach' in Late Soviet Philosophy*, edited by Vesa Oittenen and Andrey Maidansky, Leiden: Brill, 2015, pp. 17–28.

Chapter 17:   'Activity, Action and Self-Consciousness', *Educational Review*, 7, no. 1 (2018), pp. 91–9. Republished by kind permission of Taylor & Francis.

Chapter 18:   'Freedom and Second Nature in *The Formation of Reason*', *Mind, Culture, and Activity*, 19, no. 2 (2012), pp. 172–89. Republished by kind permission of Taylor & Francis.

  The bridge passage between Chapters 4 and 5, and footnote 7 in Chapter 6, contain short extracts from 'Lessons from Ilyenkov', *Communication Review*, 1, no. 2 (1995), pp, 155–78. Republished by kind permission of Taylor & Francis.

Bibliography

Akselrod, Luibov (Ortodoks) 1927, 'Otvet na "Nashi raznoglasiya" A. Deborina', ['A Response to A. Deborin's "Our Differences"'], *Krasnaya nov'* [*Red Virgin Soil*], 5: 136–63.

Allen, Barry 1994, *Truth in Philosophy*, Cambridge, MA: Harvard University Press.

Annas, Julia 2011, *Intelligent Virtue*, Oxford: Oxford University Press.

Anscombe, G.E.M. 1957, *Intention*, Oxford: Basil Blackwell.

Arsen'ev, Anatoly S., Evald V. Ilyenkov, and Vasily V. Davydov 1966, 'Mashina i chelovek, kibernetika i filosofiya', ['Machine and Human Being, Cybernetics and Philosophy'], in *Leninskaya teoriya otrazheniya i sovremennaya nauka* [*Lenin's Theory of Reflection and Contemporary Science*], pp. 265–85, Moscow: Politizdat.

Asmus, V.F. 1929, *Ocherki istorii dialektiki v novoi filosofii*, [*Essays on the History of Dialectics in Modern Philosophy*], Moscow-Leningrad: Gosudarstvennoe izdatel'stvo.

Bakhurst, David 1982, 'Action, Epistemology and *The Riddle of the Self*', *Studies in Soviet Thought*, 24, 3: 184–209.

Bakhurst, David 1986, 'Thought, Speech and the Genesis of Meaning: On the 50th Anniversary of Vygotsky's *Myshlenie i rech*'', *Studies in Soviet Thought*, 31, 2: 102–29.

Bakhurst, David 1991, *Consciousness and Revolution in Soviet Philosophy: From the Bolsheviks to Evald Ilyenkov*, Cambridge: Cambridge University Press.

Bakhurst, David 1992, 'Soviet Philosophy in Transition: An Interview with Vladislav Lektorsky', *Studies in Soviet Thought*, 44, 1: 33–50.

Bakhurst, David 1995a, 'Lessons from Ilyenkov', *Communication Review*, 1, 2: 155–78.

Bakhurst, David 1995b, 'On the Social Constitution of Mind: Bruner, Ilyenkov and the Defence of Cultural Psychology', *Mind, Culture, and Activity*, 2, 3: 158–71.

Bakhurst, David 1995c, 'Wittgenstein and Social Being', in *The Social Self*, edited by David Bakhurst and Christine Sypnowich, pp. 30–46, London: Sage.

Bakhurst, David 1997a, 'Activity, Consciousness and Communication', in *Mind, Culture and Activity. Seminal Papers from the Laboratory of Comparative Human Cognition*, edited by Michael Cole, Yrjö Engestrom and Olga Vasquez, pp. 147–63, Cambridge: Cambridge University Press.

Bakhurst, David 1997b, 'The Philosophy of Activity', *Russian Studies in Philosophy*, 36, 1: 47–56.

Bakhurst, David 2002, 'Skromnoe velikolepie Vladislava Lektorskogo' ['The Quiet Brilliance of Vladislav Lektorsky'], in *Sub"ekt, poznanie, deyatelnost'. K 70-letiju V.A. Lektorskogo* [*Subject, Cognition, Activity: Essays on the Occasion of Vladislav Lektorsky's 70th Birthday*], pp. 79–106, Moscow: Kanon+.

Bakhurst, David 2005a, 'Strong Culturalism', in *The Mind as a Scientific Object. Between Brain and Culture*, edited by Christina E. Erneling and David Martel Johnson, pp. 413–31, New York: Oxford University Press.

Bakhurst, David 2005b, 'Il'enkov on Education', *Studies in East European Thought*, 57, 3–4: 261–75.

Bakhurst, David 2011, *The Formation of Reason*, Oxford: Wiley-Blackwell.

Bakhurst, David 2012, 'Freedom and Second Nature in *The Formation of Reason*', *Mind, Culture, and Activity*, 19, 2: 172–89.

Bakhurst, David 2015a, 'Training, Transformation and Education', *Royal Institute of Philosophy Supplement*, 76: 301–27.

Bakhurst, David 2015b, 'Understanding Vygotsky: Critical Notice of Jan Derry, *Vygotsky, Philosophy and Education*', *Language, Culture and Social Interaction*, 5: 1–4.

Bakhurst, David 2016a, 'Education and Conversation', in *Education and Conversation*, edited by David Bakhurst and Paul Fairfield, pp. 5–25, London: Bloomsbury Academic.

Bakhurst, David 2016b, 'Reply to Rödl, Standish and Derry', contribution to the symposium: 'Second Nature, Bildung, and McDowell: David Bakhurst's *The Formation of Reason*', *Journal of Philosophy of Education*, 50, 1: 123–9.

Bakhurst, David 2019a, 'Punks versus Zombies: Evald Ilyenkov and the Battle for Soviet Philosophy', in *Philosophical Thought in Russia in the Second Half of the Twentieth Century*, edited by Vladislav A. Lektorsky and M. Bykova, pp. 53–78, London: Bloomsbury Academic.

Bakhurst, David 2019b, 'Activity and the Formation of Reason', in *Philosophical Thought in Russia in the Second Half of the Twentieth Century*, edited by Vladislav A. Lektorsky and M. Bykova, pp. 233–43, London: Bloomsbury Academic.

Bakhurst, David 2022, 'Philosophy, Activity, Life', *Filosofiya nauki i tekhniki* (*Philosophy of Science and Technology*), 27, 2: 31–45.

Bakhurst, David, and Christine Sypnowich, eds 1995, *The Social Self*, London: Sage.

Batishchev, Genrich S. 1990a, 'The Activity Approach in the Captivity of Substantialism', in *Activity: Theories, Methodology, and Problems*, edited by Vladislav A. Lektorsky, pp. 89–92, Orlando, FL, Helsinki, Moscow: Paul Deutsch.

Batishchev, Genrich S. 1990b, 'The Category of Activity: Inexhaustible Possibilities and Limits of Applicability', in *Activity: Theories, Methodology, and Problems*, edited by Vladislav A. Lektorsky, pp. 7–14, Orlando, FL, Helsinki, Moscow: Paul Deutsch.

Batishchev, Genrich S. 1990c, 'Not by Deed Alone', in *Activity: Theories, Methodology, and Problems*, edited by Vladislav A. Lektorsky, pp. 169–75, Orlando, FL, Helsinki, Moscow: Paul Deutsch.

Bennett, Maxwell, Daniel Dennett, Peter Hacker, and John Searle 2007, *Neuroscience and Philosophy: Mind, Brain and Language*, New York: Columbia University Press.

Bennett, M.R., and P.M.S. Hacker 2003, *Philosophical Foundations of Neuroscience*, Oxford: Blackwell.

Bibler, Vladimir S. 1975, *Myshlenie kak tvorchestvo* (*Vvedenie v logiku myshlennogo dialoga*) [*Thought as Creativity (An Introduction to the Dialogical Logic of Thought)*], Moscow: Politizdat.

Bibler, Vladimir S. 1991a, *Kant–Galilei–Kant* [*Kant–Galileo–Kant*], Moscow: Mysl'.

Bibler, Vladimir S. 1991b, *Mikhail Mikhailovich Bakhtin ili poetika kul'tury* [*Mikhail Mikhailovich Bakhtin or the Poetics of Culture*], Moscow: Progress.

Bibler, Vladimir S. 1991c, *Ot naukoucheniya – k logike kul'tury. Dva filosofskikh vvedeniya v dvadtsat' pervyi vek* [*From the Theory of Science – to the Logic of Culture. Two Philosophical Introductions to the 21st Century*], Moscow: Politizdat.

Blakemore, Sarah-Jayne, and Uta Frith 2005, *The Learning Brain: Lessons for Education*, Oxford: Blackwell.

Blunden, Andy 2016, 'Translating *Perezhivanie* into English', *Mind, Culture, and Activity*, 23, 24: 274–83.

Bochenski, Jozef M. 1963, *Soviet Russian Dialectical Materialism* (*Diamat*), translated by Nicolas Sollohub, Dordrecht: Reidel.

Brandom, Robert 1994, *Making it Explicit*, Cambridge, MA: Harvard University Press.

Brandom, Robert 2002, *Tales of the Mighty Dead: Historical Essays in the Metaphysics of Intentionality*, Cambridge, MA: Harvard University Press.

Bruer, John T. 1997, 'Education and the Brain: A Bridge Too Far', *Educational Researcher*, 26, 8: 4–16.

Bruer, John T. 2002, 'Avoiding the Pediatrician's Error: How Neuroscientists Can Help Educators (and Themselves)', *Nature. Neuroscience Supplement*, 5: 1031–3.

Bruner, Jerome 1983, *In Search of Mind*, New York: Harper & Row.

Bruner, Jerome 1990, *Acts of Meaning*, Cambridge, MA: Harvard University Press.

Bruner, Jerome 1991, 'The Narrative Construction of Reality', *Critical Inquiry*, 18: 1–21.

Bruner, Jerome 1995, 'Meaning and Self in Cultural Perspective', in *The Social Self*, edited by David Bakhurst and Christine Sypnowich, pp. 18–29, London: Sage.

Bruner, Jerome 2001, 'In Response', in *Jerome Bruner: Language, Culture, Self*, edited by David Bakhurst and Stuart Shanker, pp. 199–215, London: Sage.

Brushlinskii, Andrei V. 1994, *Problemy psikhologii sub"ekta* [*Problems of the Psychology of the Subject*], Moscow: Rossiiskaya akademiya nauk – Institut psikhologii.

Bubner, Rüdiger 2002, 'Bildung and Second Nature', in *Reading McDowell: On Mind and World*, edited by Nicholas Smith, pp. 209–16, London: Routledge.

Bukharin, Nikolai I. 2005, *Philosophical Arabesques*, translated by R. Clarke, New York: Monthly Review Press.

Burnyeat, Myles 1980, 'Aristotle on Learning to be Good', in *Essays on Aristotle's Ethics*, edited by Amélie Rorty, pp. 69–92, Berkeley, CA: University of California Press.

Changeux, Jean-Pierre, and Paul Ricoeur 2002, *What Makes Us Think?*, Princeton: Princeton University Press.

Clark, Katerina, and Michael Holquist 1984, *Mikhail Bakhtin*, Cambridge, MA: Harvard University Press.

Craig, Edward, ed. 1998, *The Routledge Encyclopedia of Philosophy*, 10 vols, London: Routledge.

Daniels, Harry 2015, 'Mediation: An Expansion of the Socio-Cultural Gaze', *History of the Human Sciences*, 28, 1: 34–50.

Danto, Arthur C. 1981, *The Transfiguration of the Commonplace: A Philosophy of Art*, Cambridge, MA: Harvard University Press.

Davidson, Donald 1984a, 'Mental Events', in his *Essays on Action and Events*, pp. 207–25, Oxford: Oxford University Press.

Davidson, Donald 1984b, 'On the Very Idea of a Conceptual Scheme', in his *Inquiries into Truth and Interpretation*, pp. 183–98, Oxford: Clarendon Press.

Davis, Andrew 2004, 'The Credentials of Brain-Based Learning', *Journal of Philosophy of Education*, 38, 1: 21–35.

Davydov, Vasily V. 1972, *Vidy obobshcheniya v obuchenii* [*Types of Generalisation in Learning*], Moscow: Pedagogika.

Davydov, Vasily V. 1986, *Problemy razvivayushchego obucheniya: Opyt teoreticheskogo i eksperimental'nogo psikhologicheskogo issledovaniya* [*Problems of Instruction and Development: An Attempt at Theoretical and Experimental Psychological Research*], Moscow: Pedagogika.

Davydov, Vasily V. 1990, 'Yes, We Need a Monistic Theory of Human Existence', in *Activity: Theories, Methodology, and Problems*, edited by Vladislav A. Lektorsky, pp. 149–55, Orlando, FL, Helsinki, Moscow: Paul Deutsch.

Davydov, Vasily V. 1999, 'The Content and Unsolved Problems of Activity Theory', in *Perspectives on Activity Theory*, edited by Yrjö Engeström, Reijo Miettinen and Raija-Leena Punämaki, pp. 39–52, New York: Cambridge University Press.

Derry, Jan 2004, 'The Unity of Intellect and Will: Vygotsky and Spinoza', *Educational Review*, 56, 2: 113–20.

Derry, Jan 2013, *Vygotsky: Philosophy and Education*, Oxford: Wiley-Blackwell.

Dewey, John 1934, *Art and Experience*, New York: Capricorn Books.

Dewey, John 1938, *Experience and Education*, New York: Kappa Delta Pi.

Diderot, Denis 1916 [1744], 'Letter on the Blind for the Use of Those Who See', in *Diderot's Early Philosophical Works*, edited by Margaret Jourdain, Chicago: Open Court.

Dubrovsky, David I. 1968, 'Mozg i psikhika' ['Brain and Mind'], *Voprosy filosofii* [*Questions of Philosophy*], 8: 125–35.

Dubrovsky, David I. ed. 1989, *Slepoglukhonemota: Istoricheskie i metodologicheskie aspekty. Mify i real'nost'* [Blind-Deafness: Historical and Methodological Aspects: Myths and Reality], Moscow: Filosofskoe obshchestvo SSSR.

Dubrovsky, David I. 1990, 'Psikhika i mozg: resul'taty i perspektivy issledovanii' ['Mind and Brain: Results and Perspectives of Research'], *Psikhologicheskii zhurnal* [*Journal of Psychology*], 11, 6: 3–15.

El'konin, Daniel B., and Vasily V. Davydov 1966, *Vozrastnye vozmozhnosti usvoeniia znaniya* [*Developmental Possibilities in the Acquisition of Knowledge*], Moscow: Prosveshchenie.

Emerson, Caryl 1983, 'Bakhtin and Vygotsky on the Internalization of Language', *Quarterly Newsletter of the Laboratory of Comparative Human Cognition*, 5, 1: 9–13.

Engels, Friedrich 1968, 'Ludwig Feuerbach and the End of German Classical Philosophy', in *Marx-Engels Selected Works in One Volume*, pp. 584–622, Lawrence and Wishart: London.

Engeström, Yrjö 1999, 'Activity Theory and Individual and Social Transformation', in *Perspectives on Activity Theory*, edited by Yrjö Engeström, Reijo Miettinen and Raija-Leena Punämaki, pp. 19–38, New York: Cambridge University Press.

Engeström, Yrjö, and Reijo Miettinen 1999, 'Introduction', in *Perspectives on Activity Theory*, edited by Yrjö Engeström, Reijo Miettinen and Raija-Leena Punämaki, pp. 1–16, New York: Cambridge University Press.

Fairfield, Paul 2016, *Teachability and Learnability: Can Thinking Be Taught?*, London: Routledge.

Fleer, Marilyn, Fernando Luis Gonzalez Rey, and Nikolai Veresov, eds 2017, *Perezhivane, Emotions and Subjectivity: Advancing Vygotsky's Legacy*, Singapore: Springer.

Foot, Kirsten A. 2002, 'Pursuing an Evolving Object', *Mind, Culture, and Activity*, 9, 2: 132–49.

Frank, Semyen L. 1910, *Filosofiia i zhizn'* [*Philosophy and Life*], St. Petersburg: Zem'lia.

Frank, Semyen L. 1964 [1917], *Dusha cheloveka* [*The Human Spirit*], Paris: YMCA Press.

Franks, Paul W. 2005, *All or Nothing: Systematicity, Transcendental Arguments, and Skepticism in German Idealism*, Cambridge, MA: Harvard University Press.

Fraser, Jennifer, and Anton Yasnitsky 2016, 'Deconstructing Vygotsky's Victimization Narrative: A Re-Examination of the "Stalinist Suppression" of Vygotskian Theory', in *Revisionist Revolution in Vygotsky Studies*, edited by Anton Yasnitsky and René van der Veer, pp. 50–69, London: Routledge.

Frolov, Ivan T. 1983, 'Zhizn', smert', i bessmertie' ['Life, Death, and Immortality'], *Voprosy filosofii*, no. 1: 183–98 and no. 2: 52–64.

Gadamer, Hans Georg 1999 [1960], *Truth and Method*, 2nd edition, translated by J. Weinsheimer and D.G. Marshall, New York: Continuum.

Gibson, William 2008, *The Miracle Worker (Play)*, New York: Scribner.

Graham, Loren R. 1987, *Science, Philosophy and Human Behaviour in the Soviet Union*, New York: Columbia University Press.

Gurgenidze, G.S., and Evald V. Ilyenkov 1975, 'Vydaiushcheesya dostizhenie sovetskoi nauki' ['An Exceptional Achievement of Soviet Science'], *Voprosy filosofii* [*Questions of Philosophy*], 6: 63–84.

Hakkarainen, Pentti 1999, 'Play and Motivation', in *Perspectives on Activity Theory*, edited by Yrjö Engeström, Reijo Miettinen, and Raija-Leena Punämaki, pp. 231–49, New York: Cambridge University Press.

Halbig, Christoph 2008, 'Varieties of Nature in Hegel and McDowell', in *John McDowell:*

Experience, Norm, and Nature, edited by Jakob Lindgaard pp. 72–91, Oxford: Blackwell.

Haugeland, John 1995, 'Mind Embodied and Embedded', in *Having Thought: Essays in the Metaphysics of Mind*, pp. 207–37, Cambridge, MA: Harvard University Press.

Hegel, G.W.F. 1952 [1820], *Philosophy of Right*, translated by T. Knox, Oxford: Clarendon Press.

Hegel, G.W.F. 1956 [1837], *The Philosophy of History*, translated by J. Sibree, New York: Dover.

Hegel, G.W.F. 1971 [1830], *Philosophy of Mind: Being Part Three of the Encyclopedia of the Philosophical Sciences*, translated by W. Wallace and A. Miller, Oxford: Clarendon Press.

Hellbeck, Jochen 2009, 'With Hegel to Salvation: Bukharin's Other Trial', *Representations*, 107, 1: 56–90.

Herzen, Alexander I. 1956, *Sobranie sochinenii v tridtsati tomakh* [*Collected Works in Thirty Volumes*], Vol. 9, Moscow.

Holquist, Michael 1983, 'The Politics of Representation', *Quarterly Newsletter of the Laboratory of Comparative Human Cognition*, 5, 1: 2–9.

Honderich, Ted, ed. 1995, *The Oxford Companion to Philosophy*, Oxford: Oxford University Press.

Hornsby, Jennifer 1997, *Simple Mindedness: In Defense of Naive Naturalism in the Philosophy of Mind*, Cambridge, MA: Harvard University Press.

Hughes, Robert 1980, *The Shock of the New*, London: BBC.

Ilyenkov, Evald V. 1960, *Dialektika abstraktnogo i konkretnogo v 'Kapitale' Marksa* [*The Dialectics of the Abstract and the Concrete in Marx's 'Capital'*], Moscow: Nauka.

Ilyenkov, E.V. (1961) *La dialettica dell'astratto e del concreto nel Capitale di Marx* [*The Dialectics of the Abstract and the Concrete in Marx's 'Capital'*], translated into Italian by Vittorio Strada e Alberto Sandretti, with a preface by Lucio Coletti. Milano: Feltrinelli.

Ilyenkov, Evald V. 1962, 'Ideal'noe' ['The Ideal'], in *Filosofskaya entsikolopediya, tom. 2* [*Philosophical Encyclopaedia, volume 2*], pp. 219–27, Moscow: Sovetskaya entsiklopediya.

Ilyenkov, Evald V. 1964, 'Vopros o tozhdestve myshleniya i bytiya v domarktistskoi filosofii' ['The Question of the Relation of Thinking and Being in Pre-Marxist Philosophy'], in *Dialektika – teoriya poznaniya* [*Dialectics – The Theory of Knowledge*], pp. 21–54, Moscow: Nauka.

Ilyenkov, Evald V. 1967, 'From a Marxist-Leninist Point of View', in *Marx and The Western World*, edited by N. Lobkowicz, pp. 391–407, Notre Dame: University of Notre Dame Press.

Ilyenkov, Evald V. 1968a, *K voprosu o prirode myshleniya (na materialax analiza nemetskoi klassicheskoi dialektiki)* [*On the Question of the Nature of Thought (Materials for the Analysis of German Classical Dialectics)*], Moscow: Akademiya nauk.

Ilyenkov, Evald V. 1968b, *Ob idolakh i idealakh* [*Of Idols and Ideals*], Moscow: Politizdat.

Ilyenkov, Evald V. 1968c, 'Psikhika i mozg' ['Mind and Brain'], *Voprosy filosofii* [*Questions of Philosophy*], 11: 145–55.

Ilyenkov, Evald V. 1969, 'Mind and Brain', *Soviet Studies in Philosophy*, 8, 1: 87–106.

Ilyenkov, Evald V. 1970, 'Psikhika cheloveka pod "lupoi vremeni"' ['The Human Mind Under "the Magnifying Glass of Time"'], *Priroda* [*Nature*], 1: 87–91.

Ilyenkov, Evald V. 1974a, *Dialekticheskaya logika: ocherki istorii i teorii* [*Dialectical Logic: Essays in its History and Theory*], Moscow: Politizdat.

Ilyenkov, Evald V. 1974b, 'Gegel' i germenevtika (Problema otnosheniya yazyka i myshleniya v konceptsii Gegelya)' ['Hegel and Hermeneutics (The Problem of the Relation of Language and Thought in Hegel's Philosophy)'], *Voprosy filosofii*, 8: 66–78.

Ilyenkov, Evald V. 1977a, 'The Concept of the Ideal', in *Philosophy in the USSR: Problems of Dialectical Materialism*, translated by Robert Daglish, Moscow: Progress.

Ilyenkov, Evald V. 1977b, *Dialectical Logic: Essays in its History and Theory*, translated by H. Campbell Creighton, Moscow: Progress.

Ilyenkov, Evald V. 1977c, 'Stanovlenie lichnosti' ['The Genesis of Personhood'], *Kommunist*, 2: 68–79.

Ilyenkov, Evald V. 1979a, 'Problema ideal'nogo' ['The Problem of the Ideal'], *Voprosy filosofii* [*Questions of Philosophy*], 6: 145–58; 7: 128–40.

Ilyenkov, Evald V. 1979b, 'Shto zhe takoe lichnost'?' ['What is Personhood?'], in *S chego nachinaetsa lichnost'* [*Where Personhood Begins*], pp. 183–237, Moscow: Politizdat.

Ilyenkov, Evald V. 1980, *Leninskaya dialektika i metafizika pozitivizma* [*Leninist Dialectics and the Metaphysics of Positivism*], Moscow: Politizdat.

Ilyenkov, Evald V. 1982a *The Dialectics of the Abstract and the Concrete in Marx's 'Capital'*, translated by Sergei Surovatkin, Moscow: Progress.

Ilyenkov, Evald V. 1982b, *Leninist Dialectics and the Metaphysics of Positivism*, translated by F. Williams, London: New Park.

Ilyenkov, Evald V. 1984a [1969], 'Chto tam, v Zazerkal'e?' ['What's There, Through the Looking Glass?'], in *Iskusstvo i kommunisticheskii ideal* [*Art and the Communist Ideal*], pp. 300–24, Moscow: Iskusstvo.

Ilyenkov, Evald V. 1984b [1964], 'Gegelevskaya kontseptsiya krasoty i istiny' ['The Hegelian Conception of Beauty and Truth'], in *Iskusstvo i kommunisticheskii ideal* [*Art and the Communist Ideal*], pp. 324–32, Moscow: Iskusstvo.

Ilyenkov, Evald V. 1984c, *Isskustvo i kommunisticheskii ideal* [*Art and the Communist Ideal*], Moscow: Iskusstvo.

Ilyenkov, Evald V. 1984d [1960], 'O "spetzifike" iskusstva' ['On the "Specifics" of Art'], in *Iskusstvo i kommunisticheskii ideal* [*Art and the Communist Ideal*], pp. 213–24, Moscow: Iskusstvo.

Ilyenkov, Evald V. 1984e [1964], 'Ob esteticheskoi prirode fantasii' ['On the Aesthetic

Nature of the Imagination'], in *Iskusstvo i kommunisticheskii ideal* [*Art and the Communist Ideal*], pp. 224–77, Moscow: Iskusstvo.

Ilyenkov, Evald V. 1984f [1972], 'Proidena lu tablitsa umnozheniya?' ['Have we Done our Multiplication Tables?'], in *Iskusstvo i kommunisticheskii ideal* [*Art and the Communist Ideal*], pp. 206–12, Moscow: Iskusstvo.

Ilyenkov, Evald V. 1991a [1979], 'Dialektika ideal'nogo' ['Dialectics of the Ideal'], in his *Filosofiya i kul'tura* [*Philosophy and Culture*], pp. 229–70, Moscow: Politizdat.

Ilyenkov, Evald V. 1991b, *Filosofiya i kul'tura* [*Philosophy and Culture*], Moscow: Politizdat.

Ilyenkov, Evald V. 1991c [1979], 'Filosofiya i molodost'' ['Philosophy and Youth'], in his *Filosofiya i kul'tura* [*Philosophy and Culture*], pp. 18–30, Moscow: Politizdat.

Ilyenkov, Evald V. 1991d [1977], 'Soobrazheniya po voprosu ob otnoshenii myshleniya i yazyka' ['Reflections on the Question of the Relation of Thought and Language'], in his *Filosofiya i kul'tura* [*Philosophy and Culture*], pp. 270–74, Moscow: Politizdat.

Ilyenkov, Evald V. 1997a, *Dialektika abstraknogo i konkretnogo v nauchno-teoreticheskom myshlenii* [*The Dialectics of the Abstract and the Concrete in Scientific Theoretical Thinking*], Moscow: Rosspen.

Ilyenkov, Evald V. 1997b, 'The Question of the Identity of Thought and Being in Pre-Marxist Philosophy', *Russian Studies in Philosophy*, 36, 1: 5–33.

Ilyenkov, Evald V. 2002a, 'O prirode sposobnosti' ['On the Nature of Ability'], in *Shkola dolzhna uchit' myslit'* [*Schools Must Teach How to Think*], Moskva: MPSI.

Ilyenkov, Evald V. 2002b, *Shkola dolzhna uchit' myslit* [*Schools Must Teach How to Think*], Moscow-Voronezh: Modek.

Ilyenkov, Evald V. 2007a, 'A Contribution to a Conversation About Meshcheryakov (November 20, 1975)', *Journal of Russian and East European Psychology*, 45, 4: 85–94.

Ilyenkov, Evald V. 2007b, 'On the Nature of Ability', *Journal of Russian and East European Psychology*, 45, 4: 56–63.

Ilyenkov, Evald V. 2007c, *Schools Must Teach How to Think. Special Issue. Journal of Russian and East European Psychology*, 45, 4: 3–94.

Ilyenkov, Evald V. 2009a, 'Dialektika ideal'nogo' ['Dialectics of the Ideal'], *Logos*, 69, 1: 6–62.

Ilyenkov, Evald V. 2009b, *The Ideal in Human Activity*, Pacifica, CA: Marxists Internet Archive.

Ilyenkov, Evald V. 2014, 'Dialectics of the Ideal', in *Dialectics of the Ideal*, edited by Alex Levant and Vesa Oittinen, pp. 25–78, Leiden: Brill.

Ilyenkov, Evald V. 2017, *Ot abstraknogo k konkretnogo. Krutoi marshrut. 1950–1960* [*From the Abstract to the Concrete: A Steep Route. 1950–1960*], edited by Elena E. Illesh, Moscow: Kanon+.

Ilyenkov, Evald V. 2018a, *Ideal'noe. I real'nost'. 1960–1979* [*The Ideal. And Reality. 1960–1979*], edited by Elena E. Illesh, Moscow: Kanon+.

Ilyenkov, Evald V. 2018b, *Intelligent Materialism: Essays on Hegel and Dialectics*, edited and translated by Evgeni V. Pavlov, Leiden: Brill.

Ilyenkov, Evald V. 2019, *Abstraktnoe i konkretnoe. Sobranie sochinenii tom 1* [*Abstract and Concrete. Collected Works, Vol. 1*], Moscow: Kanon+.

Ilyenkov, Evald V. 2020a, *Kategorii. Sobranie sochinenii, tom 2* [*Categories. Collected Works, Vol. 2*], Moscow: Kanon+.

Ilyenkov, Evald V. 2020b, *Ideal. Sobranie sochinenii, tom 3* [*Ideal. Collected Works, Vol. 3*]. Moscow: Kanon+.

Ilyenkov, Evald V. 2020c, *Dialekticheskaya logika. Sobranie sochinenii, tom 4* [*Dialectical Logic. Collected Works, Vol. 4*]. Moscow: Kanon+.

Ilyenkov, Evald V. 2021, *Dialektika ideal'nogo. Sobranie sochinenii, tom 5* [*Dialectics of the Ideal. Collected Works, Vol. 5*]. Moscow: Kanon+.

Ilyenkov, Evald V. 2022, *Filosofskaya entsiklopediya. Sobranie sochinenii, tom 6* [*Philosophical Encyclopedia. Collected Works, Vol. 6*]. Moscow: Kanon+.

Ilyenkov, Evald V., and Valentin I. Korovikov 2016, *Strasti po tezisam. Evald Ilyenkov i Valentin Korovikov o predmete filosofii (1954–1955)* [*The Passion of the Theses. Evald Ilyenkov and Valentin Korovikov on the Subject of Philosophy (1954–1955)*], edited by Elena E. Ilesh, Moscow: Kanon+.

Jensen, Eric P. 2008, 'A Fresh Look at Brain-Based Education', *Phi Delta Kappan*, February: 409–17.

Jones, Peter 1994, 'Evald Ilyenkov and the History of Marxism in the USSR', *History of the Human Sciences*, 7, 4: 105–18.

Joravsky, David 1961, *Soviet Marxism and Natural Science*, London: Routledge & Kegan Paul.

Joravsky, David 1978, 'The Construction of the Stalinist Psyche', in *Cultural Revolution in Russia*, edited by Sheila Fitzpatrick, pp. 105–28, Bloomington: Indiana University Press.

Joravsky, David 1989, *Russian Psychology*, Oxford: Blackwell.

Kagarlitsky, Boris 1989, *The Thinking Reed: Intellectuals and the Soviet State from 1917 to the Present*, London: Verso.

Kant, Immanuel 2007 [1803], 'Lectures on Pedagogy', in his *Anthropology, History, and Education*, edited by G. Zöller and R.B. Louden, translated by R.B. Louden, pp. 437–85, Cambridge: Cambridge University Press.

Kaptelinin, Victor 2005, 'The Object of Activity: Making Sense of the Sense-Maker', *Mind, Culture, and Activity*, 12, 1: 4–18.

Kaptelinin, Victor, and Bonnie Nardi 2006, *Acting with Technology: Activity Theory and Interaction Design*, Cambridge, MA: MIT Press.

Kern, Andrea 2020, 'Human Life, Rationality and Education', *Journal of Philosophy of Education*, 54, 2: 268–89.

Klyamkin, Igor, and Alexander Tsipko 1967, 'Muzhestvo mysli' ['The Courage of Thought'], *Komsomol'skaya pravda*, 8 December: 2.

Korovikov, Valentin I. 1990, 'Nachalo i pervyi pogrom' ['The Beginning and the First Pogrom'], *Voprosy filosofii [Questions of Philosophy]*, 2: 65–8.

Korovikov, Valentin I. 1998 [1990], 'Nachalo i pervyi pogrom' ['The Beginning and the First Pogrom'], in *Filosofiya ne konchaetsa ... iz istorii otchestvennoi filosofii 20 veka: tom 2 1960–80-e gody [Philosophy Does Not End ... From the History of Russian Philosophy in the 20th Century: Vol. 2, 1960s–80s]*, edited by Valdislav A. Lektorsky, pp. 472–9, Moscow: Rosspen.

Kozulin, Alex 1984, *Psychology in Utopia*, Cambridge, MA: MIT Press.

Kozulin, Alex 1986, 'Vygotsky in Context', in L.S. Vygotsky, *Thought and Language*, translated, revised, and edited by Alex Kozulin, Cambridge, MA: MIT Press.

Kozulin, Alex 1990, *Vygotsky's Psychology: A Biography of Ideas*, Cambridge, MA: Harvard University Press.

Kozulin, Alex 2016, 'The Mystery of Perezhivanie', *Mind, Culture, and Activity*, 23, 4: 356–7.

Kripke, Saul 1982, *Wittgenstein on Rules and Private Languages*, Oxford: Blackwell.

Krylatov, Yuri D. 1988, *Azbuka chutkikh ruk [An Alphabet for Keen Hands]*, Leningrad: Leningradskii vosstanovitel'nyi tsentr VOG.

Leibniz, Gottfried Wilhelm 1981 [1705], *New Essays on Human Understanding*, translated by P. Remnant and J. Bennett, Cambridge: Cambridge University Press.

Lektorsky, Vladislav A. 1980, *Sub"ekt, ob"ekt, poznanie [Subject, Object, Cognition]*, Moscow: Nauka.

Lektorsky, Vladislav A. 1984, *Subject, Object, Cognition*, translated by Sergei Syrovatkin, Moscow: Progress.

Lektorsky, Vladislav A. ed. 1990, *Activity: Theories, Methodology, and Problems*, Orlando: Paul Deutsch.

Lektorsky, Vladislav A. 2012, *Filosofiya, poznanie, kul'tura [Philosophy, Cognition, Culture]*, Moscow: Kanon+.

Lektorsky, Vladislav A. 2018, *Chelovek i kul'tura: Izbrannye stat'i [Man and Culture: Selected Essays]*, Petersburg: SPbGUP.

Lenin, Vladimir I. 1960–78, *Collected Works*, 4th English edition, 38 vols, Moscow and London: Lawrence and Wishart.

Leontiev, Aleksei N. 1977, 'Activity and Consciousness', in *Philosophy in the USSR: Problems of Dialectical Materialism*, pp. 180–202, Moscow: Progress Publishers.

Leontiev, Aleksei N. 1978 [1975], *Activity, Consciousness, and Personality*, Englewood Cliffs, NJ: Prentice Hall.

Leontiev, Aleksei N. 1980 [1935], 'Ovladenie uchashchimisya nauchnymi ponyatiyami kak problema pedagogicheskoi psikhologii' ['The Acquisition of Scientific Concepts by School Pupils as a Problem of Pedagogical Psychology'], in *Khrestomatiya po vozrastnoi i pedagogicheskoi psikhologii* [*Handbook of Developmental and Pedagogical Psychology*], Vol. 1, Moscow: MGU.

Leontiev, Aleksei N. 1981, *Problems of the Development of the Mind*, Moscow: Progress.

Leontiev, Aleksei N., and Alexander R. Luria 1968, 'The Psychological Ideas of L.S. Vygotskii', in *Historical Roots of Contemporary Psychology*, edited by Benjamin B. Wolman, pp. 338–67, New York: Harper & Row.

Levant, Alex, and Vesa Oittinen, eds 2014, *Dialectics of the Ideal: Evald Ilyenkov and Creative Soviet Marxism*, Leiden: Brill.

Levitin, Karl 1979, 'The Best Path to Man', *Soviet Psychology*, 18: 3–66.

Levitin, Karl 1982, *One is Not Born a Personality*, translated by Yevgeni Filippov, Moscow: Progress Publishers.

Levitin, Karl 2009, *One is Not Born a Personality*, revised edition with a preface by Michael Cole, translated by Yevgeni Filippov, Kettering, OH: Erythrós Press.

Lobastov, Gennady V., ed. 2004, *Eval'd Vasil'evich Il'enkov v vospominaniyakh* [*Evald Vasilevich Ilyenkov Remembered*], Moscow: RGGU.

Locke, John 1975, *An Essay Concerning Human Understanding*, edited by P. Nidditch, Oxford: Oxford University Press.

Luntley, Michael 2018, 'Plays the Thing: Wherein We Find How Learning Can Begin', *Journal of Philosophy of Education*, 52, 1: 36–53.

Luria, Alexander R. 1979, *The Making of Mind*, Cambridge, MA: Harvard University Press.

MacIntyre, Alasdair 1981, *After Virtue*, London: Duckworth.

Maidansky, Andrey 2018, 'Kommunisticheskii ideal Il'enkova i real'nyi sotsialism' ['Ilyenkov's Communist Ideal and Real Socialism'], in E.V. Ilyenkov, *Ideal'noe. I real'nost' 1969–1979*, pp. 398–413, Moscow: Kanon+.

Maidansky, Andrey 2020, 'Review of Anton Yasnitsky and René van der Veer, *Revisionist Revolution in Vygotsky Studies*', *Studies in East European Thought*, 72, 1: 82–95.

Maidansky, Andrey 2023, 'Commentary: Ilyenkov versus the Leviathan', in *Ilyenkov: Cosmos and Practice*, edited by Sascha Freyberg and Alexander Rozhkov. Venice: Verum Factum.

Maidansky, Andrey, and Vesa Oittinen, eds 2015, *The Practical Essence of Man: The Activity Approach in Late Soviet Philosophy*, Leiden: Brill.

Malinovsky, A.A. 1970, 'Nekotorye vozpazheniya E.V. Ilyenkovu i A.I. Meshcheryakovu' ['Some Objections to E.V. Ilyenkov and A.I. Meshcheryakov'], *Priroda* [*Nature*], 1: 92–5.

Mandel'shtam, N. 1970, *Vospominaniya. Kniga pervaya* [*Recollections. Book One*], Paris: YMCA Press.

Marcuse, Herbert 1958, *Soviet Marxism: A Critical Analysis*, New York: Columbia University Press.

Marcuse, Herbert 1978, *The Aesthetic Dimension*, Boston: Beacon.

Mareev, Sergei N. 1994, *Vstrecha s filosofom E.V. Ilyenkovym* [*An Encounter with the Philosopher E.V. Ilyenkov*], Moscow: Znanie.

Marx, Karl 1968 [1845], 'Theses on Feuerbach', in *Marx-Engels Selected Works in One Volume*, pp. 28–30, London: Lawrence and Wishart.

Marx, Karl 1971 [1844], 'On James Mill', in *Early Texts*, translated by David McLellan, pp. 188–203, Oxford: Basil Blackwell.

Marx, Karl 1977, *Economic and Philosophical Manuscripts of 1844*, Moscow: Progress.

Marx, Karl 1982 [1867], *Capital*, Vol. 1, Harmondsworth: Penguin.

Marx, Karl, and Friedrich Engels 1968 [1848], 'Manifesto of the Communist Party', in *Marx-Engels Selected Works in One Volume*, pp. 31–63, London: Lawrence and Wishart.

McDowell, John 1979, 'Virtue and Reason', *The Monist*, 62, 3: 331–50.

McDowell, John 1994, *Mind and World*, 2nd edition with a new introduction by the author (1996), Cambridge, MA: Harvard University Press.

McDowell, John 1998a, 'The Content of Perceptual Experience', in his *Mind, Value, and Reality*, pp. 341–58, Cambridge, MA: Harvard University Press.

McDowell, John 1998b, 'Intentionality and Interiority in Wittgenstein', in *Mind, Value, and Reality*, pp. 297–321, Cambridge, MA: Harvard University Press.

McDowell, John 1998c, 'Meaning and Intentionality in Wittgenstein's Later Philosophy', in *Mind, Value, and Reality*, pp. 261–78, Cambridge, MA: Harvard University Press.

McDowell, John 1998d, *Mind, Value, and Reality*, Cambridge, MA: Harvard University Press.

McDowell, John 1998e, 'Putnam on Mind and Meaning', in *Meaning, Knowledge, and Reality*, pp. 275–91, Cambridge, MA: Harvard University Press.

McDowell, John 1998f, 'Reductionism and the First Person', in *Mind, Value, and Reality*, pp. 359–82, Cambridge, MA: Harvard University Press.

McDowell, John 1998g, 'Some Issues in Aristotle's Moral Psychology', in *Mind, Value, and Reality*, pp. 23–49, Cambridge, MA: Harvard University Press.

McDowell, John 1998h, 'Wittgenstein on Following a Rule', in *Mind, Value, and Reality*, pp. 221–62, Cambridge, MA: Harvard University Press.

McDowell, John 1998i, 'Two Sorts of Naturalism', in *Mind, Value, and Reality*, pp. 167–97. Cambridge, MA: Harvard University Press.

McDowell, John 2000, 'Responses', in *John McDowell: Reason and Nature*, edited by M. Willaschek, pp. 91–114, Münster: LIT Verlag.

McDowell, John 2002, 'Responses', in *Reading McDowell: On Mind and World*, edited by Nicholas Smith, pp. 269–305, London: Routledge.

McDowell, John 2006, 'Response to Graham Macdonald', in *McDowell and his Critics*, edited by Cynthia Macdonald and Graham Macdonald, pp. 235–9, Oxford: Blackwell.

McDowell, John 2008, 'Respones', in *John McDowell: Experience, Norm, and Nature*, edited by Jakob Lindgaard, pp. 200–67, Oxford: Blackwell.

McDowell, John 2009a, 'Deliberation and Moral Development in Aristotle's Ethics', in *The Engaged Intellect: Philosophical Essays*, pp. 41–58, Cambridge, MA: Harvard University Press.

McDowell, John 2009b, *The Engaged Intellect: Philosophical Essays*, Cambridge, MA: Harvard University Press.

McDowell, John 2009c, 'Eudaimonism and Realism in Aristotle's Ethics', in *The Engaged Intellect: Philosophical Essays*, pp. 23–40, Cambridge, MA: Harvard University Press.

McDowell, John 2009d, 'Gadamer and Davidson on Understanding and Relativism', in *The Engaged Intellect: Philosophical Essays*, pp. 134–51, Cambridge, MA: Harvard University Press.

McDowell, John 2009e, 'On Pippin's Postscript', in *Having the World in View: Essays on Kant, Hegel, and Sellars*, pp. 185–203, Cambridge, MA: Harvard University Press.

McDowell, John 2009f, 'Response to Dreyfus', in *Having the World in View: Essays on Kant, Hegel, and Sellars*, pp. 324–8, Cambridge, MA: Harvard University Press.

McDowell, John 2009g, 'Towards a Reading of Hegel on Action', in *Having the World in View: Essays on Kant, Hegel, and Sellars*, pp. 166–84, Cambridge, MA: Harvard University Press.

McDowell, John 2009h, 'Self-Determining Subjectivity and External Constraint', in *Having the World in View: Essays on Kant, Hegel, and Sellars*, pp. 90–107, Cambridge, MA: Harvard University Press.

McDowell, John 2009i, 'Wittgensteinian "Quietism"', *Common Knowledge*, 15, 3: 365–72.

McInnes, J.M., and J.A. Treffrey 1982, *Deaf-Blind Infants and Children*, Toronto: Toronto University Press.

Meshcheryakov, Alexander I. 1970, 'Poznanie mira bez sluka i zreniya', *Priroda [Nature]*, 1: 78–87.

Meshcheryakov, Alexander I. 1979, *Awakening to Life*, translated by K. Judelson, Moscow: Progress.

Meshcheryakov, Alexander I. 2009, *Awakening to Life*, translated by K. Judelson, Kettering, ON: Eryrthrós Press and Media.

Mikhailov, Felix T. 1964, *Zagadka chelovecheskogo ya [The Riddle of the Self]*, Moscow: Politizdat.

Mikhailov, Felix T. 1976, *Zagadka chelovecheskogo ya [The Riddle of the Self]*, 2nd edition, revised and expanded, Moscow: Politizdat.

Mikhailov, Felix T. 1980, *The Riddle of the Self*, translated by Robert Daglish, Moscow: Progress.

Mikhailov, Felix T. 1981, 'Predmetnost' deyatel'nosti i predmet psikhologii' ['The Object-Orientatedness of Activity and the Subject of Psychology'], in *Metodologicheskie problemy psikhologii lichnosti [Methodological Problems of the Psychology of Person-*

hood], Moscow: Akademiya pedagogicheskikh nauk sssr, Nauchno-issledovatel'skii institut obshchei pedagogiki.

Mikhailov, Felix T. 1990a, *Obshchestvennoe soznanie i samosoznanie individa* [*Social Consciousness and the Self-Consciousness of the Individual*], Moscow: Nauka.

Mikhailov, Felix T. 1990b, 'Slovo ob Il'enkova' ['A Word about Ilyenkov'], *Voprosy filosofii* [*Questions of Philosophy*], 2: 56–64.

Mikhailov, Felix T. 1995, 'The Soviet Self. A Personal Reminiscence', in *The Social Self*, edited by David Bakhurst and Christine Sypnowich, London: Sage.

Mikhailov, Felix T. 1997, *Samosoznanie: moë i nashe* [*Self-Consciousness: Mine and Ours*], Moscow: RAN, Institut filosofii.

Mikhailov, Felix T. 1998 [1990], 'Slovo ob Il'enkova' ['A Word about Ilyenkov'], in *Filosofiya ne konchaetsa … iz istorii otchestvennoi filosofii 20 veka: tom 2 1960–80-e gody* [*Philosophy Does Not End … From the History of Russian Philosophy in the 20th Century: Vol. 2, 1960s–80s*], edited by Vladislav A. Lektorsky, pp. 443–59, Moscow: Rosspen.

Mikhailov, Felix T. 2001, *Izbrannoe* [*Selections*], Moscow: Indrik.

Mikhailov, Felix T. 2003, *Samoopredelenie kul'tury: Filosofskii poisk* [*The Self-Determination of Culture: A Philosophical Quest*], Moscow: Indrik.

Mikhailov, Felix T. 2010, *Zagadka chelovecheskogo ya* [*The Riddle of the Self*], 3rd edition, Moscow: Ritm.

Minnik, Norris 1987, 'The Development of Vygotsky's Thought: An Introduction', in *The Collected Works of L.S. Vygotsky, Vol. 1: Problems of General Psychology*, translated by Norris Minnik, pp. 17–36, New York: Plenum.

Mok, Nelson 2017, 'On the Concept of Perezhivanie: A Quest for a Critical Review', in *Perezhivane, Emotions and Subjectivity: Advancing Vygotsky's Legacy*, edited by M. Fleer, G. Rey, and N. Veresov, pp. 19–45, Singapore: Springer.

Moran, Richard 2001, *Authority and Estrangement: An Essay on Self-Knowledge*, Princeton: Princeton University Press.

Motroshilova, Nelly 2009, 'An Establishment like the Institute of Philosophy is Unique. An Interview with N.V. Motrošilova', *Russian Studies in Philosophy*, 48, 1: 68–82.

Nagel, Thomas 1979, 'What is it Like to be a Bat?', in *Mortal Questions*, pp. 165–80, Cambridge: Cambridge University Press.

Nemeth, Thomas 1981, 'Review of F.T. Mikhailov's *Zagadka čelovečeskogo ja*', *Studies in Soviet Thought*, 22, 3: 212–17.

Nemeth, Thomas 1995, 'Review of David Bakhurst, *Consciousness and Revolution in Soviet Philosophy*', *Studies in East European Thought*, 47, 1–2: 144–8.

Neuhouser, Frederick 2000, *Foundations of Hegel's Social Theory: Actualizing Freedom*, Cambridge: MA: Harvard University Press.

Nietzsche, Friedrich 1913, *The Will to Power, Vol. 2*, translated by A.M. Ludovici, London: Foulis.

Noë, Alva 2004, *Action in Perception*, Cambridge, MA: MIT Press.

Noë, Alva 2009, *Out of Our Heads: Why You Are Not Your Brain and Other Lessons from the Biology of Consciousness*, New York: Hill and Wang.

Novokhat'ko, A.G. 1991, 'Fenomen Il'enkova', in *Evald V. Ilyenkov, Filosofiya i kul'tura [Philosophy and Culture]*, pp. 5–16, Moscow: Politizdat.

Novokhat'ko, A.G. 1997, 'Ob E.V. Il'enkove' ['About E.V. Ilyenkov'], in Evald V. Ilyenkov, *Dialektika ab"straktnogo i konkretnogo v nauchno-teoreticheskom myshleniya [Dialectics of the Abstract and the Concrete in Scientific-Theoretical Thinking]*, pp. 3–10, Moscow: Rosspen.

Nussbaum, Martha 2010, *Not For Profit: Why Democracy Needs the Humanities*. Princeton: Princeton University Press.

Oizerman, Teodor I. 2009, 'The Institute of Philosophy is the Country's Central Philosophical Establishment: An Interview with T.I. Oizerman', *Russian Studies in Philosophy*, 48, 1: 26–40.

Oizerman, Teodor I., and V.I. Svetlov 1948, *Vozniknovenie marksizma – revoliutsionnyi perevorot v filosofii [The Rise of Marxism – The Revolutionary Turn in Philosophy]*, Moscow: Politizdat.

Padden, Carol, and Tom Humphries 1988, *Deaf in America: Voices from a Culture*, Cambridge, MA: Harvard University Press.

Pettit, Philip, and Michael Smith 1996, 'Freedom in Belief and Desire', *Journal of Philosophy*, 93, 9: 429–49.

Pinkard, Terry 2002, *German Philosophy 1760–1860: The Legacy of Idealism*, Cambridge: Cambridge University Press.

Pushchaev, Iu. V. 2017, 'The History and Theory of the Zagorsk Experiment. Part 2: Was it Falsified?', *Journal of Russian and East European Psychology*, 55, 4–5: 301–21.

Putnam, Hilary 1975, 'The Meaning of "Meaning"', in *Mind, Language, and Reality*, pp. 215–71, Cambridge: Cambridge University Press.

Razmyslov, P. 2000 [1934], 'On Vygotsky's and Luria's "Cultural-Historical Theory of Psychology"', *Journal of Russian and East European Psychology*, 38, 6: 45–58.

Richta, R. 1969 [1966], *Civilization at the Crossroads: Social and Human Implications of the Scientific and Technological Revolution*, Prague: International Arts and Science Press.

Rödl, Sebastian 2007, *Self-Consciousness*, Cambridge, MA: Harvard University Press.

Rödl, Sebastian 2016, 'Education and Autonomy', *Journal of Philosophy of Education*, 50, 1: 84–97.

Rödl, Sebastian 2020, 'Teaching, Freedom and the Human Individual', *Journal of Philosophy of Education*, 54, 2: 290–304.

Rorty, Richard 1982, *Consequences of Pragmatism*, Minneapolis: University of Minnesota Press.

Rorty, Richard 1991, *Objectivity, Realtivism, and Truth: Philosophical Papers*, Vol. 1, Cambridge: Cambridge University Press.

Roth, Wolf-Michael 2007, 'Emotion at Work: A Contribution to Third-Generation Cultural-Historical Activity Theory', *Mind, Culture, and Activity*, 14, 1–2.

Rudneva, E.I. 2000 [1937], 'Vygotsky's Pedological Distortions', *Journal of Russian and East European Psychology*, 38, 6: 75–94.

Ryle, Gilbert 1949, *The Concept of Mind*, London: Hutchinson University Library.

Sacks, O. 1989, *Seeing Voices: A Journey into the World of the Deaf*, Berkeley: University of California Press.

Sadovskii, Vadim N. 1993, 'Filosofiya v Moskve v 50-e i 60-e gody' ['Philosophy in Moscow in the 1950s and 1960s'], *Voprosy filosofii* [*Questions of Philosophy*], 7: 147–64.

Sandomirskaja, Irina 2008, 'Skin to Skin: Language in Soviet Education of Deaf-blind Children, in the 1920s and 1930s', *Studies in East European Thought*, 60, 4: 321–37.

Scanlan, James P. 1985, *Marxism in the USSR: A Critical Survey of Current Soviet Thought*, Ithaca, NY: Cornell University Press.

Sellars, Wilfrid 1956, 'Empiricism and the Philosophy of Mind', in *Minnesota Studies in the Philosophy of Science*, Vol. 1, edited by Herbert and Scriven Feigl, Michael, pp. 253–329, Minneapolis: University of Minnesota Press.

Sellars, Wilfrid 1963, 'Philosophy and the Scientific Image of Man', in *Science, Perception and Reality*, pp. 1–40, London: Routledge & Kegan Paul.

Shvyrev, Vladimir S. 1990, 'The Concept of Activity as a Philosophical Category: Problems Involved', in *Activity: Theories, Methodology, and Problems*, edited by Vladislav A. Lektorsky, pp. 1–6, Orlando, FL, Helsinki, Moscow: Paul Deutsch.

Silyak, Anna 2001, 'Between East and West: Hegel and the Origins of the Russian Dilemma', *Journal of the History of Ideas*, 62, 2: 335–58.

Sirotkin, Sergei A. 1979, 'The Transition from Gesture to Symbol', *Soviet Psychology*, 3: 46–59.

Smagorinsky, Peter 2011, 'Vygotsky's Stage Theory: The Psychology of Art and the Actor Under the Direction of Perezhivanie', *Mind, Culture, and Activity*, 18, 4: 319–41. doi: 10.1080/10749039.2010.518300.

Spinuzzi, Clay 2008, *Network: Theorizing Knowledge Work in Telecommunications*, Cambridge: Cambridge University Press.

Spufford, Francis 2010, *Red Plenty*, London: Faber and Faber.

Stout, Jeffrey 2007, 'On Our Interest in Getting Things Right: Pragmatism Without Narcissism', in *New Pragmatists*, edited by Cheryl Misak, pp. 7–31, Oxford: Oxford University Press.

Su, Hanno, and Johannes Bellman 2018, 'Inferentialism at Work: The Significance of Social Epistemology in Theorising Education', *Journal of Philosophy of Education*, 52, 2: 230–45.

Suvorov, Alexander V. 1983, 'Problema formirovaniya voobrazheniya u slepoglukho-nemykh detei' ['The Problem of the Formation of Imagination in Blind-Deaf Children'], *Voprosy psikhologii* [*Questions of Psychology*], 3: 62–72.

Suvorov, Alexander V. 1983–4, 'The Formation of Representation in Blind-Deaf Children', *Soviet Psychology*, 22, 2: 3–28.

Suvorov, Alexander V. 1988, 'Muzhestvo soznaniya' ['The Courage of Consciousness'], *Voprosy filosofii*, 4: 68–79.

Suvorov, Alexander V. 1989, 'The Blind-Deaf and Those Who See and Hear', *Paper Presented at the World Congress for the Blind-Deaf, Stockholm*.

Suvorov, Alexander V. 2016, 'Lessons from the Zagorsk Experiment for Deaf-Blind Psychology', *Russian Education and Society*, 58, 9–10: 650–73.

Sypnowich, Christine 2000a, 'Egalitarianism Renewed', in *Canadian Political Philosophy at the Turn of the Century: Exemplary Essays*, edited by R. Beiner and W. Norman, pp. 118–30, Oxford: Oxford University Press.

Sypnowich, Christine 2000b, 'How to Live the Good Life: William Morris's Aesthetic Conception of Equality', *Queen's Quarterly*, 107, 3: 391–411.

Sypnowich, Christine 2017, *Equality Renewed: Justice, Flourishing and the Egalitarian Ideal*, London: Routledge.

Testa, Italo 2009, 'Second Nature and Recognition: Hegel and the Social Space', *Critical Horizons*, 10, 3: 341–70.

Thompson, Michael 2008, *Life and Action: Elementary Structures of Practice and Practical Thought*, Cambridge, MA: Harvard University Press.

Todorov, Tzvetan 1984, *Mikhail Bakhtin: The Dialogical Principle*, translated by Wlad Godzich, Manchester: Manchester University Press.

Tolman, Charles 1993, 'Activity Theory and the Importance of Philosophy', *Activity Theory*, 13–14: 67–70.

Tolstoy, Leo N. 1960, 'The Death of Ivan Ilych', in *The Death of Ivan Ilych and Other Stories*, translated by David Magarshack, pp. 93–152, London: New English Library.

Tomasello, Michael 1999, *The Cultural Origins of Human Cognition*, Cambridge, MA: Harvard University Press.

Tucker, Robert C. 1978, *The Marx-Engels Reader*, 2nd edition, New York: W.W. Norton.

Valsiner, Jaan 1988, *Developmental Psychology in the Soviet Union*, Bloomington: Indiana University Press.

van der Veer, René, and Jaan Valsiner 1991, *Understanding Vygotsky: A Quest for Synthesis*, Oxford: Blackwell.

van der Veer, René, and Jaan Valsiner (eds) 1994, *The Vygotsky Reader*, Oxford: Blackwell.

van der Veer, René, and Anton Yasnitsky 2016, 'Vygotsky the Published: Who Wrote Vygotsky and What Vygotsky Actually Wrote', in *Revisionist Revolution in Vygotsky Studies*, edited by Anton Yasnitsky and René van der Veer, pp. 73–93, London: Routledge.

Vasilova, T.A. 1989, 'Ivan Afanas'evich Sokolyansky', *Defektologiya* [*Defectology*], 2: 71–5.

Vasilova, T.A. 2013, 'Ob istorii obucheniya slepoglukhikh detei v Moskovskom regione' ['The History of the Education of Deaf-Blind Children in the Moscow Region'], *Klinicheskaya i spetsial'naya psikhologiya* [*Clinical and Special psychology*], 2.

Veresov, Nikolai, and Marilyn Fleer 2016, 'The Journey Forward', *Mind, Culture, and Activity*, 23, 4: 350–52.

Vitkin, Mikhail 1982, 'Marx Between West and East', *Studies in Soviet Thought*, 23: 63–74.

Voloshinov, Valentin N. 1986 [1929], *Marxism and the Philosophy of Language*, translated by Ladislav Matejka and I.R. Titunik, Cambridge, MA: Harvard University Press.

Voloshinov, Valentin N. 1987 [1927], *Freudism: A Critical Sketch*, edited by Neal H. Bruss, translated by I.R. Titunik, Bloomington: Indiana University Press.

Vygotsky, Lev S. 1929, 'The Problem of the Cultural Development of the Child', *Journal of Genetic Psychology*, 36, 3: 415–34.

Vygotsky, Lev S. 1971 [1925], *Psychology of Art*, Cambridge, MA: MIT Press.

Vygotsky, Lev S. 1977, 'Iz tet'ryadei L.S. Vygotskogo' ['From the Notebooks of L.S. Vygotsky'], *Vestnik Moskovskogo Universiteta: Seria psikhologii* [*Moscow University Record: Psychology Series*], 15: 89–95.

Vygotsky, Lev S. 1978, *Mind in Society*, edited by Michael Cole, Vera John-Steiner, Sylvia Scribner, and Elen Souberman, Cambridge, MA: Harvard University Press.

Vygotsky, Lev S. 1982a [SS 1] *Sobrannie socheninii, tom 1: Voprosy teorii i istorii psikhologii* [*Collected Works, Vol. 1: Questions of the Theory and History of Psychology*]. Moscow: Pedagogika.

Vygotsky, Lev S. 1982b [SS 2] *Sobrannie socheninii, tom 2: Problemy obshchei psikhologii* [*Collected Works, Vol. 2: Problems of General Psychology*]. Moscow: Pedagogika.

Vygotsky, Lev S. 1983a [1931], 'Istoriya razvitiya vysshchykh psikhicheskikh funktsii' ['The History of the Development of the Higher Mental Functions'], in *Sobranie sochinenii, tom 3: Problemy razvitiya psikhiki*, Moscow: Pedagogika.

Vygotsky, Lev S. 1983b [SS 3] *Sobrannie socheninii, tom 3: Problemy razvitiya psikhiki* [*Collected Works, Vol. 3: Problems of the Development of Mind*]. Moscow: Pedagogika.

Vygotsky, Lev S. 1983c [SS 5] *Sobrannie socheninii, tom 5: Osnovy defektologii* [*Collected Works, Vol. 5: Foundations of Defectology*]. Moscow: Pedagogika.

Vygotsky, Lev S. 1984a [SS 4] *Sobrannie socheninii, tom 4: Detskaya psikhologiya* [*Collected Works, Vol. 4: Child Psychology*]. Moscow: Pedagogika.

Vygotsky, Lev S. 1984b [SS 6] *Sobrannie socheninii, tom 6: Nauchnoe nasledstvo* [*Collected Works, Vol. 6: Scientific Legacy*]. Moscow: Pedagogika.

Vygotsky, Lev S. 1987a, *The Collected Works of L.S. Vygotsky, Vol. 1: Problems of General Psychology*, translated by Norris Minnik, New York: Plenum.

Vygotsky, Lev S. 1987b [1932], 'Lectures on Psychology', in *The Collected Works of L.S. Vygotsky, Vol. 1: Problems of General Psychology*, edited by Robert W. Rieber and Aaron S. Carton, translated by Norris Minnik, pp. 287–358, New York: Plenum Press.

Vygotsky, Lev S. 1987c [1925], *Psikhologiya iskusstva* [*The Psychology of Art*], edited by M.G. Yaroshevsky, Moscow: Pedagogika.

Vygotsky, Lev S. 1987d [1934], 'Thinking and Speech', in *The Collected Works of L.S. Vygot-*

sky, Vol. 1: Problems of General Psychology, edited by Robert W. Rieber and Aaron S. Carton, translated by Norris Minnik, pp. 37–285, New York: Plenum Press.

Vygotsky, Lev S. 1993a [1928], 'The Blind Child', in *Collected Works, Vol. 2: The Fundamentals of Defectology*, edited by Robert W. Rieber, translated by Jane Knox and Carol Stevens, pp. 97–109, New York: Plenum Press.

Vygotsky, Lev S. 1993b, *Collected Works, Vol. 2: The Fundamentals of Defectology*, edited by Robert W. Rieber, translated by Jane Knox and Carol Stevens, New York: Plenum Press.

Vygotsky, Lev S. 1993c [1931], 'The Collective as a Factor in the Development of the Abnormal Child', in *Collected Works, Vol. 2: The Fundamentals of Defectology*, edited by Robert W. Rieber, translated by Jane Knox and Carol Stevens, pp. 191–208, New York: Plenum Press.

Vygotsky, Lev S. 1993d [1928], 'Defectology and the Study of the Development of the Abnormal Child', in *Collected Works, Vol. 2: The Fundamentals of Defectology*, edited by Robert W. Rieber, translated by Jane Knox and Carol Stevens, pp. 164–70, New York: Plenum Press.

Vygotsky, Lev S. 1993e [1925], 'Principles of Social Education for the Deaf-Mute Child', in *Collected Works, Vol. 2: The Fundamentals of Defectology*, edited by Robert W. Rieber, translated by Jane Knox and Carol Stevens, pp. 110–21, New York: Plenum Press.

Vygotsky, Lev S. 1993f. [1935], 'The Problem of Mental Retardation', in *Collected Works, Vol. 2: The Fundamentals of Defectology*, edited by Robert W. Rieber, translated by Jane Knox and Carol Stevens, pp. 220–40, New York: Plenum Press.

Vygotsky, Lev S. 1994a [1934], 'The Problem of the Environment', in *The Vygotsky Reader*, edited by René Van der Veer and Jaan Valsiner, pp. 338–54, Oxford: Blackwell.

Vygotsky, Lev S. 1994b [1930], 'The Socialist Alteration of Man', in *The Vygotsky Reader*, edited by René Van der Veer and Jaan Valsiner, pp. 175–84, Oxford: Blackwell.

Vygotsky, Lev S. and Alexander R. Luria 1994c [1925], 'Introduction to the Russian Translation of Freud's *Beyond the Pleasure Principle*', in *The Vygotsky Reader*, edited by René Van der Veer and Jaan Valsiner, pp. 10–18, Oxford: Blackwell.

Vygotsky, Lev S. 1997a [1931], *Collected Works, Vol. 4: The History of the Development of the Higher Mental Functions*, edited by R. Reiner, translated by M. Hall, New York: Plenum Press. Reprint, partly published in Russian in 1960; full text published in Russian in 1983.

Vygotsky, Lev S. 1997b [1925], 'Consciousness as a Problem for the Psychology of Behavior', in *The Collected Works of L.S. Vygotsky, Vol. 3: Problems of the Theory and History of Psychology*, edited by Robert W. Rieber and Jeffrey Wollock, translated by René Van der Veer, pp. 63–79, New York: Plenum Press.

Vygotsky, Lev S. 1997c [1926], *Educational Psychology*, translated by R. Silverman, with an introduction by V.V. Davydov, Boca Raton, FL: St. Lucie Press.

Vygotsky, Lev S. 1997d [1927], 'The Historical Meaning of the Crisis in Psychology', in

The Collected Works of L.S. Vygotsky, Vol. 3: Problems of the Theory and History of Psychology, edited by Robert W. Rieber and Jeffrey Wollock, translated by René Van der Veer, pp. 233–343, New York: Plenum Press.

Vygotsky, Lev S. 1997e [1931], 'The History of the Development of Higher Mental Functions', in *The Collected Works of L.S. Vygotsky, Vol. 4: The History of the Development of Higher Mental Functions*, edited by Robert W. Rieber, translated by Marie J. Hall, pp. 1–251, New York: Plenum Press.

Vygotsky, Lev S. 1997 f [1930], 'The Instrumental Method in Psychology', in *The Collected Works of L.S. Vygotsky, Vol. 3: Problems of the Theory and History of Psychology*, edited by Robert W. Rieber and Jeffrey Wollock, translated by René Van der Veer, pp. 85–9, New York: Plenum Press.

Vygotsky, Lev S. 1997g [1924], 'The Methods of Reflexological and Psychological Investigation', in *The Collected Works of L.S. Vygotsky, Vol. 3: Problems of the Theory and History of Psychology*, edited by Robert W. Rieber and Jeffrey Wollock, translated by René Van der Veer, pp. 35–49, New York: Plenum Press.

Vygotsky, Lev S. 1997h [1930], 'Preface to Köhler', in *The Collected Works of L.S. Vygotsky, Vol. 3: Problems of the Theory and History of Psychology*, edited by Robert W. Rieber and Jeffrey Wollock, translated by René Van der Veer, pp. 175–94, New York: Plenum Press.

Vygotsky, Lev S. 1997i [1931], 'Preface to Leont'ev's *The Development of Memory*', in *The Collected Works of L.S. Vygotsky, Vol. 3: Problems of the Theory and History of Psychology*, edited by Robert W. Rieber and Jeffrey Wollock, translated by René Van der Veer, pp. 123–7, New York: Plenum Press.

Vygotsky, Lev S. 1997j [1933], 'The Problem of Consciousness', in *The Collected Works of L.S. Vygotsky, Vol. 3: Problems of the Theory and History of Psychology*, edited by Robert W. Rieber and Jeffrey Wollock, translated by René Van der Veer, pp. 129–38, New York: Plenum Press.

Vygotsky, Lev S. 1997k [1930], 'Mind, Consciousness, the Unconscious', in *The Collected Works of L.S. Vygotsky*, Vol. 3: Problems of the Theory and History of Psychology, edited by Robert W. Rieber and Jeffrey Wollock, translated by René Van der Veer, pp. 109–21, New York: Plenum Press.

Vygotsky, Lev S. 1998a [1933–34], 'The Crisis at Age Seven', in *The Collected Works of L.S. Vygotsky, Vol. 5: Child Psychology*, translated by M. Hall, pp. 289–96, New York: Kluwer.

Vygotsky, Lev S. 1998b [1931], 'Pedology of the Adolescent', in *The Collected Works of L.S. Vygotsky, Vol. 5: Child Psychology*, translated by M. Hall, pp. 1–184, New York: Kluwer.

Vygotsky, Lev S. 1999 [1933], 'The Teaching About Emotions: Historical-Psychological Studies', in *Collected Works, Vol. 6: Scientific Legacy*, edited by Robert W. Rieber, pp. 69–235, New York: Plenum Publishers.

Vygotsky, Lev S. 2018, *Vygotsky's Notebooks: A Selection*, edited by Ekaterina Zavershevna and René van der Veer, Singapore: Springer.

Wertsch, James V. 1985, *Vygotsky and the Social Formation of Mind*, Cambridge, MA: Harvard University Press.

Wertsch, James V. 2007, 'Meditation', in *The Cambridge Companion to Vygotsky*, edited by Harry Daniels, Michael Cole, and James V. Wertsch, pp. 178–92, Cambridge: Cambridge University Press.

West, Nigel, and Oleg Tsarev 2009, *Triplex: Secrets of the Cambridge Spies*, New Haven, CT: Yale University Press.

Wetter, Gustav A. 1958, *Dialectical Materialism: A Historical and Systematic Survey of Philosophy in the Soviet Union*, translated by Peter Heath, London: Routledge & Kegan Paul.

Wiggins, David 1992, 'Remembering Directly', in *Psychoanalysis, Mind and Art: Essays for Richard Wollheim*, edited by J. Hopkins and A. Savile, pp. 339–54, Oxford: Blackwell.

Williams, Bernard 1973, 'The Self and the Future', in *Problems of the Self*, pp. 46–63, Cambridge: Cambridge University Press.

Wittgenstein, Ludwig 1953, *Philosophical Investigations*, translated by G.E.M. Anscombe, Oxford: Basil Blackwell.

Wittgenstein, Ludwig 1969, *On Certainty*, edited by G.E.M. Anscombe and G.H. von Wright, translated by D. Paul and G.E.M. Anscombe, Oxford: Blackwell.

Wood, Allen W. 2008, *Kantian Ethics*, Cambridge: Cambridge University Press.

Wright, Crispin 1980, *Wittgenstein on the Foundations of Mathematics*, London: Duckworth.

Yarmolenko, Avgusta V. 1941, 'Psikhologiya slepoglukhonemykh do obucheniya' ['The Psychology of the Blind-Deaf Child Prior to Instruction'], *Sovetskaya nevropsikhiatriya* [*Soviet Neuropsychiatry*], 6.

Yarmolenko, Avgusta V. 1961, *Ocherki psikhologii slepoglukhonemykh*, [*Essays on the Psychology of the Blind-Deaf*], Leningrad: Leningrad University Press.

Yaroshevsky, M.G. 1999 [1984], 'Epilogue', in Lev S. Vygotsky, *Collected Works, Vol. 6: Scientific Legacy*, edited by Robert W. Rieber, pp. 245–66, New York: Plenum Publishers.

Yasnitsky, Anton 2008, 'Rethinking the Early History of Post-Vygotskian Psychology: The Case of the Kharkov School', *History of Psychology*, 11, 2: 101–21.

Yasnitsky, Anton 2018, *Vygotsky: An Intellectual Biography*, London: Routledge.

Yasnitsky, Anton, and Michel Ferrari 2008, 'From Vygotsky to Vygotskian Psychology: Introduction to the History of the Kharkov School', *Journal of the History of the Behavioral Sciences*, 44, 2: 119–45.

Yasnitsky, Anton, and René van der Veer 2016a, ' "Lost in Translation": Talking about Sense, Meaning, and Consciousness', in *Revisionist Revolution in Vygotsky Studies*, edited by Anton Yasnitsky and René van der Veer, pp. 229–39, London: Routledge.

Yasnitsky, Anton, and René van der Veer eds 2016b, *Revisionist Revolution in Vygotsky Studies: The State of the Art*, London: Routledge.

Zakydalsky, Taras D. 1993, 'Review of David Bakhurst, *Consciousness and Revolution in Soviet Philosophy*', *Philosophy in Review*, 13, 4: 134–7.

Zalkind, Aron 1931, 'Psikhonevrologicheskii front i psikhologicheskaya diskussiya' ['The Psychoneurological Front and Psychological Discussion'], *Psikhologiya*, 4, 1.

Zavershneva, Ekterina 2016, 'Vygotsky the Unpublished: An Overview of the Personal Archive (1912–1934)', in *Revisionist Revolution in Vygotsky Studies*, edited by Anton Yasnitsky and René van der Veer, pp. 94–126, London: Routledge.

Zelený, Jindřich 1980, *The Logic of Marx*, translated by Terrell Carver, Oxford: Basil Blackwell.

Zinchenko, Pyotr I. 1983–84 [1936], 'The Problem of Involuntary Memory', *Soviet Psychology*, 22, 2: 55–111.

Zinchenko, Vladimir P. 1985, 'Vygotsky's Ideas About Units for the Analysis of Mind', in *Culture, Communication and Cognition: Vygotskian Perspectives*, edited by James V. Wertsch, pp. 94–118, Cambridge: Cambridge University Press.

Index

www.ingramcontent.com/pod-product-compliance
Lightning Source LLC
Chambersburg PA
CBHW062129040426
42335CB00039B/1847